North Cyprus

the Bradt Travel Guide

Diana Darke

with Murray Stewart

edition
8

www.bradtguides.com

Bradt Travel Guides Ltd, UK
The Globe Pequot Press Inc, USA

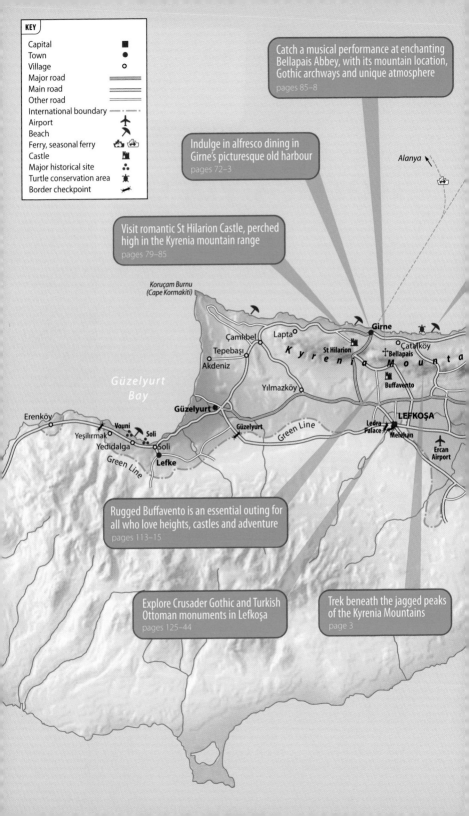

KEY

Capital	■
Town	●
Village	○
Major road	
Main road	
Other road	
International boundary	
Airport	✈
Beach	
Ferry, seasonal ferry	
Castle	
Major historical site	
Turtle conservation area	
Border checkpoint	

Catch a musical performance at enchanting Bellapais Abbey, with its mountain location, Gothic archways and unique atmosphere
pages 85–8

Indulge in alfresco dining in Girne's picturesque old harbour
pages 72–3

Alanya

Visit romantic St Hilarion Castle, perched high in the Kyrenia mountain range
pages 79–85

Koruçam Burnu
(Cape Kormakiti)

Çamlıbel   Lapta   *Kyrenia Mounta*   Girne   Çatalköy

Tepebaşı   St Hilarion   ✝Bellapais

Akdeniz

Güzelyurt Bay   Yılmazköy   Buffavento

Güzelyurt   LEFKOŞA

Erenköy   Güzelyurt   Ledra Palace   Meletan

Vouni   Soli   Green Line   Ercan Airport

Yeşilırmak   Yedidalga   Soli

Green Line   Lefke

Rugged Buffavento is an essential outing for all who love heights, castles and adventure
pages 113–15

Explore Crusader Gothic and Turkish Ottoman monuments in Lefkoşa
pages 125–44

Trek beneath the jagged peaks of the Kyrenia Mountains
page 3

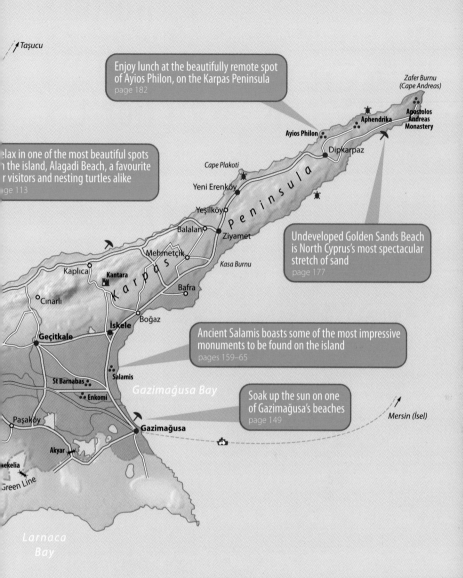

↗ Taşucu

Enjoy lunch at the beautifully remote spot of Ayios Philon, on the Karpas Peninsula
page 182

Relax in one of the most beautiful spots on the island, Alagadi Beach, a favourite for visitors and nesting turtles alike
page 113

Zafer Burnu
(Cape Andreas)

Apostolos
Andreas
Monastery

Aphendrika

Ayios Philon

Dipkarpaz

Cape Plakoti

Yeni Erenköy

Yeşilköy

Balalan

Ziyamet

Mehmetçik

Kasa Burnu

Kaplıca

Kantara

Bafra

Cınarlı

Boğaz

İskele

Geçitkale

Salamis

St Barnabas

Enkomi

Pasaköy

Gazimağusa Bay

Undeveloped Golden Sands Beach is North Cyprus's most spectacular stretch of sand
page 177

Ancient Salamis boasts some of the most impressive monuments to be found on the island
pages 159–65

Soak up the sun on one of Gazimağusa's beaches
page 149

Mersin (İsel)

Gazimağusa

Akyar

ekelia

Green Line

Larnaca
Bay

A K D E N İ Z
(M E D I T E R R A N E A N   S E A)

N

Bradt

| 0 | | 20km |
| 0 | | 20 miles |

North Cyprus Don't miss...

Crusader castles
North Cyprus's lofty castles
evidence the island's long
and troubled history;
pictured here, St Hilarion
makes for a great half-day
trip from Girne
(SA/D) pages 79–85

Karpas Peninsula
Clear, Mediterranean waters lap the
pure white sands of North Cyprus's
last wilderness (NCTA) pages 171–84

Girne Harbour
A beautiful setting, the harbour draws in most visitors for an alfresco meal at one of its many restaurants
(D/S) pages 72–3

Nature and wildlife
A dash for the sea: North Cypriot beaches find favour with nesting turtles
(NCTA) pages 10–11

Local culture
Local festivals should be a highlight for any visitor to the island. Here, folk dancers celebrate an 'Eco-day'
(MS) page 46

North Cyprus in colour

above   It is the sheer power of Girne Castle's walls that impress the most (NCTA) pages 74–6

left   Once the bustling centre for traders, Lefkoşa's Büyük Han is now a relaxing venue for a drink or some souvenir hunting (PW/S) pages 134–5

below   The Kyrenia Mountains provide a spectacular backdrop to Lefkoşa, where the Selimiye Carnii domintes the skyline (KM/S) pages 125–45

above left A sculpture near Karaoğlanoğlu commemorates the Peace Operation (NW) pages 108–9

above right The majestic abbey is the focal point in sleepy Bellapais village (A/S) pages 85–8

below left The village of Karaman is the only village in the north to have been entirely renovated by foreigners (DR) pages 109–10

below right With endless churches and historic buildings, Gazimağusa can provide a day's wanderings around what seems like an open-air museum. Pictured here, the Lala Mustafa Paşa Mosque sits on the main square (KM/S) page 154

Direct Traveller

Your holiday starts here...

Travel with the UK's leading tour operator to North Cyprus & experience the island as it should be.

- Hand picked hotels
- Private villas
- Twin centre holidays
- Dedicated rep service
- Fly non-stop direct to Cyprus
- Fly via Turkey to Ercan
- Depart from 19 UK airports

02085472857
www.directtraveller.com

ORIGINAL AUTHOR

Diana Darke first became interested in the Near East when she read Arabic at Oxford. For the last 26 years she has lived, worked and travelled extensively in Turkey and the Arab world, initially with the Foreign Office, then as an Arabic consultant. Work and pleasure have taken her to both sides of Cyprus on many occasions.

Diana has also written Bradt's guides to Syria, Oman and, most recently, Eastern Turkey. In Syria she bought and restored an old courtyard house in Damascus, which led her to complete an MA in Islamic Architecture. Her book, *My House in Damascus: An Inside View of the Syrian Revolution*, was published in March 2014. She regards it as her 'life's work'.

UPDATER OF THE EIGHTH EDITION

Murray Stewart has now completed his second update of this North Cyprus guide. Since giving up his career as a corporate restructurer with a global firm of accountants, he has also updated Bradt's *Cape Verde* guide and been published in national travel magazines, written blogs on both North Cyprus and Cape Verde, contributed prize-winning travel articles online, recovered €11 million of bank debt in Spain while working as a consultant, volunteered at the Olympic Games and Commonwealth Games, worked on the UK National Census and taught both English and Spanish. In previous guises, he has visited over 55 countries, teaching English in Mexico and Chile, being interviewed by Radio Ecuador in the midst of a civil insurrection and being threatened with a beating in Bulgaria.

Twice he has walked over 1,000km on the Camino de Santiago in France and Spain, in the process raising thousands of pounds for charity and gathering material for a to-be-published-sometime travelogue. Murray lived in North Cyprus during part of 2011, and again in 2014 to carry out this second update.

PUBLISHER'S FOREWORD   *Adrian Phillips, Managing Director*

While it's true that the north now has its holiday villas and casinos, it's still far less developed than the south, and contains some of the most unspoilt corners of the Mediterranean. I recently spent a day hiking in the Kyrenia Mountains and didn't meet a soul (unless you count a harmless whip snake); I visited one of the world's best beaches on the Karpas Peninsula; and I enjoyed several beers overlooking the harbour at Girne. North Cyprus still has appeal aplenty.

Eighth edition published June 2015
First published 1993
Bradt Travel Guides Ltd, IDC House, The Vale, Chalfont St Peter, Bucks SL9 9RZ, England
www.bradtguides.com
Published in the USA by The Globe Pequot Press Inc, PO Box 480, Guilford, Connecticut 06437-0480

Text copyright © 2015 Bradt Travel Guides Ltd
Maps copyright © 2015 Bradt Travel Guides Ltd
Photographs copyright © 2015 Individual photographers (see below)
Project Manager: Laura Pidgley
Cover research: Pepi Bluck, Perfect Picture

British Library Cataloguing in Publication Data
A catalogue record for this book is available from the British Library

ISBN: 978 1 84162 916 2 (print)
e-ISBN: 978 1 78477 127 0 (e-pub)
e-ISBN: 978 1 78477 227 7 (mobi)

Photographs AWL: Doug Pearson (DP/AWL), Neil Farrin (NF/AWL); Dave Robertson (DR); Dreamstime: Rostislav Ageev (RA/D), Senai Aksoy (SA/D); Jean Clark (JC); Murray Stewart (MS); North Cyprus Tourism Authority (NCTA); Oz Aker (OA); Shutterstock: Anilah (A/S), Debu55y (D/S), Kirill__M (K/S), nexus 7 (n/S), Ollie Taylor (OT/S), Panos Karos (PK/S), Philip Willcocks (PW/S), Valery Shanin (VS/S); SuperStock (SS)

Front cover Girne Harbour (SS)
Back cover Marble columns, Salamis (VS/S); Local man on a donkey, Karpas Peninsula (DP/AWL)
Title page Selimiye Camii, Lefkoşa (n/S); Mosaic at the Roman baths, Salamis (K/S); Wild flowers in the Karpas Peninsula (NCTA)

Maps David McCutcheon FBCart.S; some regional maps include data © OpenStreetMaps contributors (under Open Database License)

Typeset from the author's disc by Ian Spick, Bradt Travel Guides Ltd
Production managed by Jellyfish Print Solutions; printed in India
Digital conversion by www.dataworks.co.in

Acknowledgements

Murray Stewart would like to thank everyone who helped him in carrying out the update of this eighth edition. In general, a big thank you to all in North Cyprus: whatever changes have taken place in the country since the previous update, the underlying hospitality of the region's inhabitants remains undimmed. Specifically, thanks are due to Kadir Doruhan at the North Cyprus Tourism Centre in London for responding to queries; to Enver Ozdemir at Direct Traveller for his considerable help with travel logistics; and to the inhabitants of North Cyprus for sharing their knowledge, thoughts, opinions, suggestions and culture so spontaneously. In particular, thanks to Şahap Aşikoğlu, Serhan Guneyli, Selin Feza Akça, Hasan Karlitas, Türkbeg Emiradze and Ayşe Dönmezer for their assistance. Thanks also to those ex-pats who give more to North Cyprus than they take out: Alison Dowey, Tony Hutchinson, Jean Clark and Robin Snape amongst them. More than a nod of gratitude is due to Adrian and Rachel at Bradt, for giving me this opportunity, and to the project manager, Laura Pidgley. Diana Darke's original research into the history of Cyprus has stood the test of time, drawing continuing praise from many of those who care passionately about North Cyprus. The final and biggest thank you goes to my parents, Audrey and Alasdair, for everything; and to my dear friend, Sara Lister, for putting up with my long absences and even longer presences.

Contents

Introduction

The northern, Turkish-speaking part of Cyprus – 37% of the island's territory – still remains much less visited than the Greek south. No-one denies that when the island was divided in 1974, the Turks took the more beautiful and fertile region, but while holidaymakers jostled for beach space at Paphos and Limassol, for many years it was a case of spot the tourist at Girne (Kyrenia) and Gazimağusa (Famagusta). The Greek Cypriots are skilful political lobbyists and since 1974 have conducted an effective boycott of the north, presenting it as 'occupied and inaccessible'. They have done an excellent job, as both the economy and tourist industry in the north have stagnated and continue to suffer to this day. To start with, only an initiated few saw through the propaganda and went to find out for themselves, becoming loyal devotees who return each year to enjoy the wealth of cultural sites and the relaxing atmosphere.

The Greek Cypriots have also done a good job of rebuilding the tourist industry in the south, but in doing so have disfigured the landscape with concrete high-rise buildings, fast-food restaurants, associated ill-considered tourist-tat shops, and – in places – raucous nightclubs and badly behaved visitors. Less commercially minded than their southern counterparts, the Turkish Cypriots have until recently hatched few ambitious development projects of their own, and were in any event starved of the international finance needed to carry them out. For better and for worse, times have changed and are still changing. With the establishment of seven border crossing points to date, more flights into Ercan, EU money starting to filter through to improve infrastructure, and an economy supported by Turkey, the north is no longer an isolated backwater. Admittedly, North Cyprus's tourist economy still suffers from a complete ban on direct flights from anywhere other than Turkey, but the enthusiastic construction of 'casino' hotels has ensured a continuing flow of Turkish visitors from the mainland. Add to this a loyal band of European and other visitors and you have the makings of a healthy tourist industry.

Property investment has also become big business, perhaps too big: recent out-of-control levels of development represent a lesson unlearned from elsewhere in the Mediterranean. The global economic crisis of 2008 and thereafter brought the party to a grinding halt, with hundreds of empty villas, abandoned development projects and a new west-to-east road that, for a time, ended in dust. After a contemplative hiatus, things are moving again. The road to – and through – the Karpas has progressed rapidly, taking with it associated development and posing the question as to whether the warning signs of potential overdevelopment have in any way been heeded. On a positive note, there are individuals and organisations working hard to promote awareness of sustainable ecotourism, with real success.

For now, it's still possible to leave the main population areas behind and discover that the rural, tranquil charm of North Cyprus remains in place. Over the mountains from Girne and out in the Karpas, goatherds tend their flocks and the menfolk sip sweet tea between vigorous games of backgammon.

Apart from the huge casino complexes, family-owned hotels and restaurants are largely the norm, as is the warm and genuine hospitality that such establishments offer the visitor. With a good *meze* and a glass of wine, the north still offers some of the most unspoilt and welcoming corners of the Mediterranean.

Prices in North Cyprus remain reasonable. Inflation and growing tourism have nudged costs up, though the relative weakness of the Turkish lira in recent times has done much to offset the damage. Restaurant prices have been particularly susceptible, and a meal for two with wine now costs around TL100: still inexpensive, with the added benefits that the cuisine is tasty and standards are generally high. Although hotel price rises have outstripped general inflation, accommodation also remains good value, particularly in the mid-range sector popular with independent visitors, and car hire is also reasonably priced. Turkish Cypriots are very friendly and hospitable and do not as a rule hassle or pester visitors. Rates of petty crime are very low and the environment is safe and, outside population centres, pollution-free. There are daily flights from the UK to Ercan, encompassing a politically expedient touchdown in Turkey. Budget and charter airlines increasingly service the airports in the south, and a flight to Larnaca followed by an hour's airport transfer and a hassle-free border crossing barely represents an inconvenience to the visitor intending to holiday in the north. Although the vast majority of the region's visitors are Turkish, both Greek Cypriots and foreigners are once again exploring the north of the island.

The political status of the north is an emotive subject for both Greek and Turkish Cypriots, and it is not the role of a guidebook to try to analyse the rights and wrongs of this complex issue. The historical summary in *Background Information* (pages 12–17) attempts to clarify what happened and when, and interested readers will no doubt pursue their enquiries and make up their own minds. To that end, *Appendix 3* contains a non-exhaustive list of readily obtainable books on the subject. Ironically, the political situation has worked in the tourist's favour, secreting North Cyprus beyond the range of the worst excesses of mass tourism (temporarily, at least); it is here that the Mediterranean of 20 years ago can still be recaptured in places.

Ensuring that its natural environment is maintained and the genuine welcome of its people is not diminished by exposure to the negative aspects of increased tourism remains firmly the responsibility of visitors – we can all do our part in keeping North Cyprus special. Turkish Cypriots are always warm and respectful hosts, but visitors who reciprocate will be the ones who benefit most.

Since 1974, descriptions of the north have been inevitably relegated to the back pages of travel guides covering the whole island. Here, the region is given the comprehensive coverage it deserves. North Cyprus remains at a crossroads, as it has done for years, and may for many more: it is still 'another country' and, for the inhabitants of a divided island, identity is understandably an emotive issue. Turkish-speaking Cypriots possess a distinct ethnicity together with their own cultural and religious traditions. Waves of immigration from Turkey, an influx of guest workers from the Indian subcontinent and African students attending the universities, together with emigration by Turkish-speaking Cypriots to the UK and elsewhere – followed by their return – have seen Turkish-speaking Cypriots reduced to a minority in their own land. However, though the Turkish Republic of North Cyprus is only recognised by Turkey and the economic and cultural links are plain for all to see, it is definitely not the same country. In this guide, references to Turkish in the context of North Cyprus should be read simply as a method of differentiating between the subject and the Greek-speaking Republic of Cyprus.

FEEDBACK REQUEST AND UPDATES WEBSITE

At Bradt Travel Guides we're aware that guidebooks start to go out of date on the day they're published – and that you, our readers, are out there in the field doing research of your own. You'll find out before us when a fine new family-run hotel opens or a favourite restaurant changes hands and goes downhill. So why not write and tell us about your experiences? Contact us on 01753 893444 or e info@bradtguides.com. We will forward emails to the author who may post updates on the Bradt website at www.bradtupdates.com/northcyprus. Alternatively you can add a review of the book to www.bradtguides.com or Amazon.

NOTE ABOUT MAPS

Some maps use grid lines to allow easy location of sites. Map grid references are listed in square brackets after the name of the place or sight of interest in the text, with page number followed by grid number, eg: [104 C3].

KEY TO SYMBOLS

——·——	International boundary	▲	Castle/fortress
═══════	Dual carriageway	♦	Statue/monument
══════	Other main road	$	Bank
═════	Other road	⊠	Post office
=======	Minor road/track	⊞	Hospital/clinic/health centre
---------	Footpath	⊜	Internet access
■	Capital city	♪	Public telephone
●	Main town/city	✝	Cathedral/church
○	Small town/village	ℭ	Mosque
✈	Airport	ᒷ	City wall/fortification
⊞	Bus station	⚑	Lighthouse
⛴	Vehicular ferry	∴	Archaeological/historic site
⛴	Seasonal ferry	↖ ↗	Beach
P	Car park	♦	Turtle-viewing/nesting site
ℤ	Tourist information	⟻	Border checkpoint
⊖	Embassy	●	Other place of interest
♨	Museum/art gallery	▲	Hilltop/summit (height in metres)
🏛	Important/historic building		Urban park

Part One

GENERAL INFORMATION

NORTH CYPRUS AT A GLANCE

Location Island in the Mediterranean Sea, south of Turkey
Neighbouring countries Republic of Cyprus (land border); Turkey, 65km to the north; Syria, 100km to the east; and Egypt, 400km to the south (approx)
Size 224km long x 96km wide
Climate Mediterranean with hot, dry summers and cool winters
Population 294,000 (2011 census)
Capital Lefkoşa (Nicosia)
Main towns Girne (Kyrenia), Gazimağusa (Famagusta), Güzelyurt, Lefke
Economy Services-based (tourism, education)
GDP US$15,038 (income per capita, 2012)
Languages Turkish (English widely spoken)
Religion No official religion; 98% of the population is Muslim
Currency New Turkish lira (TL)
Exchange rate £1 = TL3.85, US$1 = TL2.59, €1 = TL2.86 (April 2015)
International telephone code +90 392
Time End of March to mid-September, GMT+3; winter, GMT+2
Electrical voltage 220–240 volts AC, UK-style 3-pin plug in general use
Weights and measures Metric
Flag The Turkish Cypriot flag has a horizontal red stripe at the top and bottom between which is a red crescent and red star on a white field
National anthem *İstiklâl Marşı* 'The March of Independence' (shared with Turkey)
Public holidays 1 January, 23 April, 1 May, 19 May, 20 July, 1 August, 30 August, 29 October, 15 November. See pages 44–6 for further details.

1

Background Information

GEOGRAPHY

Within its narrow boundaries, Cyprus offers a microcosm of history. Just as Constantinople was always a bridge, so Cyprus was always a stepping stone, where culture after culture left their footprints. Scarcely 224km long and 96km wide, the island has an unrivalled mix and concentration of landscapes, history and culture, and, with 768km of coastline, the sea and a beach are always close by. Turkey is the island's nearest neighbour, just 65km away, followed by Syria, which is approximately 100km distant. It is roughly 400km to Egypt and 480km to the nearest Greek island.

In the current division, the Turkish sector is undoubtedly the more beautiful. The fact that, pre-1974, 80% of Cyprus's hotels were in the Girne (Kyrenia) and Gazimağusa (Famagusta) areas, shows only too clearly where the tourist potential of the island always lay. Post-partition, the Greek Cypriots energetically set about rebuilding the south, and with the help of foreign aid and investment have now succeeded in developing Paphos, Limassol and Larnaca to be their new resort centres.

Dominating much of the northern part of the island, and rising dramatically from the coast to heights in excess of 1,000m, the Kyrenia Mountains (also known as the Beşparmak, or Five Fingers, Range) lend North Cyprus much of the striking scenery that forms the background to any number of postcards and holiday snaps. With such spectacular scenery, and a cooling breeze blowing off the Mediterranean, it's no surprise to find most of the holiday options clustered along this northern shore.

On the southern side of the Kyrenia Mountains, and comprising most of North Cyprus, the central Mesaoria Plain is notable only for its vastness and its contribution to the country's economy, and does not have much to attract visitors. From Güzelyurt in the west, the most fertile region and thronged with citrus groves, all the way to Gazimağusa in the east, the terrain is flat, dusty and uninspiring, with a mean altitude of just 70m above sea level. It is perhaps fitting that Lefkoşa, despite its enviable collection of Crusader Gothic and Turkish Ottoman monuments, should be found here. The drab, featureless suburbs of the modern town seem to blend perfectly with such an unremarkable backdrop, though the old town centre harbours many points of historical interest.

Moving east, Gazimağusa and its surroundings continue to draw a fair share of tourists away from Girne. North Cyprus has 396km – over half – of the island's total coastline, and some of the finest beaches are to be found here along Gazimağusa Bay, sweeping north from the town towards Salamis and Boğaz.

North Cyprus's final region, and surely its most treasured, is the Karpas Peninsula, a rugged finger tapering away from İskele and pointing out towards the İskenderun Bay of Turkey. With development rampant seemingly everywhere else, the Karpas is the place where you can still find small, traditional villages and the old way of life. Unspoilt golden sands, turtle beaches, itinerant donkeys and wild

THE ISLAND OF CYPRUS

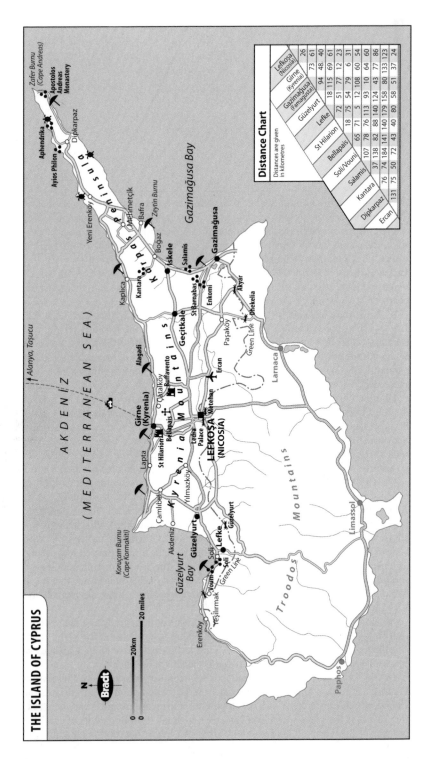

Distance Chart

Distances are given in kilometres

	Lefkoşa (Nicosia)	Girne (Kyrenia)	Gazimağusa (Famagusta)	Güzelyurt	Lefke	St Hilarion	Bellapais	Soli/Vouni	Salamis	Kantara	Dipkarpaz	Ercan
Lefkoşa (Nicosia)												
Girne (Kyrenia)	26											
Gazimağusa (Famagusta)	61	73										
Güzelyurt	48	94	115									
Lefke	40	69	77	18								
St Hilarion	61	12	51	72	75							
Bellapais	23	6	54	113	5	18						
Soli/Vouni	31	79	108	76	71	78	65					
Salamis	54	60	12	93	140	141	82	107				
Kantara	60	64	60	10	124	140	88	184	138			
Dipkarpaz	86	77	54	64	179	141	140	72	50	75		
Ercan	123	133	80	158	80	43	40	58	51	37	24	131

CLIMATE FACTS

AVERAGE MINIMUM TEMPERATURES IN °C

Jan	Feb	Mar	Apr	May	Jun	Jul	Aug	Sep	Oct	Nov	Dec
14	14	15	18	21	24	29	29	25	23	18	13

AVERAGE MAXIMUM TEMPERATURES IN °C

Jan	Feb	Mar	Apr	May	Jun	Jul	Aug	Sep	Oct	Nov	Dec
18	19	21	23	27	30	36	36	32	28	24	17

AVERAGE SEA TEMPERATURES IN °C

Jan	Feb	Mar	Apr	May	Jun	Jul	Aug	Sep	Oct	Nov	Dec
11	12	14	19	21	24	26	27	26	23	14	11

flowers continue to draw those in search of nature. You might only be a hundred kilometres or so from major civilisation but, under the stars on a clear summer's night, it could well feel like thousands.

CLIMATE

North Cyprus enjoys hot, dry summers that last from June to September. Visitors can expect more than ten hours of sunshine daily, and virtually no rain, during these months. The air is humid between June and October, particularly so in July and August. By contrast, winter can be wet, particularly in December and January: annual rainfall is around 45cm. Rivers that fill up during the wet months will be dry throughout the summer, when reservoirs lie empty. January and February are particularly cold. Snow can fall on the higher parts of the Kyrenia Mountains, but very rarely lower down.

NATURAL HISTORY AND CONSERVATION

Despite recent development, North Cyprus maintains a wide range of natural habitats and is home to several endemic species of wildlife. For the budding botanist or birdwatcher, it is a treasure trove of rarities, and for others the north boasts a fabulous array of scents, sights and sounds. The vibrancy of springtime poppies and tiny orchids, the constant chatter of cicadas, the predatory swoop of a red kite – North Cyprus has all of these, and much more.

FLORA Plant species across the north of the island number about 1,600, of which 22, including the **golden drop** (*Onosma fruticosa*), are endemic to Cypriot soil. Each season brings with it a new selection of buds, fruits and flowers.

Springtime is probably the best season for flowers, when the fields are covered with anemones, cyclamens, narcissi and wild tulips. North Cyprus plays host to nearly 30 species of wild orchids, some clinging to tree roots and rocks, showing off their unique flowers and rainbow varieties (see box, page 6). The **yellow Cyprus sun rose** (*Helianthemum obtusifolium*) crawls lazily over dry, rocky hillsides, transforming from small, hairy purple buds into pale yellow flowers. In a completely different habitat, hidden amongst the early cereal crops around Çamlıbel and Avtepe, the protected **black tulip** (*Tulipa cypria*) thrives in great numbers; it is actually dark crimson in colour, but is black inside. Up in the mountains, the scenery is transformed by a sweeping blanket of poppies, dressing the pine-covered slopes in scarlet.

As summer draws closer, the air is filled with the scent of citrus blossoms. Orange, lemon and lime groves around the Güzelyurt region are covered with white flowers, a precursor to the fruit harvest to come. **Pomegranate trees** (*Punicaceae*) blaze with their red blossoms and, as the summer draws on, tiny, fragrant, white flowers appear on the silver-leafed **olive trees** (*Olea europaea*). Legend dictates that olive trees are the safest trees to sit, relax and sleep under as, according to island superstition, evil spirits are afraid of them. The heat of the summer sun means that fruits ripen early. By August, the citrus groves are ready to harvest, the pomegranate blossoms have given way to orange fruits, olives are well on their way and the vines are heavy with grapes.

Autumn brings with it rain and colour. In shady woodland areas, look out for the **Cyprus cyclamen** (*Cyclamen cyprium*), with its white or pale pink, magenta-tipped petals. They grow only in Cyprus but are common throughout the island. Around Girne and along the Karpas Peninsula, the **late narcissus** (*Narcissus serotinus*) begins to flower in October. Its fragrant white flowers grow close to the ground on elegant green stalks, coiling and curling around the rocks. Towards the end of autumn, the **Cyprus autumn crocus** (*Crocus veneris*) appears on the northern slopes of the Girne mountain range. It has narrow, white petals and bright green leaves often laced with violet and silver stripes.

The winter months are not devoid of life either, as the **yellow oleander** (*Thevetia peruviana*) flowers break up its evergreen leaves with splashes of funnel-shaped yellow and orange blooms. Many of the autumn flowers persist throughout the winter, and on into spring. The **crown anemone** (*Anemone coronaria*) flowers late for its species but graces the foothills of the mountains south of Girne and the agricultural land around Güzelyurt from December through to April. The large petals vary in colour, appearing most commonly in red or purple shades, sometimes two-coloured and more rarely in a paler apricot pink.

FAUNA
Birds *Robin Snape*
Throughout the year, North Cyprus has plenty to offer to birds and birders alike. In spring the scrublands, forests, plains and wetlands are brimming with life after the wet winters and over 70 species are able to raise their young in these diverse habitats. In fact, two of the regular breeders, the **Cyprus warbler** (*Sylvia melanothorax*) and **Cyprus wheatear** (*Oenanthe cypriaca*), are endemic to Cyprus, breeding on the island and nowhere else. Not only does this make Cyprus important for bird conservation as Europe's only Endemic Bird Area, but it also makes the island an important destination for birders worldwide. And whilst birders visit in pursuit of endemics and endemic subspecies, opportunities for them to stumble upon other sought-after birds are plentiful.

During spring and autumn, Cyprus hosts more than 200 passage migrant species. They use the island as a fuelling station as they travel to and from their breeding grounds, stretching from the Turkish coast to the High Arctic, and their wintering grounds in the Middle East and throughout Africa. Cyprus's temperate winters also attract over 90 winter visitor species that flock to the island to escape the cold. When the size of North Cyprus is considered, its bird diversity is immense. At the right time of year, it is possible to see over 100 species in the space of a few days. This is because a huge diversity of habitats lie just a stone's throw apart, negating the necessity for lengthy travel between sites, providing more 'birds per buck' than many regional mainland sites.

In spring, migrants travelling north funnel into the Karpas Peninsula where they become increasingly concentrated before making their next sea crossing to Turkey, continental Europe and Russia. At the tip of the peninsula, migrating raptors such as the **red-footed falcon** (*Falco vespertinus*) are seen in flocks. The **pallid harrier** (*Circus macrourus*), **Montagu's harrier** (*Circus pygargus*) and **black kite** (*Milvus migrans*) are among the daily-sighted raptors heading north. Meanwhile, temporary shallow wetlands, brimming with invertebrate life and amphibians, provide perfect stop-over habitats for migrants such as **bittern** (*Botaurus stellaris*), **little bittern** (*Ixobrychus minutus*), **night heron** (*Nycticorax nycticorax*), **little** and **Baillon's crakes** (*Porzana parva/Porzana pusilla*), **garganey** (*Anas querquedula*), **ruddy shelduck** (*Tadorna ferruginea*) and a diversity of waders. Swathes of coastal *maquis* along the north and west coasts and in the Karpas Peninsula are in pristine condition and in spring these stunning habitats can be extremely rewarding with **red-backed, masked, lesser grey** and **woodchat shrikes** (*Lanius collurio/Lanius nubicus/Lanius minor/Lanius senator*) all common. **Isabelline, black-eared** and occasionally **desert wheatear** (*Oenanthe isabellina/Oenanthe hispanica/Oenanthe deserti*) can be seen in more open habitats

Through the summer the Kanlıdere waterway in Nicosia is used to irrigate crops on the Mesaoria Plain, where flowering alfalfa meadows draw in pollinators and with them insectivorous birds. Here, bee-eaters and rollers maintain nests in the mud banks of the waterways and **spur-winged plover** (*Vanellus spinosus*) and **black-winged stilts** (*Himantopus himantopus*) raise their young on the pools. **Stone curlew** (*Burhinus oedicnemus*) and **little, long-eared** and **barn owl** (*Athene noctua/Asio otus/Tyto alba*) are also common. Meanwhile, Famagusta Freshwater Lake is the only site on Cyprus where you can regularly see **glossy ibis** (*Plegadis falcinellus*), **cattle egret** (*Bubulcus ibis*), **squacco heron** (*Ardeola ralloides*) and **black-crowned night heron** (*Nycticorax nycticorax*) nesting.

During the driest months from August to October, migrants returning south continue to make use of the water offered by the Kanlıdere system, where almost anything can show up. An autumn morning at the Sadrazamköy lighthouse at the tip of the Koruçam Peninsula may yield sightings of hundreds of herons, waders, terns and raptors, in particular **honey buzzards** (*Pernis apivorus*) as they round the cape in droves on their way south. The surrounding coastal scrubland is packed with warblers, wheatears, shrikes, pipits and flycatchers, all returning from the north.

Another spectrum of species sits out the European winter on Cyprus. This includes the stunning **greater flamingo** (*Phoenicopterus roseus*) which winters at seasonal wetlands around Gazamiğusa, as do the **bluethroat** (*Luscinia svecica*), **moustached warbler** (*Acrocephalus melanopogon*), **ferruginous duck** (*Aythya nyroca*), **grey plover** (*Pluvialis squatarola*) and **curlew** (*Numenius*). Regular visitors include **pied kingfisher** (*Ceryle rudis*), **short-eared owl** (*Asio flammeus*) and **penduline tit** (*Remiz pendulinus*). On the towering walls of the Five Finger Mountains and among the three Crusader castles, **wallcreeper** (*Tichodroma muraria*) and **rock bunting** (*Emberiza cia*) can be seen.

A host of resident birds are on the island throughout the year, including the threatened **Bonelli's eagle** (*Aquila fasciata*), which builds eyries in precipices of the Kyrenia Mountains, **black francolin** (*Francolinus francolinus*), whose population in Cyprus is the only population in the EU, and **blue rock thrush** (*Monticola solitarius*). Off the Karpas islets, you may spot the **Audouin's gull** (*Ichthyaetus audouinii*).

With regard to conservation, the **North Cyprus Hunters' Federation** has in recent years taken great steps to manage its members. Hunting does go on during autumn and winter months and whilst the number of registered hunters is large, the hunt is limited to a certain number of Sundays and Wednesdays and is restricted to designated areas. The uncontrolled use of poison to curb fox populations for livestock protection has resulted in a drastic decrease in the number and diversity of nesting raptors since the 1950s.

The **North Cyprus Society for the Protection of Birds and Nature** (KUŞKOR) maintains bird records for North Cyprus, encourages bird recording and provides training in bird identification. It also raises awareness locally on bird conservation and leads campaigns against illegal hunting, trapping of birds and uncontrolled and illegal poisoning. KUŞKOR also treats and rehabilitates many injured birds each year and operates its own bird-ringing scheme. Recent projects have included the census and long-term monitoring of nesting Bonelli's eagles, an annual census of nesting Audouin's gull around the Karpas islets and the establishment of a law preventing landing at their nest sites. Additionally, it has run a project to establish sites for protection under the Birdlife International Important Bird Area scheme and, most recently, another EU-funded project to improve a major wetland for birds and birdwatchers due for completion in 2016. From October to May, monthly birding trips are arranged and visitors are welcome to attend. A small fee is collected towards the organisation, with binoculars and spotting scopes available. You can contact KUŞKOR directly via contacts at their web page (*www.kuskor.org*) which also has links to their active forum and is a good place to track sightings. For details of organised birdwatching trips, see page 48.

Further information on which birds can be seen, as well as the best times and locations at which to spot them, can be gleaned from the birdwatching brochures published by North Cyprus's Tourism, Promotion and Marketing Department and available from the North Cyprus Tourism Centres in London and elsewhere. Another good point of information is the website http://kibrisbirds.net/North-Cyprus-Birds.

Reptiles and amphibians

Although Cyprus is home to a number of varieties of snake, all of them hibernate during the winter and tend to be rather sluggish during the hot summer months. Of the harmless species, the **pink worm snake** (*Typhlops vermicularis*) looks exactly as its name suggests, the **whip snake** (*Coluber jugularis*) has a dark grey or black back and its close cousin, the **Cyprus whip snake** (*Coluber cypriensis*), is dark green. The only species to be aware of for safety reasons is the blunt-nosed viper (*Vipera lebetina*). It varies in colour but has a distinctive yellow, horny tail and is fairly common. It will not normally bite other than in defence. The village clinics stock the antidote.

Throughout North Cyprus you will see lizards everywhere. They scuttle around the ruins, bobbing their heads then disappearing into thin air before your eyes. They vary considerably in size, and some have a clear black stripe down their back. The largest species of lizard on the island is the **starred agama** (*Agama stellio*) which has a strangely proportioned body; its large head may be seen peeping out from cracks in stone walls or tree trunks.

The **European chameleon** (*Chamaeleo chamaeleon*) also inhabits parts of the north, although you would be very fortunate to see one. Our wildlife questions were met with great excitement by one resident in Lapta who had recently seen his first chameleon in the ten years that he had lived there.

Sea turtles are a species that has attracted considerable attention recently (see box, pages 10–11). Throughout June and July, turtles make the tiring journey up the beach to lay their eggs, 70–180 in each clutch, and then return to the sea having buried them safely in the sand. It is important that the temperature of the eggs stays relatively constant during their incubation period of about seven weeks. Eggs buried deeper in the sand will be cooler and the incubation period may therefore be longer. The tiny turtles have a tough start to their life, emerging from the sand during the cooler hours of the night and heading straight for the huge expanse of sea that awaits them. Human intervention can be a positive force and nesting numbers are now beginning to recover, but care must be taken by visitors to the island to help guarantee the future of the species.

Both **loggerhead** (*Caretta caretta*) and **green** (*Chelonia mydas*) sea turtles choose to nest on the beaches of North Cyprus. Approximately 10% of the Mediterranean's loggerhead turtles and 30% of its green turtles now nest in North Cyprus, making it a crucial site for the survival of both of these endangered populations.

The **Society for Protection of Turtles** (SPOT) was founded in the 1980s by the late Ian Bell (a former army major and a committed conservationist), Kutlay Keço and Celia Bell. SPOT has highlighted the importance of the island's beaches to the Mediterranean's sea turtle population, working since 1992 with conservation biologists from the University of Exeter's Marine Turtle Research Group from a base at the island's best-known turtle rookery, Alagadi Beach. Around 70 volunteers from overseas are hosted there annually. Due to this work, vast swathes of coastline have been designated by the European Union as Special Environmental Protection Areas (SEPAs) and its protected status is recognised by the North Cyprus government. As such, the main nesting sites at Akdeniz, Alagadi, Tatlısu and in the Karpas Peninsula have remained untouched by development. The Environmental Protection Department maintains signage at these sites, alerting visitors to the presence of nesting turtles; some beaches are completely closed at night.

Between 20 May and 15 September, volunteers patrol Alagadi beaches every 10 minutes from dusk until dawn, monitoring every nesting female as part of one of the world's best-established long-term monitoring programmes. All adult turtles are tagged; some are fitted with satellite transmitters and data recorders. Some of those first tagged back in 1992 are still returning to nest over 20 years later. The research results of the project have contributed significantly to the global understanding of sea turtle biology.

Volunteers also undertake daily patrols of all the nesting sites between Güzelyurt on the west coast and Balalan in the Karpas Peninsula. Here nests are located, counted, monitored and protected with a metal cage, deterring foxes and stray dogs from digging up the eggs. This work is mirrored by the Environmental Protection Department and Eastern Mediterranean University at the main nesting sites in the Karpas Peninsula and in Famagusta Bay. Prior to this nest-protection scheme, more than 80% of nests were lost to predation. Now the results of the scheme are beginning to show, with a significant rise in the number of nesting green and loggerhead turtles since 2007.

There's also increasing effort being made to involve local students in the protection work and to raise awareness about turtles among the local population. Particular attention is paid to the fishing 'industry,' as up to 1,000 turtles are accidentally caught each year.

Between 20.00 and 08.00 from May to October, Alagadi Beach is closed to the public to minimise disturbance to nesting females. Unaccompanied visitors should not attempt to visit any of the turtle beaches in the hours of darkness during these months. However, SPOT volunteers take one group of up to 15

Mammals The **Cyprus mouflon** (*Ovis musimon*) is the largest mammal on the island and is now a protected species to save it from hunters. Vegetation is perfect for herds of sheep and goats and, as you head out along the Karpas Peninsula, they may become your sole companions.

Other mammals that you may see on your travels include foxes, hedgehogs and bats. **Cyprian hares** (*Lepus cyprius*) keep themselves scarce, darting for cover to individuals per night to observe nesting turtles during June and July. To take part, you need to visit or call the SPOT headquarters in Alagadi village and book your place, preferably a week in advance as visitor places get filled very quickly. There's no guarantee of sightings, but most people get lucky and as nesting numbers are on the up, the chances are increasing year on year. The experience is amazing. Bear in mind that although the trip is essentially free of charge, SPOT rely very heavily on donations for their excellent work, so a donation or purchase of a T-shirt or other turtle merchandise from their shop goes a long way to maintaining the project. You could be waiting on a cool, breezy beach for at least an hour, so dress accordingly – June, in particular, can be very chilly at night. Visitors can bring blankets and sleep out until a volunteer wakes them and guides them to a nesting turtle. No flash photography is allowed.

From late July to late September larger groups are invited to see hatchling turtles emerge from their nests and be released to the sea during organised nest excavations and hatchling releases. These are announced each morning on SPOT's Facebook page, a link for which can be found on their website. Alternatively, visitors can drop in or phone the base to enquire. No booking is required for nest excavations: just turn up at the base at the announced time, usually late afternoon. This is the best opportunity to see and photograph baby turtles, though handling them is not possible. Hatchling releases – for which reservation *is* required – take place after 21.00, when the beach is closed to the public. Here visitors get to handle, name and release their own hatchling sea turtle under the guidance of experienced volunteers. Again, no flash photography is allowed. Due to the extreme popularity of this event, bookings are taken from noon onwards, only by phone.

SPOT also operate in Akdeniz village on the west coast, and hatchling releases are often organised there and can be arranged by phone.

Visitors are not advised to try to find nesting turtles without the guidance provided by SPOT at Alagadi or with the Environmental Protection Department in Karpas, who also occasionally guide visitors. Turtles are likely to be disturbed from nesting by inexperienced visitors and it is illegal to enter the main nesting sites elsewhere.

Truly eco-conscious visitors may consider whether they want to patronise hotels and restaurants that shine bright lights over the turtle beaches during nesting season, as this kind of development has had the most significant impact in reducing the availability of nesting habitat in North Cyprus and around the Mediterranean.

More information about the projects in North Cyprus, including how to sponsor a turtle, how to volunteer and how to make a donation towards the project work can be obtained via SPOT's website (*www.cyprusturtles.org*). Their phone is manned between June and September (m *0533 872 53 50*).

1

protect themselves from predators and thus sustaining their species. Wild Cypriot donkeys roam freely across the Karpas Peninsula, with estimates of their numbers ranging from 800 to over 2,000. They are a breed unique to the island and should be approached with caution as they are always on the hunt for food. Those involved in agriculture throughout the region resent the damage the that donkeys cause to cultivated areas.

Insects Butterflies are in abundance in North Cyprus, and many of the species are unique to the island. Spring and summer bring out the **Cyprus festoon butterfly** (*Zerynthia cerisyi cypria*) with its strangely shaped wings, and the bright, sunny-coloured **Cleopatras** (*Gonepteryx cleopatra*), which decorate mountain glades. There are numerous other species and the overall effect of colourful wings can be fantastic as they criss-cross your path or play around hotel gardens.

On any night-time stroll you can't fail to notice the hum of **cicadas** (*Cicadidae*) by the roadside. They are large, winged insects, with one species growing up to 15mm in length. They lead a strange existence, developing for years beneath the earth from grub to adult, then emerging into daylight for a 24-hour life of laying new eggs and making a lot of noise. Their method of sound production is unique as cavities either side of the abdomen resonate to produce a long droning whistle. If you do happen to see one, let it be; they are harmless and have waited seven long years for a few hours of daylight!

HISTORICAL SUMMARY

There is no specific historical section in this guide, as historical background is woven into the text as and when appropriate. The following detailed chronology is provided as a handy reference and summary and to provide a brief overview. For those who require a more detailed history of Cyprus, the books in *Appendix 3* (pages 192–3) should suffice.

6000–2500BC	Neolithic settlements. Earliest yet found is Khirokitia near Larnaca.
5800BC	Beehive huts of stone.
2500–2300BC	Chalcolithic period. Discovery of copper on island led to growth in trade.
1st Bronze Age (2300–1900BC)	Contemporary with early Egyptian dynasties and Minoan civilisations of Crete. Cyprus inhabited by people identical to those found in central Europe, Asia Minor and Syria.
2000BC	Enkomi, near Gazimağusa, major trading centre in copper, becomes capital of Alasia (as Cyprus was then called).
2nd Bronze Age (1900–1500BC)	Contemporary with middle Egyptian dynasties, Mycenaeans and Phoenicians colonising the Mediterranean. Cyprus paid tribute to them, but only the Phoenicians and Greeks colonised and left settlements. The Egyptians never occupied. Greek city states of Salamis, Soli, Marion, Curium and Paphos. Cult of Aphrodite introduced. No political link with Greece, as settlers were always breakaways from the mainland, exiles or entrepreneurs wishing to set up a new life in a different land.
1200BC	Phoenician King Hiram of Tyre invades and gathers tribute. Phoenicians rule Cyprus. Main Phoenician settlement at Kition near Larnaca.
725–575BC	Assyrian rulers, Sargon to Nebuchadnezzar. Cyprus joins them in wars against Egyptians.
525–425BC	Persian rulers including Darius and Xerxes. Cypriots join them in campaigns against Egyptians and Greeks.
411–374BC	Evagoras, King of Salamis, first native ruler. Cyprus independent after Persia and Greece sign truce. Evagoras introduces monarchy, Greek coinage and alphabet; Greek culture favoured.
350–325BC	Persia regains the island after long siege of Salamis.

335–263BC	Zeno, founder of Stoic philosophy, born at Kition. Only really great name to come out of Cyprus.
325BC	Alexander the Great. Cypriots were to send ships to Tyre to help lift siege, but sent them to Alexander instead, thus ensuring overthrow of Persians. Cyprus becomes part of Alexander's empire.
300–50BC	Hellenistic period. From Alexander's death until arrival of Romans, Cyprus is ruled from Alexandria, Egypt, first by Ptolemy, Alexander's general, finally by Cleopatra. Arsinoe (Gazimağusa) built. Fragments of Egyptian granite and statues found at Salamis. Island, united as four districts for first time, flourishes under relatively peaceful conditions.
58BC–AD330	Almost 390 years of Roman rule. Romans make Cyprus part of the province of Cilicia (southern Turkey), capital Tarsus, ruled by military governor. Roman engineers build roads, harbours, bridges and aqueducts. Prosperity enjoyed.
AD45	St Paul and St Barnabas arrive at Salamis on first missionary journey. Roman proconsul converted to Christianity.
AD100	Under Roman emperor Trajan, Jews on island (who had fled there to escape Roman persecution in Palestine) massacre 240,000 Cypriots, including St Barnabas, native of Salamis. As a result, Romans expel all Jews from Cyprus.
AD125	Under Hadrian, climax of Roman monumental art.
AD313	Emperor Constantine officially recognises Christianity. Most of Cyprus is already Christian by this time.
AD325–1191	Rule of Byzantium.
AD325–350	Empress Helena, mother of Constantine, visits on return from trip to Jerusalem. Salamis rebuilt as Constantia after severe earthquakes of 4th century.
AD395	Division of Byzantine empire into east and west; Cyprus comes under eastern half, with capital at Constantinople, but is ruled from Antioch in Syria.
AD477	Under Emperor Zeno, autocephalous Church of Cyprus is recognised, with independent Cypriot archbishop. Monastery of St Barnabas built.
AD525	Climax of Byzantine art; period of peace and unity.
AD650–965	Series of Arab raids at intervals over 300 years. Salamis destroyed, never rebuilt; many churches pillaged and torn down. Byzantine art stagnates.
1184	Isaac Comnenus, rebel Byzantine prince from Trabzon, arrives on island and proclaims himself Emperor of Cyprus. Rules for seven years in style of despot, but this is only the second time in Cyprus's history when it is independent of a foreign power.
1191	Richard the Lionheart captures Cyprus on way to Third Crusade.
1192	Richard sells Cyprus to Knights Templar to raise money for his army. Then sells it to Guy de Lusignan, last king of Jerusalem before Saladin's conquest, as a consolation for Guy's loss of Jerusalem.
1192–1489	Norman French occupation under the Lusignan dynasty. Castle and town of Nicosia built under Amaury, Guy's brother. Feudal system created, as in Kingdom of Jerusalem. Rulers take titles of King of Cyprus and King of Jerusalem (in absentia).

1225	Byzantine castles of Hilarion, Buffavento and Kantara refortified and elaborated by the Lusignan Crusaders.
1250	Cathedral of Nicosia built.
1300	Cathedral of Famagusta built after fall of Acre, last Christian toehold in Holy Land.
1325	Bellapais Abbey built. Native islanders are isolated from new wealth by ruling Catholic French-speakers and treated as serfs. Orthodox Church persecuted, humiliated and made subject to Rome and the Pope.
1375–1464	Cyprus partly ruled by Genoa. Island at war and Famagusta is ceded to Genoese as settlement. Rest of the island stays under Lusignans.
1425	Egyptian Mamelukes pillage towns and weaken Lusignan dynasty.
1464	Genoese expelled. Last Lusignan king takes Venetian bride, Catherine Cornaro, but both he and his newborn son are murdered, leaving Catherine nominally in control, while Venetian nobles arrange her retirement to Italy.
1481	Leonardo da Vinci visits, possibly advising on fortification design.
1489–1571	Venetian Republic occupation. Fortification of castles at Kyrenia, Famagusta and Nicosia. Dismantling of mountain castles of Hilarion, Buffavento and Kantara to discourage internal uprising.
1571–1878	Three centuries of Turkish rule under the Ottomans. Only resistance offered by Venetian strongholds of Nicosia and Famagusta. Islanders themselves glad to see the end of oppressive Venetian rule. Orthodox Church is recognised again and archbishopric restored. Feudal system abolished, but heavy taxes imposed, using Church as tax collectors.
1625–1700	Great depopulation of Cyprus. Plagues wipe out over half the population.
1821	Greek Cypriots side with Greece in revolt against Turkish rule. Island's leading churchmen are executed in punishment.
1869	Suez Canal opens.
1878–1960	British occupation. British take on administration of the island, ceded from the Ottomans, for its strategic value, to protect their sea route to India via the Suez Canal. In exchange, Britain agrees to help Turkey should Russia attack.
1914	Cyprus annexed by Britain when Turkey joins Germany and Austro-Hungary in World War I.
1925	Cyprus becomes British Crown colony.
1931	First serious riots of Greek Cypriots demanding Enosis, union with Greece.
1939	Greek Cypriots fight together with British in World War II, but remain set on Enosis after war is over. Turkish Cypriots, however, want British rule to continue.
1950	Archbishop Makarios III elected political and spiritual leader. Heads the campaign for Enosis with the support of Greece.
1955	Series of bomb attacks, start of violent campaign for Enosis by EOKA (National Organisation of Cypriot Fighters) led by George Grivas, ex-colonel in Greek army, born in Cyprus. Grivas takes name of Dighenis, legendary Cypriot hero, and conducts guerrilla warfare from secret hideout in Troodos Mountains. Estimated to

	have 300 men maximum, yet successfully plagues 20,000 British troops and 4,500 police.
1956	Britain deports Makarios to Seychelles in an attempt to quell revolt. Turkish Cypriots used as auxiliaries of British Security Forces, allegedly torturing EOKA captives during British cross-examinations.
1957	Field Marshal Sir John Harding replaced by civilian governor Sir Hugh Foot in conciliatory move.
1958	Turkish Cypriots alarmed by British conciliation and begin making demands for partition. Inter communal clashes and attacks on British occur.
1960	British, Greek and Turkish governments sign the Treaty of Guarantee to provide for independent Cypriot state within the Commonwealth and allowing for retention of two Sovereign Base Areas of Dhekelia and Akrotiri. Under the treaty, each power has the right to take military action in the face of any threat to the constitution. Cyprus truly independent for first time. Archbishop Makarios is first president, Dr Fazıl Küçük vice-president. Both have right of veto. Turkish Cypriots, who form 18% of population, given 30% of places in government and administration, 40% in army, and separate municipal services in the five major towns.
1963–73	Greek Cypriots view constitution as unworkable and propose changes, which are rejected by Turkish Cypriots and Turkish government. Inter communal fighting escalates and UN Peacekeeping Force sent in, but powerless to prevent incidents.
1974–76	Military government (junta) in Greece supports coup by Greek National Guard to overthrow Makarios. Makarios forced to flee. Puppet regime imposed under Nicos Sampson, former EOKA fighter. Rauf Denktash, Turkish Cypriot leader, calls for joint military action by the UK and Turkey, as guarantors of Cypriot independence, to prevent Greece imposing Enosis. The Turkish prime minister travels to London to persuade the UK to intervene jointly with Turkey, but fails, so Turkey exercises its right under the 1960 Treaty of Guarantee and lands 40,000 troops on the north coast of Cyprus. Turkey describes this invasion as 'a peace operation to restore constitutional order and protect the Turkish Cypriot community'. UN talks break down and Turkish forces are left in control of 37% of the island. Refugees from both communities cross to respective sides of the de facto border. Turks announce Federated State in the north with Denktash as leader. UN forces remain, providing a buffer between the two zones. Some 20,000 mainland Turks, mainly subsistence farmers, are brought in to settle and work the underpopulated land. Those who stay more than five years are given citizenship of North Cyprus.
1977	Makarios dies, having been restored as President of Greek Cyprus after 1974. Succeeded by Spyros Kyprianou.
1983	Turkish Federated State declares itself independent as Turkish Republic of North Cyprus (TRNC), still with Denktash as president. New state is not recognised by any country except Turkey.
1992–95	UN-sponsored talks between the two sides run into the sand, but with a commitment to resume.

1

2002–03	Concerns in Europe that a divided nation could join the European Union in 2004 prompt further UN-brokered peace talks. The plans, authored by UN Secretary-General Kofi Annan, envisioned the establishment of a Swiss-style confederation made up jointly of the two sides. Proposals included the formation of a common state with one single Cypriot citizenship and a reduction in Turkish Cypriot land from 36% to 28.5%; while the Greek Cypriots, for their part, would have to formally acknowledge that not all their refugees could return to their houses in the north. A three-year interim government was also mooted, with Turkish and Greek Cypriot representatives as co-leaders. Despite a willingness by many Turkish Cypriots to seek a solution, talks break down; Denktash rejects revised proposals within hours of having received them. In the south public opinion holds that too many concessions have been offered and perhaps as a result, February sees the election of Tassos Papadopoulos, a leader at odds with many pro-unification forces. In the north, Denktash loses much public support, many citing him as intransigent and an obstacle to successful negotiations. Perhaps to boost his popularity, Denktash makes the momentous decision to unilaterally open the border with the south as the latter moves closer to EU membership. The Greek Cypriot government reciprocates and soon thousands from the north and south are queuing to cross over to the other side.

2004 Years of political word games and cajoling from the UN come to a head on 24 April, when Cyprus goes to the polls to vote on the reunification proposals laid down by the Annan Plan. The turnout on both sides of the divide is high (84% in the north and 89% in the south), reflecting the depth of feeling that exists amongst both communities. Alas, this is the only commonality to be found – the respective votes could not have been more disparate. In the clearest sign yet that the Turkish Cypriots favour a resolution, 65% vote 'Yes' to reunification, whilst the Greek ballots yield a depressing and overwhelming 86% 'No' vote, with the Greek Cypriot government citing 'unacceptable' restrictions on property rights as an insurmountable hurdle. As a result, on 1 May the southern Republic of Cyprus ascends to full member status of the EU (with all the associated benefits). Strictly speaking, the *whole* island acceded to the treaties, but with the body of EU laws suspended *vis-à-vis* the north, which thus continues in political isolation.

2005 17 April becomes a watershed in the history of North Cyprus as Denktash stands down from the presidency he has held since the 1983 declaration of independence. His successor, Mehmet Ali Talat, is a radically different character. Reserved, softly spoken and, by eastern Mediterranean standards, still young, Talat cuts the image of a more moderate politician and carries the north's hopes for a unified and peaceful future. A fierce supporter of the UN's reunification plan, Talat's centre-left Republican Turkish Party has been gaining momentum for some time and, with anti-Denktash feeling escalating amongst the population, most agree that the time for change had arrived.

2006–08	In a surprise result, the incumbent Greek Cypriot President, Tassos Papadopoulos, is knocked out of February 2008's election race and is replaced by Communist Demetris Christofias who rides to victory on a pro-unification platform. By early April, amid tumultuous scenes, Lefkoşa's Ledra Street, once the capital's main shopping street, reopens to cross-border pedestrian traffic. September 2008 witnesses the resumption of formal direct talks towards reunification.
2009	Derviş Eroğlu is appointed Prime Minister after his National Unity Party comprehensively wins the legislative elections. While reunification talks continue, little progress is made and the result perhaps evidences a lessening of appetite for the pro-reunification agenda of Talat and the Republican Turkish Party.
2010	April's Presidential election sees Eroğlu defeat Talat, his only serious challenger. Talks on reunification continue, but apart from the opening of a seventh border crossing, little tangible progress is evident.
2011	In January, focus switches to relations between North Cyprus and Turkey. Protestors take to the streets of Lefkoşa to demonstrate against austerity measures designed to curb the North's swollen public sector. Turkey is angered by banners telling Turkey to 'go back to Ankara.' Turkey responds by appointing a new ambassador, perceived as being a hardliner. Ignoring government advice, non-violent protests and strikes are repeated in March, with an estimated 50,000 people taking to the streets once more. Western media coverage of the unrest is lost amidst the focus on the Arab Spring unfolding nearby. Meanwhile, Eroğlu and Christofias hold another round of reunification negotiations in March: it's the hundredth since September 2008.
2013	July sees the Republican Turkish Party win the most seats in the parliamentary elections.
2014	A new threat to reunification comes to a head as Greece, Cyprus and Turkey enter into dispute over rights to hydrocarbon exploration off the Cypriot coast. Israel and Egypt also take an interest. The Cypriot newspapers announce that the Cyprus talks are, once again, in crisis.

GOVERNMENT AND POLITICS

Whilst the Republic of Cyprus (the south) is internationally recognised as having the legal right of sovereignty in respect of the entire island, only Turkey acknowledges North Cyprus as a legal, sovereign entity.

Despite this precarious legal status, North Cyprus operates as a democratic republic, with a president and a prime minister who are respectively Head of State and Head of Government. Using a system of proportional representation, the five electoral districts of North Cyprus elect 50 members to the Assembly of the Republic, which shares the legislative function with the government. At the The Republic of North Cyprus (TRNC) parliamentary elections held in July 2013, the Republican Turkish Party (CTP) won 21 seats, the National Unity Party (NUP) 14 seats, the Democratic Party (DP) 12 seats and the Communal Democratic Party 3 seats. On 2 September, Özkan Yorancioğlu, the President of the CTP, was sworn

1

After years of failed negotiations and with the situation beginning to look hopeless, an announcement in early 2003 made everyone sit up and take notice. Out of the blue, on 23 April, Turkish Cypriot president Rauf Denktash declared a relaxing of the border controls between Greek and Turkish sectors. For the first time in almost 30 years, people from both sides were allowed to cross the Green Line at the Ledra Palace checkpoint and visit the other half of the island on a day trip.

For some the experience proved an emotional one as they returned to communities and met former neighbours and friends that they hadn't seen for the past three decades. For many from the north it was a chance to gaze at the comparatively lavish lifestyle of the wealthier south. For others, particularly Greeks returning to the north, it was a bewildering day as they found that their homes, for which they still had the title deeds, were now being lived in by former neighbours or, in many instances, British expats, who also held title deeds issued by the Turkish authorities. But, for almost everybody who made the trip – and in the first week of regulations over 50,000 people did – the experience was tinged with sadness as they realised that, while the move was certainly a positive step towards peace, the same intractable obstacles to a united Cyprus remained.

Quite why Denktash decided upon such a huge shift in policy – one that seemed to go against all his policies of the previous 30 years – was unclear. The official line was that border restrictions were being eased to build confidence between the two communities, though few believe that this was the only reason. One theory is that the move was designed to counter accusations abroad that the failure of the peace process was largely Denktash's fault and to repair his image on the international stage. Another suggestion is that the relaxed border policy was implemented to mollify the northern Cypriots who, opposed to his hardline stance, had taken to protesting on the streets of Girne and Lefkoşa. A third theory suggests that Denktash's motive was largely an economic one: a chance for North Cyprus to gain financially from closer contact with its richer neighbours. This premise seems all the more plausible with the Republic of Cyprus now a fully fledged member of the EU.

Some of those fiscal benefits came immediately, with an announcement by the Greek Cypriot foreign minister of proposals to allow trade between the two sides, and to enable Turkish Cypriots to work in the south.

Over a decade on from this historic development, feelings are mixed. Denktash is long gone, as is his more moderate and media-friendly successor Mehmet Ali Talat. The north has enjoyed its strongest economic growth for decades, followed by its share of woe in the tailspin of the global recession. European Union grants have funded a range of regenerative infrastructure projects and the border crossings have increased in number and proved a resounding success. But despite the crossings and the steep acceleration of the north towards modernity, a hundred rounds of negotiations across the Green Line since September 2008 have produced few discernible stepping stones towards a unified island. Many Cypriots believe that there are geopolitical forces outside their control that weigh heavily against reunification ever happening. Nor can you ignore that deep feelings on both sides of the Green Line are buried only slightly below the surface: perhaps 40 years is not sufficient time to forgive or forget the happenings of 1974.

in as the tenth prime minister leading a coalition between the leftist CTP and the centrist DP. The next general election is scheduled for April 2018. April 2010 saw the election of a new president, the incumbent Prime Minister Derviş Eroğlu, for a five-year term.

The judiciary is independent of the government in both its executive and legislative capacities.

ECONOMY

Partition in 1974 resulted in dramatic changes. Some 180,000 Greek Cypriots were rehoused in the south. With aid and investment from abroad, especially in agriculture, construction and tourism, Greek Cyprus made a remarkable recovery from the Turkish invasion and was able to provide near full employment. About 45,000 Turkish Cypriots were rehoused in the north. Some 80% of the tourist infrastructure lay in the northern zone, but a huge lack of skilled workers prevented the developments of which the south proved capable. Even now, when major investment is in hand, the majority of tourists to the north come from the Turkish mainland. With them comes no hard currency, only the volatile Turkish lira, which has suffered from rampant inflation since the 1994 devaluations. On 1 January 2005 the Turkish lira was re-indexed to correct for inflation and six zeros were dropped from the currency. The result was the new Turkish lira.

Thus, while nowhere near a third-world country, North Cyprus struggled economically for many years after partition. In more recent times, GDP per capita has increased rapidly, reaching US$15,038 in 2012. The overall economy grew by a respectable 7% in 2007, fuelled by the temporary boom in the construction and education sectors, but the upward trend was then reversed with the impact of the global recession. The economy shrank by over 3% in 2008 and a further 6% in 2009, but recovered in 2010 with a 3.6% growth.

Unemployment has also risen recently, to an estimated 12% in 2010, as construction has faltered and a lower demand for student places has had an adverse impact on the education sector. The 2010 demise of North Cyprus's national airline, Cyprus Turkish Airlines, added to the problems, affecting the tourism sector both directly and indirectly.

Despite the recent downturn, the economy is still dominated by the services sector, buoyed in particular by tourism and education. A comparatively robust – and still growing – tourist industry, together with an increased contribution from the developing universities has pushed the services sector to account for nearly 70% of GDP in recent years. Agriculture accounts for around 10% of the economy, while the contribution made by manufacturing is negligible.

Güzelyurt, the market garden of Cyprus, lies in the north and provides some employment and income. Citrus fruits are exported from here, along with tobacco, vegetables and carob nuts from other areas of Turkish Cyprus, to Turkey, Britain and Germany. Just 13% of produce is exported to the Arab world, which is perhaps surprising given its geographical proximity. Along with industrial and agricultural activities, the Güzelyurt region has historically supplied approximately 50 of the estimated 65 million tonnes of water available annually in the north. With water shortages a perennial problem, work started in 2011 on the construction of a water pipeline from mainland Turkey. This is due to become operational sometime in 2015 (see box, page 95).

For many years, negotiations were ongoing to consider Cyprus as a candidate for EU membership. The Treaty of Guarantee of 1960 (to which Britain was party) bars the island from membership of any union unless both Greece and Turkey are also members. With Greece already a member, the spotlight was shining firmly in the direction of Turkey, whose aspirations of joining the club had always foundered on its weak economy and, following years of fighting the Kurds in the east of the country, poor human-rights record.

The 2004 reunification referendum provided the opportunity for real progress to be made, but alas the chance was missed. With the Greek Cypriots voting 'No' to the UN resettlement plan, the south joined the EU anyway as the independent Republic of Cyprus whilst the north remains in political exile. Despite this, considerable EU money has been made available in the north for road development, water purification and other infrastructure projects, though this is nothing in comparison with the free-market benefits that fully fledged EU membership would provide. The ardour of Turkey itself for EU membership appears to have cooled in the face of vocal opposition from existing members, together with its own renewed economic confidence. Does Turkey need the EU, or does the EU need Turkey? If Turkey does want to join the EU party, the Cyprus debate will be a significant factor in the equation. It is worth remembering that both Greece and the Republic of Cyprus would have a veto over Turkey's membership of the community, and that other existing members are strongly opposed to it.

In the meantime, Turkish trade and financial assistance are indispensable to the economic wellbeing of North Cyprus. One recent newspaper report stated that North Cyprus's stand-alone revenues could only support 74% of its costs; another that the total debt owed to Turkey was now $7.5 billion. The public sector is hugely bloated, with salaries and associated benefits typically far more generous than private-sector pay. In an attempt to curb an out-of-control budget, the North Cypriot government announced austerity measures in early 2011, which were fully endorsed by Ankara, and Turkey has been significantly reducing the level of financial support since then. Turkish Cypriots would politely point out that the financial assistance provided by mainland Turkey is diluted by the huge number of Turks now located in North Cyprus, who benefit from it through their use of North Cypriot schools and hospitals.

PEOPLE

In 2011 the population of the whole island was about 1.1 million, of which around 60% was Greek Cypriot. The Greek Cypriots consider themselves ethnically Greek, tracing their ancestry back to the Mycenaean settlements of the 14th century BC. In its early history, the island allied itself with Greece against Persia and against the Arabs, and under the 800-year rule of Byzantium the independent Orthodox Church was established on the island.

The Turkish Cypriots are the descendants of the mainland Turks who stayed behind after the Ottoman conquest, or of settlers who came across from the mainland at that time. They are Muslim, though generally not especially devout. Since the breakdown of the 1960 Constitution they have been self-administered.

Post-1974, immigrants were brought in from mainland Turkey, often rural subsistence farmers from eastern Anatolia, to settle in the underpopulated north and work the land. Final figures published for the 2011 census suggest that the official population of North Cyprus then was 294,000, an increase of 11% since the previous census in 2006. The suspicion among most locals is that the true population figure is much higher, swollen by illegal workers and foreign students. Many estimates of the population would put it at around 500,000. According to the census figures, the official permanent populations of each of the five municipal regions were, to the nearest thousand, as follows: Lefkoşa, 98,000; Gazimağusa, 69,000; Girne, 73,000; Güzelyurt, 31,000; İskele, 23,000.

Although no split is yet available from the 2011 census, the 2006 figures show that 53% of the official population had North Cypriot citizenship, 27% Turkish citizenship, 17% dual citizenship (North Cypriot plus another) and the remaining 3% took its citizenship from elsewhere.

LANGUAGE

Turkish is the language of North Cyprus, although English is widely spoken and understood, especially in the developed tourist region around Girne. Most teaching at the universities of North Cyprus is carried out in English, thus making proficiency in the language a prerequisite for entry.

Out in the rural areas, finding an English speaker is by no means guaranteed, so learning a few essentials in Turkish – as set out in *Appendix 1*, pages 185–90 – is advisable. In the Karpas, there are a few Greek-Cypriot villages where Greek is spoken, while in the village of Koruçam, the small Maronite (Lebanese Christian) population speak a unique form of Arabic influenced by the ancient biblical language of Aramaic.

RELIGION

Turkish Cypriots are Sunni (ie: Orthodox) Muslims, but research studies have consistently shown them to be far less practising than their mainland counterparts. Islam is not a dominant force on the island. Although the call to prayer is often heard and you will find a gleaming new white mosque in even the smallest of villages, there is hardly a stampede at prayer time. As in Turkey, the secular weekend of Saturday and Sunday is followed, rather than the Muslim Friday. Shops and restaurants function as normal during the fasting month of Ramadan. See also pages 44–6.

EDUCATION

Even before partition, schools were separate for Greek and Turkish Cypriots, though there was a bi-communal school in Lefkoşa established by the British. In 1971, there were 542 Greek primary and 42 secondary schools, and 166 Turkish primary and 19 secondary schools. Schooling has been much expanded in the north since partition, with a growing number of colleges and technical schools. All of North Cyprus's universities are young, having been founded within the last 30 years, but at least until very recently, they are continuing to expand, with nearly all teaching in the English language. They offer a wide range of courses, diplomas and degrees, in many different faculties. Indeed, the fees these courses attract from the large number of foreign students (many from Turkey) have now become a significant source of income for the island. However, some foreign students bemoan the standard of teaching, the lack of accreditation afforded to North Cypriot degrees and the fact that the learning process is sometimes slowed by North Cypriot students' lack of fluency in English compared with their own.

The Eastern Mediterranean University (EMU) has established itself in Gazimağusa as an international university catering for 15,000 students from over 60 different countries around the world. Science, engineering and management

1

are the largest faculties, but it also offers courses in law, international relations, architecture and both Turkish and English literature. Programmes in tourism and hospitality are recent additions. The newly developed European University of Lefke, with 3,000 students from over 35 countries, offers courses in architecture, business administration, law, engineering and English language and literature, amongst others. Girne American University (GAU), previously called the University College of North Cyprus, now offers a full range of courses to students from 70 countries, its scope having expanded dramatically from its original position as a liberal arts college. Its main base in Kyrenia features medicine, law, dentistry and pharmacy among its faculties. It also has campuses in Canterbury in the UK, Singapore and Istanbul. The Cyprus International University is based close to the capital, claiming 8,000 students from 64 countries. The Middle East Technical University, based in Ankara, Turkey, has a new campus situated north of Güzelyurt, with a 2013–14 enrolment target of 3,500 students, while the Near East University in Lefkoşa pulls in 22,000 students from over 80 countries. Finally, the University of Mediterranean (Akdeniz) Karpasia is a Lefkoşa-based institution, which commenced in 2012 and features a faculty of aviation.

CULTURE

Although they share one language, Turkish Cypriots are proudly distinct from mainland Turks. However, the transient tourist is unlikely to distinguish the one from the other, a fact that is readily understood by the locals.

While Islam is the religion in North Cyprus, it doesn't impact as heavily upon social behaviour and cultural etiquette as it does in some of the Arabic countries. To the visitor, North Cyprus is a secular society. Alcohol is freely available and a few tourists bathe topless on some of the beaches. You will see many ladies with their heads covered, though they are generally Turkish rather than Turkish Cypriot.

With many aspects of Western lifestyles eagerly adopted, at first glance the indigenous culture may not be obvious. To experience it, a visit to one or more of the local festivals makes a good starting point. True, some of these are fairly recent in origin, but their focus is often on preserving the indigenous culture and traditions through music, dancing and demonstration of traditional arts and crafts such as baking and basket-weaving (page 46).

MUSIC Everyday life in North Cyprus is not driven by a perpetual musical beat in the way that many other cultures are. The many festivals (pages 45–6) give the visitor the opportunity to hear North Cypriot music, and some of the hotels and restaurants provide entertainment, especially in summer, which may incorporate music of a traditional nature.

Should you wish to take home a musical souvenir, then two compilations of traditional music are **Kibris Oyunlari** and **Oyun Hunalari**, both available from **Levy's CD Bar** (*160 Ziya Rizki Caddesi;* ✆ *815 72 72*) in Girne. Some of the songs are Turkish rather than Turkish Cypriot, but the distinction to the visitor's ear is marginal.

2

Practical Information

WHEN TO VISIT

North Cyprus is a year-round holiday destination, but unless you are a fan of extreme summer heat or cool winters, spring and autumn are the best times to visit. From late February until late April the island comes alive with thousands of colourful flowers, and in March and April the air is infused with the scent of citrus blossom. Rain is virtually unheard of between June and mid-September, with the midsummer months of July and August sending the mercury soaring, sometimes pushing towards 45°C.

The rainy season generally lasts from November until February, although occasional showery days do occur in October and even more so in March. December and January are the wettest months, while January and February are the coldest. April and May can yield terrific rainstorms, but you never have to wait for more than a day or two before brilliant sunshine breaks out again. If you are considering a winter visit, bear in mind that some hotels and visitor-orientated services may be closed from October to March. This is also the favoured season for restoration work on historic buildings.

HIGHLIGHTS

It's too much of a cliché to say that North Cyprus has a 'little bit of everything', but the region is certainly flexible in being able to satisfy a wide range of visitor tastes. Anyone from pure beach lovers to dedicated history fanatics – as well as those who crave more energetic outdoor pursuits – should find something to keep them happy. For the former, the white sands of the north and east coasts will prove alluring (pages 94–6 and 149), and those who are prepared to forego luxury will enjoy the more primitive ambience of the Karpas seascapes (pages 176–7). The towering Crusader castles of St Hilarion (pages 79–85), Buffavento (pages 113–15) and Kantara (pages 121–3), peaceful Bellapais Abbey (pages 85–8) and the ruined churches and crumbling walls of Gazimağusa and Lefkoşa (pages 153–8 and 129–3) will provide more than a fortnight's interest for historians. For other, more strenuous activities, both land- and sea-based, North Cyprus has plenty to offer, without – as yet – seeming to ram commercialism down the throat of the visitor. The craggy Kyrenia Mountains (page 3), the Karpas Peninsula (pages 171–84) and the flat, remote area around Akdeniz (pages 103–5) will allow the more adventurous to find a bit of welcome escape in scenic surroundings, be they coastal or mountainous; clear Mediterranean waters will tempt the swimmer, snorkeller and scuba diver.

Lovers of birdlife have ample opportunities to pursue their passion, and colourful and interesting flora such as orchids and black tulips pepper the landscapes according to season. In the summer months, nesting loggerhead turtles provide nature lovers with moments of true wonder on Alagadi Beach, while the inquisitive wild Karpas donkeys are an entertainment in themselves.

No-one who wants to get close to North Cypriot culture should depart the region without sampling one of the festivals exhibiting many of the arts and crafts that might otherwise be in danger of disappearing forever (see pages 44–6 for a full list). And even for the laziest visitor, North Cyprus presents daily opportunities to sample some of its finest treasures: culinary delights prepared with fresh fish and high-quality meats.

SUGGESTED ITINERARIES

Recent years have seen a boom in package holidays and property development, and North Cyprus now gives other Mediterranean resorts more than a run for their money when it comes to choosing a week away in the sun. Nonetheless, for those willing to circumvent an occasionally gaudy tourist veneer, the heart of what makes North Cyprus special remains the same. In such a small country, and with most people choosing to base themselves in and around Girne, all the major sights can comfortably be visited as day trips – the one exception being the Karpas Peninsula, where at least one night should be spent to experience the unique tranquillity of this unspoilt wilderness.

In addition to visiting the major attractions listed below, nature lovers will want to spend some time walking, admiring the flora and orchids (depending on the season) or birdwatching. The following suggestions are the most popular excursion options, and they assume your holiday base is in or around Girne. If your chosen base is Gazimağusa, then Vouni, Soli and Güzelyurt will be more comfortably visited if you spend at least one night in the west, whereas the Karpas could become just a day trip.

Half-day trips
St Hilarion
Bellapais
Buffavento
Beaches to east and west
Mountain monasteries

Day trips
Vouni, Soli and Güzelyurt
Lefkoşa (Nicosia)
Kantara Castle
Gazimağusa (Famagusta)
Salamis

Overnight trips
Karpas Peninsula

TOUR OPERATORS

GENERAL
A1 Cyprus Travel 1A Gateway Mews, Ringway, Bounds Green, London N11 2UT; ☏ 0800 711 7619; e sales@a1cyprus.com; www.a1cyprus.com
Alternative Cyprus 146 Kingsland High St, London E8 2NS; ☏ 020 7249 9800; e info@alternativecyprus.com; www.alternativecyprus.com
Anatolian Sky Holidays Anatolian House, 81 Warwick Rd, Solihull B92 7HP; ☏ 0844 273 3102; e sales@anatoliansky.co.uk; www.anatoliansky.co.uk

Cox & Kings Travel 6th Floor, 30 Millbank, London SW1P 4EE; ☏ 020 7873 5000; e sales@coxandkings.co.uk; www.coxandkings.co.uk
Cyprus Direct 62 Serpentine Rd, Widley, Waterlooville PO7 5EF; ☏ 0239 223 0030; e cyprusdirect@btconnect.com; www.cyprusdirectholidays.com
Cyprus Paradise 311 Ballards Lane, Finchley, London N12 8LY; ☏ 0800 170 0777; e sales@cypruspremier.com; www.cyprusparadise.com

Diplomat Travel 12 Eccleston St, London SW1W 9LT; 020 7730 2201; e sales@diplomat-travel.com; www.diplomattravel.co.uk

Direct Traveller 40–42 Hawks Rd, Kingston upon Thames KT1 3EG; 0844 414 1531; e reservations@directtraveller.com; www.directtraveller.com. See ad, 1st colour section.

The Discovery Collection 6A High St, Dunmow CM6 1AG; 01371 859 733; e sales@thediscoverycollection.com; www.discovery-collection.com

Go North Cyprus Holidays 0800 612 6600; e info@gonorthcyprus.com; www.gonorthcyprus.com

Happy Days Holidays & Tours 341 Green Lanes, London N4 1DZ; 020 8800 3836; e enquiries@happydaystravel.co.uk; www.happydaystravel.co.uk

Mercury Direct Suffolk House, Sevenoaks, Kent TN13 1XE; 0800 083 1725 or 0333 003 2812; e res.supervisors@mercurydirect.com; www.mercury-direct.co.uk

Metak Holidays Compass Hse, 36 East St, Bromley BR1 1QU; 020 8290 9293; e info@metaktravel.co.uk; www.metaktravel.co.uk

Mosaic Holidays 26 Windmill Pl, Windmill Lane, Hanwell UB2 4NJ; 020 8574 4000; e sales@mosaicholidays.co.uk; www.mosaicholidays.co.uk

New President Holidays 25 Cheston Av, Croydon CR0 8DE; 020 8406 4440; e sales@newpresidentholidays.com; www.newpresidentholidays.com

Noble Caledonia Ltd 2 Chester Close, London SW1X 7BE; 020 7752 0000; e info@noble-caledonia.co.uk; www.noble-caledonia.co.uk

Patrick Syder Travel Zenobia Hse, 23 Bowmans Close, Steyning BN44 3SR; 01903 879 737; e info@sydertravel.com; www.sydertravel.com

Transit Tours 252 High St, Orpington BR6 0LZ; 01689 832 532; e r.hatherly@transit-travel.com; www.transit-travel.com

Travelsphere Compass Hse, Rockingham Rd, Market Harborough LE16 7QD; 0844 417 1326; www.travelsphere.co.uk (email via website)

Tulip Holidays 9 Grand Parade, Green Lanes, London N4 1JX; 020 8211 0001; e info@tulipholidays.com; www.tulipholidays.com

Voyages Jules Verne 21 Dorset Sq, London NW1 6QG; 0845 166 7003; e sales@vjv.co.uk; www.vjv.com

SPECIALIST

Cricketer Holidays Beacon Hse, Croft Rd, Crowborough TN6 1DL; 01892 664 242; e info@cricketerholidays.co.uk; www.cricketerholidays.co.uk

Exodus TUI Travel House, Crawley Business Quarter, Fleming Way, Crawley RH10 9QL; 0845 163 3472; e sales@exodus.co.uk; www.exodus.co.uk

Explore Nelson Hse, 55 Victoria Rd, Farnborough GU14 7PA; 0843 634 6112; e info@explore.co.uk; www.explore.co.uk

Kudu Travel 3 Midland Close, Bradford on Avon, Wiltshire BA15 1DB; 01225 436 115; e kuduinfo@kudutravel.com; www.kudutravel.com

Maranatha Tours Trafalgar Hse, Oak Business Park, Beaumont, Essex, CO16 0AT; 01255 871 423; e info@maranatha.co.uk; www.maranatha.co.uk

Naturetrek Cheriton Mill, Cheriton, Alresford SO24 0NG; 01962 733 051; e info@naturetrek.co.uk; www.naturetrek.co.uk

North Cyprus Tour Advantage Hse, Office 1, 273 Fore St, London N9 0PD; 020 3417 6373; e info@ecoturkey.com; www.ecoturkey.com

Ramblers Holidays Lemsford Mill, Lemsford Village, Welwyn Garden City AL8 7TR; 01707 331 133; e info@ramblersholidays.co.uk; www.ramblersholidays.co.uk

Solitair Holidays Solitair House, 12 Arundel St, Manchester M15 4JP; 0844 414 4010; e www.solitairhols.co.uk. Walking & singles holidays.

Solo's Holidays 54–58 High St, Edgeware HA8 7EJ; 0844 815 0005; e travel@solos.co.uk; www.solosholidays.co.uk

WEDDING ORGANISERS Taking advantage of the almost year-round sunshine and some picturesque locations, an increasing number of visitors choose North Cyprus as the venue for their big day. For the wedding guests, it provides an excuse for a holiday, while for the happy couple there can be considerable cost savings. Note that it is currently not possible, for legal reasons, to conduct civil-partnership ceremonies or same-sex marriages in North Cyprus.

Although the marriage formalities are by no means complex, one slip-up in the required documentation could mean an expensive, wasted trip. Help is at hand, in the shape of a number of established wedding organisers:

North Cyprus Weddings m 0533 864 41 15; e info@northcyprusweddings.net; www. northcyprusweddings.net

Surya-Harrell North Cyprus Weddings m 0533 868 3867; e info@north-cyprusweddings. com; www.north-cyprusweddings.com

IN NORTH CYPRUS Despite growing opportunities for independent travel, most visitors to North Cyprus still go on package holidays. Operators and hotels offer a range of tours and activities, but do consider some of the more interesting ecotourist options that aren't part of the usual range of offerings (see box, page 175). Once you are in North Cyprus, you could try **KITSAB**, the Cyprus Turkish Tourism & Travel Agents Association (*www.kitsab.org*), which currently has around 140 local members across the region, but its website is mainly in Turkish. You may therefore be better using your chosen specialist operator to organise trips, or simply search on foot for operators in the centre of Kyrenia.

One specialist North Cyprus-based operator, run by an English couple, is **Cyprus Active** (m *0533 870 4865 or 0533 881 8993; e info@cyprusactive.com; www. cyprusactive.com*). They organise a large number of activities, from coast-to-coast walks to jeep safaris, kite-surfing, sailing and scuba-diving.

For local tour operators dealing with specific sports and recreation, see pages 48–53. If you need to book a flight or ferry ticket, **Denizkızı Travel** (*Ziya Rizki Caddesi, Girne;* ✆ *815 12 00; e info@denizkizitravel.com; www.denizkizitravel.com*) will happily oblige, as well as booking hotels and hire cars. Another well-established operator is **Cyprus Xp Group** (*Ziya Rizki Caddesi, Girne;* ✆ *815 46 81; www.cyprusxp.com*), which offers the same services and claims to get discounts on Pegasus Airlines flights.

TOURIST INFORMATION

In London, the **North Cyprus Tourism Centre** (*29 Bedford Sq, London WC1B 3ED;* ✆ *020 7631 1930; e info@simplynorthcyprus.com; www.welcometonorthcyprus.co.uk; see ad, inside front cover*) produces an occasional magazine and will send out copies of their increasingly comprehensive range of free maps and colour pamphlets, and provides a wealth of other assistance.

On the island, there are also tourist offices distributing maps and pamphlets in Girne, Gazimağusa, Lefkoşa, Yeni Erenköy and Ercan Airport, together with a small kiosk at the Locmacı Street checkpoint. The official opening hours are given in the respective sections of this book, although in traditional Turkish Cypriot style these hours are somewhat flexible and visitors should prepare for the fact that offices occasionally seem to open and close on the whim of the staff. In the USA, there are two representative offices of the TRNC. In New York, the office (*821 United Nations Plaza, 6th Floor, New York, NY 10017;* ✆ *212 687 2350*) acts as a tourist information centre, deals with visa matters and serves as the region's contact point with the United Nations, while the Washington branch (*1667 K Street, NW Suite 690, Washington DC 20006;* ✆ *202 887 6198*) operates as the de facto embassy to the USA.

RED TAPE

PASSPORTS AND VISAS British and US passport holders do not need visas for North Cyprus and a 90-day stay is permitted to all visitors. If your flight is simply transiting Turkey *en route* to Ercan and you do not leave the transit lounge, you do not require a Turkish visa. If, however, you want to leave the airport and visit Istanbul for a few hours or a few days, you will have to buy a visa, available as you exit through passport control. The visa must be bought in foreign cash, preferably sterling, though it is cheaper at US$20 to get an e-visa in advance through the government website (*www.turkishconsulate.org.uk*). For those who wish to avoid a North Cyprus stamp in their passports, there is a special form that can be requested from the cabin crew before landing, and this can then be stamped in place of the passport. This form must be retained throughout your visit. Contrary to what most people believe, a TRNC stamp in your passport does not in fact prevent a future visit to Greece or its islands. The TRNC stamp is simply cancelled with your permission on arrival in Greece.

FOREIGN MISSIONS Turkey is the only country to have a full embassy in North Cyprus. Britain, the USA, Germany and Australia have liaison offices in Lefkoşa for consular services and for cultural and social relations with TRNC.

Association Culturelle Franco-Chypriote Turque 4 Derviş Paşa Sokak, Lefkoşa; ☎ 228 33 28; e info@fransizkultur.org; www.fransizkultur.org Established in 1985 to promote cultural relations with France, holds film nights & cultural events.
Australian High Commission (Annex) 'Australia Place,' 20 Güner Türkmen Sokak, Lefkoşa; ☎ 227 73 32; e nicosia.ahc@dfat. gov.au; www.embassy.gov.au/cyprus; ⏰ 08.30–12.30 Tue & Thu only
British Council 7 Şht Üsteğmen Ünal Genç Sokak, Marmara Bölgesi, Lefkoşa; ☎ 227 49 38; e enquiries@cy.britishcouncil.org; ⏰ 08.30–13.00 & 14.00–17.30 Tue & Thu. The British Council organises some cultural events in North Cyprus, such as films & exhibitions.

British High Commission Shakespeare Av, 29 Mehmet Akif Caddesi, Lefkoşa; ☎ 357 228 61 100 (NB: this is a South Cyprus number); e nicosia. consular@fco.gov.uk; www.ukincyprus.fco.gov.uk; ⏰ 09.30–12.30 Wed only. Appointments must be pre-booked. Use phone number in emergencies.
German Information Office 29 Mehmet Akif Caddesi, Lefkoşa; ☎ 227 51 61; e nordbuero.diplo. de@gmail.com; www.nikosia.diplo.de; ⏰ 10.00– 14.00 Tue–Fri. Premises shared with the British.
Turkish Embassy Bedreddin Demirel Caddesi, Lefkoşa; ☎ 227 23 14; ⏰ 08.30–11.30 Mon–Fri
United States Embassy North Cyprus Office, 2nd Floor, 6 Şerif Arzic Sokak, Lefkoşa; ☎ 227 39 30; ⏰ 08.00–17.00 Mon–Fri

GETTING THERE AND AWAY

BY AIR There are two distinct ways of flying to North Cyprus: either 'direct' to the north, via Turkey, or via the Republic of Cyprus ('the South') and transferring across the border.

Direct to the North TRNC's airport for tourist traffic is Ercan (formerly called Tymbou). Small, but well equipped, it is situated some 24km east of Lefkoşa.

Flights from London to Ercan take a minimum of 6 hours, but don't expect much in the way of in-flight entertainment. These flights, on a range of different aircraft, are operated up to three times daily from Stansted by **Pegasus** (*www.flypgs.com*) and from Heathrow and Gatwick by **Turkish Airlines** (*www.turkishairlines.com*). The latter also fly to Ercan from Manchester, Birmingham and Edinburgh. **Atlasjet** (*www.atlasjet.com*) fly from London Luton to Ercan. Return fares on these airlines vary from £130 to over £500 according to season and availability. The 'national carrier' of North Cyprus, Cyprus Turkish Airlines, went out of business in 2010, leaving many passengers stranded or out of pocket. Since its demise, there have

2

been plentiful rumours about its resurrection under various names, but at time of writing, the rumours have come to nothing.

Irrespective of which airline you choose, all flights to Ercan have to touch down on the Turkish mainland, since TRNC is not recognised by any country except Turkey. From Europe, the touchdown points are usually Istanbul or Izmir, or occasionally Antalya or Dalaman. When touching down in Turkey, passengers for Ercan do not normally leave the plane, but simply wait on the tarmac for around 45 minutes. During peak season, these flights fill up surprisingly quickly, so you need to book well in advance if you have specific time constraints on your travel dates.

Another method for those who do not mind the hassle is to get the cheapest available flight to Istanbul then buy a return ticket to Ercan from the Turkish Airlines, Onurair or Anadolujet offices in Istanbul. However, unless you actually want to include mainland Turkey in your travels, the advent of Pegasus and Atlasjet flights to Ercan negates any cost-saving, except in the most exceptional circumstances.

The return fare for Istanbul–Ercan ranges from about £50 to £180 and is classed as an internal domestic flight. Despite this, all flights to Ercan use Atatürk International Airport rather than the scruffy domestic terminal used for other internal flights. This is a great bonus as any time spent waiting for connections is far more pleasant, Atatürk International Airport being very modern and efficient, with an extensive range of shops and restaurants. Flights to Ercan get fairly full, so it is advisable to reserve in advance, then pay and collect the tickets at Istanbul. Check-in time at Istanbul is 2 hours ahead of flight time. It may also be useful to note that, from the Turkish mainland, there are additional direct flights to Ercan from Ankara, Antalya, Adana, Dalaman and Izmir.

Ercan Airport   North Cyprus's recently revamped and functional airport is located 24km southeast of Lefkoşa, 37km southeast of Girne and 51km west of Gazimağusa. Facilities are as you would expect from a small airport: information desk (in departures), a few modest shops, airline offices, two expensive cafés, free Wi-Fi, a nonsensical number of ATMs and two car-hire companies (page 40). Most people arriving on packages will have a transfer already organised, but taxis and the Kibhas Bus Company (*www.kibhas.org*) will provide the necessary service otherwise.

Via the South   The second way of flying to the TRNC is to fly to the Republic of Cyprus, then cross the border. As it is now possible to move freely between the Turkish and Greek Cypriot sectors, this alternative has become extremely popular. With healthy competition between scheduled and charter operators, and the recent appearance of budget carriers, it can be an attractive and cheaper proposition to enter North Cyprus by this method. **British Airways** (*www.britishairways.com*) offers direct flights from Heathrow and Gatwick to Larnaca (5hrs), and flies to Paphos from Gatwick (4½hrs). **EasyJet** (*www.easyjet.com*) covers Larnaca from Gatwick and Liverpool; and Paphos from Gatwick, Luton, Manchester, Bristol and Edinburgh. Return fares on some of these routes can be as low as £80 if you book far enough in advance, but rise to a totally ridiculous £550 for short-notice reservations in peak season. It's worth shopping around though, as you or a tenacious independent travel agent could come up with return low-season charter seats to Larnaca for around £150, from a whole host of regional airports including Bristol, Glasgow, East Midlands, Exeter, Birmingham, Cardiff, Leeds-Bradford, Newcastle and Belfast.

Some Turkish and Greek Cypriot taxi drivers now hold special licences that allow them to cross the border either at Lefkoşa or Gazimağusa. From Larnaca, expect to pay in the region of £50 for the 90-minute journey to Girne. One Girne-based, English-speaking driver with the correct papers to get to and from Larnaca Airport is Ayğun Bey (m *0533 862 71 37*). Flying to Paphos will entail a long and pricey transfer to reach North Cyprus, hence Larnaca is preferred. Alternatively, some pre-booked car-hire companies in North Cyprus will send a car and driver down to collect you.

Should you want to travel on a tailored package then it's worth knowing that Direct Traveller and other operators will fly you to Larnaca and then whisk you across the border to your chosen destination in the north (page 25).

Scheduled airlines
✈ **Atlasjet** www.atlasjet.com
✈ **EasyJet** www.easyjet.com
✈ **Pegasus Airlines** ✆0845 0848980; www.pegasusairlines.com, www.flypgs.com. No UK-based office so phone enquiries are redirected to Turkey where there are a limited number of English speakers to take your calls.

✈ **Turkish Airlines** Lyric House, 149 Hammersmith Rd, London W14 0QL; ✆0844 800 6666; e info@turkish-airlines.co.uk; www. turkishairlines.com

Charter flights
✈ **Monarch** www.monarch.co.uk
✈ **Thomas Cook** www.thomascook.com
✈ **Thomson** www.thomson.co.uk

BY BOAT Fares and timetables for ferries are subject to frequent change, so check in advance if you are planning a trip that involves sea travel. The Cyprus Turkish Shipping Company operates a car ferry all year round from Mersin in southern Turkey to Gazimağusa. Currently they run three times a week in each direction, with a 12-hour journey time, departing Gazimağusa at 20.00 Sunday, Tuesday and Thursday and departing Mersin at 20.00 Monday, Wednesday and Friday. The journey takes approximately 12 hours. Single fares for foot passengers are currently TL105. Cars must be booked in advance and a standard saloon car plus driver costs TL310. The company's office is just before the military barrier by the Icon Museum in Gazimağusa. Tickets can be bought there, but not online or at travel agencies.

Cheaper and quicker routes to North Cyprus are offered by Akgünler Shipping and by a more recently established operator, Filo Shipping. Both companies operate from Girne's ferry port. To and from Taşucu in southern Turkey, the fastest ferry is operated by Akgünler for foot passengers only and carries 250 people, departing Tuesday, Wednesday and Sunday from Girne and making the crossing in 2½ hours or less, with a single ticket costing TL135. This fast ferry returns from the mainland on Mondays, Fridays and Saturdays. The same company also operates slower vehicle ferries, four times a week, departing Taşucu on Tuesday, Wednesday, Thursday and Sundays, returning from Girne on Mondays (two sailings), Thursday and Fridays. The voyage takes 4 hours in the day and up to 8 hours at night. Passenger fares are TL95, or TL115 in 'business class'. Filo also operates a thrice-weekly car ferry, departing from Girne on Mondays, Wednesdays and Fridays, with passenger fares costing TL95, returning on Sundays, Tuesdays and Thursdays. Children and student fares are cheaper; all fares quoted include taxes. Cars can be imported into TRNC without customs duty for up to one month: a permit is issued at the port of entry. The permit can be renewed for up to a year. Vehicles must be accompanied by an insurance certificate valid for TRNC, which can be bought at the port of entry.

Ferry companies Akgünler Shipping and Filo Shipping both have websites, which give full details of all fares and timings and which now allow online booking of tickets.

Akgünler Shipping Ramadan Cemil Meydani No 1, Girne; ☎ 444 43640 or 815 6002; e denizcilik@akgunler.com.tr; www.akgunler.com.tr (in Turkish only). Tickets can be booked online at a separate, English-language website, www.akgunlerbilet.com.

Cyprus Turkish Shipping (KTD) 3 Bülent Ecevit Bulvari, Gazimağusa; ☎ 366 59 95; e sales@kibrisdeniz.net; www.kibrisdeniz.net

Filo Shipping Yeni Liman Yolu, Candemir Apt No 7, Girne; ☎ 815 39 41; e filodenizcilik@hotmail.com; www.filoshipping.com. Their office is at the ferry port in Girne.

By car: access to and from Greek Cyprus

The stringent border regulations that for so long prevented free movement between the north and south sectors of Cyprus have eroded. Since 2003 both Cypriot locals and EU tourists have been able to cross at one of five designated checkpoints, open 24 hours. A further crossing at Locmacı Street/Ledra Street in Lefkoşa was opened to pedestrians in April 2008, and in October 2010 an additional crossing was unveiled by both presidents at Yeşilırmak. The formalities are straightforward – simply present yourself with your passport and complete the appropriate visa application. The current crossings are:

Metehan (aka Agios Dometios or Kermia) (Lefkoşa) This crossing handles the most traffic of the six vehicle crossings and may also be used by pedestrians.

Akyar (aka Black Knight or Agios Nikolaos) (Gazimağusa) Within the British Eastern Sovereign Base Area and open to all traffic.

Ledra Palace (aka Ledra Gate) (Lefkoşa) Right by the Green Line in Lefkoşa. Open to pedestrians, cyclists and diplomatic vehicles only.

Locmacı Street (aka Ledra Street) (Lefkoşa) This is a result of north/south rapprochement and is the newest, and perhaps the most interesting and most frequented, of the pedestrian-only crossings. The familiar repository of global high-street names that is Nicosia's Ledra Street contrasts starkly with Lefkoşa's Locmacı Street. The distance walked is insignificant, but the gulf of culture and affluence is huge (though diminishing) – truly 'east meets west.'

Dhekelia (aka Pergamos or Beyarmudu) (Gazimağusa) The other gate in the British Eastern Sovereign Base Area, again open to all traffic.

Güzelyurt (aka Zohdia, Bostanci, Morpho, Astromeritis, Morfu, Omorfo) (Güzelyurt) The crossing point with the most names. Open to all traffic.

Yeşilırmak Situated in the far west, at the end of a road partially funded by the EU. The newest crossing, open to all vehicles and pedestrians.

Private cars Privately owned cars can be driven from north to south and vice versa, as long as the driver purchases the requisite third-party insurance at the Metehan crossing point. For cars entering from the south, you have to purchase a month's cover for €25, with other classes of vehicles costing more and hire cars costing €20 for three days' cover or €35 for a month. For cars travelling in the opposite direction, cover costs around TL50 for one month.

Hire cars Some Greek Cypriot hire companies now allow rental cars to cross to the north, although the cover afforded by the increased insurance premiums needs careful scrutiny – some will cover damage up to a maximum of only £2,000–3,000 worth of damage in case of an accident, irrespective of the total repair bill.

Similarly, some North Cypriot car-hire companies will allow their vehicles to be taken into the south, though they do not actively promote this or recommend it. In the event that you break down or encounter difficulties while in the south, bear in mind that your hire company will be unable to easily assist you. If you must take a hire car south, be sure you get the necessary written permission and that you understand all the implications when you make your booking. You will need to first go to the Metehan crossing point in Lefkoşa and obtain the necessary additional insurance, without which you will be denied the right to cross the border to the south.

There are unconfirmed reports of cars with North Cyprus number plates being targeted in the south, with stones being thrown at them and bodywork being scratched. Likewise, some car rental companies in the south claim that their cars have been impounded in the north after accidents, and returned to them six months later as 'wrecks'. As it's impossible to establish the truth or otherwise of any of these reports, you would be wise to do separate hires for the south and north parts of your trip.

Crossing the border The relaxation of the border policy has led to an increase in traffic, both local and tourist, between the sectors. The scheme so far can be considered a success. However, despite recent developments to ease border regulations and make North Cyprus an altogether more visitor-friendly country, travellers should still remain vigilant against seemingly irrational and vindictive actions from police and checkpoint guards. Those visiting the south after arriving directly in the north are still deemed to have arrived illegally (though as passports are generally not stamped on either side of the Green Line, it's difficult to know how this would be determined and, in practice, this illegality is always overlooked).

When crossing the border, bear in mind that import limits on various goods apply. Travelling from south to north, goods to the value of €135 may be taken across the border before duty is payable. Any electrical goods should be shown to customs. Travelling from north to south, goods are limited to the lira equivalent of €260 (approximately TL520) before duty is payable. Travelling in either direction, no goods for resale should be carried, and restrictions on alcohol and tobacco are tight. The Foreign and Commonwealth Office website (*www.fco.gov.uk*) carries up-to-date information on applicable limits. If in doubt, ask the customs officials at the crossing-points, before you make a major purchase. There are also restrictions on carrying large quantities of cash. One Bradt reader contacted us in a state of some shock having been threatened with arrest for alleged tobacco smuggling when crossing from north to south. He eventually escaped with a fine, but such encounters can spoil any holiday. Just try to remember the politics of Cyprus – feelings still run deep and irrational behaviour on either side of the border is more likely to be the result of such ingrained disagreements than a personal vendetta against the tourist.

Those purchasing property in North Cyprus are strongly advised not to carry any deeds or documentation relating to their purchase across the land border. If these papers are discovered by Greek Cypriot authorities, at best they'll be confiscated and at worst the holders will be arrested. Under certain circumstances, the holders will be charged with the illegal purchase of Greek-owned property – an offence that can attract a substantial fine or even imprisonment. You have been warned.

All visitors are entitled to free emergency medical treatment at state hospitals, and all blood banks have been HIV screened. Many expat residents and visitors praise the quality of the medical care they receive. Note that at present there is no state system of GPs, though this is being mooted for the future. Chemist shops (Turkish *eczane*) are also capable of recommending medicines for common holiday illnesses, and many drugs such as antibiotics are available cheaply over the counter, with no need for prescriptions. Note that every edition of the English-language *Cyprus Today* newspaper lists duty chemists.

As the south part of the island is a full member of the EU, a short hop across the border will allow you to use the reciprocal rights bestowed by your EHIC (European Health Insurance Card), should you carry one. The EHIC is not valid in the north.

The **Kolan British Kyrenia Medical Center** (*220 Ziya Rizki Caddesi, Girne;* ✆ *815 59 00; www.kolanbritishkyrenia.com*) is a new, private GP clinic, accessible to all. Visitors pay TL80 for the initial consultation, but follow-up advice for the same complaint is then without further charge for the following 15 days. They also have a hospital in Lefkoşa, an emergency service at Ercan Airport and their own ambulances.

WATER Water is safe to drink in Turkish Cyprus but taste varies throughout the region, so most people prefer bottled mineral water, which is cheap, widely available and recommended. The natural springs in Lapta provide some of the purest water in the north. Water is very scarce at times on the island and visitors should respect this. The advent of piped water from Turkey should improve the situation.

VACCINATIONS No vaccinations are required for North Cyprus. However, as with any trip abroad, it is recommended that your tetanus, diphtheria and polio vaccinations are up to date. Hepatitis A vaccination may be recommended for longer trips where good food and water hygiene cannot be guaranteed. The vaccine (eg: Havrix Monodose, Avaxim) can be given even up to the day before travel and lasts for one year. A booster dose given at least six months after the first dose will extend cover for approximately 25 years. Foreign nationals intending either to work or study in Cyprus are required to undergo an HIV test. For those working in a medical setting or with children, a hepatitis B vaccine would be advised. This three-dose course can be given over 21 days when time is short for those aged 16 or over. If there's more time available (at least eight weeks), then a longer course is preferred and is essential for those under 16. There is no reciprocal healthcare with Britain, so adequate medical insurance is strongly recommended.

DIARRHOEA Diarrhoea is a common cause of illness in travellers. The most important treatment is to replace fluid loss and to prevent dehydration. Continue to eat plain foods and avoid alcohol, dairy products and anti-diarrhoea drugs unless absolutely necessary. Seek medical advice for the very young and elderly as soon as possible or if there is blood and/or slime in the stool and if you have a fever or if the diarrhoea persists for more than two days.

MOSQUITOES These can be a nuisance from spring onwards, so it is sensible to bring a DEET-based repellent. Around 50–55% DEET is considered to be the most effective.

SANDFLIES There's a risk of leishmaniasis from infected sandfly bites. These are therefore best avoided – use repellents and wear clothing that covers you up where appropriate. Infected dogs are the carriers of the disease, which can present itself either as a slow-growing skin nodule or ulcer (cutaneous form) or as a serious life-threatening fever and weight loss (Kala-azar).

SKIN IN THE SUN Heightened awareness of safety in the sun can only help towards a more enjoyable holiday for everyone. It is advisable to protect your skin from the sun's rays at all times, especially at midday. Best evidence suggests that you should use at least a factor 30.

TRAVEL CLINICS AND HEALTH INFORMATION A full list of current travel clinic websites worldwide is available on www.istm.org. For other journey preparation information, consult www.nathnac.org/ds/map_world.aspx (UK) or http://wwwnc. cdc.gov/travel/ (US). Information about various medications may be found on www.netdoctor.co.uk/travel. All advice found online should be used in conjunction with expert advice received prior to or during travel.

SAFETY

The atmosphere in the north is very relaxed and friendly. The Turkish Cypriot people are by nature easy-going, and violent crime is very rare. The aggravating hassling of foreigners by street sellers and shop owners, rampant in other parts of the Mediterranean, is blissfully absent here. If you ask for help, it will be offered willingly, but if you are just strolling and looking, you will be left to yourself. On Girne's harbour front, a waiter will try to entice you into his establishment, but it gets no worse than that. Women alone are not propositioned and it is quite safe to walk around after dark. Your privacy is respected and people keep their distance.

A few years ago, rapid growth in North Cyprus's construction industry saw tens of thousands of workers arrive from mainland Turkey, many without permits, to fuel the demand for labour. Without legal status, this workforce was open to exploitation and endured meagre wages and miserable living conditions. An inevitable rise in crime led to some headline cases in 2005, shaking the confidence of the local and expat population. In response, legislation was enacted in November 2006 making it considerably more difficult for unscrupulous employers to operate with illegal workers. In any case, the republic's labour market had reached saturation point with tens of thousands of mainland Turks working legally across all areas of the economy. A rise in crime statistics must be viewed in this context and statistically North Cyprus remains one of the safest holiday destinations, especially for those who take the usual common-sense precautions. Many expats willingly bear testimony to the feeling of safety and security there – though they are sometimes targets for the occasional scam.

Although there are in excess of 30,000 troops from the Turkish army stationed in camps here, they are highly disciplined and under strict instructions to be courteous to foreigners. At weekends, you may see groups of them harmlessly roaming the streets of Girne or Lefkoşa. Should you inadvertently stray into a military area, you will be politely escorted out and redirected; notices saying 'No photography' should always be taken seriously, as should the reduced speed limits in force when driving past: slow down, but don't stop. There are many, many military camps and occasionally they are uprooted and moved elsewhere, making it pointless to list them all here. If visiting Mavi Köşk (see box, page 98) or the Martyr's Museum in Lefkoşa (page 131), you will have to enter the surrounding camps and show your passport.

In general, you will find that the local people will bend over backwards to make you feel welcome. The Turkish Cypriots themselves make a hospitable nation, keen to please, happy to indulge in some banter, eager to ensure that visitors are content, and generally delighted to share their knowledge and opinions with the curious tourist.

SEASIDE SAFETY Although the Mediterranean is free from tidal activity, this does not mean that the beaches are free from currents (although in most situations they only run parallel to the shore, and thus pose little risk).

Some of the hotel beaches have lifeguards present, but this is not the case on public beaches. Care should be taken everywhere; awareness of the potential dangers of currents, rocks and waves may prevent any trouble. Weak swimmers should be properly supervised, and care should be exercised if you are using any inflatable swimming aids, particularly rubber rings. Litter is a problem on some beaches, so watch your feet.

DOGS AND CATS Although not exactly a danger, the large number of canine and feline inhabitants in North Cyprus is immediately obvious to any visitor. It can seem that every time you order a restaurant meal, you have unknowingly ordered a cat to come and share it with you. Many of the cats and dogs are strays that are fed and looked after by locals, who sometimes report that the local municipalities take a different attitude to the 'problem' – by exterminating them.

Some packs of dogs roam around specific areas of Girne, for example, but these do not seem to pose any overt threat to the inhabitants or tourists. Occasionally they take exception to a strange car or person visiting their 'territory', though their objection is likely to involve nothing more than a bout of barking. Your main worry should be making sure that you don't step on a dozing animal. A local charity, Kyrenia Animal Rescue (*www.kartrnc.org*) is tireless in collecting and tagging strays and welcomes any donations.

WOMEN TRAVELLERS

For foreign females, North Cyprus should be a relatively relaxed destination. Expat women and tourists report that they feel entirely safe walking around on their own after dark, there is no harassment of lone women and as a tourist destination it is untainted by the sort of expectations raised by the licentious behaviour of some visitors to other parts of the Mediterranean. Here it's all about sun, sea and sand, not sun, sea and sex.

Levels of crime against people are very low. Having said that, the usual precautions should be taken. The 'entertainment' spots to avoid are the seedy nightclubs that inhabit the roadside in usually out-of-town locations. These are basically lap-dancing joints, with prostitutes available for those who want them. It's unlikely that female visitors would stumble into one of these, but most would be uncomfortable if they did so. There are also a couple of 'motels' in the old part of Girne that also seem to have an alternative, seedy purpose.

Although the population is predominately Muslim, the dress sense for most Turkish Cypriot and Turkish women is secular. A significant proportion of the latter do wear headscarves, but you are unlikely to see a woman clad in a burqa. Visitors entering a mosque would do well to show respect by dressing appropriately: covered arms and shoulders, and avoidance of wearing short skirts, would show suitable sensitivity.

Out in the rural areas, it is a common sight to see small groups of men sitting about in the basic cafés that most villages seem to host. It is rare to see women in these establishments – presumably they are too busy working! There's no reason why foreign women shouldn't visit these village cafés, but you may be the only female present if you do.

TRAVELLERS WITH A DISABILITY

Wheelchair users will find that North Cyprus is not the most user-friendly of places. Investment in infrastructure to accompany increased tourism in recent years has led to better pavements, for example, but they are still far from easy to use and are also frequently used for the parking of cars. (On the rare occasions I saw a wheelchair during my time in North Cyprus, it was being pushed along the road, not the pavement.) Some hotels have installed ramps to allow access to bedrooms and public areas, but the situation is far from perfect.

The *Buzz* magazine, which is published quarterly and is freely available in bars and cafés, lists all the Girne restaurants, and indicates whether or not they cater for wheelchairs. It's probably best to ask at the time of booking, if you have any particular concerns.

Taxis are usually Mercedes saloon cars, comfortable and spacious for the able-bodied, but not much use for those with limited mobility. Similarly, *dolmuş* do not adapt for wheelchairs.

Needless to say, when booking through a major travel agency, advise them of your requirements in advance and you can expect to have your needs accommodated.

Although one specialist firm in the north did hire out mobility aids and wheelchairs until recently, the owner retired in 2012 and no-one seems to have taken on his sterling work.

ETHNIC MINORITY TRAVELLERS

While North Cyprus may have been internationally isolated for over 40 years, this does not mean that it's an ethnically homogeneous society. Perhaps half of the official population is from mainland Turkey, though your average visitor from Europe may not be able to distinguish between Turkish Cypriots and mainland Turks. Nevertheless, Turkish Cypriots are effectively a minority in their own territory.

Ethnic minorities are very unlikely to face hostility or harassment while visiting North Cyprus, although attitudes are not yet as liberal as in western Europe. A small but significant proportion of the student population comes from sub-Saharan Africa, the Middle East or the Indian subcontinent, which means that non-white faces are by no means a rarity in North Cyprus.

Indeed, the hotel trade around Girne employs staff from the Indian subcontinent, so your receptionist may be from India, Pakistan or Bangladesh. Some of these are working part-time to support themselves as they study, and many of the universities make use of their talents in their cricket teams! Adding to the rich ethnic mix, the significant number of British expats have in recent years been joined by an influx of property buyers and tourists from Russia, eastern Europe and the Middle East.

GAY AND LESBIAN TRAVELLERS

Despite North Cyprus being nominally Islamic, homosexuality and bisexuality are far from unknown and are – generally, at least – tolerated.

Cypriots and Turks are very tactile people, and you should not be surprised to see men hug and kiss each other (on the cheek) in public, so nothing in particular should be read into this. Ironically, other displays of public affection – such as kissing on the lips – even between straight partners, are frowned upon.

North Cyprus became the last place in Europe to decriminalise homosexual acts, when it voted in 2014 to repeal the relevant statutes that outlawed them. This resulted from many years of lobbying from various pressure groups. Changing some attitudes can, of course, take longer than changing legislation, so perhaps the best advice is still to keep overly passionate displays of your sexual tendencies, whether heterosexual or homosexual, low key when in public places. It is currently not possible to have a civil ceremony or same-sex marriage in North Cyprus.

TRAVELLING WITH CHILDREN

There are no special concerns for families choosing to holiday in the region. Where hotels do not welcome children, it is noted in this guide, though it's always worth checking at the time of booking. Some hotels have extra facilities aimed at youngsters, such as children's pools, kids' clubs and waterslides. Western food is widely available, especially around Girne, so burgers and pizza are never too far away for those youngsters who are not kebab-friendly.

WHAT TO TAKE

There's very little you need to take to North Cyprus that can't be sourced when you arrive, especially in the shops around Girne. Cosmetics, sun protection and most photographic accessories (including film and digital media) are readily available. In all but rare circumstances an adaptor plug will be unnecessary for British visitors. The electricity supply is 220–240 volts AC, and three-pin UK-style plugs are the norm.

Don't forget that North Cyprus still suffers from the misfortune of non-recognition by the international community. Whilst you're unlikely to suffer any problems, it could be worth the effort to travel with duplicates of all important documents or forms of identification – passport, airline tickets, hotel reservation, insurance documents, credit cards and the like. Leave a copy of each with somebody at home so the information is always available.

CLOTHING North Cyprus is not a dressy place and comfortable, informal clothing is best. Although nominally Muslim, Turkish Cypriots are very relaxed, and you can dress as you would when holidaying in Italy or Spain. Comfortable shoes are essential for climbs up to the mountain castles. Bikinis are fine and toplessness is increasing, especially among some nationalities on the fee-paying beaches.

From the end of October until mid-April it can be chilly, especially in the evenings. Take a light raincoat in the winter months, or an umbrella, as rainstorms are heavy.

Women may also wish to take a light scarf with them when visiting the mosques. It is not always required but it shows respect for the local culture and will make you feel more comfortable. Sometimes the mosques will provide appropriate clothing where the rules are enforced.

MONEY

In an attempt to adjust the effect of years of rampant inflation, on 1 January 2005 the Turkish lira was revalued and never were so many people demoted from the ranks of the millionaires' club in such a short space of time. Overnight, six zeros were wiped from bank accounts throughout the nation. 'Old' Turkish lira has now disappeared from circulation, though out of slow-dying habit you may very occasionally be asked for 'three million' lira instead of 'three'! In many situations, it remains fairly easy to use sterling, euros or even US dollars, at least in the towns.

CHANGING MONEY The exchange rate is better in the country and in Turkey than it is abroad. At the time of writing (April 2015), the exchange rate was as follows: €1 = TL2.86, £1 = TL3.88, US$1 = TL2.59. Travellers' cheques are no longer accepted in the banks, nor in most of the exchange bureaux. If you do find one willing to cash a travellers' cheque, the rate will be punitive. In short, don't bring them. Due to the lack of crime in North Cyprus and the fact that many places, including hotels, restaurants and petrol stations, accept sterling (and other 'hard' currencies such as euros and US dollars), some tourists choose to bring just cash in these currencies, with a credit card or two as backup. When paying in a foreign currency, you'll find that the locals will almost always know the correct exchange rate, and will be scrupulously fair in handing you the correct amount of change (invariably in Turkish lira).

However, carting large quantities of cash around is questionable practice: despite the low level of crime, there's always the risk of losing it. With cash machines in all major towns, there's no need to come armed with enough cash to sustain you during your entire stay. Instead, bring a small quantity of lira with you, and use ATMs when you need to withdraw more (although your bank will charge you a nominal fee).

There should be no need to visit an actual bank branch or moneychanger throughout your time in North Cyprus. You won't find it difficult to change your money: hotels, car-hire firms, shops and agencies will all provide this service. The banks offer the best rate of exchange, and their operating hours have extended in recent years. Generally they open at 08.00 or 08.30 and close at 15.00 or 15.30, perhaps staying open for an additional hour in summer. Some of them close for an hour and a half for lunch, though HSBC is one that stays open. Western Union facilities are available in many banks.

PLASTIC MONEY Credit cards such as Visa, MasterCard, and to a lesser extent American Express and Diners Club, are accepted by most – if not all – hotels and major restaurants, as well as petrol stations and larger shops. Turkish lira can be drawn directly from cashpoints with an international debit or credit card. In Girne, a stroll along Ziya Rizki Caddesi will reveal at least ten banks with ATMs, including – for those seeking a familiar name – a branch of HSBC with ATM, with an additional HSBC cashpoint at the side of the Dome Hotel. Both of these currently allow you to withdraw lira, pounds or euros. Most ATMs operated by the Turkish or Turkish Cypriot banks have clear instructions in English, and can be used to make withdrawals without any complications.

COSTS AND BUDGETING After a brief dip in prices in 2007, costs in Turkish Cyprus have been pushing upwards again, especially in and around Girne. For some foreign visitors, increasing costs have been offset by a weakening of the Turkish lira against many foreign currencies in the last few years. Dining out has been particularly affected by inflation. A reasonable budget for two people is around TL180–220 per day, to cover all food, drink, petrol and entry fees, but excluding accommodation and car hire. Car hire costs around TL85–120 daily in high season, and a meal out for two in a reasonable restaurant with wine will cost TL90, so eating out twice a day will considerably bump up the daily budget. During the off-season, hotel and car-hire prices drop, with lesser reductions in the two mid-seasons of spring and autumn. For information on tipping, see page 43.

Guide prices for items commonly purchased in supermarkets are:

Litre bottle of water: TL1   Postcard: TL0.80
½ litre bottle of beer: TL3   T-shirt: TL15
Loaf of bread: TL1.50   Litre of petrol: TL3
Mars bar: TL1

Prices in this guide   Unless otherwise stated in the text, prices in this guide are quoted in Turkish lira, as this is the currency that is always acceptable for even the smallest transaction. Some businesses quote their prices in euros and where this is the case, this guidebook follows suit. Sterling is a readily quoted currency in North Cyprus (and is the default currency quoted for property transactions and vehicle purchase) and is usually accepted by hotels, larger shops, restaurants and airport/ transfer taxis in the main towns. Euros and US dollars are also very welcome for most, though not all, transactions and occasionally euros are the price quoted in shops and restaurants, particularly in those close to the pedestrian border crossing in Lefkoşa. This is simply to cater to those crossing from the south, which is, of course, in the eurozone. In Girne, some restaurants also quote prices in euros, for no apparent reason. Look at the menu carefully: don't get caught out.

The lira exchange rates for sterling, euros and dollars at the date of publication are given on page 2.

GETTING AROUND

BY PUBLIC TRANSPORT   Public transport in North Cyprus is still somewhat limited and most visitors will hire a car for at least part of their stay. For those who do not want this extra cost, there is a network of *dolmuş* (minibuses) that is perfectly sufficient to get between the main towns, at least during daylight hours, provided you exercise a degree of patience. Most routes do not run to a timetable but instead set off from their start-point when the driver is satisfied that he has enough passengers. Lefkoşa is the main transport hub, and you'll find dolmuş to all of the major towns from the bus station in the north of the town, or from in front of Kyrenia Gate. Fares are very reasonable TL5 (single fare) by dolmuş between Lefkoşa and Girne, for example. Many routes are serviced by more than one operator, and buying a single ticket (rather than a return) allows you the greater flexibility to return with a different company. The main problem with public transport, however, is that many of North Cyprus's principal historic attractions are in isolated and remote locations, far from any town or village. The Crusader castles, for example, cannot be accessed other than by organised tour, self-drive car or taxi. Buses also only run once or twice per day from remote villages to the nearest major town. Hitchhiking is not unheard of, though the same potential risks apply as anywhere else in the world.

Private taxis (with yellow TAKSI signs on the roof) are also reasonably priced, charging fixed official tariffs using a meter, but they do not cruise (officially, anyway) and can only be found at taxi stands, which close late at night. There are no functioning railways. **Sightseeing tours** are widely available from numerous tour operators and these are perhaps the best options for non-drivers. Your hotel will generally have noticeboards or folders maintained by tour operators alerting you to their services.

BY CAR By far the best way to travel is by self-drive hire car (pages 40–1). All you need is a UK, other national, or international driving licence, and vehicles can be picked up and returned at Ercan Airport to avoid taxi transfer costs, which amount to at least TL90 one-way to Girne. The road network is generally good and is being regularly improved, with an increasing number of dual carriageways between the main towns. Car-hire rates are reasonable, especially off-season. Traffic drives on the left – a hangover from the British administration period. Nearly all cars are now right-hand drive, though you will see left-hand drive vehicles, imported or visiting from Turkey.

Fuel prices have decreased dramatically of late, in line with plummeting world oil prices, and are generally cheaper than in the UK and most of Europe. Petrol currently costs TL3 per litre, whilst diesel has recently become even cheaper at around TL2.70 per litre. When buying fuel, it is often easier to hand over the amount of money you would like to spend, or just to say, doldur ('fill it up'), than it is to start explaining quantities. There are, as yet, no self-service petrol stations. Stations are not hard to come by; they are dotted frequently along the main roads, both in towns and between main destinations and marked on the map issued by the tourist offices. Prices barely vary between stations. However, beware that petrol stations do not *always* update their displayed prices, particularly in remote areas. Sometimes the 'bargain' petrol you think you're getting can be 30% more than advertised.

Mention the subject of driving and some locals will throw up their hands in horror, or apologise for what they perceive as poor standards. But in all honesty, traffic generally moves slowly and driving etiquette is good. There's the occasional boy-racer, but you'll certainly experience far worse in other Mediterranean countries or on the motorways of northern Europe. Front and rear passengers must wear seatbelts by law, though this is often ignored. Just remember that the guy in the black Range Rover or Mercedes always has the right of way. Or at least, he thinks he has. Using a mobile phone while driving is illegal, though you may think that it is compulsory, given the high number of offenders. The number of operational speed cameras has soared in recent years, and a profusion of speed bumps – often unmarked – and potholes also help to slow traffic down. Speeding fines vary from around TL150–400 and you may be stopped at the airport if you have unpaid fines – or detained when re-entering North Cyprus at a later date – so slow down or pay up. Two useful words to recognise, either written on the road or on road-signs, are 'Dur' ('Stop') and 'Yavaş' ('Slow').

In some areas and at peak times, driving in North Cyprus can be a chore compared with the idyllic traffic-free days of yesteryear. But it's hardly London or Paris in rush hour. For a few years the pace of development left the road system unable to cope in some places, resulting in horrendous congestion. Around major towns, queues of traffic are to be expected at peak times. Be patient. Even outside working hours traffic in towns can still back up, and Girne's evening restaurant rush, during the holiday season, turns the roads around the harbour and old town into one big pulsating mass of idling engines – you are advised to walk if possible.

Lefkoşa to Girne is a prime commuter route and, if you can, it's wise to avoid the morning and afternoon rush hours as your journey time can be more than doubled. However, elsewhere the lure of the open road can still reveal a side of North Cyprus otherwise hidden from the casual visitor. East from Girne, there's no denying that the new north coast road has opened up remote areas of the island to tourism and associated property development, although debate still rages about the environmental impact of the project. At present the new stretch reaches just beyond

Dipkarpaz, but may extend further, almost to the eastern 'tip', during the lifespan of this edition, further reducing the journey time from Girne.

Wherever travel times are noted in this guide, they do not allow for any congestion which may be met, especially in crossing from one side of Girne to the other.

Car hire Car-hire agencies are plentiful in North Cyprus. However, in summer they can be fully stretched and it is advisable to book in advance, before you reach the country. The minimum age for rental is 25, and a valid national or international driving licence is required, together (usually) with your passport. Third-party insurance is compulsory, but fully comprehensive is recommended and is usually included, or else available for just a little extra money a day. As elsewhere in the world, insurance is invalid if you are found to be drunk at the time of an accident. All hire cars have red registration plates that are prefixed by 'Z', so they have the advantage of being immediately recognisable by the police and military, should you go astray.

Speed limit signs are in kilometres, and distance markers have now also been converted to metric. The cheapest reliable cars to hire are Ford Fiestas or equivalent, at about TL80 per day (high season, inclusive of unlimited mileage and collision damage waiver insurance), while a 4x4 Jeep may cost slightly more. Lower rates are usually available for longer rentals and during the off-season. Check that you are getting air-conditioning, though usually this is standard with the better agencies. In general, the condition of the cars will not match what you would expect elsewhere in Europe, but the corollary is that the hirer is not usually bothered about minor dents and scratches.

Something to watch is any company's promise of '24-hour guaranteed services'. It is worth checking how far the company will go to help you out in case of a problem.

Below are a selected number of car-hire agencies in the TRNC, although the tourism centre in London will be happy to provide a comprehensive list, and every hotel can organise rental for you. Most of the listed companies will deliver the car to your hotel, and collect it when you're finished. If you are travelling independently (rather than with a package), many of the hire companies will send a car and driver to pick you up from Ercan or even Larnaca airport and take you to their office to collect your vehicle, for a reasonable charge, providing you hire from them for a minimum period. If arriving at the southern airports, this is a stress-free way of getting across the border, as all the (minimal) paperwork is sorted for you.

Ercan Airport

🚗 **EVA Rent A Car** ☎ 444 71 71; m 0533 889 17 79; e info@evarentacar.com; www.evarentacar.com. Office is only open to meet incoming flights.

🚗 **Sun Rent A Car** ☎ 231 42 27; e info@sunrentacar.com; www.sunrentacar.com. The only airport office open 24/7.

Gazimağusa

🚗 **Sur Rent-A-Car** Ismet Inonu Bd; ☎ 366 47 96; e info@surcarhire.com; www.surcarhire.com

🚗 **Trip Rent-A-Car** Bus Terminal; m 0542 866 62 62; e info@triprentacar.com.tr; www.triprentacar.com

Girne

🚗 **A-One Rent-A-Car** On the road from Girne to Bellapais; m 0542 852 30 06 or 0542 851 12 35; e info@aone-cyprusrentacar.com; www.aone-cyprusrentacar.com

🚗 **Driver Rent A Car** Bellapais, based at the Tree of Idleness restaurant; ☎ 815 88 51; m 0533 840 50 00; e info@driverrentals.com; www.driverrentacar.com

🚗 **Green Rent-A-Car** 20 Karaoğlanoğlu Caddesi, Alsancak; ☎ 821 88 37; e info@greenrentacar.com; www.greenrentacar.com

🚗 **InterRent** On the road from Girne to Bellapais; ☎ 815 90 01; e inter@altinkaya-cyprus.com; www.cypruscheapcarrentals.com

MTS m 0542 880 31 41; e info@mtscar.com; www.mtscar.com
Sun Rent-A-Car Zafer Apt, 20 Temmuz Kordonboyu Av; ℓ 815 49 79; e info@sunrentacar. com; www.sunrentacar.com. See ad, inside back cover.

Lefkoşa
Sun Rent-A-Car 10 Abdi Ipekci Caddesi; ℓ 227 23 03; e info@sunrentacar.com; www. sunrentacar.com
Memo Rent A Car ℓ 227 18 59; m 0548 850 25 22; e info@memorentacar.com; www. memorentacar.com

Motorbike hire Unlike some gung-ho Mediterranean destinations of yesteryear, you *will* need to have the appropriate licence to hire a motorbike in North Cyprus. In Girne, try **The Motorbike Shop** south of the Colony Hotel on Ecevit Caddesi (ℓ 815 13 46; m 0542 850 47 87). As well as the licence, you will need a copy of your passport and a €100 cash deposit. Prices are around €16 per day.

Maps North Cyprus has for years been crying out for a decent, detailed, up-to-date map. The map provided free by the tourist offices is adequate for touring however, and should now include all new road developments. A small, red-covered pocket map, published by Rüstem in 2014, can be bought from their shop near the Saray Hotel in Lefkoşa (page 133), or from the Round Tower or Bestseller bookshops (page 52) and various newsagents in Girne.

ACCOMMODATION

Accommodation options are expanding rapidly in North Cyprus. The range covers everything from five-star hotels to backpackers', self-catering and seaside camping facilities. Many of the top-end establishments cater mainly for visitors from the Turkish mainland, although, of course, visitors from elsewhere are welcome. As a broad rule of thumb, if a hotel has a casino, the majority of its guests will be Turkish visitors on short stays, escaping the mainland ban on gambling. The smaller, family-run hotels tend to attract European and other guests, many of whom are loyal, repeat customers. Accommodation in this book is listed under each geographical region.

Prices have risen at above inflation rates in recent times. Costs do vary throughout the year, with anything up to a 50% discount during the off-season (November to March), a lower 10–20% discount during the 'shoulder' season (April and October) and a substantial discount for children. Where children are not welcome below a certain age, this is noted. In the listings, hotel rates are based on high-season costs for a double room for two people including breakfast; see box below for details. Where only a half-board or all-inclusive rate is available, this is stated.

Note that these rates are merely a guide. The chances are that when you arrive at the hotel, the rates quoted to you may differ from those given in this book, though hopefully this will be minimal. The rate you will actually pay for your hotel will depend on whether you book your accommodation at home or just walk in without pre-booking (the latter is usually more expensive), whether your accommodation is part of a package deal, how long you are staying and in what season.

HOTEL PRICE CODES

Price of a double room per night including breakfast:

$$$$$	TL400+
$$$$	TL250–400
$$$	TL170–250
$$	TL120–170
$	up to TL120

Murray Stewart

Among the casino hotels and villa developments, a new impetus is afoot to develop something altogether more sustainable. Eco- and agro-tourism are words that are turning into action, though as the Cypriots are apt to say, 'slowly, slowly' is the pace at which this is happening.

Much of the activity is out on the Karpas Peninsula, where package holidays have yet to penetrate and the rural way of life pervades. Doing more than anyone and deserving of a special mention is Lois Cemal, a Canadian expat who has settled in the village of **Büyükkonuk** with her Turkish Cypriot husband, Ismail. Lois and Ismail (*www.ecotourismcyprus.com*) are devoted to the preservation of local traditions and can help to organise eco and agro activities in the village, including wonderful courses on bread-baking, cheese-making or other Cypriot dishes, as well as crafts. Through them you can get advice on local trails and places of interest, like Yudi Natural Arch, or even just where to find a donkey to pet or ride. There is also a centre open for locals to display homemade crafts, their principles of fair trade ensuring that the artisan earns a fair price. Each Sunday between October and May the local village ladies from the Ecotourism Association set up a few stalls (⏱ *11.00–16.00*), from which they sell a variety of jams, handicrafts and unsurpassable cakes. Visitors can even join in baking bread in a traditional Cypriot oven.

Another example of sustainable development is the wonderful **Oasis at Ayfilon** (page 176). Offering simple food and accommodation in breathtaking surroundings at Ayios Philon, the appeal of this low-impact, solar-powered project is for anyone disillusioned by the ongoing development of the island. It couldn't be further removed from the resorts around Girne.

Inland from the Oasis, the village of **Dipkarpaz** plays host to a number of eco-accommodation options (page 175). Many are tastefully renovated buildings and are worthy of support and while many of the owners struggle with their English, communicating is surely part of the fun. Elsewhere, small, family-run restoration projects such as the **Lefke Gardens Hotel** (page 92) are gaining popularity, and the **Organic Farm** (page 92) in Yeşilırmak and North Cyprus's second eco-village, **Bağliköy**, offer real causes for optimism. Some UK tour operators will now take you on escorted trekking holidays through the mountains.

Just a few years ago, the very notion of having to encourage sustainable tourism in North Cyprus would have been laughable. Today, as a result of phenomenal growth and short-sighted planning, it seems essential for the long-term good of the country and its tourist industry.

Don't take ratings entirely at face value. The comparative systems used in official accommodation guides seem to reflect the attitude that 'the bigger the casino, the better the hotel'. Such flashy establishments are liberally awarded multiple stars, whilst many more attractive, friendly options are rated less favourably.

The glut of villa purchases in recent years has now resulted in opportunities for **self-caterers** to rent out villas. Try B's Hive Property Management (☎ *815 2853*; e *enquiries@bees-hive.com*; *www.bees-hive.com*), an established company that has around 30 villas of all sizes to rent, mainly around the Girne/Ozanköy area.

For those who are not too bothered about having a roof over their head, there are **campsites** at Lapta, İskele, Kaplıca, Kumyali and Salamis; local tourist offices should be able to provide details of these and they cost around TL20 per person, per night. In addition to these, the really adventurous might fancy wild camping, which is not subject to restrictions, other than it is illegal (as well as stupid) to light fires in the forests.

TIPPING In hotels, a few lira to the porter and the room cleaner is a good idea. If staying for a week or two, it is advisable to enquire whether the hotel has a tipping policy that ensures a fair distribution of tips amongst relevant staff.

EATING AND DRINKING

The range of food and restaurants on offer in North Cyprus, especially in and around Girne, is enormous, from local cuisine to Chinese, Indian, Italian and French. For those who prefer home favourites, 'British' food is very widely available in the Girne/Lapta area. You can snack on a doner kebab from a street stall or savour dinner at a chic restaurant that can hold its own with top restaurants in Europe. Whichever cuisine you choose, standards are generally very good.

Most **local specialities** will be familiar to visitors to Turkey – various *meze* (selection of hot and cold appetisers), *börek* (hot pastries stuffed with spinach, cheese or meat), kebab, *kofte* (spiced meatballs), *dolma* (stuffed vine leaves) and salads that feature aubergines, tomatoes, onions, cucumbers, peppers (sometimes *very* hot), watercress, parsley, radishes and olives. Ordering a 'full kebab', which is available at many places, will result in a seemingly endless stream of delicious dishes being delivered to your table. A Cypriot speciality – though not found on many menus – is *molohiya*, which is a spinach-like vegetable cooked with lamb or chicken. *Pilavuna* is an oven-baked pastry made with *talar* cheese, eggs and milk. Cypriot pasta can look a little insipid compared with its Italian cousin, but is nevertheless delicious.

Freshly caught sea creatures are widely offered, and include red and grey mullet, lobster, crab, mussels, bream, squid and sea bass. Fish is usually simply cooked, grilled or fried, though a few more sophisticated places offer it prepared in special sauces or as tasty casseroles. A fresh fish *meze* is a culinary highlight. Specifically Cypriot is the halloumi (or *hellim*) cheese, with that wonderful rubbery texture, often served grilled as a very tasty *meze*. There is also the crumbly white goat's cheese, and thick creamy yoghurt (excellent on meat, mixed with herbs, or as a dessert, drizzled with local mountain honey). Good-quality fresh fruit according to season includes melons, cherries, apples, strawberries, bananas, figs, grapes, oranges, grapefruits and pears. Turkish delight is available in a variety of flavours, and those with walnuts or pistachios inside are especially delicious.

To wash it all down, there's the cheap and widely available mineral **water** and the usual range of fizzy drinks, as well as delicious Cyprus lemonade (made from mandarins and lemons). Ayran (yoghurt drink) is cheap and also popular. On the **alcoholic** front, the Turkish Efes beer is very good. A local beer, Goldfassl, previously produced in Gazimağusa, is no longer available. Wine is inexpensive in the big supermarkets and in a couple of specialists on the main road between Alsancak and Lapta, and there is an ever-increasing range of European and New World wines to supplement the local and Turkish favourites. In restaurants, ordering a bottle will certainly bump up the bill quite considerably, however. The best local wine is St Hilarion (red) but it's still greatly inferior to those from the Turkish mainland, as wine-making is a recently acquired skill in the north. Of the Turkish wines,

2

those that are consistently the best are by Kavaklidere and Doluca. Kavaklidere produce the red Yakut, the white Çankaya and rosé Lâl. Doluca produce the red and white Doluca and the more upmarket red Villa Doluca. Many hotels and bars claim to make the best Brandy Sour, Cyprus's signature cocktail, a combination of mild, local brandy and lemon juice: do try one during your stay. *Raki* is the favoured spirit, clear and aniseed flavoured, drunk either neat with ice or mixed with water, when it turns cloudy, thus explaining its description as 'lion's milk'. It goes well with *meze*, fish and lamb. The Turkish *raki* is better than the local *raki*, for the same reasons as the wine. Then there's the Turkish Cypriot version of grappa, *zivana*, and if you are feeling brave, Turkish Cypriot brandy and even something that is shamelessly marketed as whisky, distilled in Gazimağusa. Turkish coffee is widely drunk, introduced here, as elsewhere in the eastern Mediterranean, by the Ottomans in the 15th century. It is drunk *sade* (without sugar), *orta* (medium sugar) or *şekerli* (heavily sugared).

Increasingly, more Western-style coffees are becoming available, and you should be able to find your favourite cappuccino or latte in the major towns. Otherwise, be aware that instant coffee is often the standard alternative offering to Turkish coffee. Tea (*çay*) is also popular with locals, served in small glasses and – unlike in some countries – not usually pre-sugared. 'English' tea is also widely available at hotels, and is offered up as the standard in more touristy establishments.

WHERE TO EAT AND DRINK As on the Turkish mainland, restaurant hours are very flexible and there is generally no problem about eating lunch at 16.00 and dinner at 20.00 if that is what happens to suit you. Opening hours are given in this guidebook only where the owner was able to state them with a degree of confidence! In Girne, you can find at least one eating establishment open at any hour. Elsewhere, lunch is available from around midday and dinner from around 18.00. Turkish Cypriots eat out a lot themselves, especially at weekends, and the whole family partakes, from grandparents to babies. For recommendations, use the listings in this guide or ask a few locals. Though the cost of eating out will depend to a large extent on personal taste and appetite, listings here include a price guide based on the average cost of a main course only, excluding drinks. Occasionally, menus and advertising boards display prices in euros, rather than lira – be aware! Although this guidebook covers the whole range of cuisines, there is quite deliberately an overrepresentation of establishments which serve Cypriot food.

TIPPING Tipping is not expected when a service charge is added to the bill, which it sometimes is in Girne and other tourist spots. If there's no service charge, a small extra amount will indicate gratitude for especially attentive service.

PUBLIC HOLIDAYS AND FESTIVALS

1 January	New Year's Day
23 April	National Sovereignty and Children's Day
1 May	Labour Day
19 May	Youth and Sports Day
20 July	Peace and Freedom Day
1 August	TMT Day (birth of Turkish Cypriot Resistance Movement)
30 August	Victory Day
29 October	Turkish National Day
15 November	Independence Day (proclamation of TRNC)

Turkey and North Cyprus follow the Gregorian calendar like the rest of Europe but, as they are predominantly Muslim, the major Islamic festivals are celebrated. The dates of these religious holidays change each year as they are calculated by the lunar system, and so move forward by about 11 days in the Gregorian calendar annually. There are two major Islamic holidays the equivalents, if you like, of Christmas and Easter. The first is Kurban Bayramı, the Feast of the Sacrifice, which commemorates Abraham's willingness to sacrifice his son Isaac. Each family traditionally sacrificed an animal (a sheep or a chicken, according to means), which was then cooked and eaten in large family gatherings. The sacrifice is rare now in North Cyprus, though the Turkish incomers sometimes continue the practice, but the gatherings are still going strong. In 2015, Kurban Bayramı will fall on 23–26 September; in 2016, on 12–15 September; and in 2017, on 1–4 September. It is always a four-day national holiday, the longest of the year. The second festival celebrates the end of fasting during the 30-day month of Ramadan and is called Şeker Bayramı, the Sugar Festival, because much sweet food is eaten. It is a three-day national holiday and in 2015 falls on 17–19 July; in 2016, it takes place on 5–7 July and in 2017, on 25–27 June. Ramadan itself is not strictly observed as a fasting month. Many restaurants and supermarkets remain open during these holidays.

FESTIVALS North Cyprus is well provided for in terms of festivals, and while you won't find anything on the scale of Rio at carnival time, a visit to one or more of the events – taking place largely between March and December –will enrich your visit to the area and give you a better understanding of North Cypriot life and traditions.

The tourist board publishes a brochure of events each year, which you can obtain from any of the tourist information offices. It lists only the months in which the festivals occur, not exact dates, as many of them are dependent on the flowering or ripening of flowers or fruit and they can therefore only be finalised a few weeks in advance. Nevertheless, it is worth enquiring as to what is coming up, perhaps as soon as you arrive in North Cyprus, or else keeping an eye on www.simplynorthcyprus. com, which shows a list of events and sometimes updates them once the dates are firmly fixed in the calendar. Some of the better-known events are described below.

Tulip festivals are held in both **Tepebaşı** and **Avtepe** in March, to coincide with the flowering of the *Tulipa cypria*, the dark crimson flower endemic to Cyprus. Although the flower is ostensibly the main event, it provides the two villages with an excuse for a bit of music and dancing, stalls serving traditional delicacies and handicrafts, and a few speeches by visiting dignitaries. The tulips themselves are protected, and to see them you'll have to wander through some of the neighbouring fields. The sight of a small crowd of local people engaging in this 'tulip hunt' is in itself a novelty.

A recently established festival celebrating the **orchid** is held on the last weekend of March in the village of **Hisarköy**.

Esentepe holds a lively **apricot festival**, usually during the last week of May and first week of June. It's a great chance to see colourful costumes and dancing, and to listen to traditional music late into the night. And to eat apricots, of course.

Also in May and June are the **International Bellapais Music Festival** (*www.bellapaisfestival.com*), which showcases performances in the spectacular setting of the abbey, and the **walnut festival** in **Lefke.**

The **Girne** area celebrates its **olive festival** in October. It's held in the little village of **Zeytinlik**, a few kilometres to the southwest of town and lasts for nearly a week. It features all types of music from teen orchestras through to Turkish pop, with a dash of folk and Latin on the way. As well as the music, there are folk dance displays, darts and table tennis tournaments, free nibbles, plays, processions, olive branch burning and basketball competitions. And, of course, a chance to taste and purchase olives and olive oil.

Güzelyurt has an **orange festival** in June and there are **folk dancing festivals**, usually in July, in **İskele**, **Lefkoşa** and **Gönyeli**, while **Mehmetçik** hosts its **grape festival** in August.

Further east, the small village of **Büyükkonuk** justifies its status as North Cyprus's first eco-village with two lively **'Eco-day' festivals**, one in June and one in October. A day packed with folk dancing, music and speeches, as well as demonstrations of how to make baskets, olive bread, straw toys and headscarves, together with broom-tying and zinc-plating, this is a true village festival that makes for an enriching experience. Over 100 stalls now participate. Canadian Lois Çemal is one of the main movers behind the festivals and will be happy to advise of the festival dates. You can get in touch with her at e delcraft2000@hotmail.com.

The celebrated **International North Cyprus Music Festival** takes place in September/October, spread between **Girne**, **Bellapais** and **Gazimağusa**, with mainly classical music.

While many of the festivals are fairly recent in origin, they are often promoting and keeping alive age-old skills and traditions. Perhaps due to the scant information available from the tourist offices, foreign attendees are scarce, though happily increasing, but the locals will welcome you if you make the effort to attend.

SHOPPING AND ENTERTAINMENT

SHOPPING Shopping can be a perfect way to spend a few hours, milling around the markets and variety of local shops, which can range from higgledy-piggledy little stores to very chic, upmarket boutiques. The best shopping is to be found in Girne, along the main street and its side roads. Lefkoşa also has good shops but they are scattered and therefore more difficult for the visitor to find and use. Shops have recently extended their opening hours and are generally open from 08.00 to around 18.00. Some grocery stores stay open virtually all night. More and more shops are now staying open on Sundays, and you'll always be able to find an open grocery store, supermarket or souvenir shop without much effort.

Traditional crafts to look out for are pottery, ceramics, leather shoes and bags, rugs and *kilims*, canvas suitcases and bags (very cheap and handy when your new purchases threaten to burst your existing suitcase), basketwork, dolls, jewellery, copper, brass and Lefkara lacework. These traditional purchases are not difficult to come by. The large souvenir shop, **Hello Basket**, in Edremit has some excellent basketware. The **Cyprus Pottery Shop** opposite The Ship Inn, on the main road west out of Girne, a few craft and local product shops on **Çanbulat Caddesi** in Girne and the shops around the centre of old Gazimağusa are other suggestions. Don't forget, too, when visiting Lefkoşa, to call in at the **Hasder Folk Arts Institute**, just north of the Selimiye Mosque (pages 136–8), which produces, exhibits and sells traditional handicrafts. The shops inside the **Büyük Han** and the **Bandibuliya** in Lefkoşa also have some interesting, tasteful crafts. **Büyükkonuk village**, in the mountains at the western edge of the Karpas, offers opportunities to purchase Cypriot items from local villagers, such as olive-oil soap, palm baskets, or bottles of olive oil and grape-almond *sucuk* sweets. For help in finding produce or crafts, contact Lois Cemal (✆ 383 2038; e *delcraft2000@hotmail.com*).

Usually, shop items are priced in Turkish lira, though occasionally in euros, and prices are frequently lower than in the UK. Prices tend to be fixed and not subject

The ancient traditional talisman of blue glass beads painted with an eye lives on in North Cyprus. Find it swinging from the rear-view mirrors of taxis, balanced above the doorways of restaurants and family homes, and set in the stone on walkways and walls.

It is widely believed that hateful looks given by one person towards another can be strong enough to bring bad luck, illness and death. Envy, hate or even extreme admiration can cause the evil eye to strike, bringing with it destruction and harm. The story goes that the smooth, rounded glass beads deflect the evil power, channelled by a hateful look, away from the victim, acting as a glass shield. They adorn jewellery and decorations and will be given away as token gifts by shopkeepers.

Not surprisingly, the myth varies from person to person, but its essence is always the same: *nazar boncuğu* (blue beads) bring with them a gift of protection and safety.

to haggling. Purchases will often be patiently wrapped, tied up with ribbon and accompanied by the traditional Turkish talisman: the evil eye (see box above).

For something other than souvenirs, keep your eye open for occasional flea markets and car boot sales that can be found along the main road between Lapta and Girne. The weekly *Cyprus Today* newspaper carries details of such events, which are often organised and frequented by British expats, selling their excess.

SIGHTSEEING North Cyprus, with its rich and far-reaching history, has no shortage of monuments and museums. Most charge an entrance fee of between TL5 and TL12, although almost all offer a significant discount to students, children and indeed war veterans – just make sure you were on the appropriate side. Although information on the lesser attractions can be sparse, many of the larger sites do offer a typed sheet of A4 explaining the site in some detail in English. An excellent additional resource are the men and women of KITREB, the North Cyprus Tour Guides Association. Highly-trained, very knowledgeable, usually multilingual and free of charge, they can be found at Kyrenia Castle, Bellapais Abbey, Lefkoşa, Salamis and other places, and using them will enhance your visits. Rewarding them with a gratuity will be appreciated.

Try to avoid the summer midday heat when looking around ruined sites, as they offer very little shade and can be scorchingly hot. Many of the sites are fascinating and, in parts, wonderfully well preserved and restored. Tour companies offer trips to most of the popular sites although, with a car, they are just as easy to visit independently.

BEACHES The whole of Gazimağusa Bay is one long sandy beach, and any hotel built along it will have excellent bathing. The northern coast is much more mixed, with sandy bays interspersed with rocky coves, cliffs and headlands. On many beaches, especially the sandy ones, you will notice clumps of eelgrass, a kind of seaweed, which accumulates and needs to be removed regularly. Local environmentalists, frequently expatriate residents, are active on beach clear-up days: the major beaches get a good clean just before the main season commences. North Cyprus does not escape the general pollution of the Mediterranean, and tar, along with plastic bottles, often mars virgin beaches. Legally speaking, all North

Cypriot beaches are public and you are entitled to sit on the sand without charge. In practice, many of the beaches are 'rented' to various hotels or restaurants, and accessing them without payment is not quite so clear-cut. Clean sand is one main advantage of using the fee-paying beaches, together with the provision of sunbeds, an umbrella and sometimes a lifeguard. You can either stump up, or try to charm your way past whoever's collecting the money. Prevailing winds are from the west, so a bay tucked into the eastern side of a promontory generally offers wind protection, the calmest water and the least tar and eelgrass.

Individual beaches are detailed with their appropriate areas. For information on beach safety, see page 34.

EVENING ENTERTAINMENT North Cyprus is not an all-night party zone. The evenings are blissfully peaceful, filled with social gatherings in restaurants and bars, which seem happy to accommodate you for hours. Live music is an added bonus and time passes with ease. Very occasionally, there are also musical performances held at Bellapais Abbey and in the Büyük Han in Lefkoşa. However, as package tourism increases so do the options, and there's now a fairly active bar scene around Girne and in the Dereboyu district of Lefkoşa. Ayia Napa it may not yet be (thankfully), but any visit in summer is likely to find a young crowd who'll give anyone a run for their money.

There are options for those seeking the delights of discotheques and casinos. Many of the big hotels offer these facilities, particularly those in and around Girne. Generally speaking, the discos are very much filled with locals and are far from being overtaken by tourists. Be warned, however, that a lot of establishments that advertise themselves as 'nightclubs' are very different from clubs back at home, and are filled with 'Natashas' (prostitutes from eastern Europe). The warning is often in the names of these places (Forplay [sic] or Monamour), which are usually by the roadside in bizarrely rural locations. Some rather more genuine, reputable discotheques are mentioned in this guide.

For details of events and musical performances on a week-by-week basis, listings can be found in the *Cyprus Today* newspaper.

SPORTS AND OTHER ACTIVITIES

Please note that some of the following activities are summer-only (usually around April–September).

BIRDWATCHING TRIPS Private or group birding trips to North Cyprus are an excellent way of maximising enjoyment of the region's rich birdlife. One respected organisation that brings birders to North Cyprus in spring and arranges private groups throughout the year is **Cyprus Wildlife Ecology** (*www. cypruswildlifeecology.com*). Their birding day-trips are a great way to see loads of different species – between 40 and 80 in a day, depending on seasons and conditions – as well as parts of North Cyprus you might not otherwise visit. Small groups travel in a 4×4, but transport is arranged for larger groups, too. Avid birders will find them at the annual Birdfair at Rutland Water in the UK, where they have a stall in conjunction with KUŞKOR, the North Cyprus Society for the Protection of Birds and Nature.

BOWLING (FLAT GREEN) A recent addition to the sporting scene, **The Olive Press** (❨ *0533 880 11 96; www.olivepressbowlingcyprus.com*) is signposted north off the main north coast road, between Lapta and Karşıyaka. All visitors are welcome and shoe- and bowl-hire are available, as is coaching for novices. Restaurant on site.

BOWLING (TEN PIN) Located on the south side of the new ring road south of Girne, the **King's Leisure Centre** (✆ 444 60 70) is a fairly recent addition to Kyrenia's attractions. Good value, with air-conditioning, a restaurant and a wide range of children's games, arcade games, a bar, restaurant and pool tables. A good place to escape the sun or – that North Cypriot rarity – the rain.

BOAT TRIPS For information on boat trips around the coast, see page 73.

CYCLING In former years, North Cyprus was as idyllic a place as any cyclist could ever hope to find. Today, with significantly busier roads, cycling along any of the major routes is likely to be a chore rather than a pleasure, and you won't see too many bicycles during your stay. Off-road, there is little in the way of well-identified trails, but there are a few restrictions, providing a lure for the adventurous. Bicycles can be rented locally at a few hotels across the island, and from **The Motorbike Shop** (✆ 815 13 46; m 0542 850 47 87) charges TL25 daily or TL140 weekly. You will also need to leave a €100 cash deposit. All prices include helmet and lock. In the Karpas, mountain bikes can be hired from **Karpas Rent A Bike** (m 0548 876 20 33) in Dipkarpaz, for around TL30 per day. Areas such as the Karpas in the east and Cape Kormakiti in the west make for pleasurable cycling destinations. **Cyprus Active** (page 26) can organise mountain biking trips. For more leisurely bike tours of Lefkoşa, see page 131.

FISHING Sport fishing with the organisation **Ladyboss** (m 0542 855 56 72; e info@fishingnorthcyprus.com; www.fishingnorthcyprus.com) might sound a bit intimidating, but the name refers to the 34ft boat, not Angela, the New Zealand owner. From June to November, a four-hour adventure to hunt for tuna, bonito

FOOTBALL: NORTH CYPRUS, WORLD CUP WINNERS … AND CURRENT HOLDERS

Murray Stewart

Despite being prevented from taking part in international football competitions – North Cyprus is not recognised by FIFA or UEFA – such formalities have not prevented the region from winning the World Cup … or more precisely, the FIFI *Wild* Cup, which was organised by a gambling syndicate to allow various unrecognised entities to compete. Step forward North Cyprus, along with such other footballing powerhouses as Zanzibar, Greenland, Tibet and Gibraltar (who became FIFA members in 2013). Surely the most bizarre entrant to the competition was FC St Pauli, a professional team from the district of Hamburg and the hosts for the competition. They entered under the name of Republic of St Pauli, but as a mere suburb, are unlikely to gain international recognition anytime soon. After defeating Zanzibar and Greenland in the group stages, and knocking out Gibraltar in the semi-finals, North Cyprus again beat Zanzibar in the final. Beset by poor attendances, the tournament has not – as yet – been repeated, meaning that North Cyprus are still World, or rather 'Wild', Champions, perhaps in perpetuity. Move over, Germany, Brazil and Argentina.

or spearfish will cost around TL180. The price includes all equipment, fishing licences and refreshments. Their office is shared with Highline Paragliding (see below), in Girne Harbour.

GO-KARTING There are two decent tracks, **CEMSA** (m *223 62 35;* e *Info@ cemsakarting.com*) on the approach road to the Near East University, which runs off the Lefkoşa to Gazimağusa road, and **Zet Karting** (✆ *866 61 73;* e *zetgroup@ kibrisonline.com*), at Alayköy, 7km east of Lefkoşa.

GOLF Located near Esentepe, the swish **Korineum Golf and Country Club** (✆ *600 15 00;* e *info@korineumgolf.com; www.korineumgolf.com*) is North Cyprus's first 18-hole golf course, developed to championship standard and 6,232m in length. Commendably, the club has invested in its own desalination plant, thus maintaining lush greens and fairways whilst avoiding adverse impact on local water supplies. Reports on the course are very favourable and the setting at the foot of the Kyrenia mountain range is truly stunning. Green fees are €85 in high season, though there are a number of packages available for those wanting more than one round and fees are cheaper if you are a member's guest. Club-, shoe- and trolley-hire are all available. There is a Golf Academy, driving range, pro-shop, restaurants, swimming pool, tennis courts and a spa. Various golf/accommodation packages are available as fully-equipped guest rooms have now been added, with all hotel facilities, including Wi-Fi and air-conditioning.

The **CMC Golf Club** (m *0533 861 02 72, 0542 851 38 84*) is a nine-hole course off the main road between Güzelyurt and Lefke, near Yeşilyurt. You access it through, bizarrely, the hospital entrance at the western end of town. It's the island's oldest club, founded in 1926. It's at the opposite end of the opulence scale from the Korineum – greens are 'browns' made of sand and oil. What it lacks in glitz it makes up for in friendliness, although it's often unmanned. Using an honesty box, it costs TL40 for nine or 18 holes. A third course is being planned as part of a new hotel complex at Çayırova in the western Karpas region.

HORSERIDING Following the recent closure of the long-established riding club at Çatalköy, horseback options are now more restricted, but at the western end of the mountains, near Karşıyaka, the **Kozan Mountain Retreat** (m *0533 845 70 70; www.kozan.orgfree.com*) also has a few horses and charges around TL80 for up to 3 hours. Beginners are accompanied; experienced riders can go unaccompanied. Maximum weight is 80kg.

KITESURFING North Cyprus is finding new adrenalin outlets for thrill-seekers and kitesurfing adds to the fun. **Kites and Bananas** (m *0542 865 88 80* or *0542 854 27 69; www.kitesandbananas.com*) organise courses run by fully qualified instructors. They operate from Akdeniz Beach, but have no permanent base there, so contact them in advance.

PARAGLIDING At **Highline Tandem Paragliding** (m *0542 855 56 72;* e *info@ highlineparagliding.com; www.highlineparagliding.com*), run by the same people as Ladyboss fishing, no experience is necessary as your English-speaking pilot takes the strain; just enjoy the view and collect the T-shirt. Daily 2-hour adventures take off from 750m above sea level in the Kyrenia Mountains. Expect to pay from TL275, including a pick-up from Girne. Their office is on the front in Kyrenia's Old Harbour.

SCUBA-DIVING Diving courses are growing in popularity in North Cyprus, with costs varying little between schools. The full PADI Open Water course (allowing you to dive up to 18m) costs around TL1,000. If you're unsure whether diving is for you, the schools also run trial dives for around TL85. In between, there are a large number of packages on offer, details of which are on the websites, listed below.

North Cyprus offers some of the best scuba-diving sites in the Mediterranean, including the underwater formations at Mansinis Reef and the ancient shipwreck at Girne, as well as providing the opportunity to photograph and feed the wildlife at Fred's Reef. Fish abound, including among their number stingray, amberjack, cuckoo wrasse, scorpionfish, bream and grouper. Bear in mind though that North Cyprus has no decompression chamber – the nearest is across the border in the south of the island. The winter months are not ideal for diving, so if it's intended to form a big part of your trip, it's best to check in advance with your chosen school.

Some of the more popular schools are:

Amphora Scuba Diving Centre
m 0542 851 49 24; e asimuygur@kktc.net; www.amphoradiving.com. Now based at Kervansaray Beach near the Merit Royal Hotel, this friendly company offers PADI & BSAC courses for beginners & experts alike. They have daily trips & dive around some of the local reefs, as well as sometimes organising diving on preserved shipwrecks just outside Larnaca in the south.

Cyprus Dive Shack m 0533 864 75 69; e www.cyprusdiveshack.com. Located at the westernmost point of Escape Beach, in Alsancak. Full range of PADI & DSAT courses, plus try-dives for beginners.

Mephisto Diving m 0533 867 37 74; e marion@mephisto-diving.com; www.mephisto-diving.com. Based at the Club Malibu Hotel, near Yeni Erenköy in the Karpas, & offering all PADI & SSI options from 1-day courses to divemaster. Multilingual instruction.

Nautilus 227 31 60; m 0533 862 98 03; e www.nautilusdivingcyp.com. Based at the Sempati Hotel, 16km west of Girne, with a range of PADI & National Geographic courses.

Scuba Cyprus m 0533 865 23 17; e info@scubacyprus.com; www.scubacyprus.com. Scuba Cyprus offers PADI & SSI courses in scuba-diving, plus try-dives, jet-skiing & boat trips. It will cost you approximately €80 for an all-inclusive try-dive day.

WALKING Information and assistance for the visitor to access North Cyprus's excellent walking opportunities have improved greatly in recent years. Whether you prefer to set off on your own or to be part of an organised walking group, the region is now better geared up to facilitate your needs. Funded by the United Nations Development Fund, a series of pocket-sized, bilingual leaflets have now been published, each detailing a circular walk. They are available free of charge from the tourist offices and many car-hire companies. Walking in North Cyprus is truly a great way to escape the relative bustle of the towns and get close to the region's diverse nature. Would-be walkers should note that there are two hunting seasons, one running from late November until the year-end and the other starting in mid-January, usually until the end of March. During the former, hunting is permissible only on Sundays, while the latter allows hunting on both Wednesdays and Sundays. For your own safety, it's advisable to check exact dates with the tourist office, as the lengths of the seasons do vary from year to year. A major consideration will be the weather, with spring and autumn being the best seasons for walking.

The Kyrenia mountain range offers some of the best walking, with many quiet forest tracks well maintained by the Forestry Department, but the area north of Akdeniz in the west, as well as the Karpas Peninsula in the east, are also favoured. Noticeboards have sprung up across the countryside with laminated trail maps and nature information. This is part of a project called Natura 2000, which is sponsored by the EU. Despite this investment, understanding the information on these boards is, at best, challenging.

For those seeking organised walks, opportunities are also improving. The longest walk in North Cyprus is the 147-mile, ten-day (or longer) coast-to-coast hike. Independent walkers could tackle this, though it would require significant planning and the carrying of camping equipment. **Cyprus Active** (page 26) can organise trips that cover this route, as can the Kaleidoskop Turizm agency. Another very useful contact is **Tügberk Emirzade** (m *0533 869 05 30;* e *http:// natureguide.wix.com/cyprus*), who has been heavily involved in the production of the leaflets mentioned above. He runs a well-stocked outdoor shop, **Agama** (*7 Fatih Sokak*), open only on Saturdays or by appointment (number as above). In addition, he goes with groups on exploration walks that last around 3 hours and that he describes as 'challenging'. They are advertisied on his Agama Wild social media pages and all can join in. He can also assist in organising other day walks for small groups. **Kaleidoskop Turizm** (✆ *815 18 18;* e *info@kaleidoskop-turizm.com; www.kaleidoskop-turizm.com*) is a reputable German agency that can organise self-guided or guided day walks and longer walking holidays. For independent walkers, they provide transport, routes and 24-hour backup phone numbers. They speak English, as do the guides provided for the guided trips. In addition, they work closely with eco/agro-tourism establishments. Another organisation that offers guided walks of varying difficulty throughout the region is **North Cyprus Walks** (m *0533 840 58 49;* e *northcypruswalk@gmail.com; www.northcypruswalk.com*).

Some further and inexpensive walking maps are available for purchase from the **Kyrenia Mountain Trail Association** (*www.kyreniamountaintrail.org*). All their trails are connected, making it possible to walk the entire distance across the north of the island. Major trails are marked out with white-painted circles, with a smaller green circle inside, often found on trees or rocks, and information boards are sometimes available at the start. However, most walkers find this waymarking confusing and a map is a more reliable information source.

Some of the loveliest shorter walks include the 1.5km walk from Malatya to İlgaz, passing a waterfall on the way; from İlgaz to Karaman, a 4km walk taking 1½ hours; along the ridge from the Five Finger Mountain pass towards the Armenian monastery; and along the ridge from St Hilarion towards Lapta. As the last two paths have now been tarmacked, the walks are slightly less attractive than they used to be, though traffic volumes are light. The last track passes a fountain at about 8km, then at 10km reaches a junction with three tracks. The middle track continues 9.2km past Mt Selvili at 1,024m to reach the tarmac road down to Karşıyaka, while the right fork leads 6.3km to Lapta; the left fork leads down to the tarmac at Akçiçek and is of less interest to walkers. For walks around Bellapais and Karaman, see pages 88 and 109.

The village of Ozanköy has many lovely walks through ancient olive groves in all directions and specifically up towards Bellapais and its abbey. Lapta is another village particularly well placed for walks into the olive and citrus groves and up into the mountains. **Büyükkonuk village** has a number of short walking routes, details of which are available at the municipality, local guest houses or from Lois Cemal (page 42). The **Theresa Hotel** (page 174) near Yeni Erenköy, has good maps of a few walks in their immediate locality.

There is an excellent book, *Walks in North Cyprus*, by Alison Dowey, which covers 30 walks of varying difficulty and length, available in Girne at the **Round Tower** (page 71) or at other bookshops, such as the **Ozanköy Bookshop** (pages 87–8) or **Bestseller** in Karakum (m *0533 845 14 92*), price TL30. Alternatively, it can be sourced in the UK from The Map Shop in Upton-upon-Severn (☏ *01584 593146*). The author also organises weekly group walks, which any visitor is welcome to attend. Contact her at e alisondowey@yahoo.co.uk for details.

WATERSPORTS Watersports are widely practised and many hotel beaches offer windsurfing, sea-kayaking, waterskiing and pedalos.

Swimming is an easy activity to come by in North Cyprus – there are plenty of beaches and most hotels have swimming pools. Specifically with children in mind, the **Lapta Holiday Club** (formerly Lapethos Resort), to the west of Lapta, has waterslides and is open to non-residents on payment of a fee (around TL20/10 adult/child).

YOGA If stretching out on a sunbed is not enough for you, contact Dharma Yoga (m *0533 825 88 80*) for pilates or yoga. Classes are held in English, so you have no excuse for non-attendance.

WEIGHTS AND MEASURES

North Cyprus used to be a total jumble of measuring systems, with all sorts of Ottoman relics in use. Happily for visitors, this has now changed. Petrol is sold in litres, bananas and apples by the kilo. The one Ottoman measure still in use is the donum, the land measure, which is a little under a third of an acre. The British administration left its heritage of driving on the left, but speed limits and distance markers are in kilometres. Hire cars may be either right- or left-hand drive (the latter are preferred by visitors from the Turkish mainland) but will almost certainly be calibrated in kilometres.

TIME

From the end of March until mid-September, North Cyprus is on GMT+3; in winter GMT+2. The usual time difference with the UK is therefore 2 hours.

PHOTOGRAPHY

While North Cyprus is not well blessed with photographic suppliers, the average visitor should be able to source what they require from a couple of shops in Girne and Nicosia. Any semi-serious photographer would do well to ensure that they bring all their spares with them: given the lack of outlets, any non-standard requests may well entail a wait for the part/spare to arrive from mainland Turkey. Likewise, many apparatus repairs will probably have to be sent overseas, and the timetable for their return will not fit into the timescale of the average holiday.

In Girne, while there are a couple of shops near the Belediye roundabout, the best place to try for batteries, memory cards and cables is **Yucel's** (*Ziya Rizki Caddesi 208*; ☏ *815 35 44*). It's located just down from the HSBC Bank and they can organise repairs and wedding photography. In Lefkoşa, **Ozatay** (*Girne Caddesi 55*; ☏ *227 45 00; www.ozatay.com*) is the best bet, situated 400m down from the Kyrenia Gate.

Apart from photos of the obvious sights (castles, monasteries, churches), there is a wealth of opportunities for other scenic shots.

North Cyprus has its share of characters and taking snaps of people is generally not a problem. When it comes to close-ups, asking before snapping is a common courtesy that should always be observed. Festivals present a great opportunity to take colourful pictures of costumed dancers and musicians.

A final word of warning: on no account should you take photos in the clearly signposted military areas.

MEDIA AND COMMUNICATIONS

TELEPHONE To telephone North Cyprus from the UK, dial 00 (international), then 90 (Turkey country code), then 392 (North Cyprus code), before dialling the relevant town code and finally the actual number itself. If dialling a North Cyprus mobile phone from the UK, dial 00 90, then the number excluding its first '0' (you do not need the 392). To dial the UK from North Cyprus it is 00 (international), then 44 (UK country code), then the town code minus the initial '0', then the number itself. For a considerable period after 1974 it was not possible to call Greek Cyprus from the north. These days as long as you use the international codes, 357 for Greek Cyprus and 90 for Turkey and North Cyprus, and appreciate the international call charges, there's no problem contacting the south.

Public telephone booths are not that common and are most easily found at main post offices in major towns. They only accept telephone cards which can be purchased from telephone offices and some retail outlets. Cards are available for TL10.

Mobile phone networks provide good coverage, and pre-pay SIM cards and top-up cards for the local networks are readily available, packaged with varying amounts of calling credit. To utilise a local SIM, Turkcell or Telsim, your mobile phone may need to be 'unlocked' from its home network. If this is the case, more specialised phone shops in Girne and Lefkoşa will be able to set you free for a small charge, but if you have a high-spec phone the cost of unlocking it can be horrendous. If you plan on using a mobile phone, even if you're just visiting for a week, a local SIM card makes immediate sense at around TL25 in order to avoid hefty international roaming charges when making and receiving calls. Remember to dial 0392 in front of all local numbers from your mobile. There's no roaming agreement between Greek Cypriot and Turkish Cypriot mobile networks, so if you're planning a trip south, or vice versa, you'll need another SIM card. UK and many other international mobile phones will roam in a shockingly expensive manner from network to network, both north and south.

North Cyprus telephone codes
Gazimağusa ✆366
Girne ✆815
Lefkoşa ✆227 or ✆228

Emergency telephone numbers
Fire ✆199
Police ✆155
Ambulance/first aid ✆112
Coastguard ✆158

INTERNET CAFÉS Access to the internet has taken off in North Cyprus, with broadband access readily available in all larger towns either via the numerous internet cafés or through hotel facilities. Most dedicated internet cafés charge around TL3 per hour, whilst an increasing number of cafés and most hotels have free Wi-Fi access for their patrons. Girne also has free municipal Wi-Fi (page 70) in places and other towns may follow suit.

Here are a few of the better-located internet cafés, usually frequented by boys playing computer games:

🖥 **Star Net** Vakiflar Çarşisi 61, Girne; m 0533 844 93 33. In the shopping arcade off Ziya Rizki Caddesi.

🖥 **Fistik Net Café** Sht Salih Cibir Sokak No 15 Kermiya, Lefkoşa; ✆227 37 27

POST Postal rates are very reasonable, with one rate for Europe and the Middle East. Postcards take about ten to 14 days to reach most European destinations, letters five to seven days. Post boxes are bright yellow and are found in the main streets of all towns and villages. When sending items to North Cyprus, the code 'Mersin 10, Turkey' should always appear, otherwise they may be misdirected to Greek Cyprus.

NEWSPAPERS The most popular Turkish-language newspaper is *Kibris*, produced daily from Lefkoşa, while the oldest national daily is *Halkin Sesi*. For English-language readers, the weekly *Cyprus Today* is the most relevant for North Cyprus. Also available are the *Cyprus Star* and *Cyprus Observer*, both published weekly in the north. The *Cyprus Weekly* is also available, but is published in the south. Elsewhere, the Northern Cyprus Hoteliers Association publishes the dual-language *Tourism Monthly*, which can be found liberally distributed around hotels and restaurants. Versions of many of the UK daily papers, printed in Greece, are available in the main towns on the day of publication.

TELEVISION AND RADIO Turkish Cypriot television and Turkish television channels are received everywhere and offer news in English plus a few imported English programmes, usually soaps. Most hotels now have a huge range of international satellite channels, and sports fanatics can nearly always find live broadcasts of all major football matches and other events, with English commentary, without much effort, certainly around Girne and Lapta. BBC World, CNN, France 24 and Al Jazeera International are the English-language news channels most widely available. For radio, the internet has changed everything and your favourite BBC (and other) channels are available online. For those without internet access, BBC World Service's main frequency is 1323Khz MW. The British Forces Broadcasting Service in the Sovereign Bases in Greek Cyprus can be heard clearly in the Gazimağusa area on 99.6MHz and 95.3MHz, and in the Lefkoşa area on 89.7MHz and 91.7MHz, as well as online at www.bfbs.com. BFBS television broadcasts may also be received by those in Lefkoşa.

North Cyprus's own main network is BRTK, with both their radio and television studios located just outside Lefkoşa. Radio programmes (105MHz) and TV broadcasts are also available online at www.brtk.com, with some in English and many other languages.

PROPERTY DEVELOPMENT

For many years, runaway development grabbed hold of the southern part of the island while investment in North Cyprus stagnated in comparison. The reluctance of the money men to invest was caused by the uncertain future of a region that was unrecognised internationally, as well as by doubts as to whether good title could be acquired to land previously owned by those Greek Cypriots who had fled to the south in 1974. While the economy of the north suffered as a result, the region was at least shielded from the ravages of frenzied construction. Change has arrived, however. A glut of holiday properties and hotels has altered parts of the tranquil landscape of North Cyprus forever, and the lessons that should have been learned from other parts of the Mediterranean, not least from Greek Cyprus, have been ignored by those hungry to make a fast buck.

Nobody can deny the rights of locals to benefit from tourism in their own land, though a great deal of the property investment has come from Turkey and Europe rather than from North Cyprus itself. And of course, much of the profit from such investments has returned overseas.

For a while the infrastructure of the region struggled to keep pace with the property development, though new pavements and the new bypass around the south and west of Girne, together with the north coast road now stretching deep into the Karpas are perhaps evidence that it is catching up. Yet even this improved infrastructure has a downside: littered along the roadside are bright new residential complexes, as well as isolated rows of empty retail units, built in hope or false expectation. At least the money invested by the EU has benefited water purification and other infrastructure projects, such as the ongoing construction of turtle research and protection centres.

With gambling illegal on the Turkish mainland, the opportunity has been taken to develop parts of North Cyprus into something of a Las Vegas-style playground, luring high rollers across from the mainland to frequent the many new casinos. The vast majority of visitors do indeed come from Turkey, often for short stays to watch their fortunes ride the roulette wheels or double or halve on the turn of a card. To cater for them, nearly every self-respecting upmarket hotel has a casino attached, each new establishment seemingly having to trump its immediate predecessor in terms of opulence (or crassness, depending on your taste).

For a while, the development bubble reached a hiatus, with even the ever-optimistic estate agents admitting that 2009 was a 'difficult' year for selling villas. As well as the troubled economic climate, uncertainty over Turkey's possible accession to the EU and lingering doubts about property title deeds caused concern. A healthy economy on the mainland, the troubles of the eurozone and the avowed opposition to Turkish membership by some existing states has led many Turks to ask: 'Why bother joining the EU?' Such uncertainty had never deterred purchasers from Britain or Germany, nor in more recent years those from Scandinavia, the Middle East and the former Soviet bloc countries. Regarding title to land once owned by Greek Cypriots, unsettling news for holiday-home owners had come a few years ago in the form of a ruling by a district court in Nicosia that a British couple who had built a villa in North Cyprus, had to demolish it and return the land to its Greek Cypriot owner. Though southern rulings are not enforceable in North Cyprus, the case then moved first to the UK's High Court and subsequently on to the European Court of Justice (ECJ). This was hardly an encouragement for prospective purchasers in North Cyprus.

With other cases looming, threatening to clog up the workings of the ECJ, Turkey – a signatory to the Court – set up the Immoveable Property Commission, intended to adjudicate the claims of Greek Cypriots deprived of their land, and to compensate them accordingly. This mechanism has brought some clarity and gained the approval of the ECJ and everyone else apart from the Greek Cypriot government, which advised its citizens not to claim. To date, around 6,000 claims have nevertheless been settled through the Commission, though there are potentially a further 10,000 still outstanding. If Cyprus's political future were to be resolved, Turkey was admitted to the EU and the still *slightly* misty clouds of land ownership vanquished, those who have already speculated and either developed or bought properties in the north might find that they hit the jackpot. Demand has picked up again, though the British have become sellers and other nationalities have moved in. One can only hope that the North Cypriot government has woken up to the fact that North Cyprus's long-held allure runs the risk of being casually blighted by a chaotic and careless scramble for easy money and a bargain-basement place in the sun. There's not much allure in a half built villa development, nor in an abandoned hotel project. Nor, perhaps, in yet another casino hotel.

Property in North Cyprus can represent good value and for those who wish to buy property, the advice has to be to thoroughly research the pros and cons, ask plenty of questions and obtain satisfactory answers. Buying a property from a well-established, reputable, English-speaking estate agent such as **Ian Smith** (℡ *822 40 53;* e *info@iansmithestate.com; www.iansmithestate.com; see ad, below*) is essential.

TRAVELLING RESPONSIBLY

North Cyprus is by no means a wealthy region, but you will not encounter extreme poverty and beggars are a real rarity. Life is nevertheless tough for some inhabitants, and one organisation engaged in a worthy cause is **SOS Children's Villages** (*www. soschildensvillages.org*). Their activities are aimed at providing support for the local community, and giving children educational access, nutritional support and healthcare. A kindergarten in Lefkoşa looks after 75 children, thus allowing impoverished parents to go to work and earn a living. Where parental care is absent, SOS endeavour to place children with a family. Donations and sponsorship are always welcome.

Part Two

THE GUIDE

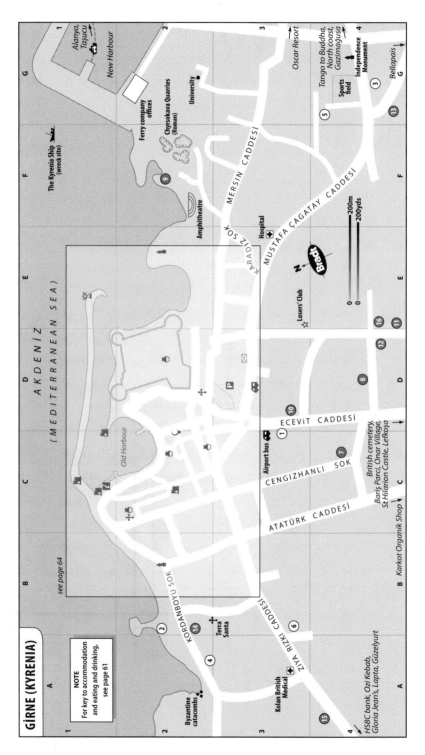

GiRNE (KYRENIA)

NOTE
For key to accommodation and eating and drinking, see page 61

see page 64

AKDENİZ
(MEDITERRANEAN SEA)

Old Harbour

Byzantine catacombs

KORDANBOYU SOK

Terra Santa

Kolan British Medical

ZİYA RIZKI CADDESİ

HSBC bank, Ozi Kebab, Gloria Jean's, Lapta, Güzelyurt

Karkot Organik Shop

ATATÜRK CADDESİ

CENGİZHANLI SOK

British cemetery, Barış Parcı, Onar Village, St Hilarion Castle, Lefkoşa

ECEVİT CADDESİ

Airport bus

Losers' Club

Hospital

KARADENİZ SOK

MERSİN CADDESİ

MUSTAFA ÇAĞATAY CADDESİ

Amphitheatre

The Kyrenia Ship (wreck site)

Ferry company offices

Chrysokava Quarries (Roman)

University

Oscar Resort

Tango to Buddha, North coast, Gazimağusa

Sports field

Independence Monument

Bellapais

Alanya, Taşucu

New Harbour

0   200m
0   200yds

Bradt

60

3

Girne (Kyrenia)

Although the economic ebb and flow has taken its toll in recent years, Girne is still the prettiest town on the island by virtue of an imposing Crusader castle and a picturesque, atmospheric harbour flanked by alfresco restaurants and bars. Hotels and villa developments may have sprouted up in the outskirts to the east and west, but Girne's old town and harbour nevertheless stand resolute against modernisation, whilst still managing to offer their many visitors all the pleasures of a well-equipped resort. To the south, the jagged Kyrenia Mountains provide the town with a spectacular backdrop and an irresistible invitation to visit both the towering hilltop castle of St Hilarion and the tranquillity of nearby Bellapais Abbey.

According to the official 2011 census, the wider municipality of Girne had 69,000 inhabitants, with just under half of those living within the town boundaries. To the visitor in high season, the town can give the impression of being even bigger, due to the large volume of tourists and general bustle.

Avoiding the crowds, the early-morning visitor can stroll the picturesque harbour area or the narrow alleys around the Djafer Paşa Mosque, stopping to savour a freshly squeezed orange juice or sip tentatively at a darkly foreboding Turkish coffee.

Eventually the town stirs into action and sets about its business with considerable bustle. From the frantic roundabout of the Ramadan Cemil Meydani – commonly known as the Belediye – to the small, diverse shops along Ziya Rizki Caddesi and Atatürk Caddesi, Girne generates a buzz worthy of any self-respecting Mediterranean resort. In the evening, would-be diners ponder the choices offered by the many fish and *meze* eateries clustered around the calm waters of the horseshoe-shaped harbour. Food is generally of a high standard, though recent price increases mean that reasonable, rather than excellent, value can be expected. After dinner, many visitors, especially those from mainland Turkey, take their chances at the flash casinos attached to the more upmarket hotels, while non-gamblers can people-watch from the outdoor cafés.

Those arriving in Girne in search of a peaceful fishing village may be disappointed – they're in the right place, just at the wrong time. But while

Girne (Kyrenia)

3

61

the tranquillity of yesteryear may have gone, the frenzied investment that has brought endless hotels and holiday apartments to the surrounding municipality has also improved the infrastructure. A fairly recently constructed bypass detours westbound-traffic from Lefkoşa around the southern fringe of Girne, avoiding the city centre and somewhat reducing the previous congestion; new pavements have smartened up the town's main shopping arteries; and a steady stream of new and revamped, chic bars and restaurants present a more spruced-up appearance to the returning visitor.

A compact and attractive resort, and the preferred base for most visitors to North Cyprus, Girne continually ups its act to try to ensure that it remains a premier tourist destination. A loyal band of visitors who return year after year provides evidence that, at least for now, it has achieved that objective.

HISTORY

Many private houses in Girne were looted during the troubles of 1974, and by 1976 only some 200 out of the original 2,500 British residents remained. Turks from the Limassol area were resettled here, and given land and property that had been Greek, in the same way that Greeks were given Turkish property in the south in compensation for their losses in the north. Some mainland Turks have also been encouraged to settle in the area, which is how the town's population level has been restored.

Indeed, settlement from the Turkish mainland was how the Turkish Cypriot community first began on the island. After the defeat of the Venetians in Cyprus in 1571, the Turkish commander Lala Mustafa Paşa chose 12,000 infantry and 4,000 cavalrymen to stay behind as colonists. A further 22,000 decommissioned soldiers and their families also went to Cyprus, along with their livestock, tools for their crafts and all their possessions. They were given expatriate allowances and tax exemptions for the first three years to encourage them to settle, as was common practice by the Ottomans throughout their conquered territories. To help in the rebuilding and repopulating process, the Ottomans especially favoured farmers, and thereafter a range of other skilled workers like weavers, cobblers, tailors, masons, coppersmiths and miners. They also favoured families with young daughters. Many settlers came from the Black Sea coastal areas of Trabzon and Sinop, and the resettlement continued intermittently until the 18th century. By the time of the British administration in 1878, there were 95,000 Turkish Cypriots living on the island.

Girne's population in the past was subject to wild fluctuations depending on plagues, droughts and other disasters. In 1814 it was recorded that a mere 15 families lived in the town, all Greeks, and that the ruling Turks would withdraw to the town's castle at night. From the 16th century, under the Ottoman administration, the population was fairly evenly balanced between Turks and Greeks. The Turks were traditionally landowners and farmers, while the Greeks were fishermen, shop owners and merchants. By 1900 the population had risen to some 1,500, and this gradually increased as Girne and the surrounding area became the favoured place of retirement for British colonial officials, living their lives of 'blameless monotony', as Lawrence Durrell put it in his autobiographical *Bitter Lemons*. The British had taken on the administration of Cyprus from the Ottomans because of its strategic importance, since the 1869 opening of the Suez Canal, in the protection of their trade route to India. Five years later, however, when Britain also took military occupation of Egypt, Cyprus ceased to be vital and was subsequently neglected, with little financial investment.

BY ROAD Thanks to some much-needed road improvements, Girne is only a 20-minute drive from Lefkoşa, 40 minutes from Ercan Airport and 70 minutes from Gazimağusa. Heading west from Girne, it takes one hour 45 minutes to reach the new border crossing at Yeşilırmak – a few kilometres beyond Vouni, the westernmost point of interest – and driving east, less than 2½ hours to reach the easternmost tip of the Karpas, making use of the new north coast road. When this road is further extended beyond Dipkarpaz, the journey time to the 'far east' is likely to shorten.

Most package tour operators provide customers with **airport transfers** between Girne and Ercan airport, or indeed from Larnaca if you fly in to the south of the island. If you do have to take your own taxi from Ercan, expect to pay around TL90 each way, slightly more at night. A cheaper alternative for the independent, solo traveller is the **bus** service run by **Kibhas Limited** (m *0533 870 78 46*). The company has a kiosk outside the airport terminal and a Girne office two doors down from the Colony Hotel. The journey costs TL13.50 and takes 1 hour 15 minutes. The bus departs around ten times per day and tickets must be bought in advance from the office, but a bit of pre-planning could save you some lira compared with a taxi. The times of buses from Ercan to Girne (and other destinations) can be found on www. kibhas.org, or on the airport website, www.ercanairport.co.uk. Some Girne car hire companies will also arrange airport pick-ups for their customers – see pages 40–1.

For local transport, *dolmuş* minibuses (or sometimes stretched Mercedes saloon cars) operate from early morning until around 19.00, with some services – particularly along the coast to Lapta – running later. These connect Girne with all major population centres in the north. Sample single fares are TL5 to Lefkoşa, TL9.50 to Gazimağusa, TL4.50 to Lapta and TL3 to Karağlanoğlu. The best place to catch them is by the Belediye roundabout, though they can also be flagged down anywhere along the main roads. Destinations are shown by a notice in the windscreen and tickets are purchased on board, with prices usually displayed clearly on a sign above the driver's head.

BY SEA Girne's **ferry** terminal lies 1km east of the old harbour, reachable by taxi. There are now only two ferry companies, following the demise of Fergün. **Akgünler** (✆ *444 43 64*) has offices on the north side of the Belediye roundabout in the town centre and also at the terminal itself. You can also book through many travel agencies as well as now online: Akgünler has an English-language option on its ticket-reservation website (*www.akgunlerbilet.com*), and promises to translate its main site (*www.akgunlerdenizcilik.com*) very soon. The fast ferry to Taşucu in mainland Turkey runs throughout the year and takes a little over 2 hours. A single fare on the high-speed, passenger-only ferry costs TL135, with the passenger fare on the slower car ferry being cheaper at TL95, vehicles extra. There are discounts for students and children. The other operator is called **Filo** (✆ *815 39 41*) and runs a car ferry to Taşucu for the same price. It has an office only at the ferry terminal, and an online booking facility in English (*www.filoshipping.com*). For further information, see page 30.

WHERE TO STAY   *Map, page 60, unless otherwise stated*

The town and surrounding area offer the best range of accommodation in North Cyprus, from self-catering to five-star hotels. Unfortunately, an upsurge in

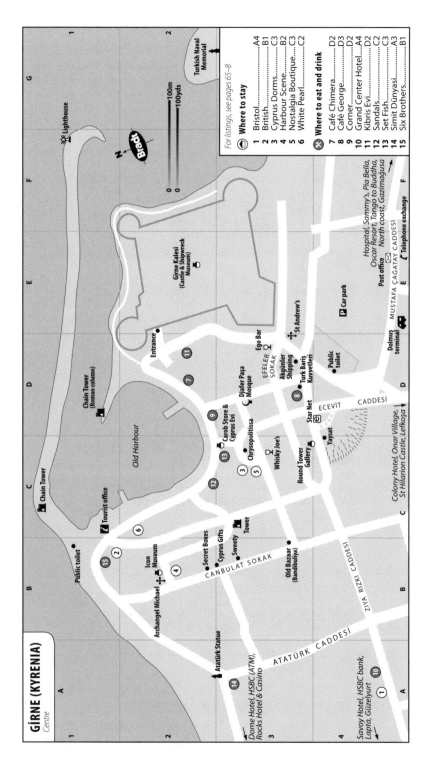

GİRNE (KYRENIA)
Centre

For listings, see pages 65–8

Where to stay
1 Bristol..................A4
2 British..................B1
3 Cyprus Dorms..........C3
4 Harbour Scene..........B2
5 Nostalgia Boutique....C3
6 White Pearl............C2

Where to eat and drink
7 Café Chimera..........D2
8 Café George...........D3
9 Corner................D2
10 Grand Center Hotel...A4
11 Kibris Evi............D2
12 Sandals...............C2
13 Set Fish..............C3
14 Simit Dünyasi.........A3
15 Six Brothers..........B1

Lighthouse

Turkish Naval Memorial

Chain Tower

Old Harbour

Chain Tower (Roman column)

Girne Kalesi (Castle & Shipwreck Museum)

Entrance

Tourist office

Public toilet

Djafer Paşa Mosque

Carob Store & Cyprus Evi

Chrysopolitissa

Whisky Joe's

Ego Bar

EFELER SOKAK

Akgünler Shipping

St Andrew's

Turk Barış Kuvvetleri

Round Tower Gallery

Star Net

Yaysat

Public toilet

Car park

Dolmus terminal

Post office

Telephone exchange

MUSTAFA ÇAĞATAY CADDESİ

ECEVİT CADDESİ

Archangel Michael

Icon Museum

Secret Boxes

Cyprus Gifts

Sweety

Tower

Old Bazaar (Bandibuliya)

CANBULAT SOKAK

ZIYA RIZKI CADDESİ

Atatürk Statue

ATATÜRK CADDESİ

Hospital, Sammy's, Pia Bella, Oscar Resort, Tango to Buddha, North coast, Gazimagusa

Colony Hotel, Onar Village, St Hilarion Castle, Lefkoşa

Savoy Hotel, HSBC bank, Lapta, Güzelyurt

Dome Hotel, HSBC (ATM), Rocks Hotel & Casino

0   100m
0   100yds

N

Bradt

investment over the last few years has led to a rash of building projects, some of them half-finished, making the fringes of Girne and parts of the coastline to the west somewhat tacky. That said, the old harbour area has fully retained its charm and will be a favourite with many visitors.

Broadly speaking, most upmarket establishments incorporate casinos and rely on a mainland-Turkish clientele who come on weekend stays to gamble, while the mid-range and budget hotels are often owner-managed and depend more on the European package-holiday market to fill their rooms. Generally, both types of hotel do their jobs very well, and many mid-range ones have loyal, repeat customers. Some hotels close for the winter months, though they don't always formulate the precise dates very far in advance, so check when making your plans.

The all-inclusive concept, popular in other Mediterranean destinations but until recently a virtual unknown in North Cyprus, is beginning to infiltrate some of the high-end hotels in the Girne region.

Except for these all-inclusives, or where otherwise stated, the price codes refer to the cost of a double or twin room with two people sharing, including breakfast. These quotes are based on the high-season summer period, and prices are often much lower out of season. Package holidays booked through a tour operator (pages 24–5) frequently represent the best value.

LUXURY $$$$$

🏠 **Rocks Hotel & Casino** (156 rooms) ☎650 04 00; e info@rockshotel.com; www.rockshotel. com. Significantly redeveloped & expanded with all mod cons, but commanding premium rates as a result. Well-appointed AC rooms, free Wi-Fi throughout, a range of bars, restaurants & cafés, deluxe spa centre, pool & large sundeck. Popular with Turkish high rollers from the adjacent casino.

🏠 **The Savoy Ottoman Palace** (128 rooms) ☎444 70 00; e info@savoyhotel.com.tr; www. savoyhotel.com.tr. A fairly new, ostentatious, city centre offering. Full Ottoman glitz, an interesting fusion with no expense spared. Pool, spa, mini-club, various restaurants (including rooftop), massive casino, use of Ada Beach Club (courtesy bus available), free Wi-Fi.

UPMARKET $$$$

🏠 **The Colony** (94 rooms) ☎815 15 18; e thecolony@arkingroup.com; www. thecolonycyprus.com. One of Girne's smartest & most tasteful hotels, well back from the harbour & with a glitzy casino. Main clientele has been Turkish businessmen, though increasing numbers of Western tourists are staying here, enjoying the excellent service, pleasant rooftop pool, spa, wellness centre & fine restaurants. All rooms come with free Wi-Fi, satellite TV, minibar & AC.

🏠 **Dome Hotel** (160 rooms) ☎815 24 54; e info@dome-cyprus.com; www.dome-cyprus.

com. Girne's most famous & longest-standing hotel, recently refurbished & set on the seafront with its own rocky promontory for sunbathing & with ladders down into the sea. Large AC rooms with satellite TV & minibar. Balconies overlooking sea or mountains. Busy cosmopolitan bar with pianist & restaurant with international cuisine. 3 pools (including children's & seawater) & sauna. Free Wi-Fi in public areas & some bedrooms. Casino.

🏠 **Oscar Resort** (254 rooms) ☎815 48 01; e info@oscarresort.com; www.oscarresort.com. This large, extended complex is set on Girne's eastern outskirts. Variety of AC, en-suite rooms with satellite TV. Self-contained resort-style hotel, with excellent facilities (some seasonal) including 3 pools, waterslides & wave machine (great for children), fitness equipment, restaurant, bar & the ubiquitous casino. Wi-Fi throughout, though at extra charge. Courtesy transport into town. Family rooms available.

MID-RANGE $$$

🏠 **British Hotel** [map, page 64] (18 rooms) ☎815 22 40; e info@britishhotelcyprus.com; www.britishhotelcyprus.com. Rooms with AC, satellite TV, minibar, some with balcony & good views to old harbour & castle. B&B only. Roof terrace & bar. Good, simple, family-run, very central base.

🏠 **Onar Village** [map, page 91] (44 rooms, plus 20 villas) ☎815 58 50; e info@

onarvillage.com; www.onarvillage.com. Very pleasant complex with indoor & outdoor pools (open according to season), consisting of villas & hotel rooms, all with balcony or terrace, AC, TV with international channels. Set on the hillside overlooking Girne. Family-run, with a once-a-day courtesy bus to town, restaurant, pool bar & library. Also has Turkish bath, sauna. Free Wi-Fi throughout & a small, private museum.

🏠 **Pia Bella Hotel** (162 rooms) ✆650 50 00; e info@piabella.com; www.piabella.com. A pleasant 20-min walk from the harbour. Comfortable rooms with AC & satellite TV, 2 swimming pools (including children's section), 4 restaurants (2 seasonal), attractive garden, pool tables, large lounge & 2 bars. Casino. Highly rated, with loyal following of mainly British holidaymakers. Friendly & knowledgeable staff. Free Wi-Fi in public areas. Rooms away from main road are quieter.

🏠 **Sammy's Hotel** (24 rooms) ✆815 62 79; e info@sammyshotel.com; www.sammyshotel. com. Situated 10mins' walk to the east of the centre. Popular, with a loyal customer base. In a residential area, but the owners make a real effort. AC rooms with satellite TV. Lovely swimming pool. Friendly staff & a good option, though not luxurious. Popular with the British. Free Wi-Fi in public areas. Reductions for longer stays.

🏠 **White Pearl Hotel** [map, page 64] (10 rooms) ✆815 04 30; e info@whitepearlhotel. com; www.whitepearlhotel.com. Dbl & twin rooms, most with balcony, all en suite with TV, AC, Wi-Fi. Superb setting on the western edge of Kyrenia harbour. Great panoramic views from rooftop bar terrace. Car hire & airport transfers.

BUDGET $$
🏠 **Bristol Hotel** [map, page 64] (18 rooms) ✆815 65 56; e bristolhotelcyprus@gmail.com; www.bristolhotelcyprus.com. Small, unassuming but friendly place on the main street. Large rooms with TV, toilet & bath or shower. Shady patio garden, restaurant & bar, Wi-Fi in public areas. Little English spoken.

🏠 **Harbour Scene Hotel** [map, page 64] (15 rooms) ✆815 68 55; e harbour.scene@ hotmail.com. A small, basic, well-established hotel. Spacious rooms, with bath or shower, AC, satellite TV, some with balcony. Good central location on Canbulat Sokak, though despite the name it's not quite on the harbour. No luxuries, but reasonable value.

🏠 **Nostalgia Boutique Hotel** [map, page 64] (28 rooms) ✆815 30 79; e nostalgiacourt@gmail. com; www.nostalgiaboutiquehotel.com. Quaint, characterful hotel in quiet backstreet, just up from the Djafer Paşa Mosque. Traditional Cypriot décor in the AC rooms (including 4-poster beds in some), all with TV. Bar & attached Gozan restaurant. Small, courtyard pool at nearby Ferman restaurant. Free Wi-Fi. Great value friendly option, slap bang in the old town.

SHOESTRING $
🏠 **Cyprus Dorms** [map, page 64] (19 rooms) m 0533 887 20 07; e cyprusdorms@ yahoo.com; www.cyprusdorms.com. Recently expanded & relocated, opposite Chrysopolitissa Church. Backpacker-style, shared washing machine, Wi-Fi, AC, but no b/fast. Open all year, dorm beds are €12 with shared bathrooms. Doubles & triples with private bath are €35 & €46 respectively. Good value.

✖ WHERE TO EAT AND DRINK

SEAFRONT *Map, page 64, unless otherwise stated*

The stunning location and ambience demand that you dine down at the harbour at least once during your stay. With the castle and the boats lit up at night, outdoor eating here is relaxed and pleasant, though more expensive than inland. Prices have escalated in recent years, meaning that better value and, indeed, quality, can undoubtedly be found elsewhere. Although there are a dozen or so restaurants with an excellent location right on the harbour, the few listed below are the ones considered to offer the best food.

Fresh fish and *meze* are the standards at most harbourside restaurants, though other cuisines are also available. Waiters will try vigorously to entice you in, but keep your nerve: it's worth strolling the harbour's length and checking out *all* the menus, as well as any live music on offer. Between April and September, booking is advisable if you want to eat at a particular establishment. In high season, harbour restaurants serve until around 23.00.

✘ Café Chimera ✆815 43 94. Next to the castle. Nice long terrace for a drink, or the usual steak, fish & chicken if you're hungry. Also children's menu & vegetarian options. Often has music, sometimes live, sometimes piped. *TL28*

✘ Corner Restaurant ✆815 33 57. Perhaps the best-rated of the harbourfront restaurants. Well-managed with varied menus featuring fresh fish & a good selection of Turkish & European dishes. *TL30*

✘ Kibris Evi m 0533 830 3333. Perched above the harbour, near the castle entrance, with narrow balconies giving an almost aerial view of the harbour. Roof terrace & some interesting old photos. Traditional Cypriot fare at very decent prices, given the first-class location. *TL23*

✘ Niazi's [map, page 60] ✆815 21 60. Opposite the Dome Hotel, so no actual harbour view, but an excellent restaurant with good service & dependable food. Deservedly a long-time favourite with tourists & locals. Order the more expensive full kebab, prepared in front of you on an open

BBQ. Once the food starts arriving, it seems it may never stop. (Niazi's Takeaway [map, page 60], on Ziya Rizki Caddesi, offers similar, cheaper food in less formal surroundings. Despite its name, it's not just a takeaway.) *TL28*

✘ Sandals ✆815 89 00. One of the better-rated restaurants along the harbourfront, with their adult menu exclusively devoted to fish. Children's options include chicken. Reasonable prices, given the location. Live music every evening. *TL30*

✘ Set Fish ✆815 23 36. On the harbour, it excels in a fresh fish set menu & is highly rated by many. Good value, though not cheap. *TL40*

✘ Six Brothers m 0542 877 08 30. Opposite the tourist office, just outside the harbour. Also known as Restaurant Marti. Unsurprisingly, it's run by six brothers, often to be seen holding management meetings in the soft chairs. Not as chic as some of the others, but a handy place for a cup of çay (tea), snack, meal & people-watching. *TL35*

AWAY FROM THE HARBOUR *Map, page 60, unless otherwise stated*

There are fewer big restaurants and bars away from the harbour but, by wandering around the cobbled streets, you'll come across numerous basic, friendly cafés with tables spilling out on to the street. Some of the better options are listed below. Although the harbour view will be absent, you could compensate for this with a rooftop view (Grand Center Hotel Restaurant) or a different waterfront setting (Eziç Peanuts). For sports fans, there are a few British-orientated cafés around the Belediye roundabout, of which the **Café George** [64 D3] has the most screens and is the most popular.

One area definitely worthy of a visit is the so-called **Turkish Quarter**, a quiet network of narrow streets off the tourist trail, yet still very central. Here you'll find traditional butchers' shops, a 70-year-old bakery and streetlife that rarely rises above the murmur of conversation and the clacking sound of backgammon games. It also houses a few high-quality restaurants that get the thumbs up from 'in-the-know' Turkish Cypriots and expats who prefer these to the harbour eateries. Prices reflect the higher standards, but are worth paying for a special occasion. Taking the street called Namık Kemal Caddesi, which starts opposite the post office, just follow the individual restaurant signs.

✘ Efendim ✆815 11 49. Styled as 'Bohemian fusion' cuisine. Divine steaks & lamb. A popular, tasteful courtyard, with creative kitchen team, relaxed ambience. Often enhanced by live music. Great place for a memorable meal. Recommended. *TL40*

✘ i Belli ✆815 46 70; A much-praised courtyard restaurant, owned & run by charming Italians. Full range of fine Italian food & wines. Smart, well run, but relaxed & informal. *TL40*

✘ Ikimiz ✆815 15 89; www.ikimiz-kyrenia. com. Run by a Cypriot mother & daughter, the name means 'the two of us'. Atmospheric setting, traditional Cypriot food with some creative twists. *TL35*

✗ No. 14 ☏815 57 69; **m** 0542 859 20 72; ⊕ evenings only, closed Sun. European cuisine, in a courtyard setting around a slightly perplexing swimming pool. *TL45*

ELSEWHERE IN TOWN

✗ Beyti ☏815 25 73; ⊕ 24hrs. On Cengiz Hanlı Sokak (the 'street of the ironmongers'), behind the Colony Hotel. Well worth a diversion for the ornate, Arabian-themed interior, this busy little place offers simple local fare of kebab & fish dishes from an extensive menu, with friendly service, low prices & generous helpings. Recommended. *TL17*

✗ Eziç Peanuts ☏815 06 92; www.ezizonline. com. Part of a small chain, this branch is 500m east of the harbour. Chicken cooked every which way, plus steaks, pastas & salads. Reasonable prices. Good seafront terrace location & chilled music for atmosphere. *TL25*

✗ Grand Center Hotel [map, page 64] ☏816 01 82; www.grandcenterhotel.com. On Ziya Rizki Caddesi, a rooftop restaurant serving simple salads, omelettes, burgers & pastas. Lunchtime, rather than evening venue. Food is good, location & prices are excellent. Views to the sea, the mountains & over the town (the elegant white mansion to the south is a military HQ). *TL15*

✗ The House ☏816 10 10; www. thehousekyrenia.com. Opposite the Colony Hotel.

A renovated residence gives a top-class setting. The Turkish President ate here on his 2014 visit. Take a full tour of the interior for a lesson in chic, but beware karaoke night on Fri. Art displays downstairs. Great food choices: steaks, kebabs, fish, salads & b/fasts. Prices are reasonable. *TL32*

✗ Ozi Kebab **m** 0533 845 52 52. When the wallet's as empty as the stomach, head out of the town centre on Ziya Rizki Caddesi for high-quality wraps at excellent prices, in a canteen setting. Free *ayran* thrown in, too. *TL12*

☕ Gloria Jean's ☏815 02 95. Out of the centre, at 19, Naci Talat Caddesi, near the Jasmine Court Hotel. Part of an expanding chain, this place has no Cypriot character whatsoever but offers a full range of hot & cold coffees, cakes & free Wi-Fi, fashionable terrace & blissful AC interior. *TL15*

☕ L'Artisan ☏815 04 67. Tucked away by the rear entrance of the Pia Bella Hotel, this small, smart, French-themed café has excellent coffees, freshly baked croissants & tempting cakes. Also has a lunch menu & divine chocolates. Free Wi-Fi. *TL12*

☕ Simit Dünyasi [map, page 64] ☏815 09 07; ⊕ 05.00–midnight daily. Part of a chain, café-cum-bakery with tasty sweet & savoury pastries, omelettes, wraps, breads & drinks. The shady roof terrace is a great place for a quick, filling snack, with sea views. Some of the longest opening hours in town. 'Instant' cappuccinos should be avoided. Snacks rather than meals, but you won't go hungry or need a bank loan here. *TL14*

NIGHTLIFE

Girne is perhaps wilder than anywhere else in the north of the island, but that doesn't mean it's a nightlife 'hotspot'. Having said that, it's got a little bit of everything if you look hard enough. And there are always those glitzy casinos, if you don't.

Most discos usually only open on Wednesdays, Fridays and Saturdays, and they don't get going until after 23.00. A peculiarity of some of Girne's nightspots is that they spend their summers at beachfront locations such as '**Ice**' and '**Locca**', both located above Escape Beach [90 C1], before migrating inland and indoors and finding a new host venue for the winter. Due to noise restrictions, some of the outdoor versions close at around 02.00. The tourist office should be able to help you track them down. At the huge out-of-town Cratos Premium Hotel (page 111), **The Cage** is a disco that attracts many fans at the weekends. For an entertaining experience, you're onto a winner at the **Losers' Club** [60 E3] (**m** *0533 862 7662*), where the host has creatively used recycled materials from around the island to transform his house into an atmospheric late-night hangout. Opening hours are 'arbitrary', the tongue-in-cheek stated aim is to be 'the rudest

Murray Stewart

At times, as the neon lures you towards another casino, the surroundings around Girne can make you feel as if you've landed in downtown Las Vegas. Why are these gamblers' paradises here? Well, as casinos are strictly prohibited in mainland Turkey, the clientele is mainly Turkish. Flights arrive at Ercan airport every weekend, depositing planeloads of eager gamblers who are then ushered off to their chosen glitzy casino – with a luxury hotel bolted on, of course.

Ironically, natives of North Cyprus are not even allowed in to gamble (that's the legal position, though it is circumvented by the keen and the desperate).

Locals officially have to content themselves with the bookies' shops that have popped up everywhere.

Like them or loathe them, the casinos bring in a huge amount of revenue to the north, though as many of the bigger hotels are Turkish-owned, it can't be said that all of the money necessarily stays on the island.

One side effect of the casino culture is that the casino-hotel guest cannot always expect the same level of warm welcome as can be enjoyed in one of the smaller, family-run, casino-free establishments. The focus of the big hotels' customer care is often the gambler, not the hotel guest, and the distinction sometimes shows at the reception desk. But those who do stay in the big hotels will have the consolation of five-star facilities: the pool, the fine restaurants. They just need to remember to keep enough money to pay the hotel bill at the end of their stay.

bar in North Cyprus' and his business card states that he and his staff are 'nervously waiting'. Expect the unexpected, but in truth it's a pleasant place to spend an evening. To find it, follow the bar's signs on the road that starts opposite the post office. Another good late-night option is **Ego Bar** [64 D3] (m *0533 842 9999*), next to the Djafer Paşa Mosque. This low-lit, courtyard place attracts a mixed crowd and moves indoors in winter to the adjacent, elegant, wood-panelled building where jazz and blues are promised.

Tango to Buddha [60 G4] (℡ *815 07 01; www.tangotobuddha.com*) is a comparatively recent, trendy arrival, on Iskenderun Av, heading east out of Girne. A lush interior provides the setting for Girne's self-styled beautiful people. Dress smartly and enjoy the cocktails, but posing is not a cheap hobby. At around midnight, it metamorphoses into a popular nightspot (and pick-up joint!)

For other late-night bars, **Bandibuliya** [64 C3], just opposite the entrance to the Round Tower Bookshop, is a venue with potential, crying out for some more activity. At present, it has a pool table, table football, a bar, a few half-hearted shops and a daytime restaurant. It is worth a before-dark visit just to see the interior of this Old Bazaar building and meet the gentleman making the freshly squeezed juice and Turkish coffee: he's been doing so for over 40 years. **Whiskey Joe's** [64 C3] (m *0533 832 3854*), just up behind the harbour, is a chill-out option, unashamedly popular with Brits, offering draft bitter and stout, a pleasant outdoor terrace and a slight Celtic theme. Friday karaoke nights are popular. Music of a more gentle, traditional flavour can be found at weekends in some of the harbour restaurants and many hotels have an entertainment programme.

The Listings section of the *Cyprus Today* newspaper is excellent for finding out what's on, though it focuses on expat activities.

OTHER PRACTICALITIES

TOURIST INFORMATION Situated on the harbour front [64 C1], the tourist office is generally open 08.00–20.00 in summer and 08.00–18.00 in winter, but don't be surprised if it isn't. This facility has improved in recent years, now providing brochures in various languages to reflect the increasing diversity of visitors. However, it still runs a poor second to your hotel or tour operator when it comes to dispensing comprehensive and accurate information or answering anything more than basic questions.

POST OFFICE The post office [64 E4] (⊕ *08.00–15.30 Mon–Wed & Fri, 08.00–13.00 & 14.00–18.00 Thu*) is on M Çağatay Caddesi behind the bus station/car park.

TELEPHONE EXCHANGE Opposite the post office, this is generally open only in the mornings.

INTERNET Girne is now awash with internet cafés, to the extent that you can't really fail to stumble upon one while strolling down Ziya Rizki Caddesi or its adjoining side streets. The rate is around TL3 per hour. Even better, however, is that Girne Municipality has recently introduced free Wi-Fi in the square in front of the smart municipality building, inside the castle and on the stretch of harbour front between the Dome Hotel and the tourist information office. The connection is called 'nethouse' and the username and password are shown automatically on the connection homepage. Most hotels now offer free Wi-Fi, as do most of the town's cafés and restaurants.

FOREIGN NEWSPAPERS Towards the town centre end of Ziya Rizki Caddesi is the small but reliable **Yaysat** newsagent [64 C4], which has the best selection of local English-language and British newspapers (page 55). The latter are printed mainly in Greece and are usually available on the day of publication. Some of the bigger supermarket branches also stock British newspapers.

SHOPPING

Shops open at 08.00 or 09.00, and while the majority then close at 17.30 or 18.00 in the winter, a significant number remain open longer. In the summer more stay open later, until 19.30 or 20.00. Gone are the days when most closed for lunch, though a few maintain this tradition. Some shops close on Sundays, but you won't have to go far on the Sabbath, or late at night, to find a grocer or supermarket that's doing business. Distances are short, so a walk round the shops can be easily fitted in whenever you have the odd half-hour to spare. Of course, as with any other opening times in North Cyprus there's a great fluidity to how rigidly they are observed.

Canbulat Sokak is a good street on which to look for souvenirs. At number 24 is **Sweety** [64 B3], which may not sound too authentically Cypriot but sells over 100 flavours of Turkish (Cypriot) delight, much of which it manufactures itself. It also stocks teas, nuts, jams and other goodies. With a mainly Anglophonic clientele, you can be grateful that the manager, Murat, won the battle with his father, who wanted to name the shop after the family surname: Yumurtacioğlu. Delicious products and fair prices. A few doors down at number 32 is newcomer **Cyprus Gifts** [64 B3], with a range of North Cypriot-made fruit preserves, Lefkara needlework, handmade soaps, olive-wood crafts and olive oil. Right next door is the wood-crafting workshop of **Secret Boxes** [64 B2] (formerly Nakkas), where Haci Avize works his magic in producing clever and beautiful boxes, chests and other wooden wonders. A market takes place every Wednesday at the **Bariş Parci** and is a good place for self-caterers to stock up on cheap fruit and vegetables. There are a few stalls selling jewellery, but apart from that it is mainly inexpensive clothes.

PLACES OF WORSHIP

Anglican services are held at the tiny **St Andrew's Church** [64 D3], by the southwest tower of the castle. A favourite with expats, there's Holy Communion at 08.00 on Sundays, followed by a Family Communion (and Sunday School) at 10.00. The midweek service sees Holy Communion at 09.30 on a Thursday. The inside of the church is beautifully maintained, a cool, shady retreat from the midday sun. The quaint **Terra Santa** [60 B2], the Hungarian Roman Catholic church opposite the Dome Hotel, holds mass every Sunday at noon.

WHAT TO SEE AND DO

A WALK AROUND THE TOWN A stroll around Girne offers a relaxing break from the beach or sightseeing. The pretty streets have a surprising range of shops that avoid tackiness, and souvenir hunting among them is a pleasure. Here and there you will come unexpectedly upon an old mosque, church or ancient tower, a relic of the town walls.

Medieval Girne was a walled town, and today the narrow wiggling streets and alleys behind the harbour still retain a slightly medieval feel, the houses huddled on top of each other. The variety fascinates: one moment you walk past a workshop where wood is crafted into furniture, the next you catch a glimpse into a private arcaded courtyard with tumbling jasmine and bougainvillea. The town walls themselves have been gradually dismantled and incorporated into other buildings, but you will still come across some of the **towers**, tucked a little incongruously beside a butcher's shop or a supermarket. The most obvious old tower is the one in the western corner of the harbour. The position of the others is shown on the map. The one beside the Municipal Market has now been converted to a crafts centre, the **Round Tower Gallery** [64 C3] (✆ 815 63 77; ⏲ year-round, but no set times), for the sale of traditional goods by locals and expats alike. It's a good place to shop for a souvenir, buy a book or get hold of some local information, but it is probably most interesting for the chance it offers to see inside one of the best-preserved and most beautifully proportioned towers in Girne.

Close behind the harbour you will find Girne's oldest mosque, the tiny **Djafer Paşa Mosque** [64 D3], frequented by a handful of faithful worshippers. Turkish Cypriots are not known for their religious fervour, and a fairly relaxed view of Islam is taken on the island. The mosque was built by and named after a Turkish general shortly after the Ottoman takeover in 1570, and is a pleasant if unexciting example of early Ottoman architecture. Below the mosque, an ancient spring has been harnessed to create an area for the ritual hand- and foot-washing before prayers.

Flights of steps connect the streets and in the area behind the mosque you will come across some very splendid old buildings, once private residences for the governor and wealthy citizens, some now converted into bars and restaurants.

Heading down towards the harbour, you'll see, on your left, the dilapidated remains of Girne's oldest church, the **Chrysopolitissa** [64 C3]. Dating from around 1500, the whole edifice is now locked up and closed off and has been left to slip noiselessly into ruin. Blink, and you may miss it. Indeed, the only sign that it was ever a building of some importance is the curious walled-up Gothic arch on its northern exterior – once, presumably, the church's main entrance.

The prominent bell tower of the Greek Orthodox church, **Archangel Michael** [64 B2], forms a landmark from many parts of town, set up as it is on a rocky outcrop. It was built in 1860, with the Turks' blessing, and the bell was even donated by a Turkish resident. The church was locked from 1974, until it reopened in 1990 as an **Icon Museum** [64 B2] (⏲ *irregular hours, but supposedly 08.00–15.30 Mon–Sat; TL5/2 adults/students*) to display some of the icons from the churches of the Girne area, previously stored in the castle.

On the opposite side of the street from the Greek Orthodox church you can see **Byzantine catacombs** [60 A2] cut into the brown limestone cliffs. In the area between the Dome Hotel and the main shopping street inland, there are some 70 of such tombs, the majority of them now covered by shops and modern buildings.

On Efeler Sokak, the street that runs down opposite the entrance to St Andrew's Church, the HQ of the Doğan Turk Birligi football club – formerly a British military chief's mansion – were being renovated at the time of writing, as part of the development of the Ego Bar. The manager has promised faithfully to retain the beautiful wood panelling and fireplaces which evoke memories of past times. Directly opposite, at the **Turk Bariş Kuvvetleri** [64 D3], former soldiers play backgammon or *okey* (a local card game), drink coffee or just keep each other company.

GIRNE HARBOUR Besides providing a fine setting for a range of eating places, alfresco or indoors according to season, the picturesque harbour also incorporates a number of curious relics of its ancient predecessor. The harbour is beautiful at all times of day, but is at its most bewitching at night. Many of the restaurants are open for food all day long.

The graceful horseshoe curve of Girne's harbour has become even more tranquil since being closed to traffic by a barrier at the west end (except for a few hours in the morning to allow deliveries). A fair proportion of the buildings enclosing the harbour are Venetian, tastefully restored to shops and restaurants on their ground levels, with apartments or the owners' accommodation above. The tourist office is itself such a restored house, with a stone vaulted interior.

Above head height to the right of the Corner Restaurant as you face it, you can see large stones jutting out with holes in their centres. In the ancient harbour, ropes were threaded through these holes for hauling boats up onto the beach.

Sticking out of the water amongst the moored fishing boats and yachts, stands a semi-collapsed squat **stone tower** , approached by a crumbling causeway. On top is a smaller tower the size of a Roman column. This was the old chain tower, from which an iron chain was suspended across the harbour entrance to block hostile shipping. The chain, though huge, was but a tiny version of that used in Istanbul to control shipping in the Bosphorus. In the old wall that rises up behind the terrace of Café Chimera, careful observation will reveal the outline of a large Gothic archway, now blocked up. Before 1400, when the moat was still full, ships used to be dragged through this archway from the harbour into the castle moat for safety or simply for repair.

Just next to the Set Fish Restaurant is the entrance to the **Carob Store and Cyprus House** (page 77). Formerly the Folk Museum, for many years this characteristic building remained closed, so the recent redevelopment is very welcome. Strolling out along the harbour wall affords you the best view back to the castle, and the difference in architectural styles is clearly visible. To the left (east) you have a good view for the first time of the taller **Crusader tower**, which is difficult to see from inside the castle or from the harbour front. Its high squared medieval crenellations and arrow slits were built with quite a different style of warfare in mind – catapults and archery – from the later more advanced tower of the Venetians, round and squat, with no arrow slits but just a solitary gun port at sea level and others on top for the newly invented cannon. From the very end of the harbour wall you can also view the eastern wall of the castle.

Walking away from the horseshoe harbour towards the Dome Hotel, you will notice a solitary granite **Roman column** [64 D1] beside the children's playground on the seafront promenade. It is something of a mystery, for though there are several Roman stone fragments to be found incorporated into churches or other buildings in Girne, this is the only granite one. There is no indigenous granite in Cyprus, and this is one of the only pieces of granite found in the whole region.

Boat trips All along the harbour front, you will find a whole host of competing boat owners offering day trips around the coastline, stopping at local bays for swimming and snorkelling. Lunch and snacks are provided on board; most trips require advance booking and leave the harbour at 10.00, returning around 16.30. Costs at present are constant along the harbour at TL70 per adult, with children at a reduced price. In high season, some also offer sunset cruises with dinner included, and even disco cruises. Check in advance exactly what type of cruise you are signing up for: party boat, or something more relaxed. The *Princess* (m *0542 877 08 31*) claims to be the biggest boat (though it is not the sole claimant), is well equipped and has had good reports. Its berth and ticket booth are next to the tourist office.

INLAND GIRNE The outskirts of Girne will be familiar to most visitors simply as an area to pass through *en route* to somewhere else. There are few sights to detain the average tourist, but the increasing urbanisation provides a few more eating options.

From the roundabout at the southern end of **Ecevit Caddesi**, you can stroll in a westerly direction towards Karaoğlanoğlu. Immediately on the left is the old British cemetery, sandwiched between new commercial properties and now somewhat overgrown. Easily missed from the road, the graveyard is of little interest to anyone other than relatives and friends of those who are commemorated there. It contains a memorial to the 371 British servicemen who died in the 1955–59 conflict that preceded independence.

Continuing in the same direction, the recent retail outlets to both sides indicate the upturn in the economy of North Cyprus. You can pick up most things along here, from household appliances to ultra-stylish furniture. Should you fancy a house to go with them, you'll be spoilt for choice amongst all the estate agents who have made this road their home.

At the Jasmine Court Hotel (being renovated at time of writing), you can choose to cut back towards the sea. On reaching the shore, it appears that this is an excellent shortcut back to the harbour, but don't be tempted to walk this way. The road leads only to the military base, and although it seems that locals come and go through the barriers at will, any tourist attempting so to do will very quickly be intercepted by rifle-toting soldiers. The best way back to the harbour is to head across to Atatürk Caddesi and then bear north. In doing so, those who are self-catering should take the opportunity to visit the **Karkot Organik Shop** (✆ *815 18 59*), just opposite the primary school on Inonu Caddesi. It stocks delicious pasta, dried foods, nuts, cosmetics and hygienic products, plus a huge range of organic baby foods. Note that not all the wine is organic. You will also find these products on sale in the larger supermarkets.

GIRNE KALESI (KYRENIA CASTLE) [64 E2] (☺ *summer 08.00–18.00, winter 08.00–17.00; the entrance fee of TL12/5 adults/students includes entry to the Shipwreck Museum housed inside the castle; you need to arrive at least 60mins before closing to be allowed into the castle*) As you approach the castle from the harbour, the sheer power of the walls impresses. Here's a castle that looks like a castle should. The huge **round tower** that confronts you is the work of the Venetians. Such fortifications were their major legacy to Cyprus, for they always regarded the island as a military outpost to protect and service their lust for trade.

Housed within the castle walls is the **Girne Department of Antiquities**, which took over custodianship of the castle in 1959. In some of the castle's locked rooms the Antiquities Department is keeping icons that were collected from churches in the Girne area pre-1974 and stored here for safe keeping. Some of these are now on display in the Archangel Michael Church (page 72).

Under British rule, the castle was also used as a police barracks and training school, and as a prison for members of EOKA, the Greek Cypriot resistance movement or the Nationalist Organisation of Cypriot Fighters (Ethniki Organosis Kyprion Agoniston). EOKA formed in 1954, and from secret headquarters somewhere in the Troodos Mountains they organised a series of terrorist and sabotage attacks against British administration, to further their aim of union with Greece, or Enosis as this union was known. Pro-Enosis propaganda was concentrated in schools, where it was easy to sway feelings. Schoolteachers were mainly Greek-trained and proponents of Greek ideology. Although Enosis did not begin as an anti-British sentiment, it gradually became so, and many people were murdered. The Greek Orthodox Church, encouraged by Archbishop Makarios, retained a strong role in the conflict, refusing to give the sacrament to those who assisted the British police or who betrayed information on EOKA fighters. In the view of impartial observers, the majority of the population were intimidated and uncertain, simply wanting the end of military rule and the return of their old, peaceful lifestyle. The Turkish Cypriots felt threatened by the prospect of union with Greece, and the seeds were sown for the inevitable intercommunal fighting. 'Greece and Turkey,' as AE Yalman, editor of the Turkish newspaper Vatan, wrote in 1960, 'have a common destiny. They are condemned either to be good neighbours, close friends, faithful allies or to commit suicide together.' Over 50 years later, their common fate is yet to be determined. On a lighter note, the castle has also featured as a film-set for Raquel Welch in *The Beloved*.

Touring the castle The ticket office sits at the head of the drawbridge, and can be reached either by steps from the harbour or from inland. Note that the services of English-language tour guides can usually be requested and are free of charge, though a gratuity is always appreciated. Ask at the ticket office as you go in. The guides will escort parties of eight or more, but smaller groups can still make use of them to provide extra information. The thorough training they undergo means that they are a wealth of knowledge and their services are highly recommended.

The moat you cross to reach the main gateway provided an inner protected harbour at times of war and was full of water until British colonial times, when eucalyptus trees were introduced to the island from Australia. Eventually, they drew the water from the moat and it is now dry.

Once inside, the scale is surprising, as you pass up a wide, almost ceremonial ramp, built by the Venetians to facilitate rolling the cannon up into place on the walls. An exit left leads off to a small Byzantine chapel (page 75). Above the inner gateway, carved into the stone, is the coat of arms of the Crusader Lusignans, the

Frankish baronial family who ruled Cyprus for 300 years in the Middle Ages and who remodelled much of the original Byzantine fort when they took it over in 1191. This coat of arms, with its combination of crosses and prancing lions, is one of the best-preserved examples on the island (a further example can be seen in Bellapais Abbey). It can be compared to the solitary Venetian winged lion to be found on the later walls and towers of Gazimağusa. Next to it, to the right, is a small room that provides a quick rundown of the history of the castle, including some interesting watercolours depicting how the harbour and town would have looked through the ages. Nearby, a local artist displays his work and there is a new pottery showroom, with pieces copied from Bronze Age originals discovered on the island. The pottery itself is in the village of Dikmen.

Just beyond the inner gateway lies the tomb of Sadık Paşa, the Turkish Ottoman admiral to whom the Venetians surrendered in 1570, and who died later the same year.

The path leads on into a dauntingly large open courtyard with a somewhat neglected garden at one end. Littering the ground are some Byzantine capitals and stones, many the size and shape of over-inflated beachballs, used in colossal catapult-like medieval weapons. Concerts were occasionally held in this courtyard, which is sheltered from the wind. In 1961 Sir John Barbirolli performed here with the Hallé Orchestra. Sadly, musical performances are no longer held here, due to concerns over potential damage to the fabric of the building. There's also a small souvenir shop, a simple and inexpensive café at the northern end of the courtyard, and new toilets on the eastern side.

A whole maze of steps, internal and external, interlink the Byzantine, Crusader and Venetian towers and ramparts of the castle. To the right of the inner entrance, a set of dark steps set into the walls leads down into the **dungeons**, which have rarely been empty in the complex series of plots and intrigues that make up the castle's past. The place was never taken by force throughout its history, though it was subjected to several lengthy sieges. The longest, in the 15th century, lasted nearly four years, and the unfortunate castle occupants were reduced to eating mice and rats. Currently the dungeons house graphic reproductions of those who were imprisoned or tortured, with one life-size model stretched over a wooden torture-wheel with his wedding tackle on full display. The budget for a recent renovation clearly did not extend to any underpants for the poor man. Also deprived of dignity is the bare-breasted model of Joanna l'Allemana, which is at the bottom of one of two deep pits. You can read about her indiscretions, and those of the occupant of the other pit, from the bilingual information boards.

If you enjoy heights and a certain amount of scrambling, it is possible to walk almost a complete circuit of the ramparts, thereby gaining the full panorama. The most photogenic stretches are definitely the **northwestern tower** and the **western wall**, with stunning views down into the harbour. Peeping out from the thickness of the wall by the northwest tower is the little **Byzantine chapel**, still with its four ancient marble columns, thought to have been taken from the old Roman town that now lies buried under modern Girne. When built, in the 12th century, the chapel stood outside the castle walls, but the Venetians gave it an extra entrance in the 16th century and enclosed it within the tower. Hence its curious position today.

Walking along the western wall inland towards the southwest tower, you will get fine views over the rooftops of Girne and the mountain pinnacles beyond. The tower itself is a remarkably advanced example of military design, built, like Gazimağusa's Martinengo Bastion, with three different heights of embrasure to allow three staggered levels of gunfire across the moat. These impressive Venetian fortifications are still in excellent condition, for they were never put to the test. In

1570, at the first confrontation since being completed around 1500, the Venetians at Girne surrendered to the Turks without a single shot being fired. They had heard of the bloody fall of Lefkoşa, and their surrender spared them the devastating siege that Gazimağusa endured. Had they not surrendered, we would doubtless not be looking at such a well-preserved monument today. The rusting gun emplacements along the ramparts are the relics of the castle's modern role in the intercommunal fighting of the last century.

Alongside this western wall are the roofless yet elegant remains of the Gothic-style royal apartments of the castle, where the French Lusignan family resided at times of unrest or during their battles with the Genoese, their maritime rivals.

From the far southeast tower you can look down on to the rocky town beach tucked underneath the castle walls, with its own café terrace. Pre-1974 this swimming spot was known as the Slab, and you had to be a member of the Country Club to use it. Set up in the greenery by itself above the bay, the former Country Club is now officially called the **Halk Evi** or People's House, and is in an area marked for redevelopment. In the area to the west of the Halk Evi, and just south of the Anglican church, is the old Ottoman cemetery. Excavations carried out here a few years ago revealed the elusive Roman town of Corineum, from which reused columns and capitals are visible here and there throughout the modern town.

Back down in the castle courtyard, more bilingual signs point the way to further displays. In the northeast corner stands the **Lusignan Tower**. To the left of its entrance is a room displaying biographies of some of the castle's prisoners during the British tenure, detailing their crimes and fates. In the tower's lower and upper sections are models of some of the various soldiers who have been garrisoned here over the years. To the right of the Lusignan Tower are renovated rooms displaying information and relics from the Neolithic settlement at Vrysi (page 119), the Kirni Bronze Age Tombs and Akdeniz village (pages 103–4). Next stop at ground level along the eastern wall is the entrance to the Shipwreck Museum (see below), before you reach the base of the southeast (Venetian) tower. A long flight of shallow steps leads under the tower to some displays depicting Venetian soldiers loading up cannons and engaging in other warmongering activities.

The Shipwreck Museum

The Shipwreck Museum Built into a couple of the great halls along the eastern wall of the castle is the much-praised Shipwreck Museum, where a 2,300-year-old **Greek trading vessel** is on display, together with its complete cargo. It is the oldest ship yet recovered from the seabed anywhere.

The ship was first discovered in 1965 by a Girne sponge diver some 1.5km off the coast from the castle, at a depth of 30m. Over the course of 1968 and 1969, a team of underwater archaeologists from the University of Pennsylvania Museum raised the vessel systematically from the seabed. It then took a further six years to reconstruct. Its cargo consisted of nearly 400 amphorae, mostly containing wine, from Rhodes and other places, 29 millstones, lead weights and around 10,000 almonds as food for the crew. It was these that enabled the carbon-dating of the ship. The reconstructed vessel is now in a separate temperature-controlled room. The pine timbers had to be soaked in a preservative bath, then dried, and the hull was sheathed in lead. No skeletons were found, so the crew is thought to have swum to safety when the ship sank.

The museum is well laid out with bilingual signage (Turkish and English) and is enhanced by the setting inside the lovely Gothic halls that form the main surviving domestic rooms of the castle. The museum was opened after the division of the island in March 1976, though most of the work was completed pre-1974.

CAROB STORE AND CYPRUS EVI [64 C3] (⏱ *08.00–17.00 daily; TL7/5 adult/student*)
Located right in the centre of the old harbour, next to the Set Fish restaurant, this is a museum of modest proportions but well worth a visit to see the interior of a Venetian-period warehouse. Most of its adjacent 15th-century contemporaries are now restaurants or cafés. The information signs accompanying the exhibits are of good quality and bilingual (Turkish/English). On the ground floor there is a giant olive press and some simply enormous storage jars, most of which came from the village of Fini. So large were the jars that the potter would take the clay by donkey from the Troodos Mountains to the customer premises and make and bake them there. Elsewhere in the museum there is naturally plenty of information about the importance of the carob (see box, page 122), some excellent old photos of the harbour and exhibits on regional pottery, carpentry, weaving, traditional clothing and Lefkara embroidery. There is also a film about life in 1930s Cyprus. A visit should take no more than 45 minutes.

SOUTH FROM GIRNE

Two sites south of Girne town make excellent excursions. Bellapais Abbey is an enchanting place, with its mountain location, Gothic archways and sense of calm. St Hilarion Castle is well worth the climb; it is the best preserved of the three mountain-top Crusader castles of North Cyprus and also the most romantic.

⌂ WHERE TO STAY *Map, pages 90–1*
The fate of two erstwhile fashionable Bellapais boutique hotels, The Abbey and The Residence, was unclear at the time of writing. Both were closed and subject to various rumours, but worth considering if they reopen.

⌂ **Bellapais Gardens** (17 bungalows)
☏ 815 60 66; e info@bellapaisgardens.com;
www.bellapaisgardens.com. Hanging on to the hillside below the abbey, set amidst orange & lemon groves & with views down to the coast. Not cheap, but comprehensive facilities including AC, satellite TV, Wi-Fi, minibar & private balcony or terrace. Spring-fed swimming pool & splendid clifftop lounge. Log fire affords a welcoming glow in the cooler months. Private parking, but the hilly location could cause difficulties for the elderly or infirm & they have no facilities for the under-12s. **$$$$$**

⌂ **Bellapais Monastery Village**
(63 rooms/bungalows) ☏ 815 91 71; e info@bellapaismonasteryvillage.com; www.bellapaismonasteryvillage.com. On the road up to Bellapais. More of a resort than any other hotel in the area, with indoor & 2 outdoor pools, jacuzzi, sauna, steam room, massage, 2 restaurants, bars & entertainment. No children under 12. All rooms have AC, satellite TV, minibar & safe. Wi-Fi in public areas. Courtesy shuttle bus to Girne, but it's still a long walk up to Bellapais village. **$$$$**

⌂ **Bella View** (26 rooms) ☏ 816 11 55;
e info@bellaview.net; www.bellaview.net. On the way up to Bellapais Abbey from Girne. Bills itself as 'The first registered luxury boutique hotel of northern Cyprus'. High-quality rooms with AC, balconies, satellite TV. Relaxed, professional service. Fine dining, à la carte restaurant featuring both Turkish & European cuisine, bar, swimming pool, Wi-Fi in all rooms, mini-golf. No children under 10 years, so worth considering if you're looking for an upmarket, child-free base outside Girne. **$$$$**

⌂ **The Gardens of Irini** (2 cottages) ☏ 815 2820; m 0533 865 82 62; e deirdremairi@yahoo.com; www.gardensofirini.com. Up the hill, close to Lawrence Durrell's former residence, former flamenco dancer & long-time resident Deirdre Guthrie rents out a cottage & converted studio, both AC (extra charge) & suitable for couples, with extra bed available. This bargain bohemian hideaway is well suited to those in search of a tranquil retreat away from the hubbub of Girne. Self-catering basis including b/fast is available for £290 per couple per week, rates for shorter stays

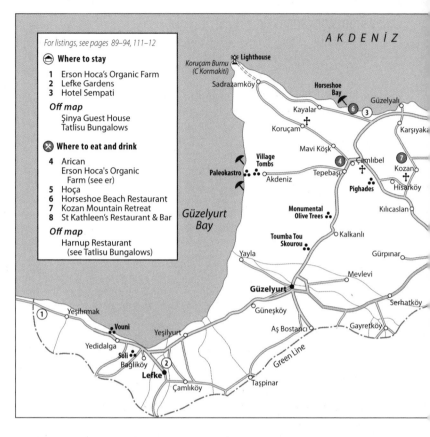

For listings, see pages 89–94, 111–12

Where to stay

1 Erson Hoca's Organic Farm
2 Lefke Gardens
3 Hotel Sempati

Off map
  Şinya Guest House
  Tatlısu Bungalows

Where to eat and drink

4 Arıcan
  Erson Hoca's Organic
    Farm (see er)
5 Hoça
6 Horseshoe Beach Restaurant
7 Kozan Mountain Retreat
8 St Kathleen's Restaurant & Bar

Off map
  Harnup Restaurant
    (see Tatlısu Bungalows)

on request. B&B also available. Non-residents welcome for drinks, snacks, light lunches &, by prior arrangement, 3-course dinners. **$$$**

Altınkaya (69 rooms) 815 50 01/2; e altinkaya@altinkaya-cyprus.com; www. altinkaya-cyprus.com. Set just off the main coast road, on the road to Bellapais, this popular complex has 2 pools & 2 restaurants, one rooftop. Rooms have AC, TV. Free Wi-Fi in public areas. Occasional live music. Courtesy bus to town. **$$**

Ambelia Village (52 rooms) 815 36 55; e management@cyprus-ambelia.com; www. cyprus-ambelia.com. Set in the mountains near Bellapais, 5km from Girne. Features 2- or 4-bed AC studios, & villas that can accommodate up to 6, in a setting of mature shrubbery, with fine views. Free Wi-Fi. Central bar & restaurant using their own organic produce as well as a bar set around a small pool. Hillside location may not suit the elderly or infirm. **$$**

WHERE TO EAT AND DRINK *Map, pages 90–1*

Bellapais village hosts several good, well-established restaurants, plus one newcomer in the shape of a renovated mill.

Bella Moon 815 43 11. Excellent family-run restaurant with peaceful courtyard setting beneath citrus trees. Friendly, attentive service & a hearty selection of *meze* & traditional Cypriot dishes, cooked in an open kitchen next to the dining terrace. *Kleftiko* special on Fri nights (needs

to be pre-ordered Thu). Free taxi service from Girne. *TL30*

Kybele 815 75 31. Here the breathtaking views of the coast are the best thing on the menu. The restaurant is the only one within the abbey grounds, with outdoor tables & indoor space,

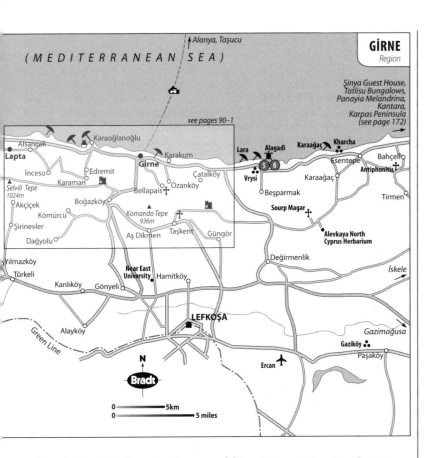

see pages 90–1

too. Particularly beautiful in the evening when atmospheric lighting of the abbey adds to an already unique setting. *TL38*

✗ Old Mill Café & Bar m 0542 873 3230 or 0533 872 1020. Follow the signs from the abbey to find this beautifully renovated, 200-year-old building, which was originally 2 mills. A bit cheaper than the others, the delicious steaks, salads, Cypriot pasta & burgers are eaten amongst the original mill machinery. Children's menu. Own car park. *TL28*

✗ Tree of Idleness (Huzur Ağaç) 815 33 80. Situated in front of the abbey & serving local & international cuisine, plus cheaper fast food. Balcony tables are cool, comfortable & offer relief from summertime heat. Beware of lingering too long under the Tree of Idleness, one of 2 that claim to be Durrell's original shady spot; a restful contentment may just give way to lethargy. Live music & belly-dancing on Sat will wake you up, though. Free taxi service from Girne. *TL35*

WHAT TO SEE AND DO
St Hilarion Castle [91 E2] (🕐 *summer 08.00–18.30 daily, winter 08.00–15.30 daily; TL9/5 adult/student; you need to arrive at least 90mins before the above closing times*) This castle and royal summer palace make an exciting and mildly strenuous half-day trip from Girne. Dieu d'Amour was the name the Frankish knights bestowed upon it, and certainly from afar its extravagantly crenellated walls and towers tumbling over the craggy hilltop evoke a fairytale vision of bygone chivalry. From within, the paths and steps wind up through the three castle sections, one superimposed on the other, culminating in the royal apartments ingeniously

sheltered in their own natural courtyard of rock. Rose Macaulay, author of *The Towers of Trebizond*, described it as 'a picture book castle for elf kings', and Walt Disney is said to have used it as inspiration for the palace in *Snow White and the Seven Dwarfs*. Some controversy exists about which of two Hilarions the castle is named after. Although Hilarion the Great is documented as having been on Cyprus in the 3rd century, some contend that the castle is actually named after a second Hilarion, who only arrived some four centuries later.

The path to the uppermost section of the castle is steep and slippery when wet, and not suitable for anyone with wobbly legs or balance. One Canadian tourist slipped and fell to his death here in recent years. Choose appropriate footwear.

A drive of 15 minutes from Girne brings you to the car park at the foot of St Hilarion; from here the walk up to the summit takes a good 20 minutes. Allow at least 2 hours to explore all the different levels of the castle. There's no restaurant, though simple refreshments (coffee, tea, soft drinks and sweets) are on sale both outside by the entrance and, during the summer, inside the castle at the Great Hall. The energetic could carry a picnic to the 732m-high summit.

On the drive back down the mountain, don't panic if the army patrol stops you next to the monument just near the military base. Far from being suspicious of what you're doing, it's much more likely that they'll simply ask you to wait whilst a tour bus winds its way up the road below.

A word of warning though. Even if you feel sufficiently energised to trek up to the summit, don't be tempted to walk from the main road, as the military are likely to take a dim view of your presence. Stick to the car, or coach, and don't stop under any circumstances.

Touring St Hilarion Castle From Girne you take the main dual carriageway out towards Lefkoşa, and as you leave the town behind, you can already pick out the distinctive shape of the Hilarion peak above you a little to the right. It was Durrell who first used the word 'Gothic' to describe the Kyrenia Mountains, and their sharp pinnacles do lend them a fine Gothic silhouette. The Troodos Mountains on the other hand, rounder and more rolling, are more naturally allied to the domes of Byzantine inspiration.

The much improved road network of the north is now such that a drive of just 10 minutes brings you to the turn-off for St Hilarion, marked by a sign to the right, shortly before the summit of the Lefkoşa pass.

From here, after appearing to double back on itself, the tarmac road winds for 2–3km and you will catch glimpses above of a soldier perched on a lofty crag, gun poised. He reveals himself on closer inspection to be made of metal. On the drive up, your eye may also have been caught by a prominent white building alone on its crag among the thickly forested hills towards Bellapais – not a magnificent private villa, but a military headquarters. The military is never far away in North Cyprus, and it is as well to accustom yourself to the idea and regard it as an interesting extra dimension to the island's sights. Don't be tempted to park in the first car park you come to; this is for the military base opposite. And don't be fooled by the presence of a solitary round tower on your right after you've passed the base. Far from being the ancient castle you've come to visit, this was built a few decades ago as a folly by a rich Cypriot who used it to gamble and entertain ladies. Now, it is under military control. Continue on the winding road. Cresting a hill, the road swoops down and on the left is a large, flat terrace, now the army's rifle range – appropriately enough, for it was here that the knights held jousts and tournaments, watched by the ladies of the court waving coloured favours from the battlements.

The next car park (on the right) is for tour buses, so continue upwards to where the tarmac road terminates in a small car park where you will find the ticket kiosk. To the west you will notice the road, signposted for the Kozan restaurant, continuing along the ridge of the mountains as it heads off to reach Karşıyaka. There is also a footpath from here down to the pretty village of Karmi (Turkish Karaman). The road of 29km to Karşıyaka now has a tarmac surface and crash barriers, which infinitely improves the enjoyment of what used to be a painfully slow and bumpy journey. It is now possible to enjoy the spectacular mountain scenery and ponder the extent of the coastal development, the vastness of the plains to the south, the abundant wildlife and finally the waves sweeping into Güzelyurt Bay without worrying about falling off the road – something that the driver of an abandoned Turkish tank clearly couldn't manage. The tank ran off the road a few years ago near Karşıyaka, irrecoverably, and is now the subject of much local interest and several postcards. If you take a picnic, a morning visit to the castle could be followed by this drive, thereby turning the outing into a day trip. Halfway along the track is a crossroads forking left for Akçiçek and right for Lapta, but you continue straight on for Karşıyaka. When you finally reach the T-junction, with the Kozan restaurant in front of you, a short detour down to the left would take you to the **Kozan** village, at one time the only village in the north with a female *muhtar* (headman). Just before reaching the village, you'll see an abandoned monastery off to your right. It has an unusual 'Star of David' marking on one of its doorframes.

Should you take the detour to Kozan, retrace your route back up the hill to the restaurant, and this time carry straight on down to Karşıyaka. The heavily ruined monastery of Sinai Vasilia overlooks the village.

Back at St Hilarion, the first section of the ascent through the castle now begins up well-laid steps and concrete paths. The **main gate** and **outer walls** were built originally by the Byzantines in the 11th century for extra defence, and these lowest parts were for the men-at-arms and the horses. In the many long sieges of medieval times this area and its cisterns were invaluable. The castle had its exposure to modern warfare too, serving in 1964 as a stronghold for Turkish Cypriots. Such were the castle's defences, even in ruin, that a garrison of boys was able to ward off the Greek attack. The Turkish army still used the castle until relatively recently, before moving out to their camp along the ridge.

Once through the main gate, the *anayol* (main road) takes you up to the left. First you will see two cisterns, one to each side, as well as the former stables, which now house the new 'Introduction Section'. This is a small visual display that briefly explains the castle's history. A few metres further on, as the path turns sharply to the right, is the **corner tower**. After a few minutes' climb you reach the **main gatehouse**, a huge and powerful arched structure that originally closed with a drawbridge.

At the end of the gatehouse passageway, a set of steps leads up to the **Byzantine church**, quite well preserved and with faint traces of **12th-century paintings** on the south (car park) side of the wall. Some restoration work was done here in 1959. It is larger than you would expect for a castle chapel, and this is because it belonged originally to a 10th-century monastery built here by the Byzantines to honour St Hilarion, a hermit who had fled to Cyprus from the Holy Land to escape persecution. He died here in a nearby cave. An old man, 'unclean in person but very holy', he sought out refuge in the mountain, with its ample water supplies. Cypriot peasantry has long believed in evil spirits, *kalikantzaroi* as they call them, which take weird and wonderful forms and have to be appeased at certain times of year by being thrown freshly baked honey doughnuts. The demons who, by popular account, had until then held possession of this mountain-top, watched the hermit's arrival with dismay and conspired to drive him off with hideous noises. His hearing was such, however, that he merely thanked them for welcoming him with music and settled down to his solitary life, leaving the nonplussed demons to look elsewhere for their doughnuts.

The area all around the church was originally the monastery, and the rooms to the north and east of it were the **buttery**, **cellars**, **kitchen**, **belvedere** and **castellan's (commander's) room**. The largest room in this group was the refectory, or main hall, used in Lusignan Crusader times as a banqueting hall. It has now been restored as the modest Café 101, selling tea and coffee, soft drinks and homemade honey. The walls are currently home to an excellent display of wildflower photographs, the work of the café's proprietor Mustafa Gürsel. The echoing walls and huge vaulted ceiling and rafters of the hall preserve an atmosphere of bygone days, with a large fireplace at the far end. Doors lead on to its narrow vertiginous balcony with benches and small tables offering a splendid panorama down over Girne and the coast. On a hot day this as an excellent spot to enjoy an ever-present cool breeze, sink one of Mustafa's cold drinks, take a rest and absorb the view. On clear days, especially in winter, the snow-covered Taurus Mountains of mainland Turkey can be seen, some 100km distant. Ongoing renovation work in the surrounding rooms has included the fitting of new windows and the provision of electricity, allowing the installation of various static tableaux illustrating life in the castle during its heyday. The significance of the café name '101' comes from the alternative name for the castle, '101 Houses'. Some elderly locals still refer to the castle by this name, which refers to the number of houses believed to have been inside the original fortifications. However, Buffavento and Kantara also carry this nickname, which rather undermines its claims to historical accuracy.

Immediately below is another series of rooms, thought to be **barracks** built for the 14th-century Crusader knights, which are curious in that their floors follow the contours of the natural bedrock below. Along from these, to the east, are the **summer royal apartments**, accessible by way of a new wooden staircase.

From the refectory in the central, middle section of the castle, you now continue to the uppermost and in many ways most intriguing part: the **winter royal apartments** and **watchtowers**. The path zigzags steeply up on uneven rock steps. In the heavy rains and floods of 1968 it was washed away completely, and access to the castle summit was impossible. Just as the path begins, notice below you to the right a huge open cistern designed to collect winter rainfall.

At the top of the path, turn right and you now enter the royal area by passing through a **Crusader archway** guarded on its right-hand side by a tower. Somewhat overgrown with trees and bushes, this area was the main courtyard, cleverly sheltered by being wedged between the twin peaks of the summit. These peaks gave the mountain its first name of Didymos (Greek for twin), from which the non-Greek-speaking Crusaders arrived at the corruption 'Dieu d'Amour'.

The tumbledown buildings immediately to your right on entering are the royal **kitchens** and **waiting rooms**. In the centre of the courtyard you may stumble across, but hopefully not into (thankfully it's railed off), a stagnant cistern sunk into the rock, and beyond it, at the farthest end, are the winter royal apartments themselves, closing off the western side of the courtyard.

To reach these you can either follow the path straight on through the undergrowth and climb the steps to the south side, or take the path to the right, passing another – this time empty – cistern before climbing some steps to the first-floor gallery. Whichever route you choose, you emerge on to what is certainly the most evocative spot in the castle, a partly collapsed but elegant gallery, still retaining two Gothic tracery windows, one with charming stone window seats on either side. Popularly known as the **Queen's Window**, it is here that Queen Eleanor, the scheming queen of the Lusignans, is said to have sat. Today the view over to the west is a spectacular one, with the little white picture-book village, still known by its Greek name of Karmi, though more properly Karaman, in the foreground. The village was leased by the Ministry of Tourism to foreigners wishing to restore and live in old-style village houses (pages 109–10). In the northern section of the gallery, there is a further decorative window.

Returning to the front part of the courtyard, the sure-footed can now climb the rugged steps and clamber along the ramparts and ruined tower to the southern peak, the highest point at 732m. You'll know when you've arrived as there's a reassuringly congratulatory sign to this effect. The rickety iron railings have been replaced with a chunkier, more robust handrail that makes the ascent an altogether less daunting prospect than used to be the case. Nevertheless, it's neither for faint hearts nor high heels.

Just outside the courtyard area as you begin the descent, another set of rough steps leads off to your right to ascend the 14th-century **Prince John's Tower**, a powerfully built watchtower on a rocky crag. It was from here that the gullible Prince John of Antioch in 1373 flung his faithful Bulgarian guards to their death, after receiving a fabricated warning about them from Queen Eleanor. All but one were dashed on the rocks below, and it was he who survived to tell the tale.

In the structure of the castle, each of the three defensive sections was self-supporting, with its own cisterns and supply depots. All of the three castles in the Kyrenia range – St Hilarion, Buffavento and Kantara – were originally built to defend against Arab raids. From the 7th to the 10th century, the Arabs launched a succession of raids on Cyprus and all along the coast of Turkey. The worst was that conducted in 806 by the Caliph Harun ar-Rashid of *One Thousand and One Nights* fame, in which the Arabs ravaged much of the island and abducted 16,000 people as prisoners, including the archbishop and many other ecclesiastics. The goals of the raids were booty and prisoners, never to conquer and rule. The Arab armies still had many Bedouin in whom the tradition of 'raiding' (Arabic ghazwa) was deeply rooted as a way of life. With the fighting for the Arab empire largely over, they had to find an alternative outlet for their energies and these raids were sanctioned by their leaders as a convenient method of keeping the armies fit and trained. The continuing raids had a marked effect on the population distribution, causing people to leave the coast and move inland to the hills.

St Hilarion Castle served as a place of refuge and summer residence for the island's kings for some 400 years after this. It was not only to escape the heat of Nicosia that they came here, but sometimes also to flee great plagues. In the summer of 1349 the Black Death swept the island and the royal entourage beat a hasty retreat from Nicosia to the safe and healthy heights of Hilarion. Estimates of the number of people who died range from a quarter to half of the island's population. The castle has, like its sisters Buffavento and Kantara, been a ruin since the 16th century, when the merchants of Venice, whose preoccupations always lay with the sea, methodically dismantled it to deter any troublesome insurrections that might arise in the island's interior and thus distract them from their trading activities.

'Happy is the country that has no history' goes the saying. Cyprus, Gordon Home's 'unhappy shuttlecock', has too much (page 192). (A 2010 survey, reported in *Cyprus Today*, claimed that Turkish Cypriots were among the unhappiest people in Europe: hard to believe for anyone who's experienced their optimism, warmth and genuine hospitality.) Cyprus's geographical location as a stepping stone to the

East from the Western viewpoint, and to the West from the Eastern viewpoint, has condemned it always to be the victim of predatory powers. Throughout its long past, Cyprus raised revolts against its rulers of the day, but they were nearly always quashed. Only on two occasions before 1960 did Cyprus experience independence. The first was in 367BC under the first king of the island, Evagoras, and the second was in 1184 under Isaac Comnenus.

Independence was, however, not necessarily any better for the Cypriots themselves, and it was in fact under the despotic rule of Comnenus that they suffered especially. Yet by a twist of fate, the rashness of this despot led to the Crusaders becoming rulers of the island. Cyprus was ruled at that time from Constantinople, by a Byzantine official sent to the island as local governor. Even so, the island continued to be unceremoniously raided: three times in the 12th century, first by Raymond of Chatillon, then by Egyptian bandits, then by Raymond, Prince of Antioch.

Isaac Comnenus was the nephew of the Byzantine emperor, and after a family dispute he fled to Cyprus and had himself proclaimed, through force and guile, the ruler of the island. He starved and robbed the wealthy, murdered, and ravished young virgins at whim. His tyrannical seven-year rule was thus chronicled:

> The island groaned beneath this scourge of fate, and he reduced the Cypriots to such a state of despair that all were ready to welcome anything which afforded a means of escape from such tyranny.

His violence and temper met their match, however, in the person of Richard the Lionheart. Richard was on his way to the Holy Land in the Third Crusade in 1191 when some of his ships were wrecked off the Cypriot coast. Isaac Comnenus rushed to the scene and seized the booty. In the process, however, he unwisely insulted two of the passengers: Berengaria, Richard's betrothed, and Joanna, his favourite sister. Enraged at Isaac's effrontery, Richard, who had had no intention of conquering Cyprus, pursued Comnenus and unceremoniously defeated him. Isaac's daughter was locked up in St Hilarion. Richard despatched his knights to take the rest of the island and in turn helped himself to large quantities of booty, as was customary. He stayed on the island long enough to marry the dark-eyed Berengaria, daughter of the King of Navarre, and one tradition recounts that Isaac, gift-wrapped in gilt chains, was brought to the queen as a wedding present.

Though generally presented as a hero, Richard was in fact not much different from Cyprus's previous rulers. The Archbishop of Sinai, chronicling events in 1766, described him as a 'bloodthirsty beast', lamenting that the poor Cypriots 'had escaped the wolf to fall into the jaws of the bear'. On leaving the island, Richard sold it to the Knights Templar for 100,000 byzants (the medieval gold currency of Europe), to raise money for his army and the crusade. The knights, however, found it more of a handful than they bargained for, and after only a year they begged Richard to buy it back.

The English king had already received nearly half the sale price and did not wish to lose his money. Instead, he persuaded Guy de Lusignan, a Frankish nobleman who had been King of Jerusalem before it was lost to Saladin, to take it on in compensation for the loss of the Kingdom of Jerusalem. De Lusignan accepted, and his family retained the kingship of the island for the next three centuries, until 1489. De Lusignan's reign was always feudal in style, and did not represent an improvement for the Cypriots. They were serfs with no rights or privileges, working the land and heavily taxed to pay for the extravagances of the nobles. Some were even bartered by their masters in exchange for dogs or horses.

Also subjugated at this time was the Greek Orthodox Church of Cyprus, scorned by the French-speaking Latin Catholic rulers. Its treasures were robbed and its bishops burnt as heretics when they refused to bow to Catholic dominance and recognise the Pope in Rome as head of all Christendom. The appointment of an Orthodox archbishop was banned, and it was in these centuries that the Greek Orthodox monasteries, hidden away in the mountain ranges, were established. Cyprus had long been a refuge for Christianity during difficult times in the Holy Land, and when the last Christian stronghold of Acre fell in 1191, Cyprus took on the role of Latin Christianity's easternmost outpost, becoming the trading centre of the eastern Mediterranean and bringing its rulers much wealth and prosperity. The relics of this prosperity are left to us today in the cathedrals of Lefkoşa and Gazimağusa, the castles of St Hilarion, Buffavento and Kantara, and the unrivalled Bellapais Abbey.

Bellapais Abbey [91 F3] (☉ summer 08.00–19.00 daily, winter 08.00–15.30 daily, arrive 30mins before closing time; TL9/5 adult/student; entry is by ticket at the kiosk. Excellent, free guides are available to show you around, speaking Turkish, English, German & Greek & they don't even expect a tip)

The beauty of Bellapais is legendary; when Lawrence Durrell bought a house here, he felt 'guilty of an act of fearful temerity in trying to settle in so fantastic a place'. Set in the foothills of the Kyrenia Mountains just 10 minutes southeast of Girne, the mainly 13th-century Crusader abbey is a must-see during any stay in North Cyprus. A well-timed, early morning visit to avoid the crowds will allow you to fully soak up the tranquillity and enjoy the panoramas over Girne.

Those who knew Bellapais before the 1950s speak disparagingly of the encroaching commercialisation of the abbey. There are indeed several cafés and souvenir shops beside the abbey, and even a restaurant inside it, but they can all be counted on the fingers of one hand, and the narrow streets of the village will scarcely permit more than this. Parking can sometimes be a little tricky, particularly if your visit coincides with a classic-car rally, though there is a large and free open parking area just beyond the abbey. Beware of sitting under the famous **Tree of Idleness**, an ancient mulberry by the abbey entrance, one of two trees claiming the title, lest you are struck down with the indolence for which the villagers are famed. Bellapais, Durrell was told, was synonymous with laziness and the villagers lived for so long that even the gravedigger was out of a job.

At least 2 hours should be allowed for the visit, starting from Girne, and the most special time is sunset, when the place is alive with the glowing silhouettes of arches. 'The dawns and the sunsets in Cyprus,' wrote Durrell, 'are unforgettable – better even than those of Rhodes which I always believed were unique in their slow Tiberian magnificence.' Durrell himself would frequently see the dawn, for when he ran out of money for renovating his house, he took a job teaching English in a Lefkoşa school, which meant he had to get up at 04.30.

Any time from mid-morning to late afternoon should be avoided if at all possible, as the abbey is swamped with tour parties and the seductive atmosphere of calm is lost amidst a frenzy of clicking camera shutters. If, however, you have no other means of transport, such a tour may be your only means of reaching the village (though a taxi is always an option). It should be noted that most tour buses eject passengers near the army camp, leaving a long uphill trek of about ten to 15 minutes to reach the abbey itself.

If you are especially fortunate, your visit may coincide with one of the concerts occasionally held in the abbey refectory: a more picturesque musical backdrop is hard to imagine. Later, after a stroll, you could stay on for dinner at one of the nearby restaurants and soak up the abbey, illuminated in its own surrealistic halo.

Sipping wine on the terrace, you may wonder if you are hallucinating as a tractor trundles by towing a grand piano.

The annual **Bellapais Music Festival** (*www.bellapaisfestival.com*) is held in May and June. In 2014 it attracted classical performers from as far afield as Argentina, Russia and Israel. Apart from the festival, there are ad hoc musical performances at other times of the year, including opera and displays by whirling dervishes. Reasonably priced tickets are generally available from various outlets in the village and in Girne: see the website for more information. Tickets can also be bought on the door, if the performance is not sold out. If you can get into a recital, the atmosphere and location are likely to rival anything you have experienced elsewhere.

Touring Bellapais Abbey
'Bellapais' is actually a corruption of '*Abbaye de la Paix*', or Abbey of Peace. Although its precise origins are obscured in the mists of history, the abbey was probably founded at the very beginning of the 13th century, but Bellapais was a significant site of habitation even in Roman times. Major additions were made to the structure in the 14th century. When making the 5km drive from Girne through olive and carob groves and ever-increasing development, few are prepared for the vista that hits them as they round the last corner before Bellapais village. There, rising up from the mountain on its natural terrace, like a mirage, is the Gothic masterpiece of the island, and indeed of all the Levant. Rarely has a place so lived up to its name, for this remarkable abbey is imbued with a sense of tranquillity and peace so powerful it is almost tangible. The road winds through the narrow streets of Bellapais village to reach the tiny square in front of the abbey. From here the path leads in from the ticket kiosk past the main entrance of the church (page 87) to the abbey enclosure through a pretty and colourful garden, and on to what was once the abbey kitchen and is now a restaurant and café, tastefully tucked into the side and with excellent views of the abbey and down over the coastline. In the abbey courtyard, the fine-pencilled cypress trees, 'emblems of grief and eternity' as eminent travel writer Colin Thubron called them, were planted only in 1940, but they are now home to hundreds of sparrows whose incessant chirping is sometimes the only sound to greet you as you enter.

Thoughtfully placed at the refectory door, by the lovely tracery windows of the cloister, lies a fine, white **marble sarcophagus** of the 2nd century AD, carved with dainty figures and foliage. Here, by the refectory door, the fastidious monks would wash their hands before meals. The first monks here were Augustinians, displaced from their custody of the Holy Sepulchre Church in Jerusalem by the arrival of Saladin in 1187. Fleeing with them were some canons of the Order of St Norbert, whose white habits lent Bellapais its other name of the White Abbey. Initially, the strictness of the abbey was exemplary, and converts were drawn from far afield.

Gradually, however, worldly values began to infiltrate. The mellow beauty of the abbey was not the natural bedfellow of asceticism, as Thubron wryly observed on his first visit: 'The spirit here feels more like a ripe fruit than a soldier of God.' Stories of the monks' misdeeds gathered momentum: as they took not just one, but two and three wives, and would accept only their own sons as novices. By the time the Genoese arrived in 1373, the abbey was ripe for pillaging, and much of its treasure was abducted. The Ottoman invasion of the 16th century destroyed more of the abbey, but the Turks allowed the Greeks to use the church after the monks were driven out. The abbey church, in fact, continued to be used as the village church until 1974.

Prior to the Ottoman takeover, the village of Bellapais had scarcely existed, but its numbers were swelled by the sudden influx of Greeks fleeing Kyrenia. The daughters of the monks also played their role in the growing population.

Though the church was still used, the abbey itself was a ruin from the 16th century onwards, for what the Turks did not destroy, the arriving Greeks plundered as a most convenient quarry for building their new houses. Early travellers observed cows grazing in the cloisters. The British army contributed by using the place as a military hospital after 1878, cementing over the refectory floor and at one time setting up a shooting range, evidenced by the bullet holes in the eastern wall.

This **refectory**, with its lovely fan-vaulted ceiling and perfect proportions, must have been one of the finest dining halls in the East. Carved into the thickness of the wall is a pulpit from which the monks were addressed throughout meals. High on the end wall, a rose window casts an attractive patterned light. On the marble lintel above the entrance are three well-carved sets of coats of arms – the prancing lion of the Lusignans on the right, Jerusalem in the centre, and the royal quarterings of Cyprus on the left. The abbey **church**, which runs the length of the cloister on the opposite side to the refectory, is still used now for occasional services and has been opened to the public again, revealing the lovely iconostasis (wooden partition separating the nave from the altar area) and wooden carving on the pulpits. Pre-1974 accounts describe it as remarkably unchanged from its original 13th-century structure, apart from the iconostasis which was added by the Greek Orthodox Church in the 16th century.

There are three stairways up to the **abbey roof**: one is near the church entrance on the garden side, and the other two are long, straight vaulted staircases running up on the church side of the cloister. One of these latter was the nightstair, used by the monks to come down from their dormitories at midnight for prayers. Today the roof forms an excellent viewing and vantage point from which to look down on the cloister with its melancholy cypresses and colourful garden, and across to the sea beyond.

From the car park (TL3, though the kiosk is sometimes unmanned) behind the abbey to the east, you have the best view of the heavily ruined **undercroft** with its simple vaulting and damaged rose window to the north. Beside it in the southeast corner, is the **chapter house**, used like an administration office for the abbey. This merits closer inspection because of its eccentric Gothic stone carving, featuring wriggling sirens, monsters embracing or fighting, and a monkey and cat in the foliage of a pear tree.

The **village of Bellapais** still claims a fair number of foreigners among its residents, especially in the newer villas that have grown up on the outskirts. Its closeness to Girne and natural beauty and tranquillity make it an obvious choice, and its image and popularity were certainly enhanced by Lawrence Durrell's purchase of a house there in 1953, and his subsequent book about the island and its troubles, *Bitter Lemons*, published in 1957. **Durrell's house** still stands at the top of the steep road that runs up from the Tree of Idleness, opposite the 1953 water trough, and has been lovingly restored and superbly maintained by the current owner. Inside, there are some decorative furniture pieces and a garishly coloured bathroom suite. Occasionally, there are talks about Durrell by members of the owner's family when they are visiting from the UK, which is usually in September/October. Details can be obtained by email enquiry (e *shorrockmatthew@yahoo.co.uk*) or from information pinned to the door of the house. The sprawling village of Ozanköy beneath Bellapais has become fashionable for foreigners purchasing and converting traditional homes, turning it into a thriving expat community. This influx has now spawned the much-needed **Ozanköy Bookshop** (📞 *815 28 53;* e *ozankoybookshop@gmail.com;* ☺ *closed Sun*), run by British expats and selling a good range of fiction and nonfiction, including local history, cuisine and walking guides. It also operates a book exchange and, given the dearth of English-language options in the region, is well worth a visit if your holiday reading supplies dry up. It serves drinks, snacks and British-style meals with daily specials and offers free Wi-Fi. They also organise talks and other activities. Visitors are welcome.

Those with accommodation in Bellapais may be interested to know that it has its own car-hire agency: **Driver Rent A Car** (815 88 54; m 0533 840 50 00; e info@driverrentals.com; www.driverrentacar.com) together with a couple of small bars, traditional barber shops and the Tatlisulu grocery shop. A gentle stroll through the backstreets will reveal these and other places of interest. The **Gardens of Irini** (page 77) is a peaceful place for a drink, away from the high-season hordes of visitors.

Doğanköy Even closer to Girne, and really an eastern suburb of it nowadays, is the village of Doğanköy. With the help of the *muhtar* and some assistance from Girne's municipality, the local community have pulled together and raised the funds to restore a small church, originally Byzantine but latterly used as a Greek church. Beautifully whitewashed and with tended gardens, the building is now a venue for talks, arts exhibitions and wedding blessings. It is unremarkable inside – the icons were removed pre-1974 – but its greatest value is perhaps in demonstrating what can be achieved when there is a display of initiative, willing and a well-targeted use of funds. It is clearly signposted from the village and if anyone wants to see inside, the caretaker Paula Shirley is willing to unlock it (m 0533 830 32 56).

Heading west from Girne, initial impressions are not encouraging: hordes of estate agents line the main road, together with endless shops selling would-be contents for your newly acquired residence. But a day or two spent trundling off to the west of Girne eventually offers the chance to see a different kind of Cypriot scenery, notably the highly fertile plain of Güzelyurt with its citrus and banana plantations. The area also produces strawberries and watermelons. There are many good swimming beaches and a wide variety of historical sites to see, ranging from the sultry hilltop Persian palace of Vouni to the Bronze Age sanctuary at Pighades and the Roman fish tanks at Lambousa, near Lapta. None of the antiquities are in themselves spectacular, but they are all from different periods and offer an interesting diversity.

Distances are mercifully short in North Cyprus, and driving at a gentle pace it takes no more than an hour to reach Güzelyurt, and a further 45 minutes to arrive at the Persian palace of Vouni. This rocky summit is the westernmost place to visit, and the best policy on a day's outing from Girne is to drive first to this, then to work your way back eastwards. That way, if you run out of daylight and still have some places to visit, they will at least be closer to home for subsequent visits. In the summer months it is perfectly realistic to make leisurely morning visits to Vouni and Soli, then to take lunch at one of the beach restaurants near Soli (at Yedidalga). After lunch there will still be time to see Lefke, Güzelyurt, Pighades and probably Lapta on the way home. In winter, with shorter daylight hours, the afternoon itinerary may have to be curtailed, as it is too dark after 17.00 to do any sightseeing.

WHERE TO STAY *Map, pages 90–1, unless otherwise stated*

If you're not basing yourself in Girne, you can rely on public transport to some extent to get into town, though services become less frequent the further west you go. For maximum convenience and minimum fuss, a rental car is strongly recommended. Between Girne and Lapta there are plenty of good restaurants and in the height of the season the area does have a certain buzz, though it can't match Girne itself. For those who want to head to Lefke and the far west, there are a couple of interesting accommodation options.

Karaoğlanoğlu, Edremit, Karaman (Karmi), Zeytinlik & around

Merit Park Hotel (285 rooms) 650 25 00; e info@merithotels.com; www.merithotels.com. Perhaps less glitzy than some of its upmarket competitors, this all-inclusive still offers the inevitable casino together with multiple swimming pools, plush spa, AC rooms, free Wi-Fi & all the facilities you might expect. Located a few kilometres west of Girne, in Karaoğlanoğlu, the construction seeks to echo Girne's Crusader castle in style & proportion. Claims an international clientele, but off-season visitors are mainly Turkish. **$$$$$**

The Hideaway Club (32 rooms & suites) m 0542 855 07 71; e info@hideawayclub.com; www.hideawayclub.com. At the entrance to Edremit, 5km west of Girne, this is a truly lovely, refurbished, smart yet informal place with a divine 22m freshwater pool & very comfortable, wonderfully appointed choice of rooms & suites, each with fridge/minibar, phone, TV, AC & a balcony or terrace. Free Wi-Fi in public areas. Great views to sea & mountains. Recommended. **$$$$**

Kemerli Konak Boutique Hotel (18 rooms) 815 63 36; e info@kemerlikonak.com; www.kemerlikonak.com. In Zeytinlik village, just southwest of Girne, this is a new, smart & tastefully furnished hotel with handmade furniture. Swimming pool with children's section. Rooms all have balcony with mountain or sea view, TV, minibar, AC. Adjacent Archway restaurant is top-notch, though not cheap. **$$$$**

Pine Bay Club (20 villas & apts) 822 30 32; e info@pinebay.com; www.pinebay.com. Located on the main coast road, on the west side of

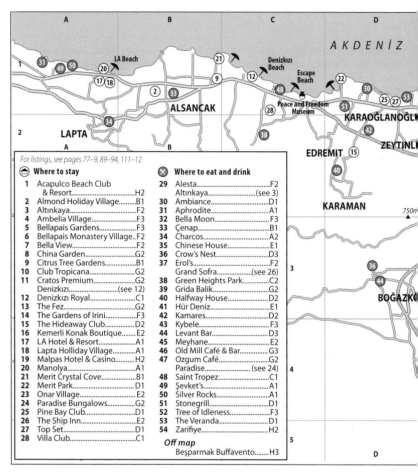

Karaoğlanoğlu. Refurbished & expanded in 2012. Accommodation is equipped with satellite TV, phone, kettle, AC & mini-fridge. The club also has 2 pools, an à la carte restaurant, free Wi-Fi access & an adjoining sports bar. **$$$**

🏠 **Top Set** (72 rooms) 📞822 22 04; e info@topsethotel.com; www.topsethotel.com. A little west of Girne, on the sea side of the road near the centre of Karaoğlanoğlu, with a variety of rooms, many overlooking the modest beach. Restaurant, pool & children's pool. All accommodation is centrally heated & has AC, shower & WC, minibar, balcony or terrace, phone & satellite TV. Free Wi-Fi in some public areas. **$$$**

🏠 **The Ship Inn** (79 rooms) 📞815 67 01; e info@theshipinn.com; www.theshipinn.com. Tudor-style hotel with rooms & a few 2-bedroom self-catering villas, all with AC, heating, kettle, satellite TV & patio or balcony. Popular with loyal British clientele, well served by public transport. Friendly staff. Large outdoor pool, indoor pool & children's pool, tennis court & beer garden. Free Wi-Fi in lobby. 1.5km west of Girne centre. Good restaurant, with weekly entertainment. See ad, 2nd colour section. **$$**

Alsancak & around

🏠 **Merit Crystal Cove** (277 rooms) 📞650 02 00; e info@merithotels.com; www.merithotels.com. East of Alsancak, North Cyprus's first all-inclusive hotel, but not the last. High-spec rooms, plus every possible amenity, including pool, beach, fitness centre, spa & wellness centre, sports facilities, many restaurants & bars. Free Wi-Fi. Shuttle bus all day to Girne. There are 2 further Merit all-inclusives nearby (page 89), including one 'adult-only' option. **$$$$$**

🏠 **Denizkızı Royal & Denizkızı Hotel**
(55 & 57 rooms) ☎ 821 26 76; e info@denizkizi.
com; www.denizkizi.com. A 4-star hotel with
3-star neighbour 13km west of Girne, overlooking
a picturesque beach. One or other of the hotels
closes in winter, depending on refurbishment
requirements. The Royal has some suites with
jacuzzis; both offer swimming pools, fitness centre
& watersports facilities, including the Nautilus
dive school, & beach bar. Wi-Fi access in public
areas costs TL20 per week. HB basis only.
$$$$** & **$$$

🏠 **Almond Holiday Village** (33 villas,
rooms, cottages) ☎ 821 28 85; e info@almond-
holidays.com; www.almond-holidays.com. Very
friendly, Turkish-Cypriot place to the east of Lapta,
with a variety of smart & recently renovated
accommodation units) built round a pool (with

children's area), all set back 200m from the main
road to avoid traffic noise. Some rooms not
suitable for those with limited mobility. Facilities
include AC, satellite TV, fridge. Free Wi-Fi in public
areas & most accommodation units. HB & FB
available. Recommended. **$$$**

🏠 **Villa Club** (31 apts & villas) ☎ 821 84 00;
e info@villa-club.com; www.villa-club.com.
Away from the noise of the main road between
Karaoğlanoğlu and Alsancak, set amongst orange
& lemon groves, this is a quiet idyll surrounded by
fountains providing the welcome, cooling sound
of running water during the hot summer months.
Swimming pool. Rooms are equipped with bath or
shower, phone, minibar & AC, terrace or balcony. Free
Wi-Fi in public areas, satellite TV in villas. The self-
catering villas for 2–6 people are available from TL460
for 2 nights (min booking), apts are cheaper. **$$$**

🏠 **Citrus Tree Gardens** (29 bungalows & apts) ☎821 28 72; e citrus@kktc.net; www.citrustreegardens.com. Small, family-run complex, around 10km from Girne. With a pool, AC & restaurant. **$$**

Lapta & beyond

🏠 **Lapta Holiday Club** (formerly Club Lapethos) (208 rooms) ☎821 36 56; e info@laptaholidayclub.com; www.laptaholidayclub.com. On the main coastal road in Lapta. Recently renovated and due to open in mid 2015, this is now all-inclusive. Still needs investment, but the aquapark, with various slides, is a draw for those with children & the new rooms are of a high standard. **$$$$**

🏠 **Hotel Sempati** [map, page 78] (35 rooms) ☎821 27 70; e info@hotelsempati.com; www.hotelsempati.com. Located on the main road, 13km from Girne, this friendly 3-star hotel has a large swimming pool, restaurant & café-bar, just 150m from the beach. All rooms are en suite & have satellite TV, AC, phone & minibar. Free Wi-Fi in lobby. **$$$**

🏠 **LA Hotel & Resort** (91 rooms) ☎821 89 81; e info@la-hotel-cyprus.com; www.la-hotel-cyprus.com. On the main coastal road in Lapta, rooms are equipped with TV, AC, shower, minibar & phone. Free Wi-Fi in public areas. Has its own narrow, sandy beach, with beach bar. **$$$**

🏠 **Manolya Hotel** (61 rooms) ☎821 84 98; e info@manolyahotel.com. Turkish-Cypriot owned

& run, on the coast road in eastern Lapta. Rooms have free Wi-Fi, satellite TV & AC. Family rooms available, but not really child-orientated. Varied restaurant menu. Swimming pool & small beach. Twice-weekly live entertainment in season. **$$**

Lefke & the west

🏠 **Erson Hoca's Organic Farm** [map, page 78] (5 rooms) m 0533 861 53 04 or 0533 868 29 89; e reservation@cyprusorganicfarm.com; www.cyprusorganicfarm.com. As west as you can get, Cyprus's only organic farm & a perfect haven of peace. About 16ha of tranquillity, set around an imposing & beautiful new building. Welcoming hosts, tasteful rooms. Rooms have no TV, no Wi-Fi & no AC. No swimming pool, either, but the sea is a mere 2km down the hill. Walking trails, & you can pick your own fruit & veg. Recommended. **$$**

🏠 **Lefke Gardens** [map, page 78] (21 rooms) ☎728 82 23; e lefkegardenshotel@gmail.com; www.lefkegardenshotel.org. A place of character, tucked away below the main road in Lefke, from which it's signposted. The main building is an Ottoman house dating from 1923, restored & tastefully decorated by the current owners, the Taskin family. The rooms at the back of the courtyard behind the swimming pool are new, but still very homely. All accommodation is en suite & comes with satellite TV, minibar, free Wi-Fi & AC. Could do with a lick of paint, but still a bargain. **$$**

🍴 **WHERE TO EAT AND DRINK** *Map, pages 90–1, unless otherwise stated*
The 15km of coastline west from Girne is the most developed stretch in the north, with restaurants and hotels in abundance. There's Chinese, French and Indian, and some 'characterful' establishments as well. One restaurateur claims to have counted over 400 catering establishments in a 24km radius of Girne! East of Lapta, you're spoilt for choice; west of Lapta eating places are fewer and farther between. There is, however, a pleasant cluster of beach restaurants near Yedidalga, before Vouni, offering a simple fare of *meze*, kebabs and fish, with willing service. The following are just a select few.

Karaoğlanoğlu, Edremit, Karaman (Karmi) & around

🍴 **Ambiance** Karaoğlanoğlu; ☎822 28 49; www.ambiancecyprus.com. Seafront establishment, much-revered international cuisine. Pleasant terrace, pool & beach. Children's & vegetarian options. Call to book. *TL40*

🍴 **Chinese House** ☎815 21 30. Popular with the expatriate community, this lovely Chinese & sushi restaurant is situated opposite The Ship Inn. *TL30*

🍴 **Crow's Nest** m 0533 885 76 35; 🕐 closed Wed. Located at the heart of Karaman (Karmi) in more ways than one, this friendly expat pub is a fine establishment, serving pub grub including Sun roasts & Fri evening fish & chips. Booking for both events essential. Large-screen TV, dartboard, open fire in winter. *TL25*

🍴 **Grand Sofra (The Ship Inn)** ☎815 67 01. The restaurant forms part of this family-run, traditional, English-style hotel between

Karaoğlanoğlu & Girne, serving an excellent selection of international & local cuisine, cocktails & beers. Live entertainment weekly, with a set menu package. Booking is advisable. *TL35*

✕ **Halfway House** ✆822 33 14. A lovely little stop if you're walking to or from Karaman (Karmi), the Halfway House is another *meze* place where the beer's always cold & the welcome friendly. There's no menu, as they use seasonal ingredients, but the deal includes 14 starter courses! 'No booking, no cooking' is the motto, so you must call ahead. *TL40*

✕ **Hür Deniz** m 0533 868 88 38. Located just west of the Ship Inn, a fish restaurant that's nearly always busy, so booking essential. Open 7 days, with a huge selection of dishes. The day's fresh catch is displayed in a fridge, priced by the kilo & served with *meze*; the other menu items are mainly frozen, but still good quality. Some question the service, however. *TL36*

✕ **Kamares** Located between the coast road & the ring road on the road that connects Karaoğlanoğlu & Karaman; m 0533 857 58 57 or 0542 861 26 17; ⏰ lunch & dinnertime, closed Mon. If you're homesick for a curry, this new place is the classy option. Wide choice of favourites & specials, plus children's & vegetarian choices, well-priced wine list. *TL30*

✕ **Levant Bar & Restaurant** ✆822 25 59 or 0533 821 56 64; ⏰ closed Mon. Karaman's swish restaurant does a short lunch menu, English cuisine in the evenings & 3-course lunch on Sun. Outdoor terrace in the summer, open fire in winter. Reservation advisable, & a necessity for Sun lunchtime roasts. *TL30*

✕ **Meyhane** m 0542 874 56 78. Heading west, take the Zeytinlik turn-off, 1km after The Ship Inn & follow the signs. Evenings only, except Sun when there's a *kleftiko* lunch. Standard meat dishes in a pleasant setting, but if you're hungry, you could take on the challenge of the full meze. *TL28*

✕ **Stonegrill Restaurant** ✆822 20 02. On the left of the main road as you head west, a somewhat sterile interior, but it compensates with seafood & great steaks, which you cook yourself on a hot stone at the table. Slightly more expensive than some places & it seems to cater mostly for tourists, but a sociable way to eat nonetheless. The generous *meze* is almost a meal in itself so make sure you go with an appetite. *TL35*

✕ **The Veranda** ✆822 20 53. Seafront restaurant & beach bar in Karaoğlanoğlu serving steaks & local cuisine from a beautiful location. Advisable to book at weekends. *TL35*

Alsancak & around

✕ **Altınkaya** ✆821 83 41; m 0542 886 98 86. Overlooking the sea near Invasion Beach, 8km west of Girne, this is reckoned to be the best & longest-established speciality fish restaurant on the island. It is very popular with the local people & offers a set *meze* with your own choice of fish. Prices vary considerably, depending on your selection. *TL40*

✕ **Çenap** ✆821 84 17; ⏰ evenings only. Up the hill in the heart of Alsancak village, a simple local place full of character that only serves a full Cypriot menu & *meze* too. Booking advisable. *TL28*

✕ **Green Heights Park** m 0533 851 75 57. Follow the signs off the main road for Botanical Garden & you'll end up here. As well as a good restaurant, you can use the pool (TL10 extra) & jacuzzi, play darts, table tennis, badminton or chess & admire the plants & birds in the compact garden. Has interesting old photos of Girne, too. A day out in itself. *TL30*

✕ **Saint Tropez** ✆821 83 24; www.saint-tropez-cyprus.com. Some say it's the best restaurant on the island, but it's not cheap. It's certainly easy to find, thanks to its 8m mockup of the Eiffel Tower in the front yard. Serves up a wide selection of classic French & other continental dishes, many with very rich sauces. Charming owner Hussein offers unbeatable customer service. *TL45*

Lapta & beyond

✕ **Aphrodite** m 0533 860 69 70 or 0533 853 87 92. Near to the Hotel Sempati, signposted on the sea-side of the main road. When you reach the collection of automotive wrecks, then you've arrived. Çemal, the owner, can reasonably be described as a local legend. Always dressed in combat fatigues, he may ride his horse into the dining room while you're enjoying your meal. Expect the unexpected, but his *meze* is as good as any, nearly all his food is homegrown & he makes his own passable wine. *TL30*

✕ **Arican** [map, page 78] m 0533 848 77 22 or 0533 880 88 18; ⏰ evenings only Mon–Sat. Set in the former cinema in the centre of Çamlıbel, this is an unpretentious but popular restaurant with excellent food. Don't be deterred by the rustic surroundings or basic décor: the food is excellent. Mixed kebab is recommended. *TL25*

✕ Charcos m 0533 876 30 07. Difficult to find, but worth the effort, this serves standard kebabs & fish dishes, plus (if pre-booked) *kleftiko* & vegetarian meals. The house is a beautifully restored centuries-old dwelling – ask to see the photos. Hostess Cristina has done all the murals herself. Mainly British clientele. Good value, given all the extras that are included. To find it, ask in Lapta village for directions: it's near the police (*polis*) station. *TL26*

✕ Erson Hoca's Organic Farm [map, page 78] m 0533 861 53 04 or 0533 868 29 89; e reservation@cyprusorganicfarm.com; www.cyprusorganicfarm.com; ⏰ closed Tue. Just west of Yeşilırmak, a great setting for a lazy lunch. All fruit & veg is organic & sourced on the farm. Delightful hosts, wonderful food, a place to sample fine Cypriot cuisine in utter tranquillity. Weekends are busiest, but booking advised at all times – it's a long way to end up being turned away. *TL30*

✕ Horseshoe Beach Restaurant [map, page 78] m 0533 861 66 64. On the road west towards Kayalar, a great stop for a swim & lunch. Apo is a genial host, cooking up fish & lamb on his grill. Or you can rent a BBQ & picnic table for TL25. The museum-like interior is worth a browse. *TL30*

✕ Kozan Mountain Retreat [map, page 78] m 0533 845 70 70; www.kozanexperience. weebly.com; ⏰ summer Tue–Sun, winter (Nov–Apr) Sat & Sun only. Follow the Kozan signposts from Karşıyaka for 4km to the mountain top. Great views & mountain air. Goat *kleftiko* on Sun. Sources produce from the local village. Bring your own food & they'll rent you a table & BBQ set in their lovely picnic area (TL20). Organic produce & crafts for sale. Horseriding available by appointment. Yoga classes, walking trails & mountain biking as well. *TL30*

✕ Şevket's 821 80 77; ⏰ daily. West of Silver Rocks, this modest but well-established place specialises in homely Turkish Cypriot cuisine. The rustic *meze* features sublime fried cheese. Also fresh fish, vegetarian & cocktails. If they're quiet, chew the fat with charming Şevket himself, & learn a bit about pre-partition Cyprus. Swimming pool for use of guests, so do a few lengths before you tuck in. *TL25*

✕ Silver Rocks 821 89 22; ⏰ daily; closed end Dec–Mar. Situated in a lovely spot almost on the beach just to the west of Lapta, this is a popular place, run by Ibrahim Seyhun, serving a wide variety of Turkish & European dishes. Customers get free use of pool & beach. *TL28*

BEACHES

Denizkızı (*Entry TL10, allows use of beach & swimming pool*) 'Belonging' to the hotel of the same name, but open, like all the hotel beaches, to fee-paying non-residents (page 48). Some 9km from Girne, a sandy bay with safe, sheltered swimming. There are bamboo umbrellas, showers and changing cabins, as well as a beach café and children's play area. A variety of watersports, including diving, is offered by **Nautilus Dive Centre** (page 51).

Escape Beach Club (*Entry TL20, includes parking & use of a sun umbrella, sunbed & cushion*) 5km west of Girne. You can drive the car right down to the beach from the main road, by following the sign for Yavaz Cikartma, next to the Altınkaya Restaurant. The reasonably priced Escape Beach Club Restaurant is at the end of the long sandy bay. The water is shallow and safe for children desperate to use air-mattresses and dinghies – there is an island, known as Golden Rock, protecting the entrance to the bay. It is so close that you can wade across to it. If you just want to swim and then sit on the sand, you should be able to avoid the entrance fee – in theory. Watersports are available.

Horseshoe Bay (*Entry free*) 20km west of Girne and 2km before Kayalar. No sunbeds, and the shingle beach is often swamped in eelgrass, but this otherwise perfect bay is ideal for a pre-lunch snorkel. The restaurant is a good one, too (see above), or you can rent a barbecue and picnic table for TL20.

You might think that, even in a divided land, something as basic as water supply would prove to be a 'neutral' or even unifying topic. Not so.

Since the 1960s, the idea of bringing water by pipe from the Turkish mainland to alleviate the drought-prone island has been mooted. Back then, many poured scorn on what was seen as simply another fanciful project, but all that has changed with the arrival of a water pipeline from mainland Turkey in 2014. To accommodate the new supply, a huge new dam has been built above Gecitköy, with water to be piped up and stored in the reservoir before being distributed around the island.

At an estimated cost of nearly 1.5 billion TL, and with a 60-mile-long section running under the ocean, the pipeline is hailed as a marvel of engineering and welcomed – at least by those north of the Green Line. In the Greek-Cypriot south, the suggestion that some of the water could be offered to them is met with more than a degree of suspicion. Although the whole of Cyprus suffers from water shortages, many Greek Cypriots believe that the pipeline simply reinforces Turkish influence, increases the North's dependence on Turkey and gives the Turkish Cypriots more power to their 'bargaining elbow' in the seemingly endless round of reunification talks. Others believe that any offer to supply water across the Green Line would be accompanied by an attempt by the Turks and Turkish Cypriots to muscle in on the lucrative natural gas reserves recently discovered off the southern coast.

So while residents and farmers are already looking forward to benefiting from the opening of the pipeline, Greek Cypriots will have to continue to invest in further desalination plants and pray for rain. Whether the new supply of water to the North will play any part in the reunification of the island remains to be seen. Whoever ultimately benefits, the infrastructure to pipe the water around the north, at least, is expected to be in place by the end of 2015.

LA (*Entry TL10*) Just opposite the hotel of the same name, a narrow but popular strip of sand with sunbeds, umbrellas, use of the pool and a snack bar with pricey Wi-Fi.

Towards Koruçam Burnu (Cape Kormakiti) All along this stretch of wild coastline, west from Kayalar, there are small sandy and rocky bays backed by the cliffs. Attractive, deserted and secluded, they are also often difficult to reach, involving a scramble down from the road and a longish walk. The area around the cape itself near the lighthouse used to be military and prohibited, but was demilitarised a few years ago and is now approachable.

If you're driving from the Girne direction, the turn-off towards Kayalar signifies a brief respite from north coast overdevelopment and the start of how things used to be. As the road sweeps around the coastline, affording superb panoramic views, it's a welcome relief to see open land ahead and, by local standards, an absence of litter. Driving here is a joy, and will definitely lift the spirits of anyone who wondered just where the 'real' North Cyprus actually was.

Pressing on after the **Horseshoe Beach Restaurant** (page 94), it is clear to see why locals and visitors alike favour this stretch of road, meandering as it does towards old Kayalar. Unfortunately, even here the builders have been busy and the old village now sits in uneasy proximity to new development that has been thrown up by the roadside. Once you reach Sadrazamköy, where there's a simple restaurant, you can turn inland to Koruçam or continue along the track to the tip.

WHAT TO SEE AND DO The description given here starts with a brief account of the route westwards to Vouni, then gives the site details starting from Vouni and working eastwards back towards Girne. As throughout North Cyprus, the roads are in good condition, with the towns and sites being, by and large, clearly signposted.

The road first follows the thin, developed coastal strip for 20km or so, before it then begins to climb as it winds inland through wooded hillsides. Leaving the valleys behind, you have a fine view below to a huge new dam, one of many that the north Cypriots are now building to harness the water that is lost in a flash after a heavy downpour: no river in Cyprus flows all year round and water is a scarce resource. For most of the year it comes from the mains for only 2 hours a day, and in July and August sometimes not at all. Residents and hotels get round this by having extremely large tanks on the roof, but the much-vaunted water pipeline from Turkey is eagerly awaited.

At the top of the climb you arrive at **Çamlıbel**, a heavily garrisoned town. One of its military camps hides the mysterious **Mavi Köşk** (see box, page 98), where there is a major fork in the road: straight on to Lefkoşa, and right to Güzelyurt and Lefke. The road straight on is the one you need to take to visit Pighades, just 2km away, on the return journey, but for now, you fork right.

Leaving Çamlıbel on its hilltop, the road drops down into the adjacent valley. **Güzelyurt** is set in the heart of this vast and fertile river plain, the centre for the island's citrus plantations. Your arrival at Güzelyurt is marked by a fine example of 20th-century British engineering – a 1904 tank engine, rusting gently just to the left of the road within the confines of the new Festival Park. This curiosity is a leftover of the line built by the British that used to operate from Gazimağusa via Lefkoşa to Morphou. The last train ran in 1951. Continuing straight along the main road, you reach the centre of town with the unmistakable Byzantine dome of the Ayias Mamas Church and the municipal museum beside it, both set in the centre of a huge roundabout (and both described in detail on the return journey). The forks to the left from the roundabout lead back towards Lefkoşa, but you continue straight on, following signs for Lefke.

From Güzelyurt the drive on, through lush plantations, takes a further half-hour to reach the sweep of **Güzelyurt Körfezi** (Morphou Bay), with its distinctive **iron jetties**, relics of the copper-mining operations. Ships would tie up alongside these jetties and be loaded with copper for export, mainly to West Germany. Copper was Cyprus's most important natural resource, and the Greek name for it, kupros, is even thought to be taken from the name of the island. Cyprus was known throughout ancient times for its copper, supplying the Egyptian pharaohs and producing more than any other Mediterranean country. The rich mines here of Skouriotissa and Mavrovouni were first worked by the ancient Greeks and then the Romans, but after that lay disused for centuries until they were reopened in 1923. The Cyprus Mines Corporation, an American outfit, worked the mines until partition, when the ore was nearly exhausted anyway. Their supervisors marvelled at the extent of the Roman diggings, and the depth of their galleries and shafts, especially in view of the lack of ventilation. Slaves were used, of course, to work the mines, so safety standards were hardly a consideration. In Roman times Christians from Palestine who refused to renounce their faith were also sent down the mines. Careful observation of the landscape will reveal it to be largely composed of Roman slagheaps, for they are said to have left more than a

right   The beautiful interior of Ayias Mamas, whose Byzantine dome dominates Güzelyurt town centre (NF/AWL) pages 102–3

below left A fresco in the beautiful Antiphonitis Monastery, located deep in the forest of the Kyrenia Mountains (DR) page 117

below right The many abandoned churches of the Karpas Peninsula signify that the area's population was once predominantly Greek Cypriot (NCTA) pages 177–84

bottom Undamaged and complete, St Barnabas Monastery is a peaceful haven, with some interesting icons on display (NCTA) pages 167–8

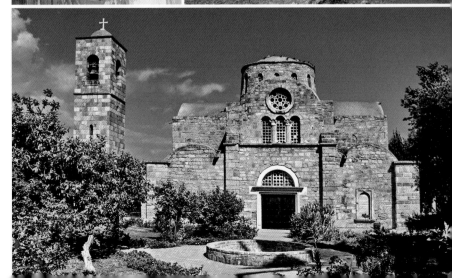

above left The Queen's Window looks down to the north coast from the imposing St Hilarion Castle built by the Crusaders to repel the threat of Arab raiders (DR) page 83

above right The steep hike up to Buffavento Castle rewards the intrepid with stunning views (VS/S) pages 113–15

below Kantara Castle offers magnificent views over both sides of the Karpas Peninsula, and on a clear day as far as Turkey and the mountains of Lebanon (r/S) pages 121–3

above   Cypriot donkeys roam freely in the Karpas Peninsula (NCTA) page 11

left   The European chameleon (*Chamaeleo chamaeleon*) is a rare sight in North Cyprus (JC) page 9

below left   The many varieties of tiny orchid announce the North Cypriot spring with a dash of colour (NCTA) page 6

below right   The starred agama (*Agama stellio*) is the largest species of lizard on the island (PK/S) page 9

above left   Once thickly forested, the Mesaoria Plain now resembles a semi-desert (DR) pages 144–5

above right   The remote Karpas Pensinsula has an abundance of wildlife and flowers (NCTA) pages 171–84

below   Alagadi Beach is a top nesting site for turtles (JC) page 113

above left **Traditional Cypriot skills, such as basket-weaving,**
and **are still kept alive, and baskets make for**
above right **authentic and colourful souvenirs**
(NCTA) page 46

left **Delicate embroidery is a North Cypriot speciality**
(NCTA)

below **Away from the main population centres,
goatherds tend their flocks as if time stands still**
(NF/AWL)

above Olives have been on the Cypriot menu for years; here, they're cooked before being dried in the sun (MS) page 43

right Local men meet to play backgammon, Lefkoşa (DR)

below Harvest time in the orange groves near Güzelyurt, home to an orange festival in the summer (JC) page 46

above   The jagged Kyrenia Mountains are perfect for walkers, offering some of the country's best forest tracks
(OA) pages 51–3

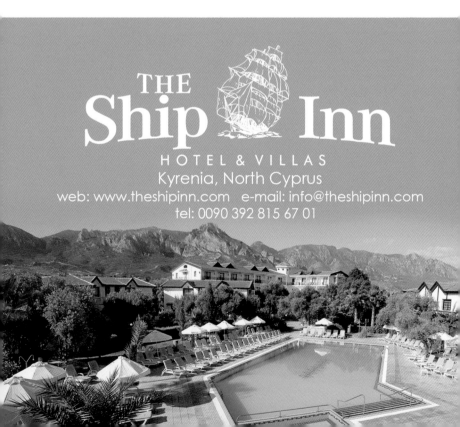

million tons of slag behind. 'Our Lady of the Slag Heaps' is one rough translation of Skouriotissa.

Shortly after the mining sites, but before the village of Yedidalga, the Roman theatre and basilica of **Soli** lie on a hillside just 200m inland from the road, signposted as usual with one of the tourist service's yellow signs. **Vouni**, too, about 8km further west along the coast road, is clearly signposted off to the right.

First the road passes a cluster of beach restaurants west of Soli, where you can eat and swim, before a steep winding ascent of a colossal hilly outcrop on the sea edge begins. Vouni Palace lies on the summit of this outcrop. The last 3 minutes are along a narrow track. Near the foot of the hill, incidentally, about halfway between Soli and Vouni, is the shell of a **modern Greek church** built in a sheltered nook to the right of the road, but badly destroyed inside. It appears never to have been completed and is covered inside and out with the vain exhortation: 'Please keep tidy'. Most mosques in Greek Cyprus are, by contrast, kept locked and clean, but the record for tolerance is poor on both sides: 117 mosques were destroyed between 1955 and 1974 by zealous Greek Cypriots.

At the foot of the Vouni hill, the main road continues westwards to the village of **Yeşilırmak**. Just as you enter the village, watch out carefully for the sign on the right for **Faces of Cyprus**, a small studio where İşmail Isilsoy carves astonishing masks made from driftwood collected on the beach. 'We Cypriots are like driftwood,' he says, explaining his choice of material. And when you consider their history, pushed and pulled from pillar to post, barely enjoying any independence, you might conclude that he has a point. Beyond this, off to the right, are a couple of beach restaurants. Until October 2010, Yeşilırmak was the westernmost point you could reach before turning back. Now, however, a new road – partly funded by the EU – twists first up and then down to a new border crossing. On the way, you should schedule a meal or even a stay at the excellent **Erson Hoca's Organic Farm** (page 92). As you reach the hilltop, you may notice some interesting-looking ruins off to your right. Resist the temptation to visit them: the short road to them ends in a military camp. At the crossing itself, you can hop across into South Cyprus, if all your personal and vehicle papers are in order. Some 8km further west, inaccessible and surrounded by Greek Cypriot territory, is the curious Turkish Cypriot pocket of **Erenköy** (Greek Kokkina). Today only troops live in this fiercely Turkish Cypriot enclave, all the original villagers having been evacuated to Yeni Erenköy ('New Erenköy') on the Karpas Peninsula. These villagers had resisted an attack by General Grivas and 3,000 Greek soldiers in 1964 and were supported in their struggle by student volunteers who included a young Rauf Denktash, the future TRNC president.

Having arrived at the westernmost point, the site descriptions now begin from Vouni eastwards.

Vouni (*ticket kiosk* ⊕ *summer 08.00–18.00 & winter 08.00–15.30; TL7/5 adult/ student*) This is the only Persian palace in Cyprus, indeed in the Mediterranean, and it lies on a spectacular hilltop overlooking the sea. However, the remains of the palace are scant, and the imagination has to be called into play.

The dizzy views down to the sea on the way up are stunning, with the rocky island of Petra Tou Limniti in the foreground. It was on this island that Cyprus's earliest inhabitants lived, and traces of a pre-Neolithic settlement were found there by the same Swedish expedition in the 1920s that excavated Vouni and Soli. Local folklore holds that this is the rock (as indeed are all the small rock islands off Cyprus's shore) that the hero Dighenis tossed onto the ships of the Arab raiders of the 7th century.

The heavily guarded perimeter fences of Çamlıbel's army camp hide a secret, the precise origin of which, though hardly ancient, has been lost in an obfuscating mêlée of conflict and hastily rewritten recent history. To investigate the mystery you'll need photo ID, a credit card (!) for the TL3 entrance fee, and to sign the register to pass beyond the gun-toting sentries and into a twilight zone of Cyprus's past. Mavi Köşk, or the Blue House, is testament to one man, Byron Pavlides, though for all their amiable manner it's likely that your Turkish military guides will be unsure even of this fact. The site is closed on Mondays, for cleaning. The army's story is that Pavlides was a gunrunner for Greek Cypriot EOKA terrorists and the house was sited in its lofty position in order to oversee the arrival of weapons shipments at the coast below. They will also state that the building contains secret escape passages and storage rooms concurrent with its usage as a hub for terrorist activity. It's further suggested that rather like a paranoid pharaoh, Pavlides ordered the house's architect, his own brother, and the unfortunate workforce to be shot upon its completion. Given the extreme circumstances, one could perhaps sympathise with Pavlides's rationale if not his actions in this excess. However, there's little evidence to support the story. What's beyond dispute is Pavlides's eccentric nature, manifest in the unique design and colour scheme of Mavi Köşk. Exploring the house, it'll be for you to judge whether the blue walls, blue-painted furniture, kitsch mock taverna with colour-coded tables and chairs, combined with a multitude of 1970s-style bathrooms, sunken fountains and, for its time, sophisticated air-conditioning reflect a ruthless and violent criminal mastermind.

What is known is that Byron Pavlides was a wealthy businessman, holding the dealership franchises for a number of automotive manufacturers across Cyprus. The house was built in 1973 and was not the first 'coloured' house that Pavlides was responsible for, having first conceived the 'White House' near St Hilarion, now also in the domain of the Turkish military.

Returning to the myth, following the 1974 invasion Pavlides escaped from Mavi Köşk by the skin of his teeth via an escape tunnel. All Turkish soldiers found was a locked safe that proved to contain a single golden key, the significance of which remains tantalisingly unknown to this day. Pavlides was not heard of again until 1986 when a rumour arose that he had died in Sicily, shot dead at a Mafia meeting by a Turk.

As with most of these historical sites, in return for your entrance fee you get a handy brochure in English. There is no refreshments stall here, so bring your own supplies, especially liquid in the summer months. Vouni is a good spot for a picnic. Allow 45 minutes for a full walk around.

Touring Vouni In Greek, the name Vouni means mountain peak, and it was built on this summit specifically to dominate and spy on the city kingdom of Soli down below, which had at that time aligned itself with the Greeks in a revolt against Persia. The palace was only in use for some 70 years, for in 380BC it was destroyed by fire and not lived in again.

Reduced today to little more than its foundations, the 5th-century BC palace of Vouni may disappoint at first. Do not dismiss it too quickly though, for if you take the trouble to walk round slowly, you will be surprised how it can be transformed, by careful observation and a little imagination, into a magnificent royal residence. The clear information signs may help to obliterate any palatial atmosphere, but they do at least provide a handy guide to the rooms. Ruined but gracious walkways, broad stairways and ample courtyards all hint at the opulent oriental lifestyle enjoyed here, and the elaborate **water system** is a marvel of 5th-century BC engineering. Everywhere there are ingeniously cut channels and very deep wells, ensuring running water in all the main rooms. In the extreme northwest corner, there is a **water closet** beside a deep cistern, which in its day was probably far more luxurious than its modern counterpart could ever aspire to be. Lower down the hill are the **baths**, with one of the earliest-known saunas. There were 137 rooms in all.

The path from the ticket office leads straight into the area identified as the **royal apartments**, and from these a broad flight of seven steps leads down into the huge open courtyard, which is the generally photographed view of Vouni. At its farthest end stands the strange carved stone **stele** which resembles an altar but was in fact designed to hold a windlass over the cistern wellhead. In the bulbous centre of the stone is an unfinished likeness of Athene.

The Swedish excavators made a series of finds in the palace that testified to the lavish lifestyle of the occupants. As well as statues and bronzes, they discovered quantities of silver and gold treasure in the form of bracelets, bowls and coins. One local story tells of noblemen dining here and leaving their silver spoons behind, and villagers still refer to it as 'the eating-place of the lords'. Much silver treasure was found in a terracotta jar that seemed to have been deliberately hidden under a staircase. Some of this treasure, including Persian-style snake-head bracelets, can be seen in the Cyprus Museum of Greek Nicosia.

Beyond the palace area, at the highest point of the hill, stands a military trigonometry point, 250m above the sea, and nearby are the scant remains of a temple to Athena where the Swedish excavators found several sculptures, notably an endearing bronze cow, now also in the Cyprus Museum.

The serene and lovely location encourages much wildlife. Lizards up to a foot long leap around on the walls and butterflies sun themselves gaily in sheltered corners. All around flourishes the yellow aromatic Johanniskreuz bush, well known for its stomach-calming qualities when drunk as a tea.

Soli (*ticket kiosk* ⊕ *summer 08.00–18.00, winter 08.00–15.30; TL7/5 adult/ student*) The Roman site of Soli boasts the best-preserved mosaic and marble floor in northern Cyprus in its basilica, and nearby beach restaurants offer a pleasant stop for lunch and a swim.

The site lacks grandeur and its setting, though raised up overlooking the bay, is a bit scruffy and uninspiring. The theatre is the only other monument to have been excavated besides the basilica, and has been rather over-restored.

About 45 minutes should be allowed for a tour. There are no refreshments available, and Soli is not a particularly good picnic spot.

Touring Soli Coming from Vouni, look out for the yellow Soli sign to the right just after the village of Yedidalga. The turn-off lies directly opposite the rusting iron jetty, hovering above the water like a swan's neck, leaning forlornly over the sea.

Just to the left of the ticket kiosk you can see the **cathedral/basilica**, with its beautiful **mosaic** and **marble floor**. Among the marble remnants, you can still see some magnificent colours: columns in deep brick-red marble with swirls of white, or cool greeny-white slabs on the floor.

The majority of the mosaics are geometric in design, with red, white and dark blue as the predominant colours. Sadly, these colours have faded due to long exposure to the sun (the roof was only erected in the late 1990s). A new wooden walkway – useful for disabled visitors – has recently been erected, allowing closer inspection of the mosaics. The centrepiece is a lovely white swan or goose-like bird surrounded by flower motifs, with four small blue dolphins and a pretty multi-coloured duck.

At the far end of the basilica a huge tumbled column gives some idea of the size of the whole structure, the full length of which must have been close to 200m. The baptistry area was also mosaic, but only with geometric patterns. In the apse itself is a Greek inscription set in an oblong panel, entirely in mosaic. Nearby is a deep well, and scattered all around are thousands of fragments of marble flooring.

The **theatre**, dating from the 3rd century AD, lies a few minutes' walk higher up the hill, approached by the tree-lined path. Facing out to sea, it stands on the same site as the theatre of the original Greek city of Soli before it, which had a similar capacity, some 4,000. The town had reached its zenith under the Romans, but was destroyed in the Arab raids of the 7th century. The heavy restoration carried out in the 1960s by the Cyprus Department of Antiquities has somewhat ruined the atmosphere. Everything was reconstructed except the orchestra floor and the platform of the stage buildings, so the seats, rebuilt to diazoma level (ie: halfway), are all new. The original seats, it is said, were carried off in the last century to help build the quaysides of Port Said. Local school performances are occasionally held here.

Above the theatre on the nearby hill to the west are the extremely scant remains of a **temple to Aphrodite and Isis**, and it was here that the famous, if armless, 2nd-century BC statue of Aphrodite was laid bare by a Canadian team of archaeologists. She is now on display in the Cyprus Museum of Greek Nicosia. Her likeness is often to be seen on wine bottles, stamps and the like – Aphrodite, goddess of Love, symbol of Cyprus, born from the waves breaking on the shore near Paphos. The other theory that she was born of Uranus's castrated testicles, is not nearly so widely advertised …

Love hath an island,
And I would be there;
Love hath an island,
And nurtureth there
For men the Delights
The beguilers of care,
Cyprus, Love's island;
And I would be there.
      Euripides, *The Bacchae*

Nothing of the original 6th-century BC Greek city remains today, and the theatre and basilica are the only visible parts from the Roman city. The rest awaits excavation.

The dazzling jewellery of the **Golden Leaves of Soli**, now safely displayed on the upper floor of the museum in Güzelyurt (page 102), were of course excavated here in 2005–06.

Back on the main road, head east briefly and take the signpost to the right for **Bağliköy.** Wind upwards for 3km and you'll reach the village, recently designated as North Cyprus's second eco-village, after Büyükkonuk (page 42). The ecotourism association here is run by the womenfolk, who staff a small café from which they also sell some local products such as fig jam, apple jelly and (more potently) *zivana*. Restoration work has taken place to all the British-era water fountains, which bear Queen Elizabeth's 'ER' marking, and the traditional mud-brick walls of several houses are apparent. The village was once famed for its grapes and there are plans to replant vines.

In the meantime, the village has already established its own September eco-festival, with music, dancing and traditional foods. A beautifully renovated house, the **Bağliköy Bagevi** (m *0548 841 31 45;* **$**) serves as a restaurant and also has some very reasonable rooms to let.

Lefke Set in one of the lushest and most fertile pockets of the island, Lefke is a pretty and unspoilt rural Turkish town that pays little attention to tourists but boasts a new university and three mosques, an unusually large number for North Cyprus. Its citrus fruits are said to be the juiciest on the island, aided by the abundance of water. Dates and walnuts are celebrated in festivals here. The nearby reservoir is a favourite spot for local picnics.

Lefke is about 5km inland from Soli and the total detour from the coast road to see it need take only about 40 minutes. There is one characterful hotel in Lefke, the Lefke Gardens Hotel (page 92) and one that is quaint but not for staying in (!), though no restaurants of note.

Touring Lefke Follow the sign from the coastal settlement of Gemikonağı that points inland about 2km east of the Soli ruins. The approach to the town is heralded by an incongruously stately stretch of dual carriageway with well-tended gardens at the side and a cloaked Atatürk (the founding father of modern Turkey) on horseback rearing up as the centrepiece. This ceremonial entry lasts about 500m, and the town proper then begins as the road winds first down and then up again to reach the core of the town. Predominantly Turkish since well before 1974, its 3,800 inhabitants have suffered no displacement or uprooting. Lefke today remains a relaxed and friendly place, sprawling over several hillsides.

The best way to see it is therefore by car. Arriving at the centre, denoted as ever by a few groups of coffee-supping, chin-wagging locals, you come to a fine colonnaded building on the right, constructed as a **British storehouse** and now giving up its space to a few shops, a chemist and the time-warped **Hotel Vasif Palas**. It's worth venturing into the reception area of the hotel to admire the interesting collections of photos, newspaper articles and curiosities that adorn the walls. The accommodation itself is the wrong side of primitive, and an overnight stay could only be recommended for the intrepid. About 100m further up the road is a circular water tank, built to commemorate the coronation of King George VI in 1937. By turning off the main street to the left just opposite this monument, you can wiggle down through a whole maze of narrow lanes lined with picturesque old houses. One lane passes a fine old **aqueduct** some 4m high. Water is everywhere in Lefke, and gurgles in little water channels that run beside the streets.

Returning to the main street, as you begin to drive uphill out of the village you'll see an old mosque in sandy-coloured stone surrounded by colourful gardens, its minaret topped with an aluminium cone. This is Lefke's main mosque, and in its garden lies one of the loveliest Turkish tombs in Cyprus, the **tomb of Piri Osman** Paşa who died in 1839. Built of white, elaborately carved marble in the dervish style with tall turbaned top, its centre is blackened from the smoke of candles, for every time the women of the village ask a favour of the local saint – a husband, a male child, a cure for illness – they leave a lighted candle on the tomb.

Taking the time to drive a little further afield in Lefke, especially down in the valley, you'll cross a wide riverbed beside which stands a derelict small Greek chapel, raised up next to a grand and excellently maintained house, evidently the seat of the local landowner. A relatively new claim to fame is the mausoleum of **Sheikh Nazim Haqqani Kibrisi**, who died in 2014. The Sheikh had a worldwide following and was also known for occasionally (and obviously incorrectly) predicting the end of the world. His resting place certainly attracts some of his fans, but the casual visitor may be deterred by some of the people demanding money outside the building, the claims of some locals that those devotees lurking inside the building are 'overeager', and especially by the inexplicable sale of hunting-knives and camouflage clothing outside the entrance. (The mausoleum is only mentioned here because some locals do enthusiastically suggest a visit to this 'tourist attraction'.)

Güzelyurt (Morphou)

The Turkish name of Güzelyurt means 'beautiful place', but it is referring less to the town itself than to the surrounding area, where beauty is virtually synonymous with fertility. Some 80% of the island's citrus groves were concentrated here, and in the first few years after 1974, the Turkish Cypriots had neither the manpower nor the expertise to tend them. Many trees died from neglect or disease, but by 1980 the situation was under control, and exports of citrus fruits began an upward trend. At one time this was the stamping ground of the juice and canning magnate Asil Nadir, a Turkish Cypriot millionaire fugitive. Unfortunately, as the citrus groves increased in size and number, the development of irrigation techniques could not keep up, leading to water contamination along the coastline.

Touring Güzelyurt Arriving from the west at the large central roundabout of the town, you drive into the little car park in front of the museum, a smart white building beside the Ayias Mamas Church. The guardian of the **Güzelyurt Museum** (⊕ *summer 08.00–18.00, winter 08.00–15.30; TL7/5 adult/student for entry to museum & church*) has the key to the church. A visit to both takes about an hour or so.

The museum opened in 1979 and contains downstairs a remarkable assortment of stuffed animals of the island, including pelicans and other birds, reptiles, foxes, rabbits and sheep. Particularly memorable, if somewhat grotesque, are the aberrant lambs: freaks of nature, one with eight legs, one with two heads on its tiny frail body. Upstairs is the archaeological section, with finds from nearby Bronze Age sites, notably Toumba Tou Skourou and Soli. The room in the far corner is the most interesting, containing both a 2nd-century statue of Artemis, whose unusual, multi-breasted form will be familiar to anyone who has visited Ephesus on Turkey's west coast, and some exquisite and remarkably well-preserved gold jewellery, including the glistening **Golden Leaves of Soli**.

Outside, the guardian will take you across the courtyard of **Ayias Mamas Church**, round the edge of what are now the disused 18th-century monastic cells. A modern wing of this accommodation was, pre-1974, one of the Bishop of Girne's residences.

Inside the church, it is as if the service had only just finished. The walls and iconostasis are resplendent with icons, many of them Venetian and all of them in excellent condition. One reader describes the church perfectly as, 'a Miss Havisham of a church, frozen in time'. A 'new' icon, originally from Tatlısu, was brought out of storage in 2014 to be displayed here. The church is certainly well worth a visit.

The tomb of Ayias Mamas himself is on a side wall beside the entrance. In the centre of the sarcophagus is a wooden flap that lifts to reveal two holes where, according to the guardian, 'the Greeks poured oil inside'. Tradition held that the saint's body exuded an oil that cured earache and calmed stormy seas, an oil that was collected from these two holes. Ears, in silver and in wax, still hang beside the tomb, their owners waiting patiently to be healed.

Ayias Mamas was a popular saint who earned the undying respect of the Cypriot peasantry in the 12th century by refusing to pay his poll tax. He is always shown in icons riding on a lion, because the story goes that when his Byzantine ruler sent for him to be brought before the court and punished, the saint rode in astride a wild lion and was promptly exempted from his taxes for life. Around 14 churches are dedicated to him throughout the island. As the patron saint of tax avoiders, Mamas's popularity may well be eternal, and universal.

Some 6km north of town stands the new campus of the **Middle East Technical University** (METU). The campus is an offshoot of the main site, located in Ankara, Turkey, and plays host to around 1,500 students, with plans to double that number. The continued investment in education in North Cyprus reaps huge benefits by way of fees from overseas students, and here it provides a welcome diversification for a local economy that relies so heavily on citrus fruits. On your way out of town, the **Festival Park** is a well-tended, pleasant piece of greenery that makes a good picnic spot. It hosts concerts, sporting events and the annual orange festival in May and June.

Toumba Tou Skourou The site of this other town, like so many Bronze Age settlements, is not of interest to the layman, and only merits the detour for the real archaeological enthusiast. Its name is known from its finds displayed in the Güzelyurt Museum. There's no guardian, so the site is always accessible. The visit will detain you for no more than 30 minutes, from the point where you turn off the main road.

Touring Toumba Tou Skourou Leaving Güzelyurt in the direction of Girne, look out for the yellow sign pointing along an old tarmac road leading off to the left opposite a new row of shops. Taking an unsignposted right after 600m, between two buildings, you'll find this rough track ends in a clearing; immediately after this are the ruins as excavated by Harvard University and the Museum of Fine Arts from 1971 to 1974. The area all around is littered with potsherds, and the huge holes left by the giant pithoi (earthenware jars) are in some ways more impressive than the pithoi themselves. Also found on the site were Minoan pottery, Syrian cylinder seals and some African ostrich eggs. The setting, surrounded by citrus trees a long way from any village, lends a certain charm to the site.

Kalkanlı Monumental Olive Trees The main road continues east across the plain before climbing up to the village of Kalkanlı. From here a steep descent begins, winding down into the next valley. Just over 1km east of town you reach the sign for the Monumental Olive Trees. Turning off the road and following the rough track for a further 1km will bring you to an information board, explaining the movement to protect the precious trees, some of which are over 500 years old. This is a great place for a short walk or a picnic. There are tables, though no refreshments or other facilities. Back on the main road, there is now a short journey towards Tepebaşı and Çamlıbel.

Akdeniz Village Tombs and Paleokastro As you approach the mound of Tepebaşı, a tarmac road leads off to the left towards the bay of Güzelyurt, signposted Akdeniz, just after the petrol station. (A new signpost promises that this road will lead you to the 'Akdeniz Visitor Centre', but must have been erected in hope: no such place exists!) This is the road you must take to reach these sites. It is 15km from the main road to Paleokastro and the total return visit will take one or two hours.

Akdeniz itself, contrary to its name (which means Mediterranean), is not on the coast, but some 2km short of it. Its Greek name was Ayia Irini, and this is the name that is well known from the Ayia Irini sanctuary displays in the Cyprus Museum in Greek Nicosia. The village has a couple of small grocery stores and a café run by Erol Akcan, who also sells handicrafts and paints and has produced a detailed illustrated history of the village and its people, soon to be translated into English. Ask to see it, as the photos are fascinating.

The Akdeniz Village Tombs are signposted from the far end of the village, and the recent abandonment of the Turkish military camp that previously dominated the headland has made visiting Paleokastro ruins possible without having to enlist the help of soldiers or having to show your passport. If you have to ask for directions, you may strike it lucky and find someone to help, but some locals seem oblivious to the existence of the sites and are unlikely to even recognise their names.

Both the sites are remarkable for what was found at them, but since these finds have been removed to museums, there is little of interest left for anyone except the specialist. The 2,000 clay figures from Paleokastro are among the most intriguing exhibits on display in the Cyprus Museum of Greek Nicosia.

Paleokastro itself lies in an attractive spot on a clifftop overlooking the sea, and has beautiful beaches immediately to the north and south. Those who assisted in the original excavation of Paleokastro confirm that the structures were head-high when the army arrived, but claim that military traffic has reduced them to rubble. Certainly, there is now little to see.

Touring Akdeniz Village Tombs

As you reach Akdeniz village, take the road down past the left-hand side of the mosque, heading towards the coast. After 200m, you'll see a battered yellow sign for the tombs. Take the right-hand fork here, fork slightly right again and head up towards a large farm, which you leave to your right, then take the left-hand fork for about 500m until you see the fenced-in site on your left. It's a rough track, not to be undertaken in or just after wet weather, unless you're in a 4x4. There's no information to accompany what are in effect a few tombs, only a couple of signs giving dates. Apart from the two marked tombs, the first of which was discovered only in 1988, it should be noted that the area immediately to the west and north is dotted with various carved rocks and other ruins, all fairly modest but indicative that the population here was once more extensive than a quick glance might indicate. Some gold was found here, and a local myth holds that buried somewhere nearby is enough gold to see Cyprus through seven years of famine, should such misfortune ever occur. This may explain some of the less-than-professional recent digging that can sometimes be seen in the shrubbery!

Touring Paleokastro

Assuming you visit the Akdeniz Village Tombs first, reaching Paleokastro is straightforward. After the tombs, continue along the same track for a further 100m, then turn right at the T-junction on to another track, heading for the sea. The abandoned military camp will soon become visible on the headland to your right, and you should park 100m before reaching it.

To the layman it is no more than a huddle of foundations with one deepish well from which a tunnel is said to have led off towards the sea below. Excavated in 1929, the 2,000 votive figures were found around the temple altar. Of these, only two were female, a few hermaphrodite and the remainder male, most of them shown wearing conical helmets. They have been dated to 750–500BC.

Having come this far, you will see immediately to your right a beautiful **beach**, sheltered and probably deserted. There are no facilities (and thankfully rumours of hotel development have so far come to nothing). On the lookout for barbed wire, you can continue to the abandoned military building itself, touch the gun turret that pokes out of the ground, and gaze along another beach – longer and less sheltered – which stretches to the south towards Güzelyurt. To access this beach, a road is signposted from below Akdeniz village and takes you the 2km down to it, and the **Caretta** restaurant (☉ *summer only*) which offers sunbeds and umbrellas. This is a turtle-nesting beach so it is closed to visitors at night. The whole area to the northwest of Akdeniz is rough terrain, but is beautiful and with fine beaches. At present, it is totally unspoilt, and a protected area. Rough tracks make it inaccessible. Pessimists believe that it can only be a matter of time before it is opened up to development.

Having returned to the main Girne–Güzelyurt road, you could take the small fork up into the village of **Tepebaşı**, just for some variation in the route. This and Koruçam (to the northwest on the Cape Kormakiti Peninsula) were both Maronite Christian villages, and Tepebaşı was badly damaged in the intercommunal fighting. Many of the village houses near the centre are derelict and crumbling. Higher up the hill, close to the main road, the large, modern domed church now serves as a hospital and clinic for the military. Today, Tepebaşı is best known for its black tulips, whose flowering in March is celebrated with a local festival. **Koruçam** (Kormakitis in Greek) remains the main Maronite village on the island, and these Lebanese Christians continue to use their huge church of Ayios Georgios freely: the Turks never had any quarrel with the Maronites. The people still speak an ancient Arabic language. It's not a problem to visit the church, which took 100 years to build (1841–1941), and was renovated in 2003. If it's locked ask around at the nearby café for the key (but the side door is usually open). The priest will happily hold a conversation with you – in French! New street signs have been produced in three languages: Turkish, English and Greek, as many Greek Cypriots come to visit relatives here. A smaller church, St George's, is also being renovated with finance from the European Union.

Çamlıbel and Pighades
The short detour through Çamlıbel gives you a chance to see the abandoned monastery of Ayios Panteleimon, and then soon after, the charming little Bronze Age sanctuary of Pighades, in Cretan-Minoan style, attractively set by itself in the midst of fields.

Pighades is just under 3km outside Çamlıbel, so the total detour including the visits need take only about 40 minutes. There are no site guardians, so you can visit at any time. There are no refreshment facilities, and no information is provided.

Touring Çamlıbel Arriving at Çamlıbel from Güzelyurt, you pass an army camp on your left, then at the next T-junction turn right towards Lefkoşa rather than left towards Girne. Then take the next right to reach the **Ayios Panteleimon** monastery on your left. Until a few years ago, the monastery was within the confines of the military camp, now relocated. Much of the perimeter fence remains, but it is accessible.

Ayios Panteleimon was the patron saint of doctors. In his pagan youth he had studied medicine at Constantinople, but after his conversion to Christianity he cured the deaf, the blind and the lame by prayer alone. Following his martyrdom, his healing powers were said to have transferred themselves to his silver gilt icon at the monastery. The church was heavily restored in the 1920s, when the monastery was the residence of the Bishop of Kyrenia, and very little of any age or interest remained beyond a few icons of the saint dated 1770. The church was closed in the 1950s and is badly run-down.

Walk around this grandiose, atmospheric site, then close your eyes and use your imagination. The potential here is enormous, as a multimillion-pound renovation would transform this into something truly special – perhaps a museum and art gallery with a restaurant and gift shop. At present this potentially beautiful site is left to the curious, and to the pigeons who nest merrily inside. It can only be hoped that the longstanding rumours of an EU-backed renovation turn out to be true.

Also of interest in the area, within a military camp but accessible upon the production of photo ID, is Mavi Köşk, former home of the intriguing eccentric Byron Pavlides. The camp entrance is 1km down the road between Çamlıbel and Koruçam. Whether Pavlides was a successful businessman, gunrunner or harmless eccentric, it's not clear, but he remains a man of mystery (see box, page 98).

Touring Pighades If you're not in a hurry, a short detour will take you to this small Bronze Age sanctuary. It lies scarcely 3km along the same road that passes Ayios Panteleimon on the way to Lefkoşa. It is signposted, the sign pointing along a 200m track by a row of tall cypress trees before reaching a cluster of them set in the middle of fields.

Amongst these trees lies the **Temple of Pighades** (1600–1050BC), with its centrepiece of a small step pyramid-shaped altar, some 3m high, built from large stone blocks. It is topped with two stones in the shape of a bull's horns, strongly reminiscent of the Cretan-Minoan horns of consecration with which it is contemporary. The excavated area has revealed a double courtyard with cisterns, all surprisingly well constructed for this early date.

The road that continues southeast towards Lefkoşa across the plain is heavily militarised, each village having been largely transformed into a military camp.

At Yılmazköy (Greek Skylloura) a small road forks to the right, signposted to the former Maronite village of Gürpınar. Pre-partition maps will show the Prophitis Elias monastery here on the hillside behind the village, but the village is now within a military camp and the road terminates at the barrier. According to a trilingual, laminated notice that one of the soldiers may produce from his sentry box, there are actually two 'churches' within the camp: 'Big' Ayia Marina church and 'Little' Ayia Marina church. Ayia Marina is the Greek name for Gürpınar. Neither can be visited, unless you have prior permission from the Turkish military.

Forking left at Yılmazköy, a road leads off towards Şirinevler and beyond to the heavily ruined village of Akçiçek, with its vandalised church. Before you enter the village, a road off to the right – initially tarmacked – turns into a rough dirt track that leads over the mountain range passing first through a series of quarries before a sign optimistically points you eastwards and upwards for Lapta. This route is not for the faint-hearted, starting out rough and getting rougher. If you're in a 4×4 and aren't afraid to use it, this route makes a memorable excursion. After incalculable ruts and potholes, it will throw you triumphantly out on to the narrow tarmac between St Hilarion and the Kozan restaurant. But be warned, take a wrong turn in a non-4x4 car, or attempt it after heavy rain, and you might find yourself looking at a long walk in search of a tractor with a tow rope.

Lapta Lapta is a picturesque town, with a superb setting on several mountain terraces overlooking the sea. Here, away from the main road, you'll find a peaceful alternative to the coastal bustle, with the scent of figs and the chatter of birds or schoolchildren your only interruptions. There are many churches and three mosques in this formerly Greek town, surrounded by a mish-mash of ruined houses, restored dwellings and newly built villas. Its sister town of Lambousa on the coast, a couple of kilometres below, served in Roman times as a port, and some remains of harbour installations, like the harbour wall and fish tanks, are still worth a quick visit, though due to development they are becoming more and more difficult to access. Also down on the coast is a pretty church and a large monastery, but the former is kept locked and the latter is behind the fence of a military camp.

A drive around the town of Lapta will take about 30 minutes, as the road network is positively labyrinthine. If you have time, it's a pleasant though hilly place to take a walk. The visit to the Roman fish tanks at Lambousa will also take about 30 minutes. You can park your vehicle on the rough ground near the back of the now-defunct Mare Monte Hotel.

Touring Lapta Lapta lies about halfway between Çamlıbel and Girne, and the turn-off to it is well signposted from the main coastal road. The town is reached after about 2km, but the maze of roads leading up and down and all over the various levels of terraces amount to at least a further 5km. These **terraces** are a natural geological formation, relics of the higher sea levels, and interspersed with huge rocky outcrops, ravines and chasms. One moment you glimpse a church set up above on a cliff edge, and your next view of it is from above surrounded by orchards and still seemingly inaccessible.

If you have time and energy, a gentle stroll around the various levels will let you see the mix of old and new dwellings, as well as the lushness of some of the private gardens, and the churches. **Apostle Loukas Church**, midway up, has been nicely restored and is in use under the banner of Cyprus Art as a school of music and ballet. The school teaches the local children, and they put on summer performances at the Near East University near Lefkoşa and elsewhere. The building's restoration has been carefully carried out, and has apparently met with the approval of the Greek Orthodox Church. At Christmas, the staff, who are all Muslim, put up a tree and assemble a nativity scene.

Further up the slopes, the **Ayia Anastasia** is a fairly modern church with some icons. Otherwise, it provides a handy storage area for spare mattresses from the retirement home – formerly a hotel – that surrounds it. The setting is on a rocky crag, and the views to the coast are excellent.

Water seems to gush in abundance all over Lapta, in one place more like a waterfall than a stream, making it one of the most fertile spots in Cyprus, famous for its orange and lemon groves. Pomegranate and fig trees also adorn the slopes. A perennial spring (one of very few on the island) issues from a rock above the town, at an altitude of 280m, reached by the road which continues on above the settlement.

Under the Romans, Lapta was one of the four administrative capitals of the island. It grew still further in the 7th century, when its sister town of Lambousa on the coast was being regularly pillaged by raiding Arabs, like most coastal settlements. When the population moved up the hillside, they carried with them many of the stones from Lambousa to build their new houses at Lapta.

Today, you can still visit the ruins of **Lambousa** on a headland near the now-closed Mare Monte Hotel. Heading east on the main coastal road, turn left 300m after the ship-shaped Capitano restaurant on to Sitkiye Ekinci Caddesi and follow it for 1km before turning left. Leave the fenced-off Mare Monte to your right and park up after another 100m. It's then a 5-minute walk to the fish tanks, heading west. The area is popular with fishermen.

Start your visit on the headland, where you'll see the ingenious **Roman fish tanks**, the largest of which is about 30m by 15m. Previous visitors, stumbling on them during their evening strolls, considered the fish tanks to be the swimming pools of a hotel since pulled down or never finished. They are cut into the rock beside the harbour, and were used by the Roman fishermen to keep their catch alive and therefore fresh for market. Waves splashing over the rock ensured the water was cool and constantly renewed, and intake channels specially positioned to tally with the tides and prevailing winds guaranteed that clean water entered the tanks, while another suitably positioned exit channel guided out the staler, warmer water. These tanks were among the first Roman fish tanks to be found.

Inland from them, on the other side of the path, are the scant remains of Lambousa, sprawling over the headland. The overwhelming impression at first sight is of mounds of rubble everywhere, but this is not so much the work of Arab raiders as of illicit treasure seekers, digging for their fortunes. Lambousa in fact means 'brilliant', a name justified by the quantities of Roman and Byzantine treasure found here, notably the famous early 7th-century silver plates depicting the story of David, some of which are still to be seen in the Cyprus Museum. The place was abandoned completely in the 13th century.

The original town was founded by the Greeks in the 12th century BC, but it was the Romans who made it into a major trading centre, establishing a naval base and dockyard here. The **Roman harbour wall** is quite well preserved, visible as you walk a little further round the headland. It is still in use with a handful of small fishing boats.

Return to the main road and head back westwards for 800m, before taking the sign marked Camelot Beach to reach **Akhiropiitos Monastery** and **Ayios Eulalios Church**. While the former is still trapped inside a military camp, the latter now stands in splendid isolation on a headland, and you can walk around its well-preserved exterior.

The charming, single-domed Ayios Eulalios, named after one of Lambousa's bishops, is kept locked, but you can peer inside from a glassless window on the eastern wall. The outer structure dates from the 15th century, but inside it has fine grey marble columns supporting the nave. The Akhiropiitos Monastery is still tantalisingly just out of reach within the camp, but its considerable size is apparent from outside the fence. Its name means 'built without hands' in Greek, from the story, somewhat ironic in the circumstances, that it was transported here intact overnight from Asia Minor to save it from Muslim desecration. It was founded in the 12th century and rebuilt in the 14th century. The monastery cells were occupied in the 1960s by animals and shepherds. Rising damp had been threatening the buildings for some time before partition, but now the problem requires urgent attention.

Alsancak to Karaman
The 15km of coastline between Alsancak and Girne are now well developed, passing a series of hotels, motels and holiday villages. Inland from Alsancak, a short detour will bring you to Malatya, a hill village with a fine gorge and permanent waterfall in a grotto on its eastern edge.

Some 9km west of Girne, just east of the Altınkaya Restaurant (page 93), is a monument reminiscent of fascist architecture, its sloping concrete fingers stretching inland towards the mountains. It marks the spot referred to by the Greeks as Invasion Beach, and by the Turks as the point from which the 1974 Turkish Peace Operation was launched. Just east of this is the **Peace and Freedom Museum** (⊕ 08.00–15.30 Mon–Wed & Fri–Sun, 08.00–17.00 Thu; free admission), with a small indoor display and an open-air exhibit of guns and tanks, both Greek and Turkish, used in intercommunal fighting from 1955 to the present. Outside the quoted opening hours, it's still possible to wander among the weapons. It was hereabouts that Colonel Karaoğlanoğlu, after whom a village is now named, and his soldiers were killed in the early days of the fighting in 1974. Signage is largely bilingual and additional information is available, on request, from the small café.

Nearby, a small sculpture on the seafront commemorates the Peace Operation, whilst a helpful sign by the roadside explains the imagery. Most visitors will pass by here without a second thought, but for some it represents something of a

Murray Stewart
Distance: 4km; time: 1hr 15mins; difficulty: mainly easy tarmac under foot, a few steep sections. No refreshments en route, but time your return to the village to coincide with the pub opening (page 92).

A short walk allowing you to admire the beautifully restored village of Karaman, visit the Bronze Age tombs nearby and get up close to the towering peaks of the Kyrenia mountain range.

Park your car in the car park by the church in Karaman (no charge). Start on the north (sea-) side of the beautiful church, down some steps then turn left, under the archway and pass the village shop on your right. At the Crow's Nest pub, head left and descend some broad, cobbled steps. At the bottom, turn left and after 50m descend a further flight of steps, passing between houses. At the foot (Cypress Road), turn left again and continue westwards. The concrete road descends first gently, then more steeply. Stay on the road, ignoring two tracks off to the left, until after around 700m you reach a sharp right-hand bend. Ahead of you is a wide firebreak, a reminder of the savage forest fires that can punctuate the summer tranquillity. Here, you follow the tarmac round to the right, heading back towards the mountains.

As you reach some houses, the tarmac turns into a rough track for 100m before reaching the main Edremit–Karaman road at a T-junction, where you turn right on to the main road and continue uphill. Pass the Labores Restaurant, after which the road turns sharply right. You will see a small sign for Bronze Age tombs and at this point you leave the road, following the signs and forking left down a minor tarmac road for around 300m until it ends at a large, single-storey house. Behind this is a further sign for the tombs. About 50m on is a stone building, which protects the largest of the tombs. Although the site is small, the tombs are dated at c1900BC and are therefore older than the much more visited tombs near Salamis. After exploring, retrace your steps back to the main road at which point you turn left, uphill, and follow the road as it winds first left then right back to Karaman village and a welcome refreshment.

pilgrimage. For Turkish tourists it's a must-see, and you're quite likely to encounter coachloads of sightseers taking group photographs and laying flowers at one of the 70 headstones commemorating fallen comrades. Such visits are obviously pre-arranged, as a young Turkish soldier will then deliver a rousing speech that will be followed by a hearty round of applause and more group photography.

The road inland to Karaman forks off at the sprawling little village of **Karaoğlanoğlu**, once known as Tiger Bay by the British, which has a number of good restaurants. It lies just 5km west of Girne. From here the road climbs some 4km up into the mountains, passing *en route* the village of **Edremit** with its photogenic basket shop, a good stop for a souvenir.

Karaman (Karmi) The road ends at the picture-book village of Karaman, magnificently set beneath the outcrop of St Hilarion. Curiosity is the main thing that will push you to visit this little mountain village, curiosity to see the only village in North Cyprus that has been entirely renovated by foreigners. It also boasts a small Bronze Age site, a shop, a good bar and a restaurant (see page 92 for details).

Girne (Kyrenia) WEST FROM GIRNE

3

Karaman is a 20-minute drive from Girne, and the last part is up a narrow winding road that climbs to the village and stops there. You might time your visit to coincide with lunch or dinner, or outside the summer heat allow an extra hour or more to walk up the mountain path towards St Hilarion Castle (pages 79–85), set just above the village.

Formerly a Greek village, Karaman was badly damaged during the fighting, and after partition the Turkish Cypriot government leased the entirety to the Ministry of Tourism for development. The ministry in turn leased the houses to foreigners for renovation, and the whole place has consequently been rebuilt in old village style, inhabited by expats, most of whom have chosen to retire here. The names of some of the roads – Mulberry Way and Geranium Lane for example – and the traditional British-style Crow's Nest pub in the centre of the village give a clue as to the nationality of the majority of the residents, though many Swiss, French, German, Canadian, Swedish and Belgian people have also chosen Karaman as their home.

The 19th-century **church** is pretty much as it was pre-1974 and, although it no longer holds services, it is the venue for occasional village events. The neighbouring village of İlgaz has also been redeveloped on a similar model though not under the auspices of the Ministry of Tourism. The **Bronze Age cemetery** lies about a kilometre below Karmi. A signpost by a bend in the road points along a path leading to an enclosure boasting a number of tombs that have been dated 1900–1800BC, making them older than the Royal Tombs at Salamis. In the roofed-over **Tomb 6** you can just about make out the oldest funerary relief on the island – that of a primitive fertility goddess, heavily weathered.

A final peculiarity of the village is the number of cats present here. The reason is that the inhabitants have established a slightly reluctant reputation for looking after strays, meaning that people from outside the village bring unwanted and abandoned felines here, safe in the knowledge that the locals will look after them. As you tour North Cyprus, you'll quickly realise that there is no shortage of candidates for their care.

EAST FROM GIRNE

The excursions described in this section are among the highpoints of any visit to northern Cyprus and should not be missed by anyone who loves walking and mountain scenery.

The two Crusader castles of Buffavento and Kantara are in spectacular settings perched on craggy summits, and the derelict monasteries of Sourp Magar, Antiphonitis and Panayia Absinthiotissa are nestled in gentle folds deep in the pine forests of the Kyrenia range. As well as the beauty of the settings, the sites are of great intrinsic interest.

The trips to the mountain monasteries involve pleasant drives along twisting forest tracks, but nothing that a saloon car driven slowly cannot handle. Access to Buffavento, once 4x4 only, has been upgraded in recent years and, though a single and precipitous track, it's currently no problem for a normal saloon car. The walk to Kantara and the monasteries is straightforward and gentle, while the challenging climb to Buffavento is via steps constructed by the military, taking a good 45 minutes for the young and averagely fit. Take water with you to all these sites as facilities are seasonal or non-existent.

The trips to Buffavento and the mountain monasteries can be done in the same day, if you are feeling energetic, though it is preferable and more in keeping with the gentle pace of the island to reserve the excursions for separate days. The journey along the coast to Kantara certainly requires a full day, as the drive one-way takes a good 2 hours.

WHERE TO STAY   *Map, pages 90–1, unless otherwise stated*
Luxury $$$$$
⌂ **Cratos Premium** (408 rooms) ☏444 42 42; e info@cratospremium.com; www.cratospremium. com. Opened in 2010, this enormous establishment a few km east of Girne raised the level of opulence in North Cyprus. Wannabe James Bonds will feel at home amid dripping chandeliers & throne-like chairs. Others may feel intimidated parking their hire cars among the stretch limos. Only accepts bookings on a 'full-board plus' basis, so edging towards the all-inclusive. Indoor pool, massive outdoor pool, shops, its own port & huge casino. Choice of restaurants. AC rooms, free Wi-Fi throughout.

Upmarket $$$$
⌂ **Acapulco Beach Club & Resort Hotel** (847 rooms) ☏650 45 00; e info@acapulco. com.tr; www.acapulco.com.tr. Some 10km east of Girne, an enormous & recently expanded bungalow village offering one of the cleanest & best-maintained beaches in the area. A huge variety of rooms & bungalows is available on a HB basis only, so a less attractive option if you want to explore the island. 2-night min booking in high season. Excellent facilities for families (children's club) & for anyone who enjoys sport. Watersports, tennis, volleyball, basketball, swimming pools, aquapark. Spa, jacuzzi & Turkish bath are at extra charge, as is Wi-Fi. Last but not least, you guessed it, there is a casino. Courtesy bus to Girne.
⌂ **Malpas Hotel & Casino** (174 rooms) ☏650 30 00; e sales@malpashotel.com; www. malpashotel.com. Located near Çatalköy, another luxury option, with indoor & outdoor pools, spa & wellness centre, fitness centre, free shuttle to beach club, multiple restaurants, jazz bar, casino & live music. Variety of AC rooms, with all mod cons.

Mid-range $$$
⌂ **Club Tropicana** (14 rooms) ☏815 51 88. Small, family-run complex. Turn right 200m

before the Cratos entrance & head south for 1km. Swimming pool, attractive gardens, poolside bar, traditional home cooking, & self-catering AC apts available. British-orientated & themed, no luxury but good budget option.
⌂ **The Fez** (12 rooms) m 0533 870 77 80; e info@thefez.co.uk; www.thefez.co.uk. Just off the main coast road, take the Çatalköy turn 1.5km after Cratos, then 1st right again. Restaurant (with pool) also has AC rooms for rent, all with TV. Large screen sports bar, free Wi-Fi. No luxury, but guests speak of a wonderfully friendly welcome. B/fast is extra, but this is still good value.

Budget $$
⌂ **Paradise Bungalows** (12 bungalows) ☏824 43 97; e info@paradisebungalows.com; www.first-paradise.com. Situated down the road that runs down the west of the giant Cratos Hotel, a pleasant, friendly place with bright rooms that have AC, TV & balcony. Small pool & restaurant, satellite sports on a giant screen.
⌂ **Şinya Guest House** (3 rooms) m 0533 863 48 58; e holiday@sinyaclub.com; www.sinyaclub. com. Firmly in the ecotourism camp, on the main road near Küçükerenköy. Great base for walking, cycling (rental possible) & with other indoor & outdoor activities for adults & children. Reasonably priced restaurant. Spacious bungalows (for 2 or 4 people) have AC, TV & Wi-Fi.
⌂ **Tatlısu Bungalows** [map, page 79] (20 bungalows) m 0533 869 22 33; e info@ tatlisubelediyesi.org; www.tatlisubelediyesi.org. Situated on the old coast road, 8km east of Tatlısu, these 1- & 2-bedroomed wooden bungalows, self-catering with AC, TV & Wi-Fi, are on a pleasant, well-equipped beach & blend in better with the environment than most of the concrete developments to the west. A restaurant (page 112) forms part of the development, which is run by the municipality.

✗ WHERE TO EAT AND DRINK   *Map, pages 90–1, unless otherwise stated*
Small restaurants are slowly popping up along, and just off, the northern coast road towards the Karpas, some servicing the new villa developments that have sprung up. Of the five Alagadi restaurants, the two listed below are in the village, not at the beach, open every day for lunch and dinner, and are recommended.

✗ **Alesta** ☏815 40 91; m 0533 835 36 16. In Karakum, on the main road east just out of Girne, a

well-established Turkish-Cypriot place with fresh, tasty food, pleasant service, smart (but not fancy) décor. *Kleftiko* is as speciality. Recommended. *TL22*

✗ Beşparmak Buffavento Restaurant
m 0533 864 53 88; www.besparmakrestaurant.
com. At the top of the pass on the road between
Girne & Gazimağusa, opposite the Buffavento
Castle turn-off. Long-established, tasteful place
offering high-class kebabs with 8 *meze* dishes
included. *Kleftiko* can be ordered, with a day's
notice. Stunning mountain views. Booking
advisable – ask for a table by the window. *TL30*

✗ China Garden ✆824 43 98. Situated 5km
east of Girne, this restaurant offers evening dining
in a beautiful setting. As its name suggests, a
purveyor of oriental cuisine – with some Turkish
dishes thrown in. *TL25*

✗ Erol's ✆815 91 36. Popular restaurant near
the centre of Ozanköy offering a largely grill-based
menu with a huge selection of *meze* dishes. Soups
come highly recommended too. Book ahead in
summer. *TL28*

✗ Grida Balik m 0542 863 08 64. Directly
opposite the Cratos Hotel, possibly North Cyprus's
best fish restaurant. Kemal & wife Sevil source
fresh fish directly from fishermen along the coast,
working wonders to serve some tasty treats. The
setting is hampered by the nearby main road, but
the food is sublime. Not cheap, but worth it – &
recommended. *TL45*

✗ Ozgum Café ✆824 58 58; ⏰ morning to
late evening, closed Mon. Just north of Çatalköy
village centre, a new café with terrace. Breakfasts,
snacks & local specialities, including handmade
desserts. *TL15*

✗ Paradise Restaurant ✆824 43 97. 5km
from Girne in Ozanköy to the left (sea side) of the
coastal road. With daily fresh fish, *meze*, kebabs &
kleftiko. *TL35*

Towards the Karpas Peninsula

✗ Harnup Restaurant [map, page 79]
m 0533 869 22 33. Part of the Tatlisu bungalows
complex, signposted 'Zambak Tatıl Köyu' off the
new road 8km east of Tatlısu itself. A great location
for lunch, perched over the waves. There's a beach
with sunbeds & umbrellas. Main courses of fish or
kebabs are served with 5 *meze* dishes & salad. *TL25*

✗ Kaplica Restaurant m 0533 825 13 61;
⏰ all year. A huge place by the sea, set on one of
the north coast's best beaches. Varied menu, with
fresh fish available. *TL25*

✗ Zarifiye ✆824 53 84; m 0533 863 41 91;
⏰ closed Mon in winter. On your left as you enter
Çatalköy village centre, from the coast. Traditional
Turkish Cypriot cuisine, plus steaks, with good
views down to the sea & friendly service. *TL25*

Alagadi

✗ Hoça [map, page 79] m 0533 865 44 64.
In Alagadi village, Hoça's son fishes every night &
this is where his catch meets its destiny – happily
for diners, who travel from Girne, Lefkoşa & even
Greek Cyprus to enjoy his fish *meze*. Price varies on
what they catch. *TL30*

✗ St Kathleen's Restaurant & Bar [map, page
79] m 0533 861 76 40. In the centre of Alagadi
village, serves simple kebabs & snacks. It's named
after the ruined basilica between it & the sea. *TL30*

BEACHES
Karakum
(*Entry free*) Signposted 'Karakum Halk Plaji', a very small horseshoe
cove of sand ideal for young children, just 3km east of Girne. You'll need a keen
sense of direction to get down to the water in the right place, branching left to follow
a dirt track to the cove, which is sometimes blighted by rubbish. A good place for
fishing or an early-morning snorkel. No entrance fee, but no facilities either.

Shayna Beach
(*Entry TL10, children TL5*) A tiny strip of pleasant sand, enlarged
with wooden decking to cope with the crowds. Entry fee gets you the usual sunbed
and umbrella. Beach is cleaned daily and gets packed at weekends and in high
season, so get there early. Around 6km east of Girne, turn left off the main road
at the Cornaro fish restaurant sign. Shayna also has a popular restaurant and bar.

Acapulco
(*Entry TL25*) 'Belongs' to the holiday village, Acapulco Beach Club,
10km east of Girne. Probably the best beach on the north coast for children with its
shallow water and gentle shelving. It's also one of the most expensive, and features

a long stretch of clean sand bounded by rocky promontories. Straw umbrellas, sunbeds and watersports are available. On the eastern promontory stands the excavated Neolithic site of Vrysi (page 119). There's a self-service beach restaurant, children's playground and a tennis court.

Lara Lara is 2km east of Acapulco and is a very pretty bay with rock and sand. The cliffs behind these rock slabs are also fun to explore, with caves and other weird formations. At time of writing, the beach was closed off, as a result of the construction of the adjacent and truly enormous Lara Park Hotel. It remains to be seen how this latest casino hotel will affect the public's access to this beach and indeed its character.

Alagadi (*Entry free*) At 18km from Girne, this is the longest stretch of sand on the north coast and unquestionably one of the most beautiful spots on the island – it has now been designated a 'Halk Plaj' (public beach), so there's no access fee. Inland the view looks directly onto the five peaks of Beşparmak Mountain (page 120). Access from the main road is either through the village itself, where you'll find the turtle project, restaurants and a free car park, or further east, from a metalled road leading to a large, well-defined car park where charges apply in high season. Next to this is the reasonably priced Turtle Paradise restaurant. Alagadi is often referred to as Turtle Beach as it is a favoured spot for loggerhead turtles to come ashore and lay their eggs (pages 10–11). Volunteers try to keep the beach clean and access is limited in nesting season to guided turtle-watching groups between 20.00 and 08.00.

WHAT TO SEE AND DO
Buffavento [91 H3] An essential outing for all who love heights, castles and adventure. This is the highest of the island's three Crusader fortresses, and the most difficult to reach. However, its setting is the most dramatic of any ruin on the entire island and well worth the trip. Remember to pack your head for heights, as the final 8km of the approach are along a precipitous, though well-surfaced, road. Due to the potential for rockfall, a Buffavento visit is not advisable either during or immediately after heavy rain. The steep climb on foot from where the road ends to the summit takes about 45 minutes, often on a concrete pathway and steps, with very little shade.
There's no longer any guardian at the castle, so in theory you can visit any time. The drive from Girne to the car park below the castle takes about 45 minutes.

Touring Buffavento The distinctive shape of Buffavento's rocky crag dominates the northern coastline and hovers ever present, beckoning seductively for most of the approach drive. Its outline bulges upwards, as if an unseen hand has struck the brow of the mountain range, making the terrain come up in an almighty bump. It was previously only approachable from the east, but the road now continues on past the foot of the castle, heading west to Taşkent. A good idea is to approach from the east, visit the castle, and then continue the drive west to see the abandoned **Panagia Absinthiothissa monastery**, before reaching Taşkent and linking up with the main road back to Girne.
By car, you leave Girne on the Gazimağusa road, following the coastal strip eastwards for some 10km, until you reach the fork left towards Esentepe and the Karpas. Take the right fork, staying on the main Gazimağusa road as it heads inland and begins to climb up into the mountains, approaching the distinctive Beşparmak Mountain to the left of the road, with its five rocky fingers reaching to the sky. Immediately at the brow of the pass, two signposted tracks head off to the left and

right. To the left is the road to the Sourp Magar monastery, now signposted to the non-existent 'Kyrenia Mountains Visitor Centre'. To the right, and also signposted, is the Buffavento road, which you must follow for some 6km as it runs along the ridge of the mountains, giving fine views to the south over the Nicosia plain.

From leaving the main road, it takes around 15 minutes to reach the right turn that takes you up to the car park by a shady olive tree. Emphasising the rugged nature of the terrain, there's also the unrecognisable remains of a memorial which previously listed those who perished in a 1988 Turkish Airlines crash. During the final 2km you will notice that the land immediately below you belongs to a military camp. At one point the shooting range is uncomfortably close, and very occasionally the military will close the road. After 6km of careful driving, you reach the junction, with a yellow sign clearly indicating the castle.

On emerging from the car at the olive tree, the sheer silence of the place is striking. Above you on the summit are the distant crenellations that are your goal. Below you is the **Ayios Chrysostomos Monastery**, not actually visible until you've reached the first level of the castle. From that higher vantage point, you can see the yellow ochre painted walls peeping out from behind the hill that obscures it when viewed from lower down, and a tall old cypress tree that stands by its door. According to local tradition, a queen who suffered from leprosy lived apart in the high castle, and her dog, her only companion, caught the disease from her. Slowly, however, he was cured, for he had discovered, at the foot of the mountain, a mineral spring with miraculous healing powers. The queen followed him to the spring and was herself cured, whereupon she had the monastery built beside it in gratitude. Today, some of the oldest henna plants on the island are said to grow around the monastery.

Other traditions have the Empress Helena, mother of Constantine, as founder, but at any rate what remains of the monastery is now largely modern. The double church still has some frescoes of the 11th and 12th centuries which are among the most important on the island. It also retains a magnificent double door, built entirely without nails and set in a frame of carved marble, dated to the 16th century. The monastery is not accessible to visitors these days, as it is firmly within a military area, but a North Cyprus television documentary revealed the inside to viewers. It showed the frescoes whitewashed up to a height of 1.7m; this was, according to the military, a deliberate act to protect them. The frescoes were restored in 1972 with great skill by the Dumbarton Oaks Byzantine Institute of Harvard University, and their condition under the whitewash is therefore likely to be good. Any faces of Apostles that appeared higher than 1.7m had wallpaper put over their eyes by the soldiers, in accordance with the Muslim belief that the Apostles must be blinded. Also out of bounds is the **12th-century church**, now heavily ruined, lower down the hill below Chrysostomos, on the road to Güngör (Koutsovendis), with its faded fresco of the *Lamentation over the Body of Christ*.

Back at the castle, apart from a brief explanatory sign in the car park, there's no further information available, nor are there any facilities. Taking water with you is strongly advised, and is essential on a hot day. From leaving the car, the steep walk up to the first gateway takes 30 minutes. The path is rocky, so appropriate footwear should be worn. Like at St Hilarion, the castle is divided into an upper and a lower ward, though the ruins are far less complete here than at Hilarion. From the gateway, the climb up to the summit, mainly on steps and often wonderfully vertiginous, takes a further 15–20 minutes. The summit is 955m-high, and even the Chrysostomos Monastery at 620m is nearly three times higher than Bellapais. In the last century the ascent was distinctly trickier than it is on today's path, as shown in the following description by a Spanish traveller:

The peak itself is a rock nearly perpendicular on every side. There was no further trace of a path, so we climbed this natural wall, taking advantage of jutting rocks, projections, holes, anything to which our hands and feet would cling. Sometimes we had to help one another with a stick, or the guide would stop to see where he could get the best foothold, so as to get over the parapet in front of him; and to complete the picture, we had always beside us a horrible precipice.

Disparaging comments are often made about the paltry nature of the ruins at Buffavento, along with jokes about its name 'buffetted by the wind' meaning that everything on the summit has been blown away. Yet the ascent to Buffavento, because of the terrain and the stupendous location, means that, if anything, it makes an even deeper impression than the other two Crusader castles, and the wonder is how anything was ever built up here at all. For a time in the early 1970s a guardian was posted up here, but he has since abandoned his lonely job.

You arrive now at the deserted first section of the castle, entered by a fine **arched gateway**. Inside is a cluster of chambers, one of which is built over a cistern. The red tiles used in the arches around the doorways are reminiscent of the Seljuk style of mainland Turkey.

Right on the summit are the remains of a **chapel** and a few other buildings, but most memorable are the staggering views, often through wisps of cloud, over the coast and back towards Lefkoşa and the Troodos Mountains beyond.

Like Hilarion and Kantara, Buffavento was constructed as part of a chain of defence against the Arab raids in Byzantine times. The Byzantine despot king of the island, Isaac Comnenus, fled here to escape the clutches of Richard the Lionheart at the time of the Third Crusade. Isaac's daughter surrendered it and herself to Richard in 1191, and the castle was thereafter fortified by the Lusignan Frankish knights and maintained as a prison called Château du Lion. The Venetians dismantled it fairly thoroughly in the 16th century to deny the islanders any chance of using the inland stronghold in any revolt against them. The Venetians' own interest was restricted to the coast, and they had no desire to maintain costly garrisons in these inland castles.

The mountain monasteries
The ruined monasteries of Sourp Magar, Antiphonitis and Panagia Absinthiotissa all have superb settings deep in the forest of the Kyrenia Mountains, and make wonderful spots for peaceful picnics and mountain walks. Sourp Magar has some interesting decorative features, and Antiphonitis still has extensive frescoes. A couple of other ruined monasteries in the area don't really justify a visit.

Improvements to the roads in recent years mean that getting to the monasteries now presents no problems, even for saloon cars. The roads are narrow and twisty, but well surfaced. The final 1km of track to all the monasteries is quite steep in gradient. Should you break down, you are a long way from help, but the isolation is part of the attraction. The drive from Girne to Sourp Magar is about 55 minutes. Immediately beyond the Sourp Magar turn-off, the road continues eastwards on winding tarmac and, following signs for Esentepe, you reach a bright yellow sign, from which it's a further 4km to Antiphonitis. Including time for walking and full exploration, as well as a picnic, a total of 4 hours for the excursion should be allowed. After Antiphonitis, you can continue east for 1km and take the twisty road signposted for Bahçeli, which takes you down to the coast road and back to Girne. As for the third monastery, Panagia Absinthiotissa, this sits in a different part of the Kyrenia range, though is still easily accessible by taking the main dual carriageway

Girne–Lefkoşa road, forking off east at Bogazköy and heading east as far as Aşaği Taşkent. From there, the monastery is reached by following the Buffavento sign, opposite the grocery store at the western end of the village. As an alternative, it can be visited as an add-on to Buffavento, by taking the right turn at the junction just down from the castle car park.

The trip is worthwhile not only to see the monasteries, of which only one is in a reasonable condition, but also to savour the tranquillity and beauty of the forest. Once you've forked off the main Gazimağusa road, you may well not encounter another car for some time. Indeed the only time the mountains get busy is on summer weekends or public holidays, when the picnic tables at the nearby Alevkaya (Halevga) Forest Station can be full of local families having an outing. Very few, however, visit the monasteries, which are also utterly abandoned save for a guardian at Antiphonitis, there to protect the frescoes.

Sourp Magar If you've visited Buffavento in the morning, and are still feeling robust and ripe for adventure, all you need to do to visit Sourp Magar is retrace your route and cross the main road at the brow of the hill to continue eastwards along the crest of the range. (You may want to stop at the excellent, timbered Buffavento Restaurant (page 112) sitting by the turn-off, which does good-value local cuisine and sits in a pleasant location.)

The narrow road makes for a scenic drive into the forest, with far-reaching views down to the sea. The turn-off to the monastery, after 8km, is hidden amongst the trees of a picnic site, which has barbecue facilities. There are car parks on both sides of the road. Should you arrive at a T-junction, just nearby to the Alevkaya (Halevga) Forest Station, then you've gone about 100m too far. At the entrance to the turn-off there's a barrier that's sometimes padlocked, though the key is available from the Herbarium (page 117). Without the key, you'll have to leave your car at the top and make the steep 15-minute walk down the tarmac road. After 5 minutes, you'll catch a glimpse of the buildings below. (Coming back up will take you longer, and water is essential when the weather's warm.) The atmosphere and superb location, nestling into the crook of the wooded mountains with distant views of the sea, make this monastery an unforgettable spot. Yet as you step down into the terraced courtyard, the desolation that greets you is enough to make you weep. Here in the beauty and silence of the mountains lies this gutted carcass, traces of its former splendour apparent at every turn – in the smashed tiles, the neglected citrus trees and the broken stairways.

Although the last monks left early in the 20th century, a resident guardian ensured, until 1974, that the place was maintained, and it was even possible for visitors and mountain wayfarers to spend the night in the monks' old rooms. The Armenian community in Nicosia used it as a summer resort, and orphans of the 1895–96 massacres in Turkey were sent here to be educated by the monks. On Sourp Magar's feast day, the first Sunday in May, the place was the scene of much festivity. The monastery used to own 10,000 donums (a donum is about a third of an acre) of land covered in carob, olive and pine trees, and crops and vegetables were grown on the terracing below, with the help of an elaborately constructed irrigation system. Now abandoned and unguarded, the monastery has been the victim of wanton vandalism. The monastery church has had its altar hacked to pieces and the Armenian tilework, the only decorative ornamentation left here, has been prised off the floor and smashed.

First founded in the year 1000, the current buildings date from the 19th and 20th centuries. The Armenian name Sourp Magar refers to the Egyptian hermit Saint

Makarios (AD309–404), whose Coptic (Egyptian Christian) monastery still stands in the Wadi Natrun between Cairo and Alexandria. This Cypriot monastery was originally Coptic, but was passed to the Armenian Church c1425.

Mystery monastery In the mountains some 15 minutes' walk above the road from the Armenian monastery is an unnamed monastery, heavily ruined and thought to date from the 12th century. Beside it is a very old and unusual tree tethered with iron ropes. The spot is difficult to find without a local guide.

Antiphonitis (☉ *summer 08.00–17.00 daily; winter 08.00–15.30 daily; TL7/5 adult/student; this is the only monastery of the 3 with an entrance fee, which goes towards the upkeep of the monastery & the provision of facilities – café & toilet*) Coming from Sourp Magar, take a left at the T-junction immediately beyond. Before doing so, you could take the right fork for 100m or so and visit the **Alevkaya North Cyprus Herbarium** (☉ *09.00–18.00; admission free*), a little museum of 800 local plant specimens pressed or preserved by Dr Deryck Viney, an expatriate resident of Karmi, a project aided by the Forestry Department. If you arrive outside the opening times, asking around might unearth the forester, who will let you in anyway. There is also a pleasant restaurant here, the **Alevkayasi Café** (☏ *0548 845 57 34 or 0533 865 98 61*) which rents barbecue equipment and supplies for TL20, or serves meals if you don't fancy cooking.

For Antiphonitis, double back up the hill from the herbarium and take the right fork at the junction to follow the Esentepe signs eastward, staying on the tarmac all the way and ignoring the sign down to Karaağaç. Travel for 11.5km, until you reach a junction with a large, bright yellow sign for Antiphonitis. Turn right, and continue for another 4.5km until you reach a huge incongruous electricity pylon, and a junction where the monastery is signposted down to your left. This steep but well-surfaced road leads you directly down to Antiphonitis, nestling below in a fold of the mountain, its red-tiled dome protruding unmistakably from the surrounding green.

Architecturally, Antiphonitis is of far greater merit than Sourp Magar, and the lovely **Byzantine church**, centre of the monastery until 1965, dates to the 12th century, when it was built by a monk from Asia Minor. The porch and graceful **Gothic loggia** (open arcade) were added in the 15th century under the Lusignans, and inside the derelict shell you are staggered to see exquisite frescoes with their colours preserved surprisingly well. It was in the wall paintings of such tiny rustic churches, tucked away in remote places, and often financed by private donors, that Cypriot Christian art achieved its own distinctive style, and such frescoes are today its finest legacy.

The **dome** reveals itself, on close examination, not to be a perfect circle, but its disproportionately large size gives it fine acoustics, if you fancy a bit of chanting. Appropriately, the name Antiphonitis means, loosely translated, Christ who Responds. High up in the dome is the lovely deep blue background of the Christ Pantokrator, and on the south wall is the unusual Last Judgement scene, both from the 15th century. In the southwest corner are the main, early 12th-century frescoes. In recent years two professional attempts have been made, probably by locals under the instruction of international art dealers, to steal sections of these frescoes. These two sections can be identified quite clearly, squares of about half a metre each way, cut into the walls. One of the attempts failed, and the cut-out section crumbled, disintegrating into pieces on the ground. The other is now probably part of a private Byzantine art collection in some distant part of the world.

From Antiphonitis you can, if you are based in Gazimağusa, take the forest track eastwards from the pylon for 500m to reach a further crossroads at which you continue straight on. Some 300m later there is yet another junction, and from here you can fork to the right, downhill some 6km to reach the village of Tirmen where the tarmac begins again. This dramatic descent can be driven with care in a saloon car, though the villagers are generally rather startled to see visitors approach from the mountain heights.

If you are based in Girne, you can retrace your route for a few kilometres before turning down to Esentepe. Returning from this direction, you may spot, about halfway back along the forest track, the forlorn little red dome of a derelict Greek church, overgrown with scrub, with no apparent route to it. An alternative route is via Bahçeli (page 115).

Apati This church is in fact all that remains of the 16th-century Apati Monastery, and as you get closer and pass underneath it, you will notice a poor but driveable track forking off to the left, which brings you to within a 5-minute scramble of it. Set on a wide grassy terrace, it is empty of frescoes and full of goat droppings.

The old village of **Esentepe** (Greek Ayios Amvrosios), just 15 minutes' drive below Antiphonitis, was noted for its weaving and woodwork. Beside the church in the village square are a couple of restaurants offering simple fare. From here, the drive back to Girne takes 25 minutes.

Panagia Absinthiotissa This is the least visited of the mountain monasteries, lying as it does on the southern flank of the Kyrenia range and therefore difficult to incorporate into another itinerary. The only maps to mark it are old Greek ones: none of the currently available maps admit to it at all. Nevertheless, it's simple enough to locate. The monastery itself was originally Byzantine and stands on a platform at a height of 510m, directly above the village, previously Maronite, of Taşkent (Vouno), now inhabited largely by Turkish Cypriot refugees from the south. In the centre of the village is a small museum displaying photos of atrocities committed during an attack on the village by Greek Cypriot EOKA fighters in 1963.

From the top of the village a tarmac road leads north towards Buffavento and, after a few kilometres, there's a picnic area on your left and the monastery on your right. A seasonal café provides drinks and snacks. If approaching from Buffavento, follow signs from the crossroads below the castle car park towards Taşkent, and the monastery will appear on your left after a ten-minute drive.

All around the monastery church are numerous outbuildings, indicating that quite a prosperous monastic community once flourished here. The church itself is mainly 15th century and structurally is in a good state of repair following some restoration work in the 1960s. Inside, virtually all traces of the frescoes have now disappeared, the main murals having been stolen post-1974, probably by professional black-market traders. By comparison with many European countries, North Cyprus does not suffer unduly from the curse of graffiti, but you will find plenty adorning the walls here.

Coastal route to Kantara
The 77km drive to Kantara is a magnificent one eastwards, taking the Esentepe turn-off along the scenic coast. Development here, particularly of villas, has accelerated in recent times but the density of construction is still nothing in comparison with the shoreline west of Girne. In the main you can enjoy a feeling of freedom the further east you travel. The castle of Kantara itself makes a fitting climax to the trip, perched dramatically astride the ridge, with commanding views over the sea on both sides.

The new road is superb to drive, and a considerable improvement on the old single-track route, although it is inevitably threatening to usher in developments that pose risks to the environment. The extended road now runs along the coast as far east as Balilan, then turns inland and continues to Yeni Erenköy and on to Dipkarpaz.

The drawback of a fast road is that it becomes all too easy to get detached from the landscape through which you are driving. There are plenty of tracks running down to the sea, allowing you to connect with parts of the old coastal road and visit beaches with countless swimming or picnic opportunities. The temptation is to stay on the tarmac and race through to your destination, but time spent exploring the side roads will yield some worthwhile discoveries. If you turn on to the old road north and east of Tatlısu, for example, you can hug the coast briefly to just beyond Kaplıca, admiring the coastal rock formations, sandy coves and the odd abandoned carob warehouse or church. As resources are being concentrated on the new road, excursions on to the lesser roads demand that you remain vigilant for potholes, and a 4x4 is preferable, though not essential.

Hazreti Ömer Tekke (⏰ *09.00–20.00 daily; free admission*) A few kilometres east of Girne, and exactly 1.8km after the monolithic Cratos Hotel, a small white sign points off left to the coast to 'Hz Ömer Tekkesi', a delightful little Ottoman mausoleum set on a headland, where seven Muslim saints are buried. English-language information boards enhance the experience. Can be busy at times of religious festivals. The tarmac track leads down some 2km through a housing estate to the whitewashed shrine at the end of a rocky bay.

Vrysi Leaving the main Gazimağusa road that heads inland, you can continue straight on along the coast, following the signpost to Esentepe. Barely 1km later, after passing a military camp, you come to **Acapulco Beach** (pages 112–13).

On the eastern headland of the bay is the Neolithic site of Vrysi, excavated from 1969 to 1973 by Glasgow University. Clusters of primitive stone houses were uncovered, thought to have been inhabited between 4000 and 3000BC by Neolithic people from Cilicia on the Mediterranean coast of Turkey opposite Cyprus. Among the finds, 250 bone needles and 62,000 fragments of pottery indicated that the Vrysins were weavers and potters rather than fishermen. To the layman today, the site is of little interest and almost looks more impressive from below when swimming in the sea. Persistence is required to find it, as most hotel staff are blissfully unaware of its existence. Behind the huge hotel restaurant complex, turn left towards the sea and carry on past the rear of the restaurant's kitchens. Emerging on to the tiny headland, you'll stumble across the sunken remains. The protective fence has fallen over, and visitors are, alas, free to clamber about on the fast-crumbling walls. There is recent evidence that the ever-expanding hotel is diminishing this site and only an extreme enthusiast will find anything of interest. Without greater awareness and a commitment to protect heritage sites such as this, you have to fear for their future. You'll find better information about Vrysi from the displays at Kyrenia Castle than you will do at the site itself.

Alagadi Soon after Acapulco Beach, you'll pass the signs to the currently closed **Lara Beach** (page 113). After this, there is not much of note along the coast until you reach the area known as Alagadi, some 18km from Girne. The potential for this stretch of coastline, the longest stretch of sandy beach on the northern coast and in a beautifully wild setting with the Beşparmak Mountain as backdrop, is enormous. The area is also characterised by extensive sand dunes.

For a number of years, conservationists have been concerned about development of the area around Alagadi, because of the threat to turtles who currently favour it to come ashore and bury their eggs in the sand. The construction of the new north coast road disturbed several nesting beaches, and the improved access to the area is now expediting the rate of property development. Although these loggerhead sea turtles are the subject of several active conservationist projects, it is too soon to say what the long-term impact of the development will be.

There's now a metalled road, identified by signs for the turtle conservation project, leading to a clearly defined parking area, complete with litter barrels! There's also a barrier that closes off the beach to public access from 20.00 to 08.00 during the May to October turtle-nesting season (see pages 10–11 for more details). The long sandy beach is quite magnificent, dominated by the spectacular Beşparmak Mountain. Two local legends surround this five-fingered mountain: sometimes it is seen as the handprint of the Greek hero Dighenis, left behind as he grabbed hold of boulders to toss on to the Arab pirates; sometimes as a testimony to woman's fickleness, as the handful of mud that the man threw at the woman when she rejected him. Another track leads off to the small village of Beşparmak at the foot of the mountain, and the energetic can, if they wish, make an assault on its northern face.

Peeping round the western headland, a significant disfigurement to the landscape is the ugly electric power station, built unconscionably close to the sea, the first one of its kind constructed in North Cyprus. The north of the island currently gets some of its electricity from the south, in exchange for water, but this situation will change once the north has completed more power stations. Many locals complain about the cost of electricity, which is significantly higher than it is in the UK, for example.

Kharcha ruins This is another pretty beach, though now almost entirely swamped by new development, that has the added interest of archaeological ruins. It's situated some 22km from Girne, just 1km west of the sign inland to the village of Karaağaç. To locate the ruins, take a small access road on the coastal side of the main road, exactly 3km east of the entrance to the Korineum golf course, and on the eastern side of the new development. After 100m on this road, turn left, then right down a rough track that leads you to the west side of the bay. The few modest ruins are now barely visible. On the eastern side of the bay are an **old Roman jetty** and a section of narrow sunken road. All around are fragments of pottery and crafted stone blocks.

This is the harbour and ancient town of Kharcha, traces of which lie scattered over the hillside to the east of the path. With time and patience you can still see, among the scrub and rocks, **cisterns** and **tombs** cut into the rock. One tomb, difficult to find and set underground, still bears a carved face on its lintel.

Along the coast, as you drive further east, you will notice ruined shells of large buildings such as that near Esentepe, just where the fork goes off inland. These are old **storehouses** for carobs and generally date to the 19th century when carobs were exported in large quantities (see box, page 122).

Panagia Melandrina Some 3.5km east of the sign that points inland off the main road to Esentepe, you can take a rough track following a signpost down the side of a development called Paradise Village. Judging by its apparent abandonment, it's unlikely to ever be either a paradise, or a village. Park the car 500m down the track and a quick scramble up the slope takes you to Panagia Melandrina. This church is believed to be 15th century and formed part of a monastery complex. It is now subject to 'emergency measures' with the whole structure being braced together with supports. For the casual visitor it is unremarkable and only a tour around the outside is possible.

Aphrodision and Galounia The pretty drive meanders eastwards along the coastline, passing a few modern ruins, the large hulks of buildings that were going to be hotels or villa complexes, now abandoned for lack of trade along this lonely shore. Old maps mark an ancient site called Aphrodision here on the coast, just at a kink in the road near the fork to Tatlısu, but nothing remains of it save a few rubble foundations. The same is true of Galounia, 18km further east, at the point where the road heads inland. Both are said to have been the capital of the Hittite kingdom of Cyprus in 700BC.

Inçirli Cave An excursion inland can be taken after the coastal road passes the village of Küçükerenköy, to visit the Inçirli Cave. This natural cave, the biggest in North Cyprus, lies a short drive from the village of Cinarli and while it is obviously not 'new', it now has a ticket office and commands an entrance fee. Although the cave runs to a depth of 250m, access is currently possible only to 70m, but there is still an impressive display of geological formations, including stalagmites and stalactites.

Panagia Pergaminiotissa (⊕ 08.00–17.00; admission free) Back on the coast road, some 4km beyond the sign inland to Tatlısu, a signpost directs you off to this 12th-century restored and recently reopened church. Previously walled-up, it is now manned to protect the frescoes which are once again open to visit. The space is now used to display and sell handicrafts.

Kantara At Kaplıca, one fork of the new road heads inland towards Kantara, just after passing signs for the **Kaplıca Hotel**, which is set on its own lovely sandy beach, a good spot for lunch and a swim (map, page 172). You then turn up the pine-lined street towards the beacon-like white minaret of the new Rauf Denktash Mosque. The castle beckons from its ridge up above, and the drive from here up a twisting road to reach it takes another 30 minutes.

As you reach the summit of the ridge, you enter the little village of Kantara, strongly reminiscent of the Greek summer resorts of the Troodos. There used to be hotels here, but the decline in visitors since 1974 has meant that only the **Kantara Guest House and Restaurant** remains. It's not a bad option for lunch, and as there are no refreshments at the castle itself, it's your only option if you haven't brought a picnic.

A narrow tarmac road now runs eastwards along the top of the ridge to end below the castle walls by the ticket office. If the guardian is there, you might well find him cooking on his gas stove or playing backgammon with his friend from the mountain fire rescue team. A more convivial place to work is hard to imagine. From here a path, a mixture of steps and earthy ground, brings you to the main castle gateway in just 5 minutes.

Kantara Castle (⊕ summer 08.00–17.00 daily; winter 08.00–15.30 daily (supposedly); TL7/5 adult/student) The relative ease of the approach makes Kantara Castle in some ways less exciting than its two sister castles, St Hilarion and Buffavento, and its altitude, at 724m, is also the lowest of the three. It is, however, unique in having splendid views to the sea on both sides, being sited as it is on the beginning of the island's tapering peninsula, the 'Panhandle', or more correctly the Karpas (Turkish Kırpasa). On clear days, especially early in the morning, you can glimpse the distant mountains of mainland Turkey and even, in winter, the snows of Lebanon, 160km away. For a castle, a better location is hard to imagine. The

CAROBS

North Cyprus is said to produce the best-quality carobs in the world, and the pods or locust beans are exported to the UK as animal fodder. The small beans inside the black runner-bean-like pod are used to make gum, photographic film and a variety of other items. The tree itself has very hard wood and is used for cartwheel hubs and agricultural tools. Altogether it is a valuable tree, earning its description as 'black gold'. The pods when ripe have a distinctive smell, strong and sickly like squashed black beetle, and the Cypriots make a kind of black treacle from them. The smell was evidently enough to deter fleas, for on St John's Day, 18 July, the peasants would roast carobs and jump over the fire singing: 'Fleas, fleas, depart, for the old man is coming with his club'. Carobs are also sometimes known as 'St John's bread'. Whatever the true benefits of the carob, they almost certainly do not include the fanciful claims of the leaflet that accompanies the jars of carob powder on sale in Lefkoşa and elsewhere. Amongst these are enhanced sexual performance and appetite, 'natural doping', prevention of arrhythmia and lung cancer – though disappointingly in the latter's case, only 'up to 90%'.

word kantara is Arabic for arch, and accurately describes the sheer rock walls on which the castle is built, making it accessible only from the east. Here, the entrance is guarded by twin towers, and steps climb up to the iron gate that leads into the castle enclosure.

Inside, the castle is surprisingly elusive, as the ground plan had to adapt to the rocky contours. Locally the castle was referred to as the House of 101 Rooms (as was St Hilarion), and the popular Muslim belief was that anyone who entered the 101st room would suddenly find themselves in paradise and unable to go back through the door. Unlike its sister castles, it is not divided into upper and lower wards, but the summit of the mountain rising up in the centre means that the western half of the castle is not visible at all as you enter. Having clambered up to the summit, you will discover paths leading off through the trees and undergrowth to reach a group of three chambers, the **living quarters**, one of which has an emergency exit from the castle. Underneath are two large cisterns still full of water.

Returning along the southern wall, the first building you reach is a medieval **latrine**, barely visible now. The huge **northeast tower**, the highest constructed point, is accessible at its lower level, which is well preserved and with a fine row of arrow slits in its thick, windowless walls. The upper floor of the tower is not accessible.

From the ruined chamber at the very summit, messages were transmitted using a system of flares after dark, first to Buffavento, and thence to St Hilarion. At its solitary Gothic window, villagers claim to see a queen sitting gazing out towards her lost country. She has been there, they say, for the last 500 years, since the castle was abandoned. For 50-odd years in the 19th century, she shared the castle with a hermit called Simeon. The orientation of the castle is towards Gazimağusa, an hour's horseride away, and when the Genoese had seized Gazimağusa from the Lusignans in the 14th century, Kantara was a refuge for many a prisoner who escaped. The Lusignan lords lived in true feudal style on the island, and on fleeing Palestine brought with them their semi-oriental ways and habits. With the fall of Acre in 1291, the last Crusader foothold in the Holy Land was lost, but the knights had grown accustomed to their Eastern titles and luxurious lifestyles. Here in the grand quarters of their castles, princes of Antioch, Tyre and Galilee, and counts of Jaffa, Beirut and Caesaria, pursued the pleasures of the chase, hunting mouflon (mountain goats) with tame leopards. The manes and tails of the horses were dyed red with exotic henna, as were the tails of the hunting hounds. One count of Jaffa had more than 500 hounds, with a servant tending to each pair.

Also somewhere within this enclosure, 13 Greek monks were sentenced to death by the Lusignan Crusaders who established the Catholic Church as the official church of the island. The Greek Orthodox bishops were therefore forced to comply with Catholic beliefs, and when the outspoken ones did not, they were, as a contemporary historian described it, 'condemned to be tied by the feet to the tails of horses and mules, and thus dragged over the rough stones in the market place, or the river bed, until the flesh was torn from their bones, and then burnt'.

It is from this time that most of the remoter mountain monasteries date, built far away in the mountains, where the devoted could pursue their faith safe from Catholic interference and persecution.

Alternative return route If you're based at Boğaz, a pleasant, winding drive of 35 minutes brings you out, via the villages of Turnalar and Yarköy, to the coast at Boğaztepe. If you are at Gazimağusa or Salamis, the more direct route is via Ardahan and İskele.

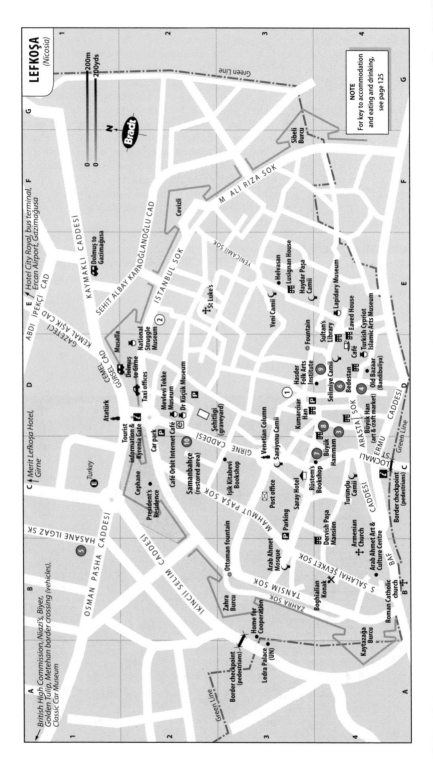

LEFKOŞA
(Nicosia)

Green Line

0   200m
0   200yds

N

Bradt

NOTE
For key to accommodation and eating and drinking, see page 125

British High Commission, Niazi's, Biyer, Golden Tulip, Metehan border crossing (vehicles), Classic Car Museum

Merit Lefkoşa Hotel, Girne

Hotel City Royal, bus terminal, Ercan Airport, Gazimağusa

ABDI IPEKCI CAD
KEMAL AŞIK CAD
GAZETECI CAD
GÜRSEL CAD
CEMEL CAD
KAYMAKLI CADDESİ
SEHIT ALBAY KARAOGLANOGLU CAD
OSMAN PASHA CADDESI
HASANE ILGAZ SK
İKINCILI SELIM CADDESİ
ISTANBUL SOK
M ALI RIZA SOK
YENICAMII SOK
GIRNE CADDESİ
MAHMUT PAŞA SOK
ZAHRA SOK
TANSIM SOK
S SALAHAI ŞEVKET SOK
ARASTA SOK
CADDESİ
CADDESI
BAF

Dolmuş to Gazimağusa
Dolmuş to Girne

Turkey

Sibeli Burcu

Cevizli

St Luke's

Helvasan
Lusignan House
Haydar Paşa Camii
Lapidary Museum
Eaved House
Turkish Cypriot Islamic Arts Museum

Yeni Camii
Fountain
Sultan's Library
Café

National Struggle Museum
Musalla

Atatürk
Taxi offices
Mevlevi Tekke Museum
Dr Küçük Museum
Car park

Hasder Folk Arts Institute
Selimiye Camii
Bedestan
Old Bazaar (Bandibuliya)

Tourist information & Kyrenia Gate
Cephane
President's Residence

Café Orbit Internet Café

Samanbahçe (restored area)

Işik Kitabevi Bookshop

Sehitligi (graveyard)

Venetian Column
Sarayonu Camii
Kumarciar Han
Büyük Han (art & craft market)

Rüstem's Bookshop
Büyük Hammam

Saray Hotel
Post office

Parking

Turunçlu Camii

Ottoman fountain

Dervish Paşa Mansion
Armenian Church

Arab Ahmet Mosque
Arab Ahmet Art & Culture Centre

Zahra Burcu
Boghialian Konak
Roman Catholic church
Kaytazağa Burcu

Border checkpoint (pedestrians)
Home for Cooperation
Ledra Palace (UN)

Green Line

Border checkpoint (pedestrians)

LOKMACI
ERMU ST

Green Line

Border checkpoint (pedestrians)

1 2 3 4 5 6 7 8 9 10

4

Lefkoşa (Nicosia)

In the featureless Mesaoria Plain that surrounds Lefkoşa, there is little to detain the visitor. Lefkoşa itself is the worthwhile destination, with a fascinating collection of Crusader Gothic and Turkish Ottoman monuments set within the old Venetian fortifications. Selimiye Camii and the cluster of half-a-dozen or so buildings in this immediate area form the heart of old Lefkoşa. They were nearly all originally Christian Crusader structures, converted by the Ottomans in the 16th century to Muslim or secular functions. Lefkoşa was the Gothic capital of the Lusignan kings, and they graced it with magnificent palaces, churches and gardens. Much was destroyed in pillaging through the centuries by Venetians, Genoese, Egyptians and Turks, and earthquakes helped wreak the final havoc.

The end result, with its medley of Christian and Muslim ideas, cathedrals turned into mosques, Greek foundations topped by Turkish roofs, churches reworked as public baths and archbishops' palaces reincarnated as municipal offices, is what makes Lefkoşa memorable today.

Anyone who is attracted by all things Turkish should spend a day in Lefkoşa. Here, within the walls of the old city, are the island's major Ottoman monuments, many of them either still in use or renovated (or being renovated) as museums. Apart from the renovated buildings, the town has a kind of shabby charm. If you poke around the backstreets, particularly on a Sunday, the peace will be gently interrupted only by the sound of a caged bird, the chatter of children or an animated conversation between persons unseen behind shuttered windows. On other days, you may stumble across a carpenter, a tailor or other craftsman, plying their trade as if caught in a time gone by. Lefkoşa is divided into Greek and Turkish sectors by the euphemistically named 'Green Line', erected by the UN, an ugly barrier built from barbed wire and corrugated iron, cutting across the heart of the old walled city. (The Green Line gets its name from the fact that it was originally drawn on a map in green ink by a British army officer.) The sight of streets barricaded and houses bisected has a certain eerie fascination and few will visit Lefkoşa without taking a look at the Green Line. Of course, it's now possible to cross over to the south, and those who do so will be struck by the difference. Where Turkish Lefkoşa retains an old-world charm and sense of individuality, Greek Nicosia has rapidly pursued the EU dream, with a liberal sprinkling of international coffee shops, high-street boutiques and fast-food outlets providing every tourist with a home-from-home experience. But like all facelifts, the effect is only skin deep – the heart of Greek Nicosia has long since relocated from inside the walls to the new high-rise suburbs of the commercial city.

GETTING THERE AND AROUND

On the main highway, funded by the Saudi Arabians, it takes a mere 20 minutes from Girne to Lefkoşa, and many people who work in Lefkoşa commute with ease in half an hour from Girne. Gazimağusa is a 50-minute drive away. It is therefore possible, especially from a Girne base, to visit the major monuments of Lefkoşa in half a day, but it will be more leisurely and enjoyable to spend a whole day there. What's more, history fans may decide to stay overnight and take two days to absorb the museums and monuments in a more relaxed manner.

Dolmuş run regularly to Lefkoşa from the other major towns in North Cyprus. Currently, it will cost you only TL5 to or from Girne. Dolmuş set out from the Belediye Meydani in Girne (the central roundabout with the sculpture of the doves in the middle) and drop passengers off just outside the Kyrenia Gate, also the pick-up point for your return trip. From Lefkoşa to Güzelyurt/Gazimağusa, the *dolmuş* operate from the main bus terminal between the hours of 06.30 and 19.00, with singles costing TL10 and TL9 respectively. Services are roughly every 30 minutes, or hourly on Sundays. For Gazimağusa only, you can also get the bus at an alternative terminal, only 2 minutes' walk from Kyrenia Gate. It's unlikely that you'll need a **taxi** within the city walls, but for trips further afield, there are a couple of booking offices just to the left as you enter town through the Kyrenia Gate. One of these is NATO Taxis (\ *227 15 55*) who, despite the name, have no known endorsement from the intergovernmental military alliance, but who do speak a little English and quote around TL65 for a journey to Girne or to Ercan Airport.

Traffic around Lefkoşa can be heavy, but **driving** into town is still straightforward. From Girne, head directly over the first roundabout with the Gazimağusa road and initially follow the signs for Ledra Palace. The road continues straight on and passes through the suburb of Ortaköy before eventually branching left and widening to four lanes – position yourself in the right-hand of the four lanes, branch right and you'll arrive at the Kyrenia Gate on your left. Passing through the gate there are several options for parking, all signposted. You can take a right at the roundabout once you've passed the gate, then the first left, where you'll find a car park (TL10 all day). If you need to park nearer to the centre, continue straight ahead at the roundabout towards the Venetian column, bear left just after the column and then right towards the Kumarcılar Han. As you arrive, an 'Oto Park' sign will point the final few metres. The car park behind the Han currently charges a whopping TL30 for 24 hours. Although locals seemingly park anywhere – including on pavements – parking wardens do operate and fines cost TL150.

It is easy to **walk** around within the walled part of Lefkoşa, and the main attractions are closely packed together. Distances are small and the twin minarets of the Selimiye Camii, always rising above the rooftops, act as dependable homing beacons. The major monuments are clustered around the Selimiye, so a leisurely circuit of them need take no more than 3 or 4 hours (though aficionados of history will need longer). Take heed that, depending on which map you use, streets and places of interest may well have different names, which adds to the challenge of competent navigation. It is worth noting that Lefkoşa is blessed with the highest temperatures in the north, with humidity and its inland position making it a very uncomfortable place at midday in high summer.

WHERE TO STAY   *Map, page 124*

The choice of places to stay in Lefkoşa has increased in the last few years, but you're still far from being spoilt for choice. At least the options available to the visitor now extend from budget to top-end, but the choice within each of the categories is somewhat limited. The two luxury chain-hotels detailed below have all the benefits you would expect, but cater mainly to a business clientele. Both are located well outside the old city walls, though they are served by public transport during the day.

In addition to the below, the ugly but central **Saray Hotel** was yet again being restored at the time of writing. Its eighth-floor bar/restaurant is worth a visit for the great views, but its focus on casino – rather than hotel – clients casts doubt on its suitability for non-gambling visitors. Within the city walls, there are many pensions offering very cheap dormitory accommodation and rooms, though these are very basic and many are so dodgy that even those staying in them may advise you against checking in! But if you're feeling brave, look for the ubiquitous 'pansiyonu' signs.

🏠 **Golden Tulip** (142 rooms) ✆610 50 50; e info@goldentulipnicosia.com; www. goldentulipnicosia.com. A fairly new & tasteful hotel, spacious rooms, indoor & outdoor pools, spa, fitness centre, 2 restaurants, casino, free Wi-Fi throughout. **$$$$$**

🏠 **Merit Lefkoşa Hotel** (116 rooms) ✆600 55 00; e info@merithotels.com; www.merithotels. com. Indoor & outdoor swimming pools, spa, fitness centre, free Wi-Fi, 4 restaurants, with great views from the Ottoman one on the top floor. **$$$$$**

🏠 **Hotel City Royal** (80 rooms) ✆228 76 21; e info@city-royal.com; www.city-royal.com. Handy for the bus station, but a 10min walk from town. Popular with Turkish businessmen. Rooms are fine, though unexceptional. Rooftop sun terrace, indoor pool & spa, 3 restaurants, Wi-Fi throughout. **$$$**

🏠 **Swallow Boutique Hotel** (3 rooms) ✆223 44 66; m 0542 853 66 42; e info@swallowboutiquehotel.com; www. swallowboutiquehotel.com. A delightful old building, renovated by an architect. A few mins' walk from Kyrenia Gate. Rooms have AC & private bath, grouped round a peaceful inner courtyard. **$$**

🏠 **Aksaray Pansiyonu** (12 rooms) ✆228 46 48; e aksarayhotel@hotmail.com; www.aksaraypansiyon.com. A good-value budget/ backpacker option on Mecidiye Sokak in the heart of the old quarter. Genial English-speaking owner Ali Koç has run it for over 20 years. Not luxury, but all rooms have bathrooms, AC & free Wi-Fi. There's a great inner courtyard for alfresco b/fast, washing machines & endless satellite channels on the TV. You can borrow bikes & Ali can organise car hire. Family rooms are available. See ad, page 145. **$**

✗ WHERE TO EAT AND DRINK *Map, page 124*

Eating options are slowly expanding in Lefkoşa, but the choice will never match that in Girne. There are few options within the old city walls and at the time of writing, the **Boghialian Konak Restaurant** [124 B4], once one of the capital's finest, was still under renovation. Housed in a beautiful building on Victoria Street, if it ever reopens it is worth visiting for the building alone. If you are on a budget, there are a number of tiny *köfte* joints outside the rear entrance to the Büyük Han that will successfully fill the stomach for around TL10.

At times, it can seem that the town has gone to bed early, such is the lack of evening activity. For those seeking some more action, a 10-minute stroll down Osman Paşa Caddesi should satisfy. Here you'll find the district of Dereboyu, home to a cluster of stylish bars and restaurants. Few of these give even a cursory nod to Cypriot or Turkish culture, the exceptions being Biyer and the branch of the ever-reliable Niazi's. But if you need a burger, pizza, European-style coffee, ice-cream or just to feel younger or more western, then this should be your chosen destination in the capital. There's even an Irish bar, of sorts.

✗ **Ada Mutfaği** ✆227 86 84. One of the eateries clustered around the Büyük Han's main entrance, serving a good range of Cypriot favourites at good prices & with shade from the sun. *TL16*

✗ **Bibliotheque** ✆444 33 00; m 0533 833 71 65. Brand new for 2014, a welcome addition to the rather quiet Old Town evening scene. Huge investment has seen a (largely) tasteful renovation, with a roof terrace to enjoy. International cuisine with sushi, steaks, pizzas, pasta, burgers & more. Quality is good, atmosphere is relaxed, though it transforms into a disco after 23.00 on Wed, Fri & Sat & stays open till 03.00. Be aware that some prices here are given in euros. *TL28*

✗ **Biyer** ✆229 17 50. In Dereboyu, this traditional restaurant has served up good-value *meze* for over a decade. It has a separate fish menu, too. Its newer, adjacent café is cheaper, targeted at the young crowd & has more varied fare, such as salads & burgers, & also has live pop/rock music Fri & Sat, while the main restaurant enjoys more traditional vibes. *TL25*

✗ **Nenemin Evi** ✆227 89 19. ⊕ 08.00–05.00 Mon–Sat. Translates as 'My Grandmother's House', & though the setting is hardly traditional, the daily-changing menu serves up some great Cypriot dishes. Try the *molohiya*. Little English is spoken. *TL20*

✖ **Niazi's** ☎228 88 55. 10 mins' walk from the Old Town on Osman Paşa Caddesi, an outlet of the dependable chain, which has branches in Girne & Gazimağusa. Great kebabs & more expensive steak/fish dishes. *TL25*

✖ **Old Mosaic** ▭ 0533 873 76 35. Quirky & characterful, set in a restored house that lay empty for 35 years. Owners Işmail & Dilek also run the antiques shop opposite, so this courtyard restaurant is full of interesting artefacts. Standard kebab fare, plus vegetarian options. Across from the main entrance to the Selimiye Camii. *TL28*

✖ **Rüstem's** ☎228 35 06; ▭ 0533 875 42 42; ⏲ lunchtimes only. Above the bookshop of the same name, excellent fresh & tasty Cypriot fare cooked by the owner's wife. Popular with businessmen, a daily-changing menu keeps things interesting. Coffee & dessert included, so good value. High-ceilinged dining room, packed bookcases & hands-on management add to the already pleasant experience. *TL20*

✖ **Sabir Restaurant** ☎227 34 70; ⏲ daytime only, closed Sun. Ornate décor suggests fine dining. Think again: there's no menu, only *şiş köfte* on offer & alcohol is strictly on request. Still, it's been here since 1955, so they're doing something right. To find it, turn right out of the Büyük Han's main entrance. *TL15*

✖ **Sabor** ☎228 83 22. Great location next to the Selimiye Camii. Classy food featuring Spanish, Italian, Japanese, steaks, salads & more. Add in a relaxed ambience, tasteful Latino music & outside tables frequented by the beautiful people. Free Wi-Fi. *TL25*

✖ **Sedirhan Restaurant** ☎228 14 39; ⏲ daily, hours vary according to season. A great location, acceptable food. Light refreshments or reasonably priced salads & kebabs in the relaxing oasis of the Büyük Han's courtyard. *TL20*

▭ **Simit Dünyasi** ☎229 01 50. On the main street near the Kyrenia Gate. Part of a reliable chain, with an array of breads, pastries & cakes, as well as a variety of coffees, it's the place for a tasty snack (rather than a meal) while sightseeing. *TL14*

SHOPPING No serial shopper should descend on town with huge expectation. Nevertheless, there are opportunities to pick up some genuine local handicrafts at the **Büyuk Han** [124 D4], **Old Bazaar (Bandibuliya)** [124 D4] and **Hasder Folk Arts Institute** [124 D4]. The small shops on **Arasta Sokak**, near the Locmaci Street crossing, are stuffed with cheap clothes and fake designer trinkets. For anything modern and chic, shoppers should head down Osman Pasha Caddesi into the **Dereboyu** district, where some familiar (and genuine) household names can be found. On Sundays, the open space in front of the bus terminal is turned into a **market**, colourful and lively by North Cypriot standards. It is firmly focused towards local customers, with fruit and veg and clothing, but a visit makes for a pleasant interruption to what is otherwise Lefkoşa's sleepiest day of the week.

WHAT TO SEE AND DO

THE CITY WALLS The modern suburbs offer little to the visitor besides standard shopping, but as you approach the centre from the north, the one-way system does a wide loop and sweeps around to bring you in through the fine medieval walls at the Girne Gate, which now stands isolated like a traffic island. It looks more like a bewildered little chapel than a major gateway, as cars and trucks pass by either side of it, through the two breaches in the walls made by the British in the 1930s. An Arabic inscription above the gate reads:

> O Muhammad, give these tidings to the Faithful; Victory is from God and triumph is very near. O opener of doors, open for us the best of doors.

In 1878, when the British annexed the island of Cyprus, it was here that the Turkish doorkeeper permitted the British officers to enter the capital. This colourful character, Ali the Cock, as he was known, also made history by living to the age of 121. Today, the gate has found a new purpose as the home of the city's **tourist office** (⊕ *08.00–17.00 Mon–Fri, 09.00–16.00 Sat–Sun, although this is not a certainty*). A newly produced map and directions are given freely. On Mondays, Wednesdays and Fridays, an English-speaking guide waits here at 10.00 to escort you, free of charge, around Lefkoşa's main attractions. The service will greatly enhance any visit, and surely deserves a decent gratuity.

Between the gate and the **Atatürk statue** are a few huge **iron cannons**, several more of which can be found displayed in public gardens or on the ramparts. They were British, made in about 1790 at the Woolwich Arsenal, and were used in the Napoleonic wars in Egypt, later finding their way here after being acquired by the Turks.

Lefkoşa has been a walled city since medieval times, but the walls in their current manifestation are the work of the 16th-century Venetians, who were intent on bolstering Cyprus in its role as a major outpost in the Mediterranean to secure their trade routes. The medieval Crusader walls before then had been tall with high towers to defend against catapults and arrows, but with the coming of gunpowder, the priority in wall design was to make maximum use of cannons. Hence the **Venetian walls** are not high but colossally thick, to allow cannons to be rolled up the ramparts. The population in Venetian times had shrunk, and the circumference of the Venetian walls shrank with it from 5km to 3km. Historical records show that the demolition this entailed meant that many Gothic buildings were razed and some 80 Crusader churches lost.

The wide **moat** area below the walls was never intended for water, but rather as open space where, unprotected, the enemy soldiers could be fired at as they approached. In times of peace, the town's dung and rubbish was tossed over the walls as natural fertiliser and good yields of corn were obtained. Today, these open spaces serve well as football grounds or public parks, or occasionally, alas, as dumping grounds. From the air or using Google Maps they still define the outline of Lefkoşa's walls very clearly. At regular intervals around the circumference of the walls are 11 huge bastions, six of them now in the Turkish sector, five in the Greek. Of the three fortified gates, the **Famagusta Gate** and the **Paphos Gate**, now in the southern, Greek sector, were always larger than the northern **Girne Gate**, reflecting the relative importance of the sizes of the ports in Venetian times.

The Venetians, belying the beauty and grace of their architecture, were nevertheless unsympathetic rulers. Having built their magnificent fortifications, they proceeded to bleed the islanders of every last drop of revenue, even resorting to such ruses as selling the serfs their own freedom. A Christian abbot at the time spoke for the rueful islanders when he wailed, 'We have escaped from the grasp of the dog [the Lusignan king] to fall into that of the lion [the Venetian lion of St Mark].' The Venetians acquired the island through diplomatic trickery, manoeuvring to have the Lusignan James II marry the daughter of a Venetian patrician, Catherine Cornaro. Her husband and later her son were then poisoned, leaving the hapless queen nominally in charge of the island. In 1489 she was persuaded to retire to Asolo and hand the island over to the Venetian Republic. The Venetian nobles then ruled for the next hundred years, until they lost the island to the Turks in 1571.

Unless you are feeling energetic, it is best to drive a quick circuit of the walls on the internal ring road. Forking east (left) on entering the Girne Gate, you can follow the northern perimeter and pass some older-style houses before the road ends at the slogans of the Green Line barricading the street ahead and bisecting the Flatro Bastion.

THE NICOSIA TRAIL In a city so brutally divided by the Green Line, anyone could be forgiven for thinking that the 'Blue Line' was some kind of bad joke. It's not. Somebody thought it was a good idea to paint an incongruous blue line around the streets of Lefkoşa to direct tourists from one sight to the next. Though the blue paint has flaked off in many places, the 4.5km Nicosia Trail starts and finishes at the Girne Gate and takes 1–2 hours at a gentle stroll, not allowing for time spent at sights *en route*. Truthfully, the old city isn't big enough to warrant a guided path, and in any case it's often more rewarding to find places for yourself. Having said that, if you should get lost you can always follow the line and eventually you'll arrive at somewhere you recognise, and it could be useful if you're short of time. In a few years, the blue line will have disappeared; the Green Line, sadly, is likely to outlast it.

OLD NICOSIA CYCLING TOUR If walking isn't your thing, you could take to two wheels and enjoy a city tour that crosses the divide, picking out the highlights from north and south Lefkoşa. Starting at the Home for Cooperation, inside the buffer zone at the Ledra Palace crossing, the 3-hour tour is gentle and suitable for all. Prices are reasonable and bikes can be hired. You will need your passport or ID card. Contact Constantinos in advance for more details (m *357 995 85497;* e *armoconst@hotmail.com*).

MARTYRS' MUSEUM (NATIONAL STRUGGLE MUSEUM) [124 D2] (🕐 *08.00–15.30 Mon–Fri only; free admission; as it's firmly within a military camp, ask the helpful guards at the entrance for permission to enter, & be prepared to leave some form of photo ID & any mobile phones/cameras with them*) From the Girne Gate, follow the inside of the walls a few hundred metres to your left (east), to find the museum, the entrance to which is towards the far end of the whitewashed military camp building. It's dedicated to the battles of 1974 and the formation of North Cyprus. Many of the information labels have been translated into English to accompany exhibits that consist mainly of rifles, oil paintings and gruesome photos. A visit won't detain you for long.

MEVLEVI TEKKE MUSEUM [124 D2] (🕐 *08.00–15.30 Mon–Wed & Fri, 08.00–13.00 & 14.00–17.00 Thu; TL7/5 adult/student*) Returning and continuing towards the heart of the city along the main road, you soon come to the **Monastery of the Whirling Dervishes** or Mevlevi Tekke Museum, dedicated to the mystic order of Islam founded by Mevlana, a Persian-Turkish poet of the 13th century. It is the only monastery of its kind on the island, and your eye will be caught by its low-rise domes immediately to your left after the roundabout just inside the Girne Gate. Street parking outside is supposedly reserved for visitors to the museum.

The early 17th-century building was in use as the dervishes' monastery until the 1920s, when Atatürk banned them along with other monastic orders in his determination to make Turkey a secular state. The Turkish Cypriots followed Atatürk's policy and closed the tekke. The remaining dervishes now have their headquarters in Aleppo, Syria. Though much of the original complex was destroyed, the meeting room and part of the shrine were restored in 1963 and reopened as a museum of dervish paraphernalia.

Entering through the arch from Girne Caddesi, you pass through a courtyard flanked by headstones leaning against the whitewashed walls. The ticket booth is straight ahead; opposite is the entrance to the **meeting room**. The wooden floor is the original one on which the dervishes danced, and at one end stairs lead up to the charming wooden gallery where the long-robed musicians played their eerie trance-inducing music, a piped version of which is usually playing in the background when you visit, adding some much-needed atmosphere to the display. (If not, ask for it to be switched on!) H V Morton described the scene thus:

> The dancers are dressed in long, high-waisted, pleated gowns that fall to the ground. They wear tall brown felt cones on their heads. Each one, as he begins to turn, stretches his right arm straight up, the palm held upwards to the roof, while the left arm is held stiffly down with the palm towards the earth. The head is slightly inclined to the right shoulder ... The dance symbolises the revolution of the spheres, and the hands symbolise the reception of a blessing from above, and its dispensation to the earth below.

On the walls you'll find a useful rundown of the history and beliefs of the order. In one corner are the kitchen and dining area, while leading off from another is the galleried **mausoleum** of the 16 tombs of the Mevlevi sheikhs, row upon row, as if in mirrors endlessly duplicated. Only six of these tombs have been positively identified. Above them are the domes so conspicuous from the street.

GIRNE CADDESI AND THE SARAY HOTEL Retracing your steps to the main street, immediately on the left is the building of the **Dr Küçük Müzesi** [124 B2], a small museum dedicated to the memory of Fazıl Küçük, one of the most prominent activists ever to champion the cause of the Turkish Cypriot people. In particular, Dr Küçük stressed the importance of Turkey's association with North Cyprus, without which, he proclaimed, the island would never be able to live in peace. He became the first vice-president of Cyprus in 1959. The museum was closed throughout 2014, but plans for renovation were in place and it should be receiving visitors by late 2015.

On display in a shabby room is a hotchpotch collection of medals, photographs, paintings, swords and general artefacts of little significance to the casual observer. Possibly of more interest will be the English information that the friendly curator will happily provide if you ask, which explains in detail the life and times of Dr Küçük. Perhaps most significant of all is his statement that adorns the front of the leaflet: 'Turkish Cypriots! Turkey will never abandon you to foreign hands ... Be sure that you are going to live in this country under your own flag for eternity and look towards tomorrow with hope ...' Given the underlying tension between Turkey and North Cyprus, evidenced by street demonstrations as recently as 2011 (page 17), it will be interesting to see whether the relationship remains so unequivocal.

Continuing south along the bustling main street, down the small street to your left, behind the Mevlevi Museum, is the **Şehitligi**, the mass grave of the martyrs of Turkish Cyprus. (Actually, most of the bodies have been removed from this site, though according to the sign 160 are still interred here.) The bodies are of those who perished fighting the Greeks in 1963 and 1974. It's a peaceful spot away from the bustle of the main drag, but is of little interest otherwise.

Returning to Girne Caddesi, 20m further south on the opposite side of the street you can see a small, domed, stone water cistern in the heart of the **Samanbahçe district**, down the alley beside the Simit Dünyasi café. The district is actually one huge social housing project, funded largely by the local mosque, with low rent for the inhabitants. In the middle of its first intersection is a water fountain, now unused, which used to be policed – so it is said – by two hefty women happy to accept bribes from queue jumpers. As some of the bribes were cake, this may explain their heftiness.

Following the blue line from the fountain, you come to Polis Sokak. A few metres to the right is a well-stocked bookshop with English-language titles, **Işik Kitabevi** [124 C3] (*Polis Sokak 14;* 227 74 43; *www.isikkitabevi.net*), which is well worth a visit. Retracing your steps to follow the blue line, at the end of Polis Sokak you soon reach the small **Atatürk Square**, recognisable by its solitary grey granite column, probably carried from Salamis. In Venetian times it carried a lion of St Mark, but the Turks overturned it in the conquest of the island. The British replaced the lion with a copper globe, which is still perched on top. Around the square are the pleasant government offices, including the law courts, built by the British colonial rulers from sand-coloured limestone blocks, with elegant arcades and verandas.

Straight on beyond the square you will see the tall Saray Hotel, an ugly 1960s block whose saving grace is a roof terrace on the eighth floor, that provides excellent views over all Lefkoşa. The hotel is frequently closed for renovation, but it's worth taking the time to go up to the terrace for a drink, as this is the closest you will come to a detailed aerial view of the town.

From the rooftop, you'll be struck by the situation of Lefkoşa on the flat expanse of the Mesaoria Plain. The only dramatic topography is where the plain collides with the jagged ridge of the Kyrenia Mountains, forming the picturesque northern backdrop. Somewhat less picturesque is the colossal slogan gouged out of the closest south-facing hillside by the military: Ne Mutlu Türküm Diyene, 'How happy is he who can say he is a Turk'. The slogan is said to be an adage of Atatürk, who suggested that a true Turk was anyone living within the territory of Turkey, irrespective of ancestry or ethnicity. As such, the military are seen to be preserving the memory of Atatürk through such a display of patriotism. However, as with all stories in Cyprus there are two sides to the coin. Over a period of weeks, and in the dead of night, it is claimed that the Turks secretly created the slogan by painting rocks, which they subsequently replaced, face down, before sunrise. Can it be mere coincidence that, on the eve of Greek National Day, scores of troops scaled the hillside to invert the stones and reveal, clear to see for all Greek Cypriots in Nicosia, such a defiant and provocative message? (Just to highlight the divide further, the hillside lights up the outline of the national flag at night, ensuring that Greek Cypriots have a good eyeful.)

The next thing to strike you from this aerial vantage point is the difference between the Greek and Turkish sectors. To the south, in the area beyond the old walled town, is a distant sea of high-rise blocks, testifying to the relative apparent prosperity and development of the Greek sector; new buildings outside the walls in the Turkish sector are much more modest and thinly spread. To the west (right) as you stand with your back to the twin minarets of the Selimiye Camii, is a distinctive, long, four-storeyed building with white-framed window arches, the famous **Ledra Palace Hotel** [124 A3], now occupied by UN forces and a major pedestrian crossing point between the Turkish and Greek sectors. Ledra was the name of the original ancient settlement on which Lefkoşa now stands.

Just behind the Saray Hotel is the **Sarayonu Camii** [124 C3], the most centrally located mosque in Lefkoşa. Dating back to the Byzantine period, the mosque was converted from its original use as a Latin church, and restored to a considerable extent in 1902.

If you walk south from the Saray Hotel, you can cross the street to **Rüstem's Bookshop** (Rüstem Kitabevi) [124 C4], a well-stocked bookshop and the oldest in Lefkoşa. It's a good place to grab an English-language title and has coffee, a pleasant garden area, free Wi-Fi and an excellent lunchtime restaurant (page 129).

BÜYÜK HAMMAM [124 C4] (m *0548 830 08 81; www.grandturkishhamam.com;* ⊕ *opening times on website; men-only, women-only & mixed sessions, prices vary from TL35 for bathing only to TL100 to include an exuberant massage*) Recently renovated, this is a lovely building. Forking left immediately after the bookshop, you walk down a narrow street, on the right-hand side of which, after less than 100m, you will see the Büyük Hammam (Great Baths), its entrance sunk well below pavement level. This was the level of the street in the 14th century, and the elaborate entrance portal carved in stone is now all that survives of the church of St George of the Latins, the original incarnation of this building before the Ottomans converted it to a Turkish bath. The sunken level means that the carving on the entrance arch presents itself for a close inspection of its intriguing mix of Gothic, Italianate and Muslim elements.

In 1989 these baths were reopened as functioning establishments, the government having rented the premises to private individuals to run, and, following yet another recent further renovation, they are once again being used by locals and tourists. The minimum time needed for the whole process of heating up the body and allowing it to sweat freely in the hot room is about an hour. Once this stage has been reached you can either give yourself a self-service wash, using the camel-hair glove provided, or prostrate yourself on a stone slab for massage and the removal of several top layers of dirt and skin by the vigorous glove-rubbing of the masseur or masseuse.

In the large domed room you enter from the street, a huge nail high above floor level marks the height reached by the 1330 flood of the River Pedieos, in which 3,000 people drowned. There is another *hammam* in the town centre, opposite the Turunçlu Camii. It is male-only, cheaper and more traditional, but lacks the opulence of its rival.

KUMARCILAR HAN [124 D4] Continuing past the Büyük Hammam, you arrive after some 50m at a little square, on the far side of which is the battered and unkempt Kumarcılar Han, or Gamblers' Inn, built around 1600. Like all caravanserais, the entrance used to lead into an open interior courtyard, where the merchants would gather with their donkeys or camels, having arrived bearing their goods for sale. Inside, all the services they required were on hand: not only accommodation, in the upper rooms of the arcaded courtyard, but also stabling for the animals below, along with food and refreshments, and blacksmiths and leatherworkers for repairs. You can still view the courtyard, now overgrown, through the grille in the front door. The building was under renovation at the time of writing. A proposal to turn it into a casino was thankfully rejected, though its intended purpose once the current renovation is complete remains unclear: some say 'boutique hotel', others that it will become a Büyük Han Number Two, full of cafés and shops.

BÜYÜK HAN [124 D4] (⊕ 08.00–21.00 Mon, 08.00–midnight Tue–Fri & 08.00– 16.00 Sat; ⊕ opening hours are variable & may shorten in winter) A few steps further down the street, away from the front door of the Kumarcılar Han, is the entrance to the Büyük Han (Great Inn), a *khan* that has been fully restored and is looking splendid because of it. This, the largest of the khans on the island, was built by the Ottomans in 1572, the year after they seized Cyprus from the Venetians. It was built on the orders of Mustafa Paşa, the first Ottoman governor general of the island. From the outside, the high windows of the downstairs rooms, even though they were only stables, lend a defensive feel to the building, and indeed their role was partly one of protection for the merchants and their goods from brigands and thieves. The British were not slow to see its possibilities, and used it as Lefkoşa's Central Prison in colonial times until 1893.

In the centre of the open courtyard is an octagonal **miniature mosque** with a fountain for pre-prayer ablutions. The other distinctive feature of the khan is the tall **chimneys**, topped with metal pointed cones, as each of the 68 upstairs rooms

THE LAST PUPPETEER?   *Murray Stewart*

Mehmet Ertuğ couldn't find a suitable apprentice. As the last shadow puppeteer in North Cyprus, that's a shame, as it could mean his admirable art has already faced the final curtain on the island.

Not that there *are* any curtains, for Mehmet is a practitioner of *karagöz* or shadow theatre. Dating back to time immemorial, this art was introduced to Cyprus in the 16th century by the Turks. Mehmet's puppets are beautifully made from camel skin and treated with a chemical to make them transparent. Their brightly coloured shadows are then projected on to a white screen, illuminated by a bright light.

Many of the stories have been scripted by Mehmet himself. They have set characters, based around conflict between Karagöz, the commoner, and Hacivat, the educated and slightly pompous scholarly gentleman. The performance is composed of a prologue, a dialogue, a main play and a short epilogue, and the stories are lightened with a variety of songs and humour. The use of tambourines, bells and reed pipes, together with a variety of voices, adds to the fun.

Mehmet remembers a pre-television era when itinerant puppeteers would visit the village of his childhood to enthral the children. Now, however, he believes he is the only one left, and his attempts to find a successor have proved to be in vain.

'A young man will turn up on a Friday and expect to do my Saturday show!' he says, bemoaning the unreasonable expectations and impatience of youth. His tiny theatre is on the first floor of the Büyük Han and is set out with around 50 seats. But in 2014, Mehmet fell ill and had an operation. Before his hospital treatment, he performed on Saturday mornings to an audience of enraptured children. Now, he intends to return just to show some DVDs of his art. His live performances are perhaps merely a remnant of a bygone era, sadly gone forever. Unless, of course, this magical man makes a miraculous recovery or can conjure up that elusive apprentice.

had an open fire for the merchants to keep warm at night. Lefkoşa, pitilessly hot in summer, exposed as it is to the extremes of the plain, is also fiendishly cold in winter with icy winds. Today, the khan has been resurrected as a thriving **arts centre**, a superb collection of galleries, workshops and curios. Until 2014, you could even see a traditional show of Turkish Cypriot shadow theatre (see box above), though it remains to be seen whether the puppeteer recovers from illness to continue his art. With a couple of pleasant courtyard cafés, it's the ideal spot to pick up a few tasteful souvenirs or just take a break from sightseeing. It is also illuminated at night.

THE BEDESTAN [124 D4] (⊕ *10.00–15.00 Mon–Fri, 10.00–13.00 Sat; TL3*) Turning right from the entrance of the Büyük Han, follow the narrow street south and then left, to see rising up before you the renovated façade of the Bedestan, originally a Gothic church of the 14th century. It was formerly two churches, and served as the Greek Orthodox cathedral during Venetian times. The Bedestan was converted by the Turks to serve as a grain store and clothes market (bedestan means covered market). Its interior has been tastefully restored, and is in use as a cultural centre, with details of the renovation project displayed around the walls.

Perhaps the Bedestan's most noteworthy feature is its **entrance portal**, elaborately carved. Especially fine are the gargoyles, their mouths grotesquely shaped to act as spouts for the rain gutters. The gargling noise of the water bubbling through their throats has given us our word 'to gargle'. The British in 1879 put forward a plan to convert the Bedestan into an Anglican church, but the Muslim community rejected this as it would have been provocatively close to their mosque. Now it houses a few old photos of Cyprus and some information boards about the building, the proportions of which remain the main attraction. There are also occasional performances of whirling dervishes. On the street corners near the Bedestan are a couple of simple kebab restaurants for those in need of nourishment.

TURKISH CYPRIOT ISLAMIC ARTS MUSEUM (KIBRIS TURK ISLAM ESERLER MÜZESI) [124 D4] (🕐 *10.00–15.00 Mon–Fri; TL7/5 adult/student*) Just behind the Bedestan, down the side of the mosque, is this newly opened, small museum. Most of the exhibits here, which include 17th-century carpets, calligraphy, clocks, candles and letters from Sultans, come from Turkey, but there are also contributions from Lebanon and France. Of particular interest are the Tombak-style candle bases. As these were gilded using poisonous mercury, the craftsman was effectively committing suicide by creating them. Needless to say, this form of manufacture is no longer undertaken! Information signs are not yet all in English, though this is a work in progress and the curator is a mine of additional information.

SELIMIYE CAMII/ST SOPHIA CATHEDRAL [124 D4] The Bedestan has a certain curiosity value; however, as you approach it from the Büyük Han you'll inevitably find your attention drawn away from the Bedestan to its more complete and magnificent neighbour, the Selimiye Camii, once upon a time the St Sophia Cathedral.

The best place from which to survey the outside of the cathedral is the simple, almost rustic **garden café**, residing in a fine old two-storeyed crenellated building with Gothic windows that was once the **Chapter House**, and reached by walking between the cathedral and the Bedestan. This quiet spot has a superb view of the cathedral's south wall with its flying buttresses, and gives you space to relax and appreciate the soft golden stone, harmonising with the background of the green cypress trees and the deep blue sky.

French craftsmen began work on the construction of the cathedral in 1209 and, thanks to the stability of its flying buttresses, it still stands today despite the earthquakes of the 15th, 16th and 18th centuries. The roof is flat, a concession to the geography and climate of the Orient, but a curiosity in a building that in all other respects resembles the great Gothic cathedrals of France.

The cathedral of St Sophia is, architecturally, the most important monument in Lefkoşa (Greek or Turkish), with its superb carving and sculpture in the **triple-portalled porch** and the colossal high **west window**. The twin towers were never completed, which meant that they were able to serve admirably as foundations for the two tall Ottoman minarets added by the Turks after 1571. In appearance these additions, labelled incongruous by purists, have been likened to candles with their snuffers in place.

Today, as it has done for more than the last 400 years, the cathedral serves as Cyprus's principal mosque, and the greatest celebrations of the two major Muslim festivals, Seker Bayramı and Kurban Bayramı (equivalents, if you like, of the Christian Christmas and Easter), are conducted here. Its name-change from Aya Sofya Camii took place only in 1954, when the mufti, the religious head of the Muslims of the island, renamed it the Selimiye Camii in honour of Selim II, the sultan in whose reign Cyprus was conquered by the Turks. Since 1959 the muezzin has been spared the climb up 170 steps to the minaret gallery every day, five times a day, to summon the faithful to prayer, by the introduction of an automatic recording played through a loudspeaker.

The mosque is open and can be visited anytime, though it is best to avoid the midday prayers on a Friday. During other daily prayer times you can visit but must keep silent. As in all mosques, shoes must be removed at the entrance. No special dress is required, as Turkish Cypriots take a much more relaxed view of bare heads and arms. Inside, the whitewashed interior seems stark, but the beauty of the proportions in the high-pillared nave is, if anything, enhanced by the absence of decoration.

Colour comes in the form of the carpets, predominantly reds and greens, none older than this century and all orientated towards Mecca. This direction is indicated by the highly colourful mihrab or prayer niche in the southern wall. The green wooden structure in the centre of the nave is the prayer platform where the prayer leader or imam stands during services, and the closed lattice gallery in the north transept is where the women, the few who come to the mosque, are penned. Unlike churches, where the bulk of the congregation tends to be female, worshippers in mosques are almost always men.

All Christian symbols and decorations were stripped from the cathedral, inside and out, when the Turks conquered Lefkoşa in 1570, save for one or two **tombstones** hidden underneath the carpets at the far (eastern) end of the cathedral (if you show an interest, a local will help to locate them for you). The Turkish commander, Mustafa Paşa, even had the graves opened and the bones scattered randomly. Paolo Paruta, a Venetian historian and statesman, recorded the events thus:

> He destroyed the altars and the images of the saints, and committed other bestial and cruel acts for which he was much blamed even by his own people.

Venetian historians wrote many such accounts, none of which enhanced the Turks' reputation for clemency. The Ottomans had already taken Syria, Egypt, Rhodes and Constantinople before they turned to Cyprus. With a huge fleet and over 100,000 men, they landed at Limassol, which they quickly pillaged and burnt, before moving on to Lefkoşa, the capital.

Hearing of the advance, the terrified government gathered the men, women and children within the walls. The Venetian governor at the time was one Nicolo Dandolo, 'a man whose ineptitude was so apparent, his supineness so glaring that it verged on treachery', as one historian wrote. The odds were hopeless. Within the walls were 76,000, of whom only 11,000 were capable of fighting. The strength of the walls was such, however, that the siege lasted 48 days before the city fell. In the marketplace of Lefkoşa a funeral pyre was made of the old, the infirm and any others who were unsuitable as slaves, and the acrid smoke filled the city for days. When the Ottoman ships returned to Constantinople, they were bulging with as many slaves and as much gold and jewels as they had been able to cram aboard. Over 20,000 Turkish soldiers were left behind to settle on the island, and more were subsequently encouraged to emigrate from the mainland.

The Turks retained control of the island for the next three centuries, and despite much mismanagement, along with nature's contributions of famine, drought and plague, there were some important developments. The Greeks were given more autonomy than they had ever enjoyed under any previous ruler. The feudal system imposed under the Lusignans and perpetuated under the Venetians, in which the

4

peasants were forced to work without pay for several days a week, was abolished. The everyday life of Cypriots was also made easier by such foundations as water fountains distributed all over the cities for the first time. The Turks rarely went in for building fancy, self-glorifying edifices like Roman triumphal arches or Egyptian pyramids. Their legacy lay in social welfare buildings, like aqueducts, mosques, tekkes, caravanserais, schools, libraries and baths.

No attempt was made to impose Islam on the native population. The Latin Catholic priests were expelled, and the Greek Orthodox Church was restored. The Greeks in fact tore down many Latin Gothic churches and the remainder were turned into mosques or stables. The Turks gave the Orthodox archbishop the responsibility for collecting taxes from both Greek and Turkish elements of the population, and in return the Church was itself exempt from any tax it collected in excess of the tribute specified. It was from this practice that the habit was established of the archbishop being regarded as the de facto head of the Greek Cypriots, a role which was frequently misused from then until Archbishop Makarios, under whom the Cypriot Church overreached itself for the last time. William Turner, a British diplomat staying on the island in 1815 wrote:

> In short, these Greek priests, everywhere the vilest miscreants in human nature, are worse than usual in Cyprus, from the power they possess. They strip the poor ignorant superstitious peasant of his last para, and when he is on his deathbed, make him leave his all to their convent, promising that masses shall be said for his soul.

Skirting round the cathedral from the northern side, you will notice to the right a small fountain set in a pointed arch. Many of these **Ottoman fountains** can be seen on street corners all over old Lefkoşa, and two of them are even still in use. The one on Tanzimat Street is especially fine.

THE SULTAN'S LIBRARY (*At the time of going to press, the library had been closed to the public for several years, with little apparent prospect of reopening*) Skirting the south wall of the cathedral between it and the Bedestan, past the garden café, you walk under the arch of one of the massive buttresses to reach the Sultan's Library situated at the back of the cathedral. It was named after Sultan Mahmoud, who had it built in the early 19th century.

When the library is accessible to visitors, the guardian opens up its tall doors that lead into the single square room covered from floor to ceiling with bookcases. The gilded **ceiling rail** under the little domed roof has inscriptions from a poem dedicated to the sultan. From the library, you can study the back end of the cathedral/mosque, with its elaborate **doorway**, now closed. In the mixture of elements so typical of Lefkoşa, Greek white marble columns flank the doorway, with pictures of green cypress trees either side of Arabic texts from the Koran.

Should it reopen and you are lucky enough to be visiting when the shelves are full, you'll find a collection of books in Turkish, Arabic and Persian. Unfortunately, the books often seem to be housed elsewhere. If you do manage a visit, you may wonder if it's worth the admission fee, although a visit to the **Lapidary Museum** is included in the price.

LAPIDARY MUSEUM [124 E4] (⏰ *08.00–15.30 Mon–Wed & Fri; 08.00–13.00 & 14.00–17.00 Thu; TL5/2 adult/student*) Directly behind the Sultan's Library, through a pair of large wooden doors, the Lapidary Museum can be found. The guardian used to open these doors on an ad hoc basis by means of an enormous key that stretched from his wrist to his elbow, but today the museum has more customary scheduled opening times and a regular guardian to take your money. Inside this Venetian nobleman's house, the English colonial rulers, with their love of antiquities, gathered together fragments of stonework from Lefkoşa's ancient palaces and churches.

The place is now little more than a storeroom for all manner of carved stone, covering all eras and styles, from gargoyles to headstones to Corinthian capitals, stacked one on top of the other against every wall. In the open courtyard is the most interesting exhibit, the mildly diverting Gothic **stone tracery window** in 'Gothic Flamboyant' style, flanked with a face on either side, which forms the centrepiece of the back courtyard. This is the last surviving relic of the Lusignan palace that once stood on the site of the government offices beside the Venetian column in Atatürk Square, near the Saray Hotel. The Turks adapted it for their use and called it the serail, or palace. A traveller in 1845 described it as 'a poor crumbling lumber chest, with hanging doors, rotten floors, and paper window panes', and so when it fell into total disuse, only the Crusader stonework remained intact. The museum will be of most interest to architecture enthusiasts.

HASDER FOLK ARTS INSTITUTE [124 D4] (⏰ *summer 08.00–12.30 & 13.30–17.00 Mon–Fri, 08.00–13.00 Sat; free admission*) A worthwhile detour on the way back towards the Selimiye Camii is the Hasder Folk Arts Institute. Initially supported by the UN Development Programme to preserve traditional Turkish Cypriot crafts, it is now independent of such funding. Inside you'll find a dedicated and talented group of locals turning out a range of high-quality goods. If you want a souvenir of your holiday, their handmade collection of carvings, costumes, art and basketwork provides a broad selection from which to choose, and you'll be making a fitting contribution to help conserve local culture. They also run classes teaching traditional skills.

EAVED HOUSE (SACAKLI EV) [124 D4] (⏰ *08.00–15.30 Mon–Wed & Fri, 08.00–13.00 & 14.00–17.00 Thu; free, though charges may apply during exhibitions*) The Eaved House lies just 10m to the south of the Sultan's Library. Its name comes from the large eaves that overhang the courtyard. The house has its origins sometime in the Middle Ages, though you'll have trouble recognising anything from that era in the construction today. Most of it seems to be typically late Ottoman in style, and indeed the '1932' inscription above the door gives a better clue as to the date of much of the building. Fully restored, the house is now a lovely centre for culture and the arts, with gallery space, conference facilities and outdoor seating areas. Regular exhibitions are held here, and at such times catering facilities might also be provided. The delightful curator, Gürsel Sezgin, is a fount of local knowledge and will happily chat about Lefkoşa's colourful history – or any other subject!

HAYDAR PASHA CAMII/ST CATHERINE'S CHURCH [124 E3] Returning to the Lapidary Museum, you can follow the road that runs to the north along its left-hand wall to bring you, after 100m or so, to the Haydar Paşa Camii, originally St Catherine's Church and instantly recognisable by the Gothic windows and the tall minaret. The stone is the same sandy limestone as that used in all these Gothic buildings, and the distinctive mellow colour helps it to stand out from the later surrounding buildings. After the cathedral, this is the most important of Lefkoşa's mosques/churches, unusual architecturally because of the many tall arcaded windows requiring extra buttresses to strengthen the walls. The style, dating back

Lefkoşa (Nicosia) WHAT TO SEE AND DO

4

to the 14th century, is another example of Gothic Flamboyant design. The building has at last undergone internal restoration,UNESCO funding for the project having been withdrawn post-1974, and now serves as a private art gallery, though with events few and far between. Unless there's an event in progress, it's closed (though, architecturally, the exterior is still interesting). At one stage it was used as a marriage registration office. Facing the front of the church, turn around and you will see a grand colonial edifice. This magnificent building houses the Ministry of Tourism, amongst other departments. It is not open to visit, but you might ponder why some of the grandest constructions have been reserved for the functions of the administrative classes.

LUSIGNAN HOUSE [124 E3] (⊕ *08.00–15.30 Mon–Wed & Fri; 08.00–13.00 & 14.00–17.00 Thu; TL7/5 adult/student*) Heading north past the western side of St Catherine's, on the corner of a kink in this small but busy road is the restored Lusignan House. Dating back to the 15th century, the house is a typical, if rather grand, dwelling of its time, being a simple two-storey structure, with the second floor reached by a staircase that ascends from a small rectangular courtyard. The (now bricked-up) arches in the back wall suggest the building had an Eastern connection. The rooms themselves have been simply furnished with reproductions of the Lusignan and Ottoman era, including, in one room, a splendid old gramophone from the early years of the 20th century. Renovations were yet again under way in 2015, so the house may soon reveal further glories.

At this point in your wanderings, and especially if ongoing renovations have partially thwarted your ambitions, console yourself with a visit to **Helvasan** [124 E3] (*Yeni Camii Sokak 1E*). The modest shop front does scant justice to the delicacies inside, where varieties of delicious *helva* are on sale at modest prices. This tahini-based confectionery has been made by the same family for five generations.

YENI CAMII [124 E3] Those whose appetite for mosques/churches is not yet sated can walk on for a further 20-minute circuit to see the Yeni Camii and St Luke's. Heavily ruined, with only a staircase and one fragmented arch remaining, the Yeni Camii was once a 14th-century church. It owes its dilapidated state to one of the more demented Turkish governors, who tore it down in the 18th century in a frantic search for buried treasure. The name means New Mosque, given to it because the temporary mosque built afterwards on its site had to be constructed almost from scratch.

ST LUKE'S [124 E2] Formerly a church, St Luke's stands in the middle of an open playground area and is now in occasional use as a workshop for goods crafted by the **Hasder Folk Arts Institute**, whose main showroom is next to the Selimiye Camii (pages 136–8). Unlike the other churches described, it was never a converted mosque, since it was in fact built under Turkish rule, like many other churches, in the 18th century. In style it is Byzantine, with a bell tower. If you're in luck, there may be someone there when you visit, though it is usually unmanned and the interior is of limited architectural interest.

TOWARDS THE ARMENIAN CHURCH AND THE GREEN LINE Returning to the Bedestan, a more interesting diversion can be made to see the old quarter in the western area of walled Lefkoşa, where the best examples of Ottoman and British colonial houses are to be found. Retracing your steps up the bustling street west from the Bedestan, instead of forking right to pass the entrance of the Büyük Han, you keep heading west, straight on, passing through a pedestrian precinct shopping area selling jeans and all sorts of other clothes and shoes. This is **Arasta Sokak**, interesting in itself both for a spot of retail therapy and for its proximity to the Green Line. Just at the end of Arasta Sokak is the **Turunçlu Camii** [124 C4], the mosque built in 1825 by the governor of Cyprus, Seyit Mehmet Aga.

Keeping on this westward course, passing through an area of engineering workshops and scrapyards, you will come after some 300–400m to a car park, across which, in the distance, behind a fence, rises the bell tower of the lovely **Armenian Church** [124 B4]. An extensive restoration of the church has now been completed, though it remains perplexingly closed. The proposed work to the adjacent convent has halted after being covered in scaffolding. It was originally a Benedictine convent and the walls conceal an unfinished Gothic cloister. The abbess in the 14th century was involved, so the story goes, in an intrigue to murder the regent, the Prince of Tyre, and was accused of sheltering the assassin. Soldiers broke down the gates and threatened the holy sisters with death and dishonour. The abbess appealed to the papal legate for protection, and she and her nuns were finally spared.

The convent was much altered and repaired over the centuries, and was in use as a salt store when the Turks gave it to the Armenians. The area here around the Paphos Gate had long been the Armenian quarter.

Behind the Armenian church and just on the Greek side of the Green Line is the **Roman Catholic church** [124 B4], recognisable by its distinctive spire. A walk down this street is to be recommended for the succession of lovely houses it offers. Aptly named **Victoria Street**, the houses were built from the time of the British occupation in 1878, and their distinctive features are the **curved ironwork balconies** above their huge doorways. No 73 Victoria Street is a good example, built in 1923. Continuing south, you can walk down the street towards the Green Line, where you can peek into no-man's-land through the bullet-riddled fence. There's also the splendid **Boghialian Konak Restaurant** (page 128), if it reopens.

Whilst wandering down Victoria Street, your eye may be drawn towards the large blue footprints leading off the main Nicosia Trail. Following these down a side alley will lead to the **Arab Ahmet Art & Culture Centre** [124 B4], established as part of the regeneration programme and to help boost community relations on both sides of the divide. It has now been taken over on a five-year lease by the Girne American University who have invested in its further development. It hosts occasional shows or exhibitions, so if you're lucky there might be something to see. In the meantime there is a café and a modest toy museum, which is as much in need of donations as visitors: if you have some old toys, preferably with an interesting story to accompany them, please take them along! A video, showing the use of the exhibited traditional Lefkoşa street toys, should be available shortly.

A few steps round the corner, one of the most surprising sights in Lefkoşa has now disappeared, hopefully temporarily. In a town where life seems to be painted in a series of monotone sandy yellows and browns, artist Farhad Nargol-O'Neill created an enormous **mural** on the east-facing gable end of the Culture Centre with vivid colours illuminating the area like the brightest of spotlights. Entitled *Ode to Aphrodite and Hala Sultan*, the fresco reflected the culture of the people of Lefkoşa – two bodies coexisting in the same space and a corresponding mural exists on the south side of town. Described as 'cubist symbolism', the piece combined the Hellenistic image of Aphrodite, the goddess of love who was reputed to have emerged from the surf off the shores of Cyprus, with Hala Sultan, aunt of the prophet Muhammad. Nargol-O'Neill was selected from a series of candidates to create the work and both murals were completed with the help of youngsters from both north and south. Unfortunately, the Cypriot sunshine exacted a heavy toll on the paintwork and the whole wall has now been whitewashed over! But Nargol-O'Neill has vowed to replace it. Watch that space.

The Green Line is in fact a somewhat euphemistic description of the barrier of bricks, barbed wire and corrugated iron that divides the old city into two roughly equal halves, abruptly bisecting streets that used to run straight on, rudely separating houses that were once neighbours. In the suburbs of Lefkoşa, it is extended by the Red Line, becoming the Attila Line once out of the city.

DERVISH PASHA MANSION [124 B4] (⊕ *08.00–15.30 Fri–Wed, 08.00–13.00 & 14.00–17.00 Thu; TL7/5 adult/student*) Facing out over the car park towards the Armenian church stands the renovated Dervish Paşa Mansion, opened in 1988 as an ethnographic museum. Dervish Paşa himself was the editor of *Zaman* (Time), the first Turkish newspaper in Cyprus, which was introduced in 1891. The house dates back to 1807 and, immaculately presented with whitewashed walls and blue woodwork and rafters, is laid out in a room-by-room recreation of an early 19th-century mansion. Downstairs are the service rooms: kitchens and stores, with displays of cooking utensils and agricultural implements; while upstairs are the living quarters, furnished with relics of a lavish lifestyle: embroidered bath-towels, exquisitely delicate purses, fine old carpets and sumptuous clothing including some classic platformed mother-of-pearl bath-shoes. In the pleasant, open courtyard are the baths and washrooms.

ARAB AHMET MOSQUE [124 B3] Forking north (right) up Victoria Street (Salahi Sevket Sokagi) after the Dervish Paşa Mansion, you will arrive at the Arab Ahmet Mosque at the corner of the next major road intersection, set on the left in a lush graveyard. What seem at first glance to be Roman columns in the neat gardens are in fact tall tombstones of various eminent *paşas*, the fine white marble originally from Beirut. The mosque is a typical example of 19th-century Ottoman, restored in 1955, and the spot is attractive more for its trees and graveyard than for the building itself. Inside are the usual whitewashed walls with medallions near the dome bearing the names in Arabic of Abu Bakr, Umar, Uthman, Ali, Hussein and Hassan, the first caliphs of Islam. The pulpit is, as so often, painted green, the colour of Islam, and beside it is the mihrab, the prayer niche that indicates the direction of Mecca, so that the faithful can orientate themselves correctly during prayer. The crass modern carpets conceal the **tombstones** of some Frankish knights, reused in the floor paving as conveniently large slabs. The mosque guardian will pull back the carpets if you ask to see. If at this point you should need a rest, you could do a lot worse than sit in the immaculately tended **garden courtyard**. If the mosque door is locked when you arrive, it will be opened at prayer time.

LEDRA PALACE [124 A3] Heading northwest from the Arab Ahmet area it is but a short stroll to one of the city's newer 'tourist attractions', the Ledra Palace border crossing. Formerly one of the grandest hotels on the island, Ledra Palace has for many years served as the UN's Wolseley Barracks and the strain shows all too clearly. Pock-marked walls, overgrown gardens and abandoned properties mark this as the only section of no-man's-land through which civilians are free to walk.

There's nothing special about being checked in and out by the border police (just turn up with your passport), but for many this is the closest they'll ever get to a disputed military area and there's an eerie fascination with the whole process. Of course, for the locals this is all part of the routine and their casual approach helps lend an air of normality to the whole affair. Today, most visitors will wander outside Lefkoşa's walls to see this decrepit old relic, and to take in the vitriolic Greek Cypriot propaganda on the other side of the line. At this point, having reached the other side, if you have no real business in Nicosia you'll probably wonder why you bothered crossing in the first place.

Most people crossing to and from the south on foot now use the Locmaci crossing, so queues have diminished here in recent years. Ledra Palace provides a particular fascination for German tourists, who since the fall of the Berlin Wall have been captivated by the world's only remaining divided capital city. If you plan to go just for the experience, stick to early morning or later in the evening and you'll be mercifully left to your own devices.

EXIT FROM THE WALLED CITY By car, the one-way system encourages you to leave from the Saray Hotel area in a westerly direction towards the walls and then north along Tanzimat Street, where many older-style private houses can be seen. Some of these, exposed as they are to the Ledra Palace Hotel directly across from the Venetian ramparts, were targets for the EOKA terrorists, and many of the houses still bear the bullet holes. Also on this street, you will see the **Ottoman fountain** [124 B3] where the elderly women, enjoying the chance to meet neighbours and gossip, until recently collected water from the old, octagonal fountain with its fine brass taps set in elaborate panels.

Heading north inside the walls, the Mula Bastion is now a disused military area, and at the Qurini Bastion, the large white building is the president's residence. Before partition, it was designated the vice-president's palace.

MUSEUM OF BARBARISM [124 A1] (⏲ *09.00–17.00 daily; admission free*). Going out of town through the Dereboyu district on Osman Paşa Caddesi and then doglegging right on to Mehmet Akif Caddesi, you will eventually reach this gruesome museum. The significance attached to this place by Turkish Cypriots is evidenced by the extensive opening hours, free admission and the comments in the visitors' book. This was the house of Dr Nihat Ilhan, a major serving in the Cyprus-Turkey Army, whose wife and three children were murdered here in 1963. Now it is a small museum, with some information in English. It focuses firmly on the atrocities committed against Turkish Cypriot villagers in 1963 and 1964. A strong constitution is needed to look at the photos, the sole blessing being that they are only in black and white. In addition to the photographs, there are some cuttings from the international press, but little else.

THE SUBURBS As you enter Lefkoşa from the north, the main road crosses a bridge over a riverbed, almost invariably dry. No river in Cyprus flows all the year round, and the watercourses are highly seasonal: full and rushing after a heavy downpour, dwindling to a trickle shortly after. When Nicosia was founded in the 4th century BC, it lay on the banks of the Kanli (Greek Pedieos) River, and the plain all around was thickly forested.

After the river bridge, a fork can be taken to the right at the traffic lights, to follow a road that runs more or less parallel to the main street. Now Mehmet Akif Caddesi, this was once called Shakespeare Avenue and is still commonly referred to as such by the foreign community. If you're spending a night in Lefkoşa, this is the Dereboyu area, the place to head for in the evening for some lively restaurants and cafés.

Automobile enthusiasts might detour to the **Classic Car Museum** [124 A1] (⏲ *09.00–17.00, Mon–Fri; admission is supposedly TL10/5 adult/student, but the*

4

ticket desk is often unmanned) on a rainy day. It's located within the campus of the Near East University, just northwest of Lefkoşa, and houses around 50 cars, mainly British and mainly from the 1950s and 1960s. As the country villages are in any event scattered with old vehicles – most of them no longer functioning – some might question the necessity of such a museum!

ACROSS THE MESAORIA PLAIN

East from Lefkoşa, the character of the landscape changes as you enter the vast expanse of the Mesaoria Plain. It is not an area worth visiting in itself, but simply has to be crossed on the way to what in most cases will be Gazimağusa or Salamis. Some background is provided here to help relieve the monotony of the journey. Fertile but now nearly treeless, the Mesaoria was once thickly forested. Hunting wild animals was the great sport of the early rulers, and whole retinues of nobles, barons and princes would go into the forest for anything up to a month at a time, living in tents. One account written in 1336 described how the party took with it 24 leopards and 300 hawks to aid in the sport. By the 16th century, many species verged on extinction. The huge forests were gradually cut down for domestic fuel, but also for smelting in the copper furnaces throughout the ages. The abundance and ease of obtaining this fuel enabled Cypriot craftsmen to attain a high standard of metallurgy, and Alexander the Great is said to have had a Cypriot sword. Great expanses were also cleared for crop growing. The plain owed its fertility to the alluvial deposit brought down from the mountains in heavy winter rains, like the fertility bestowed on the banks of the Nile in flood. As the climate changed over the centuries, less and less rainfall occurred and the area around Nicosia became a semi-desert-like plain. In recent years, many new retail outlets and car dealerships have sprouted up along the main road.

TOURING THE MESAORIA PLAIN A more interesting route to Gazimağusa than by the main highway is via Ercan, a former military airport (previously called Tymbou). It was constructed by the British in World War II, and has now been transformed into a small but quite slick passenger terminal for all civilian flights that connect to the Turkish mainland.

Heading west from Ercan towards Gaziköy, resist any desire to follow the signs marked 'Tomb' and, even more enticingly, 'Captive tanks'. A detour here will only take you around a trail of barbed wire before you end at a military camp, where a Turkish soldier will politely and apologetically inform you that only Turkish people can visit these attractions. Why the signs are in English, therefore, is perplexing. Some 8km west of Ercan, at Gaziköy, is the only antiquity along this route, an **Ottoman aqueduct**. It runs close beside the left of the road, quite well preserved for a long stretch, beginning about 1km before Gaziköy. One of the major legacies of the Ottomans was the transformed water distribution on the island via several such aqueducts. The water was sent not just to wealthy rulers' houses, as had been the case under previous occupations, but also to public fountains in the cities and towns, introducing a higher standard of hygiene and cleanliness than had been possible before.

The villages you pass along this route have some interesting, old, rural-style, mud-brick houses, but these are now being surpassed by the development of large new dwellings. After rain, the whole area is very liable to flooding, with roads and fields becoming indistinguishable in sheets of water. Rain in Cyprus can often be violent, and it is not unusual, anytime from mid-October to mid-March, for two or three inches to fall in a day. It is mercifully brief, though, and the day after is quite likely to be bright and sunny.

Further east, Paşaköy is, like so many villages in the vicinity of the Attila Line, a bit like a military garrison. Though the forest of military barriers is a little daunting at first, you are in fact never stopped as a tourist vehicle. South of Paşaköy near the village of Erdenli (Greek Tremetousha), you may feel tempted to visit **Ayios Spiridon**, the monastery marked on some old maps. It is, however, heavily guarded, due to its proximity to the Attila Line, so do not attempt to approach it. One of the oldest and largest monasteries on the island, Ayios Spiridon was also the place where icons were sent for restoration from all over the island. As a result, it has the largest collection of valuable icons in northern Cyprus. Though these are not on view to visitors, independent archaeological authorities have been allowed in to see them since 1975 and have confirmed they are all safe and neatly catalogued.

The road on to Gazimağusa forks north through Turunçlu. If you're continuing to Salamis rather than Gazimağusa, be careful not to miss the poorly signposted fork left near Mutluyaka to save yourself the unnecessary and unsightly detour through the industrial outskirts of Gazimağusa. The traffic along this road is, by northern Cypriot standards, very busy, with many lorries and goods vehicles heading for the commercial freeport of Gazimağusa.

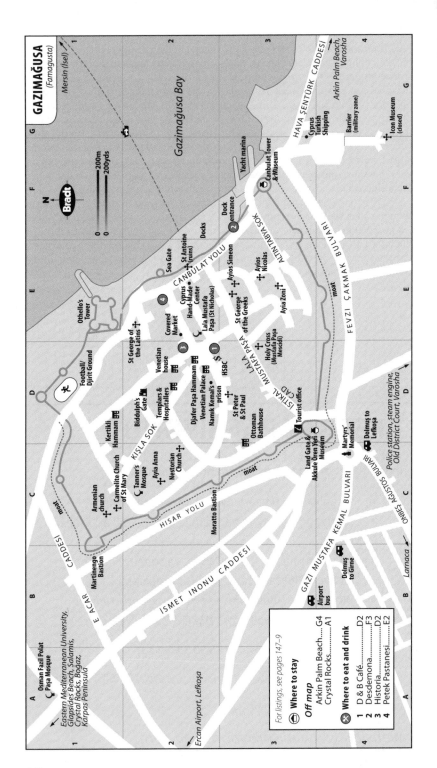

GAZIMAĞUSA
(Famagusta)

Mersin (İsel)

Gazimağusa Bay

N

Bradt

0 ___ 200m
0 ___ 200yds

Eastern Mediterranean University,
Glapsides Beach, Salamis,
Crystal Rocks, Boğaz,
Karpas Peninsula

Ercan Airport, Lefkoşa

A Osman Fazil Polat
Paşa Mosque

Martinengo
Bastion

E ACAR CADDESI

Armenian
church

Carmelite Church
of St Mary

Kertikli
Hammam

Tanner's
Mosque

KISLA SOK

Biddulph's
Gate

Ayia Anna

Templars &
Hospitallers

Nestorian
Church

Football/
Djirit Ground

Othello's
Tower

St George of
the Latins

Covered
Market

Venetian
house

Djafer Paşa Hammam

Venetian Palace

Namık Kemal's
prison

St Peter
& St Paul

Ottoman
Bathhouse

HSBC

Sea Gate

St Antoine
(ruins)

CANBULAT YOLU

Cyprus
Hand-Made
Center

Lala Mustafa
Paşa (St Nicholas)

St George
of the Greeks

Holy Cross
(Mustafa Paşa
Mescidi)

Ayios Simeon

Ayios
Nicolas

Ayia Zoni

MUSTAFA PAŞA

Dock
entrance

Docks

Yacht marina

Canbulat Tower
& Museum

HAVA ŞENTÜRK CADDESI

Cyprus
Turkish
Shipping

Barrier
(military zone)

Icon Museum
(closed)

Arkin Palm Beach,
Varosha

ALTINTABYA SOK

FEVZI ÇAKMAK BULVARI

moat

ISTIKAL CAD

Tourist office

Land Gate &
Akkule Ören Yeri
Museum

Martyrs'
Memorial

Dolmuş to
Lefkoşa

Police station, steam engine,
Old District Court, Varosha

Moratto Bastion

HISAR YOLU

moat

ONBEŞ AĞUSTOS BULVARI

GAZI MUSTAFA KEMAL BULVARI

ISMET INONU CADDESI

Airport
bus

Dolmuş
to Girne

Larnaca

For listings, see pages 147–9

Where to stay
Arkin Palm Beach.....G4
Crystal Rocks.........A1

Off map

Where to eat and drink
1 D & B Café..............D2
2 Desdemona...........F3
3 Historia.................D2
4 Petek Pastanesi.......E2

146

5

Gazimağusa (Famagusta)

If beaches are your priority, then the Gazimağusa region is for you. The immense sweep of Gazimağusa Bay is one of the finest stretches of sand anywhere in the Mediterranean. Nearly all of the eastern region's hotels are situated along this bay and have excellent beaches and watersports facilities. For sightseeing, the major classical site of the island, Salamis, is on your doorstep, as are a few lesser attractions, such as St Barnabas Monastery and the Royal Tombs. Kantara Castle is also close by and you are well placed to explore the Karpas Peninsula.

As a base for a holiday on the island, the Gazimağusa region is more limited than Girne. Most meals will probably be taken in your hotel, since the choice of restaurants is restricted and eating elsewhere becomes an excursion in itself, unless you are staying in Boğaz. Shopping is a lot less sophisticated. Visits to the major sights of the Girne area, such as Bellapais and St Hilarion, become quite lengthy trips, and trips even further west, to places such as Vouni and Soli, become impracticable without an overnight stay.

GETTING THERE AND AROUND

From Gazimağusa, the **drive** to Girne takes about one hour, and to Lefkoşa about 50 minutes. Ercan Airport is 40 minutes away. From the walled town of old Gazimağusa it takes 15 minutes to drive to Salamis. *Dolmuş* from Girne run from outside the Colony Hotel and drop passengers off outside the walled city, about 400m from the tourist office. Fares are TL9.50, one-way. Once inside the compact walled city, walking is the way to get around.

WHERE TO STAY *Map, page 146, unless otherwise stated*

Gazimağusa itself doesn't have a great deal of accommodation options, and most visitors from Girne will consider it as a day-trip destination. Those wishing to stay on this stretch of coast will probably look to the few beach hotels to the north of town, but the smart Palm Beach Hotel in nearby Varosha has undergone a recent renovation and is ideal for those seeking a beach location that is nevertheless close to town. There are a few other hotels in and around the city walls, but unless you are on a tight budget, none of them are really suitable holiday options.

Salamis Bay Conti Resort Hotel [map, page 160] (404 rooms) 378 82 00; e info@ salamisbayconti.com; www.salamisbayconti.com. Cavernous complex 11km north of Gazimağusa, well located on its own beach & a 45min walk from the ruins of Salamis. Accommodation is a mix of rooms & villas, now offered on an all-inclusive basis only. Facilities include restaurants, bars, outdoor & indoor pools, aquapark, shopping centre, Turkish bath, massage, tennis, fitness centre, watersports, enormous casino & crèche (high season only). Seasonal live music, plus entertainment for adults & children. Shuttle bus to town. **$$$$$**

🏠 **Arkin Palm Beach** (102 rooms) ☎366 20 00; e arkinpalmbeach@arkingroup.com; www.arkinpalmbeach.com. The closest decent option to the city centre: 15mins' walk, yet right on the clean, well-equipped beach. Refurbished in 2012, garish exterior but very smart rooms & it's small enough to be friendly. Spa, gym, outdoor & indoor pools, quality restaurant, beach bar. All rooms have AC, satellite TV, free Wi-Fi & balcony. Children welcome, though limited facilities for youngsters. You get a good view of Varosha's 'ghost town' from here. A few restaurants are nearby. **$$$$**

🏠 **Crystal Rocks** (62 rooms) ☎378 94 00; e info@yeldenercrystalrocks.com; www. yeldenercrystalrocks.com. On the seafront near Salamis ruins. AC, bungalow rooms, pool with waterslide, restaurant on site. Basic for the price, with mixed reviews. All-inclusive basis in summer. **$$$**

🏠 **Exotic Hotel** [map, page 160] (22 rooms) ☎371 28 81; e exoticmirillo@superonline.com; www.exotichotel.net. In Boğaz, up the coast towards the Karpas. Not *that* exotic, but a personable place that caters well for children, with a seasonal swimming pool with big waterslides, & for adults with sauna, gym, Turkish bath & jacuzzi. Small 'private' beach, large beachside restaurant. Rooms feature satellite TV, balcony, AC & free Wi-Fi. **$$$**

✕ WHERE TO EAT AND DRINK *Map, page 146, unless otherwise stated*

In and around the old walls of Gazimağusa there is a selection of kebab houses and cafés. The central square dominated by St Nicholas Cathedral is a relaxing place to sit and eat. Outside the walls there are plenty of student-focused restaurants on the main road north, near the university. Further north, the road towards Salamis and Boğaz has a number of bistro-type establishments, with Boğaz itself offering some decent fish restaurants. The construction of a new dual carriageway has made access to some of the coastal restaurants more difficult.

INSIDE THE WALLS

✕ **D & B Café** ☎366 66 10; ⏰ daily, early until late. Gazimağusa's best-located eatery is directly opposite the cathedral/mosque. Popular with the local youth, the café offers free Wi-Fi for customers & offers a roof terrace. Pizzas, burgers & salads feature among a huge selection of food. Prices remain reasonable. Wide range of cocktails. Good ice cream too. *TL20*

✕ **Desdemona** m 0533 870 48 71. Housed in a former church from the 13th century. Short menu includes kebabs, fish & full *meze*. Plenty of artefacts to gawp at while you wait. *TL18*

✕ **Historia** ☎367 01 53. Next to the cathedral, friendly service & a central location, simple but tasty Turkish food with a couple of European dishes. Delicious fresh orange & lemon drinks. *TL21*

✕ **Petek Pastanesi** ☎366 71 04. This café on Yeşil Deniz Sokagi is very much a tourist attraction in itself. If you aren't enjoying the walled city, cheer yourself up here. Legendary cakes, wonderful sticky pastries & sweets, plus reasonable & good-value sandwiches & light meals. On a hot day the downstairs water feature is a soothing companion, though the view from the 1st floor is also tempting. Free Wi-Fi. *TL14*

ELSEWHERE IN GAZIMAĞUSA

✕ **Aytotoro Meze Evi** [map, page 160] ☎378 97 74; m 0533 860 47 85' ⏰ evenings only, closed Sun. At the Salamis ruins' roundabout, take the inland turning for 1.5km. Good value, with 20 *meze* dishes to accompany your kebab. Live music Fri & Sat. *TL40*

✕ **Bedi's** [map, page 160] ☎378 82 25; ⏰ daily, lunchtimes only, though 'lunchtime' lasts from 09.00 to 20.00. Right by the car park at the Salamis ruins. Outdoor tables & friendly management. Fish & kebab are the standard choices. *TL25*

✕ **Kemal in Yeri** [map, page 160] ☎371 25 15. On the front at tiny Boğaz harbour. Decent range of fresh fish, plus usual kebab menu. Occasional live music Fri & Sat. *TL30*

✕ **Kıyı** [map, page 160] ☎371 28 81. Part of & opposite the Exotic Hotel just south of Boğaz, a well-rated seafront fish restaurant, using the catch from the nearby harbour. *TL30*

✕ Marinero Fish Restaurant [map, page 160] m 0533 862 21 40; ⊕ daily. Right on the sea, 1km south of the Salamis Bay Conti Hotel roundabout. Nothing fancy, but decent kebabs & fish. *TL25*

BEACHES

If you've decided to base yourself at one of the beach hotels around Gazimağusa, you'll have plenty of sand to lie on. Day trippers can usually make use of the hotel beaches too, but will have to pay a fee for umbrellas and loungers (though this may be waived if you buy a few drinks).

PALM BEACH 1km south of the town, this free public beach next to the hotel of the same name has clean sand and good swimming. You'll have the deserted hotels of Varosha as a unique backdrop.

GLAPSIDES BEACH Pronounced 'Glap-seed-es', this beach lies 3km north of town. It's a large stretch of sand that's free and very popular in season with locals. It's not associated with any particular hotel, but has a restaurant and club that plays host to a lively open-air disco in summer, with guest DJs.

WHAT TO SEE AND DO

The old walled city of Gazimağusa houses some of the most superb medieval architecture in the Middle East, and no less a figure than Leonardo da Vinci is thought to have been involved in the design of its colossal Venetian fortifications. Within the town walls an intriguing range of monuments, mainly churches, can still be visited.

Gazimağusa town today, with a population of around 41,000, is a fascinating hotchpotch, perpetually startling in its incongruities and juxtapositions. Here, a Leeds steam locomotive stands in front of the Turkish police station against the backdrop of skyscraper shells in decaying Greek Varosha. There, a Crusader church appears in the garb of a cultural centre, while another serves as a café. One tower built by Venetians has a museum to Ottoman military might, and another holds the ghost of Shakespeare's Othello. In the main square, the French Gothic cathedral, topped with a misshapen minaret, faces out at the façade of a Venetian palace supported by Greek marble columns from Salamis. Next door, a former Ottoman school looks across at a Turkish bath. Today's Turkish inhabitants have blended the city's relics so casually with their own daily needs, that the preservation of these monuments is almost synonymous with the routine maintenance of their public buildings and offices.

The expanse of the modern town entails an extensive industrial sprawl that belongs to a bustling port, while just outside town, the huge campus of the Eastern Mediterranean University has added a new, cosmopolitan dimension to the area. Elsewhere, the surrounding landscape is flat and featureless, and the busy commercial port means that traffic can be heavy, with many noisy goods vehicles. However, for the visitor the quiet streets of the old medieval walled town possess an understated wealth of interest.

It has been said Gazimağusa has little of the sophistication of Girne or Lefkoşa. However, a great deal of reconstruction and restoration, some UN-funded, has combined to lift the ambience of the central old town. More smart cafés and bars are in evidence of late, though whether there's the trade to support all of them remains to be seen; most tourist accommodation lies further north near Salamis. It's true that good restaurants are limited inside the walls, with much of the commerce now out by the university, but there are enough to get by.

Pick a quiet day and it's enough to sit in a public space and take in the city's remarkable architectural testament. One full day should ideally be devoted to Gazimağusa, to give yourself time to stroll in the streets of the old walled town seeking out the early churches and Venetian buildings, and to explore the walls and bastions fully. These are really Gazimağusa most remarkable features today, and if you are limited to just a couple of hours, the essentials could be reduced to a drive around the walls from the outside, noting especially the Land Gate with its drawbridge, and the Martinengo Bastion; a walk round Othello's Tower (currently being restored); and a stroll round the Lala Mustafa Paşa Mosque/St Nicholas Cathedral in the main square. The ghost town of Varosha, the once modern Greek suburb that's now a sealed-off no-man's-land, also holds an eerie fascination and is worth a quick look from the car, or from the beach if you have time. Beautiful it isn't, but it may well be unique.

Conveniently located at the Land Gate, though with limited useful information, is Gazimağusa **tourist office** [146 D3] (⊕ *summer 09.00–19.00, winter 09.00–16.00*). If you're driving, this makes the Land Gate the most sensible way to enter the old city, and, on passing through the walls, there are parking areas clearly signposted both to the left and right. Mercifully, traffic within the walls remains light and there's no problem in finding alternative parking in other areas: there are plenty of open spaces here.

THE WALLS OF OLD GAZIMAĞUSA

Any visit would best begin with a tour of the walls. Originally Lusignan Crusader, these walls were redesigned and strengthened by the Venetians, who made the square towers round and generally adapted them for cannon warfare rather than for the outmoded bow and arrow. The result was to make Famagusta one of the most impressive walled cities in the Middle East. To appreciate the walls properly it is best to drive around the moat gully, viewing them from directly below.

If you are coming into the bustle of modern Gazimağusa from the direction of Salamis, you arrive at a roundabout (easily identified by the huge new twin-minaret mosque). Before doing your tour of ruined churches and churches-converted-into-mosques, it's worth parking up here to see what a *new* mosque has to offer. This one is the **Osman Fazil Polat Paşa Mosque** [146 A1], a fine example with bright carpets and ceiling decoration. Then, continue over the roundabout and take the first left, towards the sea. This road takes you to a junction at the northern edge of the walls, to the mighty **Martinengo Bastion** [146 B1], where you continue straight ahead. Squat and muscular rather than tall and towering, these Venetian ramparts are not visible from the modern town until you are nearly upon them. Their height, some 15m, is less than twice their thickness, often 8m. At the turn of the 20th century, before industrial development had burgeoned, the imposing outline of the cathedral within the walls could be seen from a great distance as you approached. The soft brown limestone that was quarried to create the moat was then used to construct the walls, an immense task that must have taken decades; 50 years is the usual estimate. Leonardo da Vinci is recorded as having visited Cyprus in 1481, and is thought to have advised his fellow countrymen on the design.

You can get on to the track either at the arch where the road enters the walls from the north, or from beside the **Canbulat (Djamboulat) Tower** [146 F3] on the south. Although until recently it was possible to drive along the moat, the circuit is nowadays better done on foot, and in the winter months it makes a pleasant stroll of about an hour. North of the Land Gate, the moat is invariably deserted. In summer, when the heat is trapped in the airless gully, all but the hardiest would be best advised to save their energy for the walk within the walls, in itself more than sufficiently sapping. In many places around the moat, especially between the Land Gate and the Canbulat Tower, you can still find old cannonballs and other bits of metalwork left over from the Turkish bombardment. Iron was expensive and, whenever possible, the bravest soldiers would sneak into the moat at night to retrieve the cannonballs for reuse.

As for the ramparts themselves, you can still – sometimes – walk along the top of them with ease between the Canbulat Tower and the Land Gate. In the 1930s, the British colonialists, ever amused by games, engineered a nine-hole golf course on top of the ramparts, on which 'the accuracy of direction' more than made up for 'the comparative shortness of the holes'. If you're prepared to be agile, you can also walk a little way from the Land Gate towards the Martinengo Bastion. A large chunk of northern walled Gazimağusa was for a long time a military zone, rendering inaccessible four of the city's remaining churches. Relaxation of these boundaries means that today's visitors can view all of the remains up close, together with the fine craftsmanship of the Martinengo Bastion, the most powerfully built of Gazimağusa's 15 strongholds.

The **Land Gate** [146 D3] is certainly the most impressive of the bastions, with its arched stone 19th-century bridge spanning the moat. Today it also houses the tourist office, and beside it is a colossal ramp leading up on to the walls, used for rolling up the cannon. The gate has also been converted into the **Akkule Ören Yeri tourist attraction** (⊕ *09.00–15.00 Mon–Fri; TL5*), and it takes a full 15 minutes to explore its labyrinth of rooms, dungeons, steps, ramps and arches. Here and there in the ceiling, chimney holes can be seen, essential to let out the smoke that billowed up every time the cannons were fired. The cannons used by both the Venetians and the Turks during the siege of Famagusta in 1571 were more powerful than any ever used before in any other country.

It was the sheer power of Gazimağusa's walls that enabled it to hold out for ten months against the Ottoman Turks. Nicosia had fallen in 48 days and Kyrenia surrendered without a fight, as did the rest of the island, but Famagusta resisted to a degree that has become famous. The Turks, with an immense force of 100,000, approached along tunnels and trenches so deep that a man on horseback could not be seen, and so extensive that their entire army could disappear inside them. Using mines and artillery, they commenced their firing, lobbing more than 150,000 cannonballs into the city. Inside, a force of a little over 5,000 men – Venetians, Cypriots and Albanian mercenaries – waited in terror behind the walls. Using clever tactics, making lots of brief sorties, the Venetian commander managed to trick the Ottomans into thinking that his troops were far more numerous, and the siege lasted an incredible ten months before the city fell, with the besieged, weak with plague and famine, reduced to eating cats, dogs and rodents. The Turks lost over 50,000 of their men in these ten months, and their rage on final victory was expressed in the most appalling form. Surging through the gates, they overran the entire place, randomly killing men, women and children, desecrating churches and plundering houses. The Venetian commander Bragadino surrendered and was promised safe passage, only for the Turks to renege on the promise and murder him most horrifically. He was flayed alive in public, having first had his nose and ears cut off, then his body was stuffed with straw to be sent to Constantinople dangling from the prow of a ship. The Turk, when roused, may justify his epithet 'terrible'.

THE CANBULAT (DJAMBOULAT) TOWER [146 F3] Emerging from the outer wall circuit beside the Canbulat Tower, you can now turn left to enter the walls. The tower is named after one of the Turkish commanders of the siege. Here, the Venetians

had erected a huge revolving wheel spiked with knives, on to which Turks were tossed as they scaled the walls, until the gully below was choked with dismembered bodies. Canbulat rushed at the wheel, and deliberately impaled himself and his horse, thereby putting it (and himself) out of action. His fellow soldiers were thus able to breach the defences.

Today the tower holds his tomb and has been converted to a small **museum** (⊕ *08.00–15.30 Fri–Wed, 08.00–13.00 & 14.00–18.00 Thu; TL5*). As a place of pilgrimage for Turks, this tower ranks second in Cyprus only to the shrine of Hala Sultan Tekke on the lake at Larnaca. The vaulted interior, with its long hall leading to the tower at the end, is in some ways more interesting than the exhibits. These include displays of guns, 17th-century Turkish tiles and bowls, and a couple of pretty but unexceptional 15th-century Venetian plates. The attendant may give you the keys that enable you to climb the steps and get on to the roof, though there is no access to the ramparts. If the attendant is unable to produce these keys, by heading in the direction of the Land Gate it's possible to ascend the stone steps and reach the top of the wall at this southeast extremity of the fortifications, which is as good as emerging from within the tower itself.

OTHELLO'S TOWER [146 E1] In 2014, a team began work on a two-year renovation project, so the tower will be closed for part of the lifetime of this book. The description below relates to the pre-renovated tower. To reach it from the Canbulat Tower, you now continue along the dockside, passing the Sea Gate on the way to Othello's Tower. The **Sea Gate** was, along with the Land Gate, one of the two original gates of the walled city, and was built by the Venetians in 1496. The side that faces the harbour has a magnificent archway surmounted by a Venetian lion in a white marble gabled plaque. As the gate is now closed, this is only visible from within the harbour itself or by craning one's head over the walls. Note, however, that the safety barriers are less than satisfactory.

It's worth climbing the steps here for a view over the wall to the docks or back towards Lala Mustafa Paşa Mosque in the heart of the old town. Those who are tempted to walk along the top of the wall towards Othello's Tower may do so, but the process is ultimately futile as there's no way down at the other end. Inside the Sea Gate the huge, rusting portcullis is well and truly lowered, and whilst the impressively domed ceiling is worth a look, most visits will be limited to the length of time the explorer can hold his or her breath against the somewhat overpowering stench.

The emotively named Othello's Tower is not just a tower. It would be more aptly called Othello's Castle, for it was built as a fort within a fort, a citadel to defend the entrance to the harbour. One side now looks directly on to the quayside of the modern port, out of bounds to all but port traffic. In the pre-1974 days, when cruise ships and passenger ferries called at Famagusta, this citadel was the first thing that would have confronted visitors as the ship docked. Now, the ferries come only from Turkey.

The entrance to the tower today is from just inside the walls, through the gateway crowned by the white marble Venetian lion. The moat was drained of water on British instructions in 1900, because of the risk of malaria. Beside the gate is a simple **restaurant**, attractively set in green gardens with a playground. Opposite is the heavily ruined shell of **St George of the Latins** [146 E2], a fortified 13th-century church, the earliest church in the town. A little to the north, just inside the walls, is a disused football field marked on old maps of the 1960s as the Turkish polo field, Djirit.

The tower has an entry fee (see above for details) and it takes a good 20 minutes to have a proper look inside; longer, if you enjoy the fun of re-enacting Shakespeare. You may even be able to tread the boards, as staging is still in place, though due to concerns about crumbling walls, the theatrical and musical events that were held here have been (at least temporarily) suspended. Scattered about in the open courtyard are **old Turkish cannons**, recognisable by the heavy iron rings round their barrel. In several places, the iron cannonballs can be seen, along with some stone balls that were tossed by the giant catapults.

Flanking the fine courtyard are the rooms of the citadel, regal in their proportions, especially the **Great Hall** or **Refectory**, used in 1915 by Syrian refugees fleeing from the Ottoman Turks.

Although Shakespeare had never visited Cyprus, probably indeed never left England's shores, he had evidently read or at least heard of Sir Cristoforo Moro, who was sent by Venice to be governor of their colony of Cyprus in the early 1500s. Othello, the Moor of Venice, was likewise sent by his masters:

> Duke: The Turk with a most mighty preparation makes for Cyprus. – Othello, the fortitude of the place is best known to you; … you must, therefore, be content to slubber the gloss of your new fortunes with this more stubborn and boisterous expedition.
>
> *Othello*, Act I, scene iii

From Act II onwards, the setting is 'A seaport in Cyprus'. Scene III of Act II takes place in 'a hall in the castle', which must be the Great Hall or Refectory, where much revelry and drinking was ordered by Othello's herald. The tower was named Othello's Tower by the British during the colonial period.

THE WALLED TOWN Old Gazimağusa maintains a surprisingly quiet and unhurried feel, despite more shops and cafés springing up to meet perceived increasing tourist demands. The flat, dusty streets, the neglect and the randomly sprouting palm trees give the place a more Middle Eastern feel than any other Cypriot town. The Old Town population has grown to in excess of 5,000 people, all of whom have been Turkish Cypriots ever since the 16th-century siege of Gazimağusa, when a number of Turks stayed behind to colonise the island. The bombardments of the siege, however, along with the destruction wrought when the place was finally overrun, were permanent scars, and in the 18th century travellers described it as miserable and deserted, 'a confused mass of ruins and filth', with scarcely 300 inhabitants. The Ottomans also used Gazimağusa as a quarry: its ruined churches were exported as stone blocks to Egypt, prompting the retort that Alexandria is virtually Gazimağusa rebuilt in Egypt.

The state of the town and its churches cannot be wholly laid at the door of the Turks, however. In the 15th century, Venetian troops were quartered in disused churches and private houses and, later on, earthquakes also played their role. Today, an air of dereliction continues to pervade the place, as the husks of churches still tower above the modest low-rise houses, and bombed-out open areas have never filled up again.

The name Famigusta, from the Greek ammochostos, means 'buried in the sand', and the town was, until medieval times, as undistinguished as that implies. (The Turkish name Gazimağusa is more impressive sounding, for in Turkish the prefix gazi means 'victorious warrior'.) However, when Acre, the last Crusader toehold in the Holy Land, fell to Saladin in 1291, Gazimağusa received an influx of new blood and burgeoned into sudden life. As the largest natural harbour on the island and also the closest to the Holy Land, it was the natural choice: Cyprus is the only foreign landmass visible from the hills of Palestine. Protected from storms by the natural calm of the bay, Gazimağusa became virtually the only safe deep harbour left to Christendom in all the Levant. Suddenly the European kings and merchants were all concentrated here, and Gazimağusa quickly grew rich from its new role as middleman between the East and West, import/export centre of the Mediterranean, trading in perfumes, spices and ivory from the East and selling the island's produce of sugar cane, wine and silk. On the crest of the wave of wealth came the inevitable wave of immorality, and the city's prostitutes were said to be as wealthy – and as numerous – as the merchants.

Lala Mustafa Paşa Mosque/St Nicholas Cathedral [146 E2] (⊕ *summer 08.00–19.00, winter 09.00–15.30; donations requested*) Set in the main square in the heart of old Gazimağusa, the twin towers of the cathedral are visible from most parts of the old city. Making them even more distinctive is the incongruous minaret that tops one of them. There is usually somewhere to park near the main square (though the square itself is pedestrianised), and this is the best place to begin your walking tour within the walls.

The imposing western façade of the cathedral has been likened to Reims Cathedral in France, and it dominates the main square. Its towers were badly hit in the Turkish bombardment of the 16th century, and further damaged by earthquakes. Nevertheless, the cathedral is an undeniably beautiful building, its Gothic grace and elegance far exceeding that of its sister cathedral in Lefkoşa. It was built 100 years later than St Sophia, in the early 14th century, and its more delicate tracery work and ornate design reflect the more luxurious lifestyle and tastes of the ostentatious merchants of the port. The architects were themselves brought from France, and the cathedral may well have taken 100 years to complete. A tradition tells that the architects were a master and his pupil, and the master, on seeing the pupil's genius in the work, was consumed with jealousy. He invented a technical error he claimed to have noticed in the top of the towers, and having led the pupil up there to point it out in detail, pushed him headlong over the edge – the first of much blood spilt at St Nicholas. The cathedral is built from the same familiar soft brown limestone that is used in the ramparts and walls. All the Crusader and Venetian buildings are from this stone and you need only walk round the town looking out for this colour to identify all the older buildings.

The atmosphere of the square is conducive to reflection and, despite the proximity of modern buildings, nothing can detract from the overwhelming presence of the cathedral/mosque. To the left of the façade the small domed building was once an Ottoman madrasa, built around 1700. Next to it is a small shrine.

Inside the cathedral, the whitewashed walls almost serve to emphasise the superb proportions and height of the nave. The stained glass was all blown out in the bombardment and blasting of the siege, save for the high rose window in the front façade. Today, the remaining colour is supplied by the mosque accessories, painted the usual reds and greens: the raised platform for the Koran-recitation classes, the wooden pulpit or minbar, and the mihrab niche, indicating the direction of Mecca and around which all the decorative effort is concentrated, as in all mosques. If you're lucky, the keeper will take you to the northern corner of the building where, behind the screens, lies a stone slab etched with a **medieval depiction of St Nicholas**. Formerly, this slab was in the threshold of the church.

Your imagination has to work hard to recreate the splendid coronation ceremonies that took place here under the Lusignans. The custom had developed that each ruler was first crowned King of Cyprus in St Sophia in Nicosia, and then, after an elaborate and exhausting procession on horseback, was crowned King of Jerusalem here in St Nicholas, Gazimağusa being symbolically that bit closer to the Holy Land.

The huge **old tree** that looms to your right as you come out of the cathedral/ mosque main door is thought to have been planted around 1250, shortly before construction of the cathedral began. It is a type of tropical fig, originally from East Africa, and it keeps its foliage all year round except in February. The **old Venetian loggia** (open-sided arcade) facing the tree now serves as the mosque ablutions area. Beneath its circular windows are sections of friezes with barely discernable animals and garlands, taken from the cornice of a Roman temple, probably in Salamis.

Along the streets that run down either side of the cathedral/mosque you'll find a number of souvenir shops and eateries. Of particular interest is the **Cyprus Hand-Made Center** [146 E2], 200m down the right-hand side, offering a range of quality handicrafts and wooden furniture. Even if you're not buying, they can give you an excellent *Walking Tour of Famagusta* guide and a map, both free or at a nominal charge, which are far better than anything on offer from the tourist office.

The Venetian Palace [146 D2] Opposite the cathedral, on the far side of the square, is the triple-arched façade of the 15th-century Venetian Palace, supported by four granite columns that the Venetians brought from Salamis. This fragmentary relic is all that now remains of the once magnificent palace where the Venetian governor Bragadino lived. Its courtyard behind the arches was the stage for the excruciating death of the unfortunate Bragadino (page 151), a scene difficult to reconjure here in this peaceful spot filled with cafés. The building was badly damaged in the Turkish bombardment, and when the Turks took over the city, they did little to repair it. The section that remained, on the west side, was turned into a police barracks, and it still serves this function today.

Beside the Venetian façade, just to the right, also facing into the main square, notice the little **Ottoman fountain** for distribution of drinking water. The basin is an adaptation of a Roman sarcophagus taken from Salamis.

Turkish poetry aficionados can visit **Namık Kemal's prison** [146 D2] (⏱ *08.00–15.30; TL5*) in the courtyard of the Venetian Palace. In a move that has some modern analogies, the writer and poet was locked up here for over three years for criticising the sultan in Istanbul. Inside, there's nothing but four bare walls and an earth floor, while in the upstairs room are simply photos of Namık Kemal (1840–88) and his contemporaries. His writings were political and patriotic, and he wrote articles, novels, plays and essays as well as poetry, reviling the stifling lifestyle under the last sultans, loathing the legacy of 600 years of stagnant cultural values.

Namık Kemal's bronze bust stands by the cathedral/mosque, facing the square.

THE CHURCHES It has often been said that Gazimağusa had 365 churches, each one paid for by a man or woman intent on buying their place in heaven. The number of churches is indeed high, and can be partially explained by the plethora of sects that coexisted in the city. Here we have Latin and Greek, Maronite, Armenian, Coptic, Georgian, Carmelite, Nestorian, Jacobite, Abyssinian and Jewish.

Of the 17 churches still standing today, only two are in use: the **Nestorian Church**, now well restored, which underwent a recent reincarnation as the Cultural Centre of the Eastern Mediterranean University of Gazimağusa, though there is little recent sign of activity; and the cathedral church of **St Nicholas**, in service since the 16th century as Gazimağusa's main mosque, and now called Lala Mustafa Paşa (pages 154–5), after the Ottoman commander-in-chief during the siege. To visit all the churches described in the following itinerary will take you 3–4 hours on foot, but if you have only an hour, then just visit the central cluster around the main square, the **church of St Peter and St Paul**, and the huge haunting shell of **St George of the Greeks**, once the Greek Orthodox cathedral.

Church of St Peter and St Paul (Sinan Paşa Mosque) [146 D3] Following
the road away from the main square, leaving the Venetian Palace on your right, you soon reach the large, tall church of St Peter and St Paul, unmistakable with its heavy flying buttresses, essential props for the high walls. It was built around 1360 and is still in a reasonable state of preservation because the Turks always found a use for it. It was at one time a mosque, as evidenced by the ruined minaret, missing its cone, built onto the southwest corner. Under the British it was a grain and potato store. In 1964 it was restored and used as the town hall for a while, and it then served as Gazimağusa's municipal library, with a wonderfully pious atmosphere. Schoolchildren used to come here to do their homework in the peace and quiet that is difficult to find at home. Although it did become a venue for plays and recitals, it has been locked up for a while now and, despite two further recent renovations, its future remains uncertain. You can see inside through a gap in the rear doors.

The Nestorian Church (Ayios Georgios Exorinos) [146 C2] Walking on
further, leaving the church/mosque on your left, you can now follow the road as it swings round gradually to the north (right) towards the cluster of five churches that lie near the western edge of the walls, and continue in a huge lap around the town before returning to the main square.

The first church you notice, down a side street opposite the Moratto Bastion on Necip Tozu Sokagi, is the small and pretty Nestorian church, neat and well looked after. Having enjoyed a role as the Cultural Centre of Gazimağusa's **Eastern Mediterranean University**, the major university of North Cyprus, it held a Good Friday service in 2014, with many hundreds of Greek Orthodox attendees from the Republic of Cyprus and elsewhere. Earlier, it had been used as a camel stable, though as recently as 1957 it still served as a church. Its style is different from the other churches, with its unusual but attractive bell tower and small rose window. It was built for the Syrian community of Gazimağusa by a wealthy businessman, as many Nestorians were rich financiers. Inside, it was decorated with frescoes by Italian and Syrian painters of the 14th and 15th centuries. Traces of these frescoes survive on the back wall opposite what is today the stage. Originally it was called St George the Foreigner (Ayios Georgios Exorinos) to distinguish it from St George of the Greeks and St George of the Latins.

Martinengo Bastion and surrounding churches Following the path of the wall
towards the Martinengo Bastion, four churches that were previously inaccessible present themselves for closer inspection. The military have decamped from the zone that occupied a large chunk of the northwest of the city and visitors can now access the churches and the Bastion itself. However, there are none of the usual yellow information signs, and the whole area is crying out for some tender loving care.

Ayia Anna [146 C2], known locally as the **church of the Maronites**, is the first of the churches, with a sturdy belfry and a few frescoes inside. It is tiny but perfectly formed. Unfortunately the military have sealed off the doorways, which means the view from the road is almost as good as walking around the inside of the fence. Indeed, as this area has now been leased to the state's school for children with learning difficulties, you may decide not to disturb the pupils and simply look from afar.

Sharing the same fenced-off compound is the **Tanner's Mosque** [146 C2], originally a 16th-century church. Again, the doors have been blocked up with ugly materials and it's impossible to see anything.

On the other side of the road is the tall **Carmelite Church of St Mary** [146 C1], originally part of a monastery, now disappeared, for the mendicant friars. It was richly adorned with frescoes by Italian artists of the 14th and 15th centuries, and some traces remain, although the ravages of neglect have ensured that the images are indistinct to the point of near invisibility. Behind it stands the tiny 14th-century **Armenian church** [146 C1], the most forlorn of the group. It now serves predominantly as a pigeon loft. Sadly, the interior of the church is now almost totally derelict, with just a few smoke-blackened frescoes barely visible towards the tops of the walls. In what was presumably one of the Turkish army's occasional acts of preservation, the lower parts of the walls have been whitewashed, making it impossible to assess whether or not anything of worth remains beneath.

Many of these churches suffered severe damage in the 1960s and 1970s, when Turkish Cypriots came here as refugees, having been turfed out of their villages by the Greeks. Shortage of accommodation meant that some had to camp inside the churches along with their possessions and animals. Cooking fires caused blackening and damage to frescoes, while children larked about trying to prise off pieces of decoration with penknives or dislodge higher mosaics with catapults.

Behind the Armenian church, the large ramps that sweep underground lead the visitor down to the bowels of the Martinengo Bastion, named after a Venetian commander who was sent to Cyprus to relieve the Turkish siege, but who died at sea before arriving. This was to be his final resting place. From close up the imposing power of the architecture looms large, and thankfully there's a project under way to remove the ugly breezeblocks that were used to partition up the chambers, along with the equally unsightly concrete walls.

Next to the bastion is a small cemetery for civilian casualties killed in the troubles of 1964 and 1965, including the grave of one as yet unidentified person.

Some 300m beyond the Tanner's Mosque you now fork back south towards the main square to complete your circuit. On your right you can glance at the ruined **Kertikli Hammam** [146 D2], a Turkish bath with its six domes still intact.

Further on you pass on your right, just after a street junction, the structure known as **Biddulph's Gate** [146 D2], an archway built from old brown stone with three steps leading up into what was once the house of a wealthy merchant, but is now a small piece of open, scruffy wasteland. Sir Robert Biddulph was the British High Commissioner in Cyprus who stopped the gate being destroyed in 1879.

Beyond the next junction on the right is one of the very few relics of a private as opposed to a public building, the shell of a **Venetian house** [146 D2]. The Venetians were in Gazimağusa for only 82 years and the bulk of their building effort went into the fortifications. The house's exterior is elegant and pleasing, like all Venetian architecture in the style of the Italian Renaissance. By peering through the keyhole you can see into the courtyard wilderness inside. Both doors are locked and the roof has collapsed. It used to be called the Queen's House.

Up a side street to the right, just before the Venetian house, you will come to the twin churches of the **Templars and the Hospitallers** [146 D2], both orders of the Latin Church formed at the time of the Crusades in 1350, yet often at loggerheads despite their apparent embrace. The left one has been converted to a private art gallery.

Just before the main square you pass the renovated **Djafer Paşa Hammam** [146 D2], a Turkish bath built in 1605. Thick glass pieces set into the roof allowed the sun in by day, and the starlight by night. It has seen recent service as a café, but is currently closed.

From the main square you can now head off south to see the remaining four churches in a small loop. This route can also be driven, by taking the only permitted exit from the main square to the south, a narrow road that winds round to the right and takes you through a picturesque Ottoman archway, like a gatehouse with rooms above.

Southern churches By far the most impressive of these five southern churches is the huge shell of **St George of the Greeks** [146 E2], standing alone in an area of wasteland. Its roof was blown off in the Turkish bombardment in 1571, and the most damaged part is visibly the side that faces the Canbulat Tower, the direction from which the Turkish artillery was firing. The pockmarking in the walls tallies with the size of the cannonballs. Many of these can still be seen lying about in the waste ground in and around the churches of this area. Some have been put to ingenious uses, such as marking the edges of flowerbeds in manicured gardens.

You can enter the church from the southern side, through a hole in the railings. It was built as the rival cathedral for Gazimağusa's Orthodox community. Its three apses once held frescoes showing the life of Christ, and some small fragments survive in the eastern apse. In what remains of the roof, you can see the bottoms of pottery jars embedded. Their function is mysterious, but one clever suggestion is that they may have been used to improve the acoustics. Abutting the church to the south is the much smaller **Ayios Simeon** [146 E2].

Some 200m further to the south, also standing in open waste ground, is the small, 15th-century church of **Ayios Nicolas** [146 E2], still with its roof but with no frescoes inside, and further away, tucked behind it, the little dome of **Ayia Zoni** [146 E2], a church in typical rustic Cypriot style. It is now kept locked to protect the fragmentary frescoes of the Archangel Michael, and you can just glimpse them if you peer in through cracks in the door.

The final church, further to the north on Mustafa Paşa Sokak, is the barrel-vaulted church of the **Holy Cross** or **Stavros** [146 E3], long used as a store, and later as a mosque. It now has the sign 'Mustafa Paşa Mescidi' out front and its structure is severely threatened.

TOWARDS VAROSHA Opposite the Land Gate outside the walls is a large, modern roundabout. In the centre of the roundabout stands a rather gory colossal bronze **Martyrs' Memorial** [146 C4], depicting the suffering of the Turks. Driving south from here, just by the old tourist office, a wide road, previously known as Independence Avenue, leads off towards Varosha. Some 300m down this wide avenue on the left-hand side, your eye may be caught by the little **steam locomotive** that stands just behind a wire fence. A plaque announces that it was the first locomotive to be imported into Cyprus, in 1904. The little railway line on which it ran was the only one in Cyprus, built by the British, running from Gazimağusa via Nicosia to Morphou. There were passenger services, but very few Cypriots took advantage of them, being either too poor to afford a ticket or content to travel more slowly by donkey or cart. The railway's primary function was to transport the copper and chrome from the Skouriotissa mines to the port at Gazimağusa, from where they were then exported. The coal on which it ran was brought all the way from England by boat. By 1945 the railway began to fall into disrepair, and diesel trucks were found to be more economical for transporting the copper ore. The last train ran in 1951.

Beyond the locomotive are the **post office** and the derelict former **courthouse**, their architecture a testament to the British colonial period.

Following the road further south you soon come to the edge of **Varosha**, lying about 1km south of old Gazimağusa. Once an affluent Greek suburb (**varoş** is Turkish for suburb), Varosha, the 'Monte Carlo of the Middle East', grew in the 1960s to be far larger than the old walled town. While the Turkish walled town decayed, this fashionable resort of Greek Cypriots and expatriates mushroomed with hotels and holiday flats along the 6km beach of Glossa, said to be the best beach in the eastern Mediterranean. By the early 1970s it had a population of 35,000, overwhelmingly

Greeks. The annual Gazimağusa Orange Festival used to take place here in March, during which visitors were showered with as many oranges as they could eat. Varosha was famous for its orange groves and fertile gardens, and the district had so many windmills it was sometimes called the Town of the Windmills.

Now fenced off and forlorn, it was evacuated in 1974 when the Turks captured it for use as a bargaining card in any future negotiations. There was no military necessity for its capture as no Turkish Cypriots lived there. On paper it is now in the hands of the UN, but in practice the Turkish army uses one hotel as a barracks, another two as student hostels and a further one as an officers' club. Furniture looting still goes on, despite the fence, and as you peer inside you can spot many houses where boarded-up doors have been forced, window frames ripped out, and weeds are growing up through the floor. It is difficult to see how this or any other formerly Greek property could be returned. Here in Varosha, most of the houses would need total renovation and in some cases even demolition before starting again. Where Greek houses have been used and inhabited in other parts of the north, many have been sold on to foreigners who have since spent much money on restoration. After 1974 the Turkish Cypriots were given Greek houses under a government scheme to compensate for property and land they lost in the south. They were issued with a paper that gave them title to the houses and they were then at liberty to sell them. In some cases there have been several sales of the same house since 1974 and to unravel all these transactions now would be a mighty task. Prospective purchasers, beware!

You can drive south all the way along the edge of the fenced-off area, until you see the checkpoint barrier blocking your path: the Attila Line is just a kilometre or two beyond. You can return a slightly different way by forking off towards the sea whenever you can, hugging the Varosha fence throughout.

Emerging near a sea lagoon, you will see another cluster of simple restaurants. On the headland beyond it is the **Arkin Palm Beach Hotel** (page 148). Originally Greek-run and called the Constantia, it has recently been fully renovated. Set on a beautiful beach with crystal-clear waters, the setting is surreal. The other once-famous hotels, such as the Grecian, the Florida and the King George, are all within the fence and crumbling away. The Greek Cypriots, ever mindful of a commercial opportunity, run cruises from Ayia Napa for tourists to stand off and peer at the ghost city. They also organise minibus or taxi trips to a viewing platform at the village of Dherinia, from where Varosha can be discerned through telescopes and binoculars.

Another sight that tourists can no longer visit in Varosha is the **Icon Museum** [146 E3]. Previously, you simply parked your car, showed your passport to the soldiers and walked through to the museum, where the icons were housed in a fairly modern Orthodox church of Maraş. The icons are nothing special – most date from the last 50 years, with the oldest less than 300 years old – though the acoustics were impressive, particularly noticeable if one of the resident pigeons flew under the dome. Now, all you can do is observe the distant church from outside the military barrier, though things may change. To reach here, from the Canbulat Gate drive southeast and continue straight on past the northern end of Fevzi Cakmak.

SALAMIS *Map, page 160*

(☺ *summer 08.00–19.00 daily, winter 08.00–17.00 daily; TL9/5 adult/student*) Ancient Salamis, the first city of Cyprus in classical Greek times, boasts some of the most impressive monuments to be found on the island. The pleasantly overgrown ruins lie among fragrant eucalyptus and acacia trees, alongside an excellent though

5

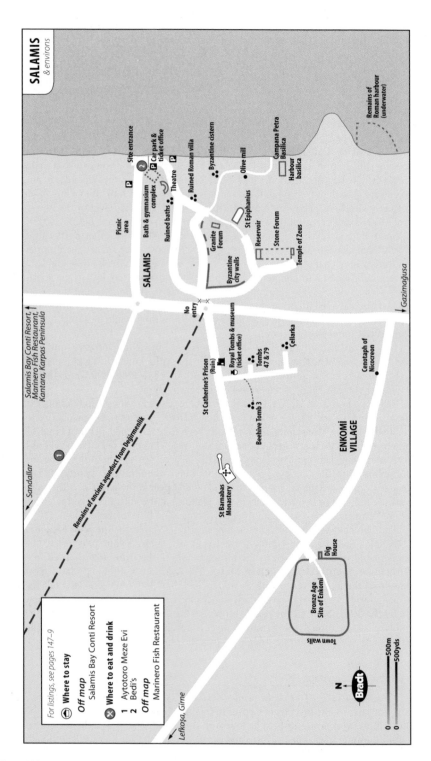

SALAMIS
& environs

Site entrance

Car park &
ticket office

P

Ruined Roman villa

Byzantine cistern

Olive mill

Campana Petra
Basilica

Harbour
basilica

Remains of
Roman harbour
(underwater)

Picnic
area

P

Bath & gymnasium
complex

Theatre

Ruined baths

Granite
Forum

St Epiphanius

Reservoir

Stone Forum

Temple of Zeus

SALAMIS

Byzantine
city walls

Gazimağusa

No
entry

Royal Tombs & museum
(ticket office)

Çellarka

St Catherine's Prison
(Ruin)

Tombs
47 & 79

Cenotaph of
Nicocreon

ENKOMİ
VILLAGE

Sandallar

Salamis Bay Conti Resort,
Marinero Fish Restaurant,
Kantara, Karpas Peninsula

Remains of ancient aqueduct from Değirmenlik

Beehive Tomb 3

St Barnabas
Monastery

Bronze Age
Site of Enkomi

Dig
House

Town walls

Lefkoşa, Girne

For listings, see pages 147–9

Where to stay
Off map
Salamis Bay Conti Resort

Where to eat and drink
1 Aytotoro Meze Evi
   Bedi's
Off map
   Marinero Fish Restaurant

N

Bradt

0   500m
0   500yds

160

narrow beach, with safe swimming. Situated 6km north of Gazimağusa, it makes an easy visit and is readily accessible.

The area covered by the site is huge: so huge that although archaeologists began work here in 1890 and have continued intermittently throughout the last century, the site is still only partially excavated. Networks of roads run across it, none signposted, and it can be fairly easy to lose your way, and difficult to get an overview as the site is so flat. A few minutes studying the map will help. Cars have recently been banned from driving through the site, so be prepared for some lengthy walking under a blistering sun. Take comfortable shoes, suntan lotion and a sunhat; the flat landscape offers precious little shade. Go well equipped with liquid refreshments, too, or else you may find yourself hallucinating that the marble basins in the gymnasium are still sparkling with cool water. If you don't fancy walking much, don't be put off: the main sites (the gymnasium and theatre) are right next to the entrance and car park where you leave the car.

The only **entrance** into the site now is the northern side entrance on the coast; the former main entrance, opposite the turn-off for St Barnabas (pages 167–8) is no longer open. It takes about 2–3 hours to visit the major parts of the site, but you could easily spend a whole day here if you wanted to explore exhaustively – much of it spent walking between different excavated areas. If you're coming from the Girne area and only have a day to devote to Gazimağusa and its environs, you could spend the morning in old Gazimağusa, then drive on to Salamis for lunch at the pleasant seaside restaurant beside the entrance – though you'll probably have time only for the gymnasium and theatre areas of Salamis before you have to return. Those based in the Gazimağusa area will probably make separate visits to Salamis and the other sites close by. Recommended times for visits would be 3–4 hours for Salamis, 2 hours for the Tombs of the Kings and St Barnabas Monastery, and one hour for Enkomi.

TOURING SALAMIS Heading north out of Gazimağusa towards Salamis, you pass, near the outskirts of town, a busy area with lots of cafés and pizza restaurants full of young people. Directly opposite is the reason – the Eastern Mediterranean University, North Cyprus's major university, offering degree courses in sciences, engineering, management and economics. The medium of instruction is English and the students are an international bunch.

The road continues north past a ridiculously ostentatious new nightclub, adorned with leaping lions and bugling cherubs (you can't miss it!), reaching Salamis after about 10 minutes. At a roundabout, take the clearly signposted road running along the northern edge of the site, which brings you out at the beach by the pleasant Bedi's restaurant, raised up overlooking the bay. Its spacious shady terrace makes a cool haven in summer. Beyond this first car park – there are two more inside – is the ticket office. Your ticket price includes a basic leaflet in English, and there is usually an English-speaking guide available to help. The service is free, but a gratuity would be appropriate. The first point of interest after the entrance is the baths and gymnasium complex. The theatre is just 100m further on and there is also a new, simple café.

These two areas together form the most spectacular part of Salamis, the part you should explore most thoroughly. They have also received the bulk of the excavators' attention. Suspiciously headless statues have been re-erected in the gymnasium and the theatre has been renovated. Though discovered in 1882 and dug erratically since then, the site was not excavated systematically until 1952. From then, work was in progress every season until 1974, when the University of Lyon excavators left. In 1998 regular work began again under the auspices of Ankara University and Gazimağusa's Eastern Mediterranean University. New structures have been revealed and abandoned digs reopened. However, as you walk around the site today you will se that vast tracts of the city remain untouched, and without a much greater resource, progress will inevitably continue slowly. The task is undoubtedly a daunting one, for Salamis was the victim of two severe earthquakes in the 4th century within ten years of each other. Tidal waves combed across the city bringing in sand and debris. Later that century, the Byzantine emperor Constantine II rebuilt it, but on a smaller scale, and renamed it Constantia in honour of himself. It suffered badly again in the Arab raids of the 7th century, and most of the population that survived the massacres moved to Gazimağusa, then called Arsinoe. Abandoned, its collapsed buildings were used as a quarry for medieval Famagusta, and the sand and vegetation reclaimed the city.

The gymnasium and baths The gymnasium is the pearl of Salamis and the glimpse of lifestyle afforded here helps to convey, more than any other monument yet exposed, the magnificence and wealth that the city must have enjoyed in Hellenistic and Roman times. As you first enter along the marble pavements, you feel the elegant colonnaded courtyard must have been the forum, the marketplace and heart of the city, rather than simply an outbuilding devoted to education and the culture of the body, the ancient Greek version of a school and health centre. It is now thought that there were originally three gymnasia, two for boys and one for girls. The open forecourt (palaestra) was where the boy athletes would exercise and train. Afterwards they would plunge in the cool water of the two pools, watched by the naked white marble statues of their gymnasiarchs or headmasters. These were wealthy citizens elected for a one-year terms to help with the school's finances, and also provided the expensive olive oil for body massage for those boys who had won free attendance by scholarship. Today these gymnasiarch statues have been replaced by women draped in robes, headless to a woman, decapitated it is thought by early Christian zealots who took the statues to be relics of the pagan religion. Nudity offended them, and all bare statues were broken up or tossed into drains. Clothed statues were just tolerable if their faces were removed. Today, the most striking statue is the handless and faceless black marble Persephone.

The **columns** of the porticoes were re-erected in the 1950s by the excavators, and on close examination the apparent harmony of the whole reveals its mixed origins, for it was destroyed and rebuilt many times in its history. In the east portico, for example, the Corinthian capitals are too small for their columns, which are taller and larger than this on the other three sides, presumably brought from somewhere else in the city by the later Byzantine builders.

The **Hellenistic and Roman latrines** are situated in the southwest corner of the palaestra, and are the largest on the island. Arranged in a semicircle, with open-plan seating for 44, they strike us today, with our prudishly solitary cubicles, as most improper. The puritanical Christians of the 4th century, too, considered them indecent, and had them walled up.

Beside the gymnasium are the colossal **Byzantine baths**, an impressive complex of tall chambers with marble and mosaic flooring and underfloor heating, so deeply buried in sand that they were only discovered in 1926. In two of the vaulted arches traces of Roman mosaics can still be seen, mainly in reds and browns. In the largest mosaic, the central figure is thought to be Apollo with a lyre and quiver below.

The walls throughout are of immense thickness, often 3m or more. Columns and capitals lie scattered about, but much of the more elaborate marble carving was taken away and is now on display in the Cyprus Museum in Greek Nicosia. Some of the finds also used to be on display at the Museum of Gazimağusa within the suburb of Varosha. Now they are doubtless heavily cobwebbed. The intricate water system, here and in the gymnasium, is a perpetual source of amazement. A 56km aqueduct brought water from the abundant spring at Kythrea (now Değirmenlik) to a large tank which can still be seen in the undergrowth. Scholars have estimated that this water system could supply the needs of 120,000 people.

The theatre   The theatre was not discovered until 1959 and archaeologists have now rebuilt it to under half its original height, 18 of the 50 rows of seats. Of these, only the first few rows are original, and the division is clear where their white limestone casing gives way to the brown limestone used in the reconstruction. Badly damaged in the earthquakes of the 4th century, many of its original stones and decorative blocks were carted off for reuse in other buildings. The marble tiles of its orchestra, for example, were taken off to renovate the nearby baths after an earthquake. The channel in the middle of the orchestra was the drainage for blood from animals sacrificed to Dionysus before each performance. With an original seating capacity of between 15,000 and 20,000 it is far and away the largest theatre in Cyprus, reflecting the fact that Salamis was the foremost city on the island for much of its history. Eschewing blood-letting, these days the theatre again hosts crowds for regular music and theatre performances.

Most of the extant ruins date from the Roman and Byzantine times, but Salamis was in fact said to have been founded in the 12th century BC by a hero of the Trojan War. Brother to Ajax, his name was Teucer, and he named the new Greek colony in Cyprus after the small island of Salamis (near Piraeus) that had been his homeland. All over the island, other heroes of the Trojan War also founded their own cities, such as Paphos, Soli, Lapithos, Kyrenia and Marion (Polis), and each was independent, ruled by its own king. At one time there were ten such tiny kingdoms on the island. Salamis was generally the most powerful, and by virtue of its excellent harbour, became the greatest commercial centre, trading with the Levant, Greece and Rome. It was the first city in Cyprus to mint its own coinage.

The forums, basilicas and other ruins   Although the theatre and gymnasium together form the most impressive part of Salamis, there are plenty of other ruins in the area that are worth visiting. A circular tour of the other major sites can be made if you have the time (a minimum of 1½–2 hours) and energy (to walk the 5km or so). Taking a left at every junction should ensure you cover most of Salamis.

After the gymnasium and theatre area, the next most impressive section of ruins at Salamis is to be found beside the **old Roman harbour**. To reach it, you head south from the theatre and fork left at the first junction of tarmac roads. Passing the sorry remains of a **Roman villa**, take the next left. Some 100m or so after this junction, on the left of the road, is an **underground Byzantine cistern** with paintings on the walls, but now kept locked. The key is held by the Gazimağusa Department of Antiquities, beside the Namık Kemal prison. The cistern consists of three interconnecting chambers, in one of which are faded water scenes of fish and sea plants with a bearded Christ above. Access involves descending a ladder with torches (supplied).

Beyond the cistern and past an old olive mill on the right, as the road heads towards the sea you will see rising up on your right the columns of the recently excavated but already overgrown basilica identified as **Campana Petra**, standing just above the sandy beach. This large, attractive building has been dated to the

4th century and has elegant columns and many beautiful geometric floor designs. The bulk of the stone is white marble and in summer the impression is of dazzling brightness as the sun glints off the sea and the gleaming stone. The most elaborate floor patterning of all is to be found in the lowest section of the basilica near the sea, where the diamond-shaped stones are set in very modern-looking swirls of colour. From the basilica, you can watch the cargo ships waiting their turn to unload at the nearby Gazimağusa docks.

After exploring the basilica, you can go on to the beach for a swim or to seek out the remains of the **Roman harbour**. In the clear shallow water are thousands of fragments of Roman sherds, and beyond, the harbour wall is still only at waist height. The main harbour of ancient Salamis in fact lies a little further south, and you can explore it by strolling along the beach and rounding the first headland.

The Stone Forum, St Epiphanius and the Granite Forum
Returning to the junction near the olive mill, take a right to return to the theatre and car park or a left to explore the rest of Salamis. Though these last ruins are unexcavated, they remain impressive and for those with the time it is pleasant to stroll around the ancient city to find them, enjoying the gentle breeze which blows in the fragrant eucalyptus trees. In spring and early summer, the walk across the gentle rise and fall of the land, alive with the yellow blossom of acacia mimosa, is especially lovely.

Most memorable, perhaps, is the **Agora** or **Stone Forum**, thought to be the largest forum or marketplace in the entire Roman Empire, with origins going back to the Hellenistic period. On the way to the forum you will come, on your right, to the foundations of **St Epiphanius**, the largest basilica in Cyprus. It was built in AD345, just after the earthquakes, by Epiphanius, the Bishop of Constantia. Utterly devastated as it is, the church still conveys its vastness. Salamis has an important place in the early history of Christianity, and St Barnabas himself was born here. Barnabas accompanied Paul on his first missionary journey from Antioch:

> For the Jews require a sign, and the Greeks seek after wisdom: But we preach Christ crucified, unto the Jews a stumbling-block, and unto the Greeks foolishness.
>
> 1 Corinthians 1: 22–23

Later, Barnabas split from Paul and came to Cyprus again with his nephew, the young John Mark. He became, according to Church tradition, the first bishop of the Church of Cyprus, and was martyred by the Jews of his native Salamis in AD75. On the site where he is buried, the St Barnabas Monastery now stands, described on pages 167–8.

Close to the basilica, just a little further north on the opposite side of the road, look out for the huge tumbled **granite columns** of another, smaller forum. These hefty 50-tonne, 6m-long columns are in the unmistakable pinkish colour of Aswan granite from Egypt.

Measuring 230m by 55m, the Agora or Stone Forum is best viewed from the temple end (ie: not from the trackside but from the far side of the ruins), though this involves a long walk, taking a left where the path forks near the Gazimağusa– Boğaz highway. Don't try to pick your way through the forum ruins, for they are heavily overgrown and somewhat dangerous. (If you can't be bothered to traipse all the way to the temple, the view from the end of the forum nearest the path is almost as good. Lying between the forum and the path is a deep, pillared reservoir that supplied the city.) The little temple, with well-crafted marble steps are still visible, is known to have been dedicated to Zeus (Jupiter), who was also the protector of the island of Salamis, the city's namesake. Having reached the temple, you must pick your way across to the temple podium, slightly raised, from where you can then look out over the forum. The column stumps lining the sides are still visible and a solitary capital remains on its full-height column to help evoke the scale of the whole. These columns would have formed part of the forum's twin arcades, protecting shoppers from the fierce heat. The central courtyard would have been filled with temples, statues and fountains.

To return to the entrance, follow the path as it loops round alongside the **Byzantine city's walls**. All around are more buildings, covered in sand and undergrowth, awaiting excavation. Sections of town wall belonging to the smaller Byzantine town of Constantia can be glimpsed here and there. Of the earlier Greek city wall, nothing remains except earth banks. Just opposite the former entrance to Salamis, next to the highway, you can still see in the scrubland a fragment of the aqueduct that brought water down from Kythrea. At the beginning of the century, parts of it were still in use.

THE ROYAL TOMBS AND NECROPOLIS OF SALAMIS   *Map, page 160*

(*The gates to the tomb enclosures are usually open, but the adjacent little museum adheres to office-like hours:* ⊕ *08.00–15.30; TL9/5 adult/student*) To the west of Salamis sprawls a huge necropolis covering some 7km². Some of the tombs that have been uncovered have been of great importance archaeologically, helping us to understand more about the beliefs and rituals of the early islanders. Chief among these finds is an unusual collection of tombs, unique on the island and interesting for their strange Homeric associations. They are less than 1km from the main site of Salamis.

TOURING THE ROYAL TOMBS   Leaving Salamis, take a left back on to the main road and then a right at the next roundabout signposted for St Barnabas Monastery. The road continues inland and takes you to the un-signposted Necropolis of Salamis after just 500m or so on your left, with the St Barnabas Monastery barely 1km further inland on the same road.

Drive up to the Royal Tombs's ticket office (follow the yellow signposts as usual) and leave your car here. Next to the ticket office is a very useful **museum**, providing you with the necessary background information to the tombs. Even if the office and museum are closed, you can usually still gain access to the tombs themselves as their gates are not generally locked. If the museum is shut, you can peer in through the windows to see the reconstructions of the bronze horse chariots and drawings showing the course of excavations and how the tombs were found. The discovery of these tombs and their accompanying chariots has yielded some evidence that would seem to confirm Salamis's origins as a Trojan foundation, and Homer's *Iliad* describes precisely such funeral pyres as were found here, piled high with jars of honey and oil, and then the four horses on top.

There are six major royal tombs and a visit to all would take at least an hour. It is not actually known whether these tombs belonged to royalty or not, but the quality and value of the objects buried with the deceased to accompany them to the next life suggest that they were very important and wealthy people.

If you are short of time you might confine yourself to three: St Catherine's Prison and tombs **No 47** and **No 79**. These last two sit directly behind the museum and are generally reckoned to be the most interesting. On their wide, sloping entrance passages are the skeletons of the horses that had pulled the deceased's hearse to the

THE CENOTAPH OF NICOCREON

Of all the tombs in the vast, sprawling necropolis that lies on the plain to the west of Salamis and Gazimağusa, **Tomb No 77** stands out for a number of reasons. For one thing it is not actually a tomb at all, there being no bodies buried there (hence its official description as a cenotaph, or memorial). For another, it lies some distance apart from the main tomb complex, in the village of Tuzla (Enkomi), just a couple of kilometres to the west of Gazimağusa.

Furthermore, the story behind the cenotaph is rather unusual. In 31BC, Nicocreon, King of Salamis, sided with Antignon against Ptolemy. This quite naturally upset Ptolemy, who besieged the city with a huge army. Nicocreon, realising that his own forces stood no chance against the might of Ptolemy, decided to commit suicide. When his wife, Queen Axiothea, heard this, she chose to kill their daughters – and persuaded the wives of Nicocreon's brothers to do the same – to prevent them from being raped by Ptolemy's soldiers. In a final act, Axiothea then burnt the palace with herself and the remains of her extended family inside.

To commemorate what they saw as a highly virtuous act – choosing death over the perceived disgrace of being violated by the soldiers – somebody (presumably the Salamians, though nobody is exactly sure) constructed this curious cenotaph. The site consists of a platform, 52m in diameter, with a ramp on one side and steps on the other three. In the centre a pyre was built, where clay statues (thought to represent the members of the royal family), rosettes and other offerings were burnt in their honour. The whole lot was then covered in earth to a depth of over 10m.

The cenotaph was finally excavated in 1965–66. Unfortunately, little remains of the site today, which sits behind the church in Tuzla and is usually locked (though you can look over the fence). The Royal Tombs Museum, however, has a reconstruction of the cenotaph, along with various statues and offerings found at the site.

grave. The skeletons are now preserved under glass cases like confectionery. The king's body was cremated and the horses were then sacrificed, still yoked together. Their death agony is evident in their contorted positions, their necks broken and twisted in panic.

The tomb known as **St Catherine's Prison** is unmistakable, with its stone vaulted hump clearly visible to the right of the road as you drive up from Salamis. It is unique in appearance because the Romans built a chapel above the original tomb, using these huge stone blocks, and dedicated it to St Catherine. Inside, pieces of church furniture like lecterns and tables still lie in alcoves.

St Catherine, the early Christian martyr of Alexandria, was born in Salamis, daughter to one of the island's puppet kings under Roman administration. She refused to marry unless her parents found her a groom as fair and learned and wise and rich as her. Her parents considered this impossible and sent her to a holy hermit, who told her the only man she could marry with these attributes was Jesus Christ. Her father was later exiled to Alexandria and the Christians on the island severely tortured. Catherine proclaimed herself of the faith and was thrown in prison, and later sent to Alexandria herself to be martyred on a gruesome, spiked wheel, cited as the origin for the name given to today's pyrotechnic Catherine Wheel. When the site was excavated in 1965, her tomb was shown to be of the same type as the others in the necropolis, dated to the

7th century BC. Like them, it has the skeletons of a pair of royal horses yoked together in the entrance passage, sent to the afterlife with their mistress.

On the opposite side of the road, the huge anthill mound with a modern gabled roof of asbestos is prominent. This was imaginatively christened **Tomb No 3** by the archaeologists working the site in the 1960s. Inside, you simply clamber down to the empty grave chamber. The remaining tombs lie behind the beehive No 3, in fenced-in areas. They are in a sorry state, overgrown and vandalised, the glass skeleton cases smashed, scarcely warranting the extra walk for the non-specialist.

THE ÇELLARKA More interesting in many ways to those who have the time is the short detour to visit the additional group of tombs known as the Çellarka. This is an area some 15m by 100m dug out in a maze of interlinking underground tombs, at least 50 in all. Some are approached by rock-cut steps down to the grave chamber, and one of the tomb doorways has a simple decoration with what looks like a fish carved into the rock.

To reach the Çellarka you simply continue along the track past the museum for 300m or so, then fork left up an equally rough track lined with oleander bushes. You arrive at a fenced-in area with a gate (usually unlocked). Don't go round these tombs after a beer too many at lunchtime, lest you slip and entomb yourself.

ST BARNABAS MONASTERY *Map, page 160*

St Barnabas Monastery (Ayios Varnavas), along with Ayias Mamas in Güzelyurt and Apostolos Andreas on the Karpas tip, is a complete monastery, preserved as it was pre-1974 and open for viewing as an **icon museum** (⊕ *summer 08.00–19.00 daily, winter 08.00–17.00, daily; TL9/5 adult/student*). A visit takes at least 40 minutes. There are toilets here, a basic but pleasant café in the gardens, and a small gift shop.

Its atmosphere is relaxed and pleasant, and it lies less than 2km from Salamis.

TOURING ST BARNABAS MONASTERY Set on the road between Enkomi and the tombs of the kings, a signpost announces the monastery and you drive up to the door opposite the attractively carved **water fountain**.

The monastery was functioning until 1976, having been lived in since 1917 by three monks, all brothers, said to be indistinguishable from one another. The youngest, a mere 79, was a painter, prolific in the production of necessarily mediocre icons, sold to visitors in order to finance monastery repairs. The other brothers, despite their age, then effected these repairs, adding the new bell tower and finishing the rooms and cells around the courtyard. The attractive **garden** and **cloister courtyard** contain quantities of carved blocks and capitals brought from nearby Salamis. Many of the rooms around the courtyard are bursting with pottery from the Enkomi site, much of it in fantastic condition. The courtyard garden is still well tended, with jasmine and hibiscus flame trees, huge pink flowering cacti and citrus trees, one of which is a chimera, producing oranges, lemons and mandarins from its different parts. Refreshments are on offer here.

The monastery church itself has also changed since the monks left. The pulpits and wooden lecterns are still in place, though the pews have been removed and it has now been converted into a gallery for the church's collection of icons. The newer, crasser ones are the work of the pragmatic painter brother. A series of four depict the story of how the Cypriot archbishop went to Constantinople to request and be granted independence for the Church of Cyprus by the Emperor Zeno. This story is especially pertinent to the monastery, as it was thanks to Barnabas that this came about. As the

Apostle who, with Paul, brought Christianity to Cyprus, Barnabas is revered as the real founder of the Cypriot Church. Born in Salamis, Barnabas returned here later with Paul and died in his native town, martyred by Jews. A number of his followers who witnessed his murder and watched as his body was dumped in marshland are said to have taken his corpse before his murderers could dispose of it properly, and brought it to this spot. Here it lay undisturbed and forgotten for centuries until its location was revealed to Anthemios in a dream in AD477.

Its rediscovery prompted the archbishop to set off to Constantinople and ask that the Cypriot Church be granted its independence. The Byzantine emperor agreed, persuaded by the gift of the original Gospel of St Matthew, in Barnabas's own handwriting, allegedly found clasped in the dead saint's arms. Zeno even donated the funds for this, the first monastery on Cyprus. Today, the self-governing Church of Cyprus ranks fifth in the world of Greek Orthodoxy – after the patriarchates of Constantinople, Alexandria, Antioch and Jerusalem, but before the patriarchates of Russia, Greece, Serbia, Romania, etc.

The monastery as it stands now dates largely to the 18th century, as the original 5th-century building was destroyed in the Arab raids. Of the icons in the church, the two rows across the top of the iconostasis show the disciples and scenes from the Bible and are thought, after recent research, to be just 200 years old. Carved capitals from Salamis peep out from the whitewashed walls, and the blackened pillar inside the painted apse is also from Salamis. Near the altar is the wax effigy of a leg, from a family whose child had an illness in this limb, hung here for the saint to cure.

Perhaps more impressive than the church is the monastery's **museum**, housed in the rooms surrounding the courtyard. Among the collection are some wonderfully complete pottery pieces from various eras from 4000BC onwards, some equally complete Roman glassware and some gold jewellery.

Outside, opposite the entrance, new excavations have revealed several deep **rock tombs** and the tree-lined road straight ahead from the monastery door leads to Barnabas's tomb. The plain-domed mausoleum was erected in the 1950s above an old rock tomb, and you can still clamber down the steps to see where the bones of Barnabas and his Gospel of St Matthew are said to have been found. These days there's a small shrine with a few lighted candles and the smell of incense to venerate the spot.

ENKOMI: BRONZE AGE CAPITAL OF CYPRUS *Map, page 160*

(⊕ *08.00–15.00 Fri–Wed, 08.00–18.00 Wed; TL7/5 adult/student*) Enkomi, the first ancient capital of the island, dated to 2000BC, is a much underrated site. Even though at first glance it looks uninspiring, the longer you stay down inside the site, the more you notice the details that gradually bring it alive. Allow anything from 30 minutes to an hour.

TOURING ENKOMI To reach the site, you drive inland (west) from the St Barnabas Monastery. The site, clearly signposted, sits immediately to the right of the first major junction you come to, opposite a water tower. At the entrance, the cluster of derelict buildings on the left were originally the French excavators' headquarters for the digs that went on here under Professor Schaeffer (excavator of Ugarit/Ras Shamra in Syria) from the 1930s until the 1960s. The site was, in fact, first excavated in 1896 by the British, who found quantities of treasure and Mycenaean pottery, now in the British Museum.

Since the late 1960s Enkomi has been neglected, though today this process has been at least arrested if not reversed. The entrance fee includes a map and brief history of the site. However, it's quite likely that apart from solemn accompaniment by the ticket collector's two dogs you'll have the island's former capital to yourself. Watch out for hidden wells and snakes.

The whole site is remarkably large, about 1km², as befits the ancient capital of Cyprus, or Alasia as it was called then. Although first settled around the beginning of the second millennium BC, the town came to prominence about 200 years later, when, according to clay tablets found at various sites around the Levant, Alasia traded with many of the region's great powers. Its main trade was in copper ingots, notably with the pharaohs of Egypt and the Hittites of Asia Minor, and Professor Schaeffer also found much evidence of Enkomi's role as a staging post between the Mycenaean towns of the Aegean and the towns of the Syrian coast. The merchants grew wealthy on this trade, and the prosperity is visible in the strikingly grand and well-built houses for this early period of history.

The town never really recovered, however, from an invasion in around 1200BC by the enigmatic 'Sea peoples', a group who feature prominently in the history of the Near East at this time but whose real identity has never been satisfactorily discovered. With the silting of its inland harbour by the Pedieos River, Enkomi fell into permanent decline, and an earthquake in 1075BC finished the town off for good. There is a story that the last inhabitants went off to found a new settlement by the coast. That settlement was Salamis.

The town is encircled by a **defensive wall**, which closely followed the line of the modern fences that ring the site today and was built to a loose grid pattern, with perpendicular streets bisecting each other at right angles. Signs tell you not to walk on the ruins themselves, and if you do stray from the main path be very careful: there are tombs and wells everywhere, with new ones opening every year.

Follow the old path down into the site and walk first along the main street, looking out for the **houses** built of large and well-crafted blocks. The whole town is littered with fragments of sherds and greeny-black pieces of stone lying about on the tops of the walls. Abandoned by human visitors, the site is alive with lizards and birdlife. All around, you will come across wells, grinding stones, cisterns and tombs. One well, some 20m deep, still has water, and all around there's evidence of a remarkably sophisticated **water system**. Especially impressive are the huge door lintel blocks and the vast door openings, sometimes 3m wide, notably into the so-called **House of the Pillar** to the left of the main street.

Also to the right of the path, look out for the large stone block in the shape of a bull's horns, highly reminiscent of the Minoan fertility symbol. The building in which it stands is known as the **Sanctuary of the Horned God**, and it was here, in the corner of the building, that the little bronze, horned statue of a god was found, often seen on pictures and now in the Cyprus Museum.

In another large house known as the **House of the Bronzes**, to the left of the main street, many finely wrought bronze objects were unearthed by the French in the 1930s, now also in the Cyprus Museum. At the extremities of the site, particularly in the north and south, large sections of the town wall can still be seen, with the foundations of fortified city gate-towers.

CHURCHES ON THE MESAORIA PLAIN

Scattered about in the countryside or in the villages of the Mesaoria Plain are a few other churches that enthusiasts may care to visit. They can be seen in a two-hour circuit from a starting point of Boğaz or Salamis, and the drive also affords the chance to see the deeply rural communities of the plain, whose lifestyle is so far removed from that of the towns and cities close by.

Starting inland from Gazimağusa towards İskele (Greek Trikomo, birthplace of George Grivas Dighenis 1878–1973, the EOKA leader), you come to the very heart of this pretty little rural town: the tiny Dominican **chapel of St James**, nearly bisected by crossroads like a sort of traffic island. Its tiny floor area and relatively high dome give it a distinctly Armenian look. After a brief stint as a tourist information office, the church is now sadly kept locked to protect the 15th-century interior and the porcelain plates set in its vaulted ceiling.

Heading out west from İskele, you come almost immediately to the 12th-century domed **church of Panagia Theotokos**, now converted to an **icon museum** (☉ 08.00–15.30 daily; TL5). Inside, it also has traces of 12th- and 15th-century wall paintings.

Continuing westwards and turning right at the main road, Sınırüstü (Greek Syngrasis) is the next village you come to, strikingly set under a small escarpment with the occasional palm tree peeping out of the fertile greenery. Here you turn left (south) and, as you leave the village outskirts, you will notice on your left a wonderfully pretty domed church surrounded by a cluster of cypress trees, approached by a derelict tarmac lane. This is the 13th-century **Ayios Prokopius**. It is now locked, though if you are persistent you might track down the *muhtar* of the village and get hold of the key. The interior has two large frescoes of St George and the Dragon on a deep blue background, and opposite is an older fresco of a saint on a horse. In recent years, the place has been cleaned up by Greek Cypriots from the south. They visit annually on 8 March to celebrate the saint's day with a festival. Returning to the Sınırüstü junction you now continue west towards Geçitkale, a large town of the plain. Its recently opened airport tends to be used only when Ercan is closed for repairs. If you veer off the new road at the first sign for Akova (Greek Gypsos), before entering the village you will pass a desecrated **Greek cemetery** on the left-hand side. Beside it is a new Turkish cemetery with the first graves dated 1987.

Turn left (south) at Akova, and at the next village, Yıldırım (Greek Milea), turn left again to head back towards the coast. Leaving the outskirts of the village, the medieval church of **Ayios Yeoryios** is to be found to the right of the road. The striking thing with all these churches is how numerous they are: the tiniest village usually boasts a church and it is quite common for larger villages to have two or three. The reason for this lies in Cyprus's history, in which the church long represented political power as much as religious devotion. During the 20th century the church bells were used by Greek-Cypriot EOKA zealots as summons or as danger signals. All the churches are now derelict or, if their location lends itself, they are turned into barns or stables. Although surveys have confirmed that Turkish Cypriots are among the least zealous Muslims in the world, there are nevertheless numerous new mosques appearing across the plain, funded from abroad.

Forking left after the church, you soon come to a junction where you turn right, following the sign for the Martyrs' Museum. In this area in 1974, a massacre of the villagers of Sandallar, Muratağa and Atlılar is documented. Each village has a mass grave and memorial, but the well-kept **museum** (☉ 09.00–15.00 Thu–Tue; free), with bilingual information, will be enough for most visitors. It is set out as a classroom and a book, *Genocide, Step by Step*, is on sale. Heading back east from here, through Atlılar and Mormenekşe, you eventually reach the coast in about 10 minutes, arriving almost opposite the entrance to Salamis.

6

The Karpas Peninsula

The Karpas has been called the nature reserve of Cyprus, with abundant wildlife and flowers, as yet still relatively untouched by encroaching development. Remote and isolated by virtue of its geographical position, it holds itself apart from the rest of the island and almost feels like a different country. If you set out to find tranquillity in North Cyprus, then you'll find it here or not at all.

The peninsula was predominantly Greek pre-1974, and boasts some exquisite early churches that shouldn't be missed. A few are still in use, as the Karpas retains a small community of Greeks, some 600 strong, who chose to stay behind after 1974, and they continue to live in and around Dipkarpaz (Greek Rizokarpaso). Driving across the sparsely populated rural landscapes, it's possible to imagine that you are heading out to the end of the earth. The corollary of its isolation is that the accommodation options and restaurants are smaller and less luxurious here, so it's best to plan and book, building your itinerary around the available facilities.

However, though the island's indigenous population of donkeys continue to lollop across the tarmac in a timeless and oblivious manner, the Karpas is opening up to tourism. At the northwestern end of the peninsula, the new road now sweeps eastwards past Kaplıca, then splits in two. One branch heads southwards, its sole purpose at present seemingly to serve the burgeoning Bafra tourist complex with its luxury hotels. The other branch continues its course eastwards, first hugging the coast, before turning briefly inland and then progressing on to Yeni Erenköy, with its new Karpas Gate Marina, and finally to Dipkarpaz. The next stage, it is rumoured, will be to roll out the tarmac all the way to Apostolos Andreas Monastery along the south coast, followed by a new road back along the north, connecting the monastery to Dipkarpaz. Logical progress, but guaranteed to increase the pace of travel in this 'slow' oasis.

Although there are no luxury hotels in the far east of the Karpas, this is surely a blessing. In this protected area, some small, characterful places that respect the environment have sprung up. If you have the time, at least one night on the peninsula is highly recommended. Standards are generally more basic here, though constantly improving, but this is more than compensated for by a friendly welcome and some excellent locations. Pleasingly, there is a growing awareness of sustainability in the region, with an increasing number of eco- and agro-tourism establishments emerging to offer something that's a world away from their five-star casino brethren. Restaurants, too, are beginning to grow in number. As well as the usual delicious kebabs, the fish here are amongst the freshest on the island: much of the fish available in North Cyprus is caught in Karpas's tiny harbours and whisked away to Girne and other towns – but not before the local restaurants have helped themselves. Petrol stations used to be sparse in North Cyprus, especially in the Karpas, but there are new rows of pumps along the peninsula, with Dipkarpaz currently the most easterly opportunity to fill up.

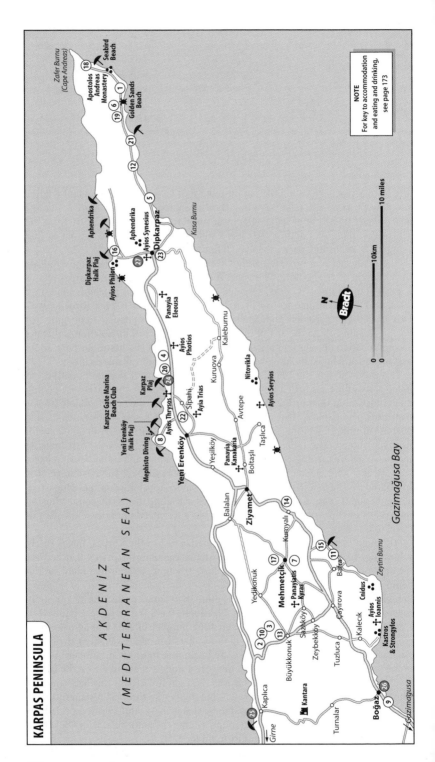

KARPAS PENINSULA

A K D E N İ Z

(M E D I T E R R A N E A N   S E A)

Zafer Burnu
(Cape Andreas)

NOTE
For key to accommodation
and eating and drinking,
see page 173

Seabird
Beach

Apostolos
Andreas
Monastery

Golden Sands
Beach

Aphendrika

Aphendrika

Dipkarpaz
Halk Plaj

Ayios Philon

Dipkarpaz

Ayios Synesius

Kasa Burnu

Panayia
Eleousa

Ayios
Photios

Karpaz Gate Marina
Beach Club

Karpaz
Plaj

Kaleburnu

Kuruova

Nitovikla

Ayia Trias

Sipahi

Ayios Seryios

Yeni Erenköy
(Halk Plaj)

Ayios Thrysos

Yeni Erenköy

Avtepe

Mephisto Diving

Yeşilköy

Panayia
Kanakaria

Boltaşlı

Taşlıca

Balalan

Ziyamet

Kumyalı

Mehmetçik

Panayia
Kyra

Yedikonuk

Zeytin Burnu

Baf tepe

Gazimağusa Bay

Çayırova

Cnidus

Ayios
Ioannis

Kastros
& Strongylos

Zeybekköy

Sazlıköy

Kalecik

Tuzluca

Büyükkonuk

Kantara

Kaplıca

Tırmalar

Boğaz

Girne

Gazimağusa

N

Bradt

0   10km
0   10 miles

There is an ATM in Yeni Erenköy, with another at the new marina and a third in Dipkarpaz. Some peninsula accommodations and restaurants do not accept credit cards, so it's best to carry sufficient cash for your needs.

It takes at least two days to explore the Karpas properly, but if you're seeking a break from the crowds and you can live without the trappings of luxury, you could base yourself here for an entire stay of sunbathing, walking, swimming and little else. In such a peaceful, slow-paced region, it would certainly be a shame to rush.

Some of the establishments offer walking trails, bike hire, cooking classes or an introduction to village handicrafts, though these activities are still in their infancy and pre-booking is advisable. The drive from Girne to Dipkarpaz takes less than 2½ hours, whereas from Salamis it takes less than two hours, and from Boğaz, 1½ hours. These timings are based on using the new, main roads where available and the narrow, winding, potholed alternatives, where they are not.

WHERE TO STAY AND EAT Map, page 172

KARPAS PENINSULA
For listings, see pages 174–6

🏠 Where to stay
1 Ali's Big Sand Beach Bar & Restaurant
2 Asut Guest House
3 Ay Phodios Village House
4 Balci Plaza
5 Blue Sea
6 Burhan's Place
7 Çelebi Garden
8 Club Malibu
9 Exotic
10 Galifes Guest House
11 Kaya Artemis Resort & Casino
12 Livana Hotel & Restaurant
13 Lois and Işmail Cemal
14 Nitovikla Garden
15 Noah's Ark
16 Oasis at Ayfilon
17 Rozagi Guest House
18 Sea Bird
19 Teko's Place
20 Theresa
21 Turtle Beach Restaurant, Bungalows & Camping (Hasan's Turtle Beach)
22 Wave Cyprus
23 *Dipkarpaz:*
   Cyprus Guest House
   Glaro Garden
   Karpaz Arch Houses
   Karpaz Ciftlik Pansiyon
   Karpaz Stone House
   Revakli Ev Guest House
   Teko's Nature House
   Villa Carparis
   Villa Lembos

❌ Where to eat and drink
24 Alev Kayali
25 Kaplica
26 Kemal in Yeri
   Kıyı (see 9)
27 Manolyam

Although facilities are more basic than in Girne, there are hotels, motels, bungalows and campsites offering some of the most beautiful deserted beaches and a very friendly welcome. The ecotourism movement's collection of low-impact accommodation options deserve support (see box, page 175).

The Bafra tourist complex, at the western end of the peninsula, is composed of a few five-star hotels: next to the Kaya Artemis (page 174), an abandoned hotel project themed on the Colosseum lies forlorn, less complete than it's ancient Roman role model and infinitely more ugly. A few kilometres to the east, the massive Noah's Ark hotel, with a shape that matches its name, is now fully open and presumably awaiting a flood. (It's unclear whether their pets' policy only admits animals in twos.) If the whole Bafra project is ever completed, it is intended that it will include a dozen five-star hotels.

Beware that some of the smaller establishments along the coast are closed for renovation and maintenance in winter, and tend to reopen only when the work is finished. Due to their modest size, they can be booked up quickly in high season: reservation is advisable at any time of year.

Places to eat are largely limited to the restaurants, bars and catering provided by the hotels, lodgings and

6

campsites detailed below. Food quality is good, centred around simple meat and fish standards, and with main courses costing in the TL25–30 range. This section takes you to the tip of the peninsula along the main road, from Boğaz and then via Ziyamet, Yeni Erenköy, Dipkarpaz and beyond.

BAFRA

🏠 **Kaya Artemis Resort & Casino** (734 rooms) 📞630 60 00; e artemis@kayatourism.com. tr; www.kayahotels.com.tr. Las Vegas comes to the Karpas, with the largest resort hotel in North Cyprus. Popular with Turkish, Russian & eastern European guests. Monstrous-sized casino. All the trappings of 5-star luxury are here, from fancy restaurants & spas to fitness & sports facilities, a pool with waterslides plus a well-tended beach. Construction of neighbouring hotels has halted. **$$$$$**

🏠 **Noah's Ark** (616 rooms) 📞630 30 30; www. noahsark.com.tr. If the faux-Roman columns of the Kaya Artemis are too bland for you, try the ship-shaped Noah's Ark. Only recently opened, there's nothing antediluvian about this hotel, least of all the prices. Every trapping imaginable, with spa, pools & aquapark. Opulence by the sea it certainly is, but cheap it certainly is not. **$$$$$**

🏠 **Çelebi Garden** (23 rooms) 📞375 55 50; e info@celebigarden.com; www.celebigarden. com. Away from the coast, & a world away from the big resort hotels. Located in Mehmetçik, a tasteful family-run hotel & restaurant, opened in 2010. Satellite TV, AC, Wi-Fi, pleasant pool & views down towards the distant sea. Suites & family units available. **$$**

🏠 **Lois and Işmail Cemal** e delcraft2000@ hotmail.com; www.ecotourismcyprus.com. Pioneers of all things 'eco' (page 42), Lois & Işmail are helpful intermediaries who will find you accommodation in local village guest houses, at very reasonable prices. **$$**

🏠 **Nitovikla Garden Hotel** (10 rooms) 📞375 61 20; m 0533 834 48 68; e info@ thenitoviklagardenhotel.com; www. thenitoviklagardenhotel.com. Situated in a 250-year-old house in Kumyali, another successfully flying the flag for eco-/agro-tourism – with an award from Italy to prove it. Rooms have AC, satellite TV, free Wi-Fi & mini-fridge. Traditional food, homemade wine, organic produce. Interesting cave restaurant, trekking, bike hire, cooking lessons. Swimming pool, views to the sea. **$$**

YENI ERENKÖY & SURROUNDING AREA

🏠 **Balci Plaza Hotel** (18 apartments) m 0533 824 00 44; e balciplaza@hotmail.co.uk; www.balciplaza.com. Some 8km beyond Yeni Erenköy, in lovely gardens with pleasant beach. Apts for 2 or 4 people, with self-catering facilities (though b/fast is included) & restaurant on site (steaks a speciality). Ramp to restaurant allows wheelchair access. AC, satellite TV. Free Wi-Fi & bikes to hire. Mountain & sea views from terrace or balcony. **$$$**

🏠 **Club Malibu Hotel** (40 rooms & 5 bungalows) 📞374 42 64; e info@clubmalibucy. com; www.clubmalibucy.com. Some 3km beyond Yeni Erenköy. A pleasant spot with a small, inviting beach & a little harbour where fishermen dock & sell their catch to the Malibu's restaurant. En-suite rooms are AC with TV, Wi-Fi & fridge. High season is HB basis only. **$$**

🏠 **Theresa Hotel** (25 rooms) 📞374 42 66; e theresahotel@hotmail.com; www.theresahotel. com. Situated 7km east of Yeni Erenköy is a basic but wonderfully friendly hotel & restaurant with a newly expanded beach. Well-stocked kitchen-garden feeds the restaurant. Try to secure a room on the 1st floor with a balcony & sea view. AC, Wi-Fi & communal TV, refurbished bathrooms. The characterful owner also has some very useful walking maps & guides, available for guests. A bargain. **$**

🏠 **Wave Cyprus** (20 rooms) m 0542 889 55 16 or 0533 889 55 16; e wavecyprus@gmail.com. Situated a few km east of Yeni Erenköy, all rooms with private bath, Wi-Fi, AC & fan. Communal TV. Good food & friendly young owner. Good value. **$**

✗ **Alev Kayali** m 0533 876 09 11, 0533 848 30 74. Ignore signs that tell you otherwise, it's located right next to the Theresa Hotel. Excellent fish, never frozen. Meat dishes too. Sea views, friendly service, cold meze included with the main course price. 'Meet before you eat' policy means you can choose your fish pre-cooking! Recommended. *TL25*

DIPKARPAZ & BEYOND

🏠 **Blue Sea Hotel** (12 rooms) 📞372 23 93; m 0533 862 11 77; e info@blueseahotelkarpaz.

Murray Stewart

The renewed focus on the ecotourism movement across North Cyprus has certainly taken firmer root in the Karpas than anywhere else. It's not hard to see why, as the region is undeveloped and ripe for a slower introduction to tourism than has happened in the concrete jungle further west.

Financial support was given a few years ago to help the renovation and construction of a dozen or so 'eco' lodgings, but a lack of marketing expertise has hindered their viability. Although facilities are more limited than elsewhere, the establishments listed here provide a good standard of comfort, excellent food, a warm welcome and a fairly rural setting. Most have between two and eight rooms, with doubles in the range TL120–160. A stay here will give you a taste of rustic North Cyprus, while supporting a worthwhile movement towards more low-impact tourism, much needed to stem the threat of overdevelopment.

Bear in mind though, that some of the owners are not based at the guest houses full-time, as they need to supplement their income with other jobs. Advance booking is, therefore, recommended.

KÜÇÜKERENKÖY

🏠 **Şinya Guest House** (2 bungalows, camping) m 0533 863 48 48; e holiday@ sinyaclub.com; www.sinyaclub.com. Offers walking trails, biking & a variety of games. AC, TV & Wi-Fi.

BÜYÜKKONUK

🏠 **Asut Guest House** (5 rooms) m 0533 874 63 08; e info@asutguesthouse. com; www.asutguesthouse.com. Rooms with TV, AC. Free Wi-Fi. Activities such as biking, hiking & fishing with advance reservation.

🏠 **Ay Phodios Village House** (3 rooms) m 0542 860 62 73; e info@ayphodios.com; www.ayphodios.com. Donkey tours, bike hire & home cooking on request.

🏠 **Galifes Guest House** (4 rooms) m 0533 830 70 96; e info@ galifesguesthouse.com. Children's play area, farm-related activities on request.

MEHMETÇIK

🏠 **Rozagi Guest House** (5 rooms) m 0533 860 82 68; e havva@rozagi.com. Self-catering available on request.

DIPKARPAZ

🏠 **Cyprus Guest House** (3 rooms) m 0533 865 37 40. Bike hire available.

🏠 **Glaro Garden** (5 rooms) ☎ 372 24 10; e glarogarden@msn.com; www.glarogarden.com. Walking, tractor safari by arrangement.

🏠 **Karpaz Arch Houses** (17 rooms) ☎ 372 20 09; e info@karpazarchhouses.com; www.karpazarchhouses.com. Larger than the others in Dipkarpaz. Walking, biking by arrangement.

🏠 **Karpaz Ciftlik Pansiyon** (5 rooms) m 0533 841 51 64; e info@karpazciftlikevi. com; www.karpazciftlikevi.com. Bread-making, walking.

🏠 **Karpaz Stone House** (4 rooms) m 0542 854 7006; e karpazstonehouse@ hotmail.com.

🏠 **Revakli Ev Guest House** (4 rooms) m 0542 874 21 60; e info@ revaklievguesthouse.com; www. revaklievguesthouse.com. Children's play area, biking, walking.

🏠 **Teko's Nature House** (10 rooms) m 0533 837 17 43; e info@tekosplace.net; www.tekosplace.net.

🏠 **Villa Carparis** (6 rooms) m 0533 837 17 43; e info@villacarparis.com; www. villcarparis.com.

🏠 **Villa Lembos** (9 rooms) m 0533 870 19 77; e info@villalembos.com; www. villalembos.com. Walking & tractor safaris available.

com; www.blueseahotelkarpaz.com. A few
kilometres outside Dipkarpaz, this splendid,
characterful hotel/restaurant is a long-time
favourite with tourists. Not luxury, but family-
run & solar powered, the hotel has some lovely
rooms, all with AC & a sea view (at least of sorts)
& balcony, with many overlooking the nearby
harbour. A renovated stone carob house will soon
provide self-catering rooms. Free Wi-Fi. Boat trips
arranged. **$$**

🏠 **Burhan's Place** (16 bungalows) m 0542
854 29 88; e burhankalin2002@yahoo.co.uk;
www.burhansgoldenbeach.com. Next door to
Turtle Beach, Burhan's perches just above Golden
Sands Beach. There's a shady restaurant & bar with
TV & Wi-Fi, as well as bungalows with AC. Tents to
rent, or bring your own. **$$**

🏠 **Livana Hotel & Restaurant** (26 rooms)
m 0533 846 09 34 or 0542 882 15 63; e info@
livanabungalow.com; www.livanabungalow.
com. Equally charming but more rustic than the
neighbouring Blue Sea, Livana offers AC rooms in
its main building or in newly renovated huts, built
on stilts. Wi-Fi in restaurant. The chance to drift
off to sleep to the sound of the sea is not to be
missed. **$$**

🏠 **Oasis at Ayfilon** (8 rooms) m 0533 840 50
82 or 0542 856 50 82; e info@oasishotelkarpas.
com; www.oasishotelkarpas.com. One of the
most stunning locations on the island – the
ancient ruins & crystal waters combine to form an
intoxicating brew. Solar-powered Oasis provides
simple but clean accommodation for those seeking
sustainable tourism. AC due in 2015. There can
be nowhere else with such a '5-star' location. All
rooms now en suite. Free Wi-Fi. Charming staff
& excellent food. Popular, so advance booking is
essential. Recommended. **$$**

🏠 **Sea Bird Restaurant** (18 bungalows)
m 0533 875 63 36; e seabirdmotel@gmail.com;
www.seabirdmotel.com. Past the monastery, Sea
Bird offers bungalows to rent, a restaurant & very

pretty curving beach. It forms the last building you
see before heading off, dust clouds behind you,
to the end of the island. Rooms are AC. Price is for
HB. **$$**

🏠 **Teko's Place** (20 bungalows) m 0533 847
33 95, 0533 863 73 65; e info@tekosplace.net;
www.tekosplace.net. Also on the monastery road,
just off Golden Sands Beach, the recently expanded
Teko's Place has AC bungalows & camping places &
offers a simple restaurant & bar. Wi-Fi throughout.
$$

🏠 **Turtle Beach Restaurant, Bungalows
& Camping (Hasan's Turtle Beach)** (20
bungalows) m 0533 864 10 63; e hasan.
turtlebeach@hotmail.com. The most 'hippy' feel
of the Golden Sands options. Bungalows with fan
& a number of tents available, as well as plenty
of room to pitch your own. Communal Wi-Fi &
TV. Hasan prepares & cooks all the food to order,
serving up köfte, kebabs, fish, etc. The sand
stretches, clean & golden, for near on 1.5km & the
sea is crystal clear. Though the beach here was
once favoured by nesting turtles, it appears that
through increased human traffic most have been
displaced. Whether you encounter turtles or not,
it's still a beautiful location. **$$**

🏠 **Ali's Big Sand Beach Bar &
Restaurant** (7 bungalows) m 0533 844 13 22;
e hakankarpaz@gmail.com. About 3km from
Apostolos Andreas, Ali's Big Sand offers new
bungalows & basic camping facilities. Rooms have
fan. Communal TV & Wi-Fi. Restaurant & bar are
excellent, set high above the beach, offering the
best breezy panoramic of the Golden Sands Beach,
far below. **$**

✖ **Manolyam** ✎372 22 09; ⏲ all year, daily.
Next door to the Arch Houses (page 175), excellent
kebabs & fish, plus a daily-changing 'village meal'
featuring traditional cooking. Main courses include
a section of *meze*. On Sat in summer, the owner's
son & his friends perform a breakdancing &
acrobatic display for open-jawed diners! *TL23*

BEACHES

While some of the Karpas's main beaches are listed below, those with an adventurous
spirit and preferably a 4x4 will discover many more. From the main road, just select
a track that heads seawards, satisfying yourself first that you won't get stuck. It's
not difficult to find a beach that's exclusively yours. The waters will be crystal clear,
though there may be a bit of rubbish and eelgrass washed ashore. The southern
coastline of the Karpas has as many beaches as the northern one, often sandy, but

most are more difficult to reach and have no amenities. Their remoteness will be an attraction for some, a deterrent for others.

The most magnificent stretch of all lies close to the tip, a few kilometres before the Apostolos Andreas Monastery. It is known as **Golden Sands** and the extent of its beach is unrivalled anywhere else in the north. Still a nesting-ground for sea turtles, it is marred only by tar and accumulated sea debris. The extreme tip of the peninsula itself is rocky and swimming there is very tricky.

KAPLICA (*Entry free to swim, sunbeds TL5*) Some 69km from Girne, a long, remarkably clean sandy beach just before the turn-off inland to Kaplıca and Kantara Castle, whose outline can be seen on the crest of the mountains above. A large, recently developed hotel stands in front of it. Good picnic spot *en route* to Kantara.

YENI ERENKÖY (HALK PLAJ) (*Entry free*) Roughly 2km after the town of Yeni Erenköy, a signposted road leads down onto the small, sandy Halk Plaj or public beach, which has a restaurant, showers and cabins that function from April to October. Out of season, it's often deserted and a bit forlorn.cccc

KARPAZ GATE MARINA BEACH CLUB (*Entry TL10, under 7s free*) If the rawness of the Karpas is getting to you already, you can make use of the smart beach club at the new marina, featuring a 33m pool, clean sand, a beach bar, restaurant and sunbeds/umbrellas. Crowded in high season.

DIPKARPAZ HALK PLAJ (*Entry free*) Right next to Ayios Philon (page 182), a beautiful stretch of sand. Public beach, no facilities, totally unspoilt.

APHENDRIKA (*Entry free*) Around 10km north, then east, of Dipkarpaz, currently at the end of the road on the northern coastline, where a group of three picturesque ruined churches stand. The walk to the sea is a long one, 1.5km to the east of the ruins across the fields. The beach is sandy with advancing dunes and is utterly deserted.

SEABIRD BEACH (*Entry free to swim, small charge for sunbeds*) Just east of the Apostolos Andreas Monastery, the temptation of perfect waters and a clean crescent of sand is hard to resist.

TOURING THE KARPAS PENINSULA

The Turks, ever since Sultan Selim first took a fancy to 'the rock called Cyprus', have regarded the island as an extension of Anatolia. The long, tapering peninsula that reached up to the northeast was described by Churchill as 'the dagger which points at the soft underbelly of Turkey'. If you choose to see in the landmass of Cyprus the shape of an oblong frying pan, you could choose to see in the Karpas the shape of the panhandle. Viewed this way rather than as a dagger, the handle is conveniently turned towards Turkey, the master who can seize it and take control.

The peninsula falls into three distinct sections. First, from the fishing village of Boğaz to Ziyamet, the least interesting section, forming a kind of transitional zone from the mainland (for details of Kantara see pages 121–3). Here you'll see vines growing and stalls in the lay-bys selling seasonal fruit and vegetables. Next, from Ziyamet to Dipkarpaz, it is scenically much prettier with smaller roads and more contours. This section also has the much publicised Kanakaria church and the early Ayia Trias basilica with its mosaic floor. Finally there is the section beyond Dipkarpaz,

6

definitely the most rewarding stretch, with the northern fork to Ayios Philon and Aphendrika, and the southern fork to the Apostolos Andreas Monastery and the very tip. In an ideal world, this section would warrant an entire day in itself, with time to picnic and enjoy one of the many deserted beaches, something that is best achieved by spending at least one night at one of the accommodation optons along the way.

Those who can devote only a day to the Karpas should head out early, beyond Dipkarpaz to Ayios Philon and Aphendrika, then drive on for lunch at the Blue Sea Hotel and take a quick look at the Apostolos Andreas Monastery, once it has been renovated. On the way back, call in at Ayia Trias in the Greek village of Sipahi. Kanakaria church is kept locked, and the key has to be extracted from the village *muhtar* or headman, so it is best to allow plenty of time: he may be out working the fields. There are many other minor churches and sites, and the more leisured visitor can take their pick from the following itinerary. For walkers, a few extra days spent here will bring its own rewards.

TO ZIYAMET   The first section of the Karpas, before Ziyamet, has the largest number of sites to visit, albeit minor, and for those with the time and inclination to explore fully, there are three possible detours from the main road.

Starting at Boğaz, the first is at the turn-off right towards the sea, opposite the sign marked inland to Kurtuluş and Ergazi. There is no signpost for the site itself: instead, pass down the left side of the massive new villa development, heading for the rugged rock protruding out of the ocean. Kalecık means 'little castle' and by the sea just 1km short of the storage tanks are the heavily ruined 12th-century twin Templar castles of **Kastros** and **Strongylos**. A few foundations and cisterns are all that remain today, so it's a detour only for the dedicated, especially as accessing the rock may require a paddle at high-tide. Nearby is the ruined **chapel of Ayios Ioannis**. In the village itself, a few kilometres further north, the school is a former Byzantine church. Kalecık is the second port of North Cyprus after Gazimağusa and before Girne, used for exporting quantities of cargo, especially the tobacco grown in the Karpas, and for importing oil. It has no passenger traffic.

At **Tuzluca**, the village on the crossroads to the north, the curious used to be able to seek out a large stone in the old churchyard. The stone had a hole in the middle and local tradition held that every Easter Monday, if the married men of the village clambered through the hole, they could check that their wives had remained faithful. Any that had been cuckolded got stuck because of their 'horns' and, having extricated themselves, rushed off to beat their wicked spouses and begin divorce proceedings. Records show that the last such event occurred in 1935. With scarcely 600 inhabitants one would have thought the opportunities for infidelity were limited, and the chances of keeping it quiet even more so, but perhaps that betrays a lack of familiarity with village life. Now, this method of checking fidelity is denied them, as the stone has been pinched.

At Çayırova (Greek Ayios Theodhoros), the next village on the way to Ziyamet, an 8km dirt track forks south to the headland of Zeytin Burnu, Olive Cape (Greek Cape Elea). Here, to the right of the track, close to the sea, are the ruins of ancient **Phoenician Cnidus** set in a natural harbour. Today the ruins are scarcely visible among the ploughed fields, but the town was inhabited from the 5th century BC until the 2nd century AD. A new golf course is planned for this area, though the opening date is not yet known.

From Çayırova you can take the fork to the north to the village of Zeybekköy, then to the right again to the hamlet of Sazlıköy (Greek Livadhia). At the foot of the hill behind this village, alone in a bucolic setting, you'll see the pretty little church of **Panayiatis Kyras**, thought to be 7th century. Follow the Mehmetçik sign from the village and it can be approached from a track to the left that starts directly opposite the cemetery. Unless you have a 4x4, you'll have to go up the track on foot for about 5 minutes. Empty and desecrated, the church has a little arched side entrance with a charming sitting area. Inside there was a mosaic of the Virgin, which has now gone as a result of the local superstition that a cube of the mosaic would, if kept in a pocket, banish pimples and spots: cheaper, it would seem, than buying cream from the pharmacy. Pigeons and their droppings will be your only companions.

A fork south from Çayırova leads to the village of Bafra. Mehmetçik itself has a hotel, but although it is the grape capital of North Cyprus – and celebrates this with a late July/early August festival – there is no other particular reason to spend time there. Some of the residents are said to have Sudanese descent, explaining the darker hue of their skins. Further north at Kumyalı a fork off to the harbour leads to a sandy beach. In the village itself, raised up on a hillock, is a small **15th-century church** built above an ancient tomb, and all around are vestiges of a classical necropolis.

BEYOND ZIYAMET At Ziyamet (Greek Leonarisso) the character of the Karpas changes, becoming much more rural and hilly. Just beyond Ziyamet, a small town inhabited largely by mainland Turks, is a crossroads, where a fork right to Gelincik will take you, just a couple of kilometres beyond, to the monastery church of Kanakaria, in Boltaşlı (Greek Lythrangomi). This fork continues all the way to Kaleburnu and Dipkarpaz. The track going north marked on most maps between Kaleburnu and Sipahi is terrible and any ideas you may have of a shortcut to Sipahi should be abandoned. Ask two locals whether it's passable and you may get well-meaning but contradictory answers.

The large Byzantine monastery church of **Panagia Kanakaria** stands on the left of the road soon after entering Boltaşlı village. The monastery outbuildings are gradually decaying and in the graveyard round the back, three desecrated graves of the last monks have now been submerged below the weeds. In the semi circular ceiling above the main entrance is a well-preserved fresco of the Virgin dated 1779. The original 11th- to 12th-century church was restored at that time, giving the church stone a (comparatively) newish look.

The door is kept locked, but you can peer through the gap or go into the village to ask the *muhtar* or headman for the key if you are really keen. Inside, a **fragment of a mosaic** of the Virgin and Child in the central apse was all that survived of the earliest 5th- or 6th-century church, making this the earliest Byzantine mosaic on the island. This is the fragment that was stolen on the instructions of black-market art dealers. Four sections, each measuring 61cm square, were chipped away. They depicted the Christ Child, an angel and the saints James and Andrew. On the black market for antiquities they found their way to Indianapolis, to an art dealer who paid US$1.1 million for them. She in turn tried to sell them to the J Paul Getty Museum in California for US$20 million, but Getty's curator notified the Cypriot authorities, leading to an international court case. Faint traces of fresco can still be made out on the walls, but the pigeons have taken over wholesale.

The drive further along this little road towards Kaleburnu is interesting for its scenery, rather than any sites along it, which are essentially minor. The stretches just before and after Avtepe are most unusual, with a dramatic drop down into a huge valley and bare rolling hills all around. Avtepe announces itself with a sculpture of giant tulips, as the village is renowned for its tulip festival in March. A track leads along this river valley to the sea, some 4km away, where a ruined 14th-century domed chapel, **Ayios Seryios**, can still be seen, to the right of the river mouth. Northeast of Avtepe there is also an unusual cave tomb of unknown date cut into a bare cliffside at a height of some 200m, and visible as you approach from afar.

The climb up to it is very tricky and should be attempted only by those who relish heights and unsure footholds. Inside are many deep corridors leading to grave chambers, cut some 26m deep into the hillside. Be sure to take a good torch. At the very back is a well shaft of immense depth, which, village tradition has it, leads either to hell or to paradise, depending on which is more deserved.

At Kuruova, bumpy tracks to the right head for the coast, winding 4km across the riverbed and through ploughed fields. One leads you to the stones of the Middle Cypriot (c1800bc) fortress of **Nitovikla**, standing a few courses high. It was excavated back in 1929. After wet weather the track is impassable for cars, as tractors gouge out great ruts that fill with water.

Next you reach the village of **Kaleburnu** (Greek Galinoporni). On the slope around it are many rock tombs, thought to have been originally Phoenician. On the eastern outskirts and high up in the rocks is an extraordinarily large **cave tomb**, which is 21m long. To locate it, it's best to ask a local, as the streets are labyrinthine.

From Kaleburnu, you can return to the main road and either continue to Dipkarpaz, or retrace your journey back to Ziyamet then north to Yeni Erenköy. (The Dipkarpaz road is now tarmacked, albeit with the occasional holiday- terminating pothole. It is scenic and peaceful, with virtually no buildings of any kind.) If you choose to return to Ziyamet, you now continue on the main road to **Yeni Erenköy** (Greek Yialousa), the second-largest town of the Karpas, with 2,500 inhabitants, the resettled Turkish Cypriots from the enclave of Erenköy (Greek Kokkina) to the west. Here you'll find the Karpas Peninsula **tourist office** (⊕ *09.00–16.00 daily*) with experienced, helpful staff.

Beyond the pleasant, rambling town with its narrow streets, the main road enjoys new tarmac again as it heads along the north coast. Just east of town, Phase One of the construction of the 300-berth **Karpaz Gate Marina** (*www.karpazbay.com*) is now complete. Although still short of yacht business, it is a full-service facility with customs, immigration, chandlery, insurance-approved repair service, cranes, plush restaurant, beach club, some watersports and shops. Phase Two will involve some form of hotel, though whether it will be low-impact or full-blown casino hotel remains unclear, as does the effect on the overall character of this area.

Some 2km from the edge of town, a track to the left leads down to the Halk Plaj or **public beach** (page 177).

After another 3km a signpost opposite the new marina directs you to the Greek village of Sipahi, with its ruined church of **Ayia Trias** (⊕ *summer 09.00–17.00, winter 09.00–15.30, both daily*). Situated on the right of the road as you enter town, the ruined column stumps of this large, early 5th-century basilica are visible from the road. The site has an entrance fee of TL5/2 (adult/student), though frequently the place is deserted and the gates left unlocked. The setting is wonderfully pastoral, in the middle of orchards and fields, and sheep are frequently to be found grazing in the aisles. The site was excavated in the 1960s to reveal a large, three-aisled structure. Few of the columns stand higher than head height, and the walls are rarely above waist height, but the memorable feature of the basilica is its mosaic floor paving. Open to the sky, its colours, mainly reds, blues and whites, are faded, but the intricate geometric designs are striking, mixed in with patterns of foliage and the occasional Christian symbol. The north aisle shows two curious pairs of sandals facing in opposite directions. The font can still be seen, and its cruciform shape is unique on the island.

The village of **Sipahi** (Greek Ayia Trias, Holy Trinity) is still home to around 130 Greeks who chose to stay behind despite partition, and as you walk about in the village you may still see old men dressed in traditional rural baggy black trousers.

Even in the times of mixed villages, Greeks and Turks always had separate schools and there was no official intermarriage between the communities. Today the non-Greek inhabitants are Turks from Trabzon and Samsun on the Black Sea. Every Wednesday, the UN Peacekeeping Force in Cyprus, the 'Blue Berets', bring in about ten tonnes of food, petrol, mail and other supplies for them from Greek Nicosia. Relatives from the Greek side can, of course, visit, though problems have occurred in the past. On one such visit, a Greek girl met and married a local Turk. The Greek Cypriots of Nicosia were outraged, convinced she had been abducted, and a band of friends marched on the Green Line in protest, demanding her return. A few months later, the girl returned to visit her parents in Nicosia, and stayed there. Her husband followed her, and was promptly deported by the Greek Cypriots. The numbers of this Greek community are, not surprisingly, slowly declining.

Retrace your route to the main Dipkarpaz road, and 3km after rejoining it you pass the renovated **Ayias Thrysos Church** on the left, with the Deks Restaurant next to it. With both an expat and a more local menu, lunch can be taken here. The beach itself is no longer suitable for swimming, due to road-building debris dumped thoughtlessly on what used to be pleasant sands. The 15th-century church is whitewashed, with no frescoes, but with some icons and wooden pews. Lower down, close to the shore, is a smaller medieval chapel, still in use, and beneath it is an even smaller cave church, probably Byzantine.

A few kilometres further on, the observant may spot the isolated church of **Ayios Photios** uphill to the right, approached by a bad but driveable track. Thought to be 10th century, the church has no door, and inside there are traces of frescoes showing figures on horseback and a saint with a halo. Some recent visitors have added their own frescoes, which at least adds a bit of much-needed colour, if not authenticity. Goat droppings form the major floor embellishment and the ceiling is adorned with swallows' nests.

Further east on the main road, a signpost to your right directs you to the monastery of **Panagia Eleousa**, 2km up a tarmacked road. It stands in an open clearing in the thick, prickly scrubland. The small, 16th-century whitewashed church has a decorated doorway, but inside the frescoes are completely covered in whitewash. Turks and Christians alike share the unfortunate habit of covering everything in whitewash. Swallows and wasps have also moved in. There is now a restaurant nearby with rooms. Return to the main road by the same route.

The main road now begins a steep ascent up a fertile valley to reach Dipkarpaz, set on a hilltop. A lot of tobacco is grown in the area, and the soil's fertility is due to the abundance of wells, for the Karpas is rich in underground water reservoirs.

FROM DIPKARPAZ TO THE TIP OF THE PENINSULA The newly widened road and spruced-up pavements may suggest otherwise, but the town of **Dipkarpaz** (Greek Rizokarpaso) has little historic interest for the visitor today, except perhaps the petrol station and a line of grocery stores selling ice creams, bread and picnic fodder. Nevertheless, it is home to a number of excellent eco-accommodations (see box, page 175) and would be a good base for peninsula exploration. The mosque towers above the church and at the top of the hill is an impressive, colonial-era, disused school. A few 18th-century houses remain, but on the whole the modern buildings are unmemorable. Set up on the hill to the left is the plain, whitewashed church of **Ayios Synesios**, still used by the Greek community, numbering around 300. The church stands on the site of the Orthodox cathedral that was built here in the 13th century when the Greek Orthodox bishop was banished from Famagusta to Rizokarpaso by the Catholic Crusaders. The town has always been predominantly

Greek, and you'll notice a prevalence of blue or green eyes in the locals. Travellers of earlier centuries imagined the place filled with exotic beauties, but most modern visitors will search in vain.

A teacher comes up from Greek Nicosia to instruct the Greek youngsters, but for college education the students have to head south.

Ayios Philon   Beyond Dipkarpaz, to reach the northern coastline, you must turn left uphill from the centre of town, passing the long white school building on your left near the brow of the hill, and follow the clear signs to Ayios Philon. Soon you'll join the tarmac road to begin the descent to the coast, 4km away.

As you head downhill, you can already see in the distance the church of Ayios Philon, standing alone on the shoreline. This was the site of the ancient city of Karpasia, founded by the legendary King Pygmalion of Cyprus. It was a flourishing Christian community until the Arab raiders burnt and sacked it in AD802. Its inhabitants fled inland at that time and Rizokarpaso grew up. Today Ayios Philon is the spectacular location of **Oasis at Ayfilon** (page 176), a sustainable ecotourism venture offering simple, excellent food and rooms by the beach.

The spot is beautifully remote, with only the sound of the sea against the rocks and the twittering of the birds. The church is set on the cliffs above a rocky bay with six solitary palm trees breaking the skyline. Traces of the old harbour wall can still be seen where you swim, the large stone blocks still extending some 100m, while the remainder of the town lies hidden under the sand dunes away to the west. Philon was the name of the 5th-century bishop who converted the inhabitants of the Karpas to Christianity. The well-preserved church complete with roof is 10th century, but beside it, open to the elements, the red, white and grey mosaic pavement and column remnants belong to a 5th-century basilica, the original church of Bishop Philon. Nearby are a few heavily vandalised Greek houses of this century. Walking either east or west will enable you to see some rugged coastline and beautiful beaches, only slightly marred by flotsam and jetsam.

Aphendrika   Beyond Ayios Philon to the east, a dead-end, potholed, tarmac road leads to Aphendrika in just 10 more minutes. There's no habitation at all on this stretch of coastline, and the tarmac turns into dirt track some 400m short of the Christian settlement of Aphendrika, where the shells of three churches clustered together can still be easily explored. Silent except for the birdsong and the buzzing of flies echoing in the ruined church, the spot is utterly deserted.

Strabo the Greek historian tells us that in 200BC Aphendrika was one of the six great cities of Cyprus, and the site is deceptively extensive. Apart from the three **churches** – Panaghia Chrysiotissa, St George and Asomatos – which date from the 12th and 14th centuries, you should also search for the **citadel**, set up on the hill east (inland), with many of its rooms cut into the bedrock.

Walking towards the west, you'll stumble on the **necropolis**, a whole area scattered with rock tombs, and the site of a temple beyond it. To the north, and a 2km walk across the fields, lies the silted-up **harbour** of the ancient city, with a lonely sandy beach. The city has never been properly excavated.

From Aphendrika, currently the furthermost point on the north coast road, it is around 100km back to Kyrenia.

Apostolos Andreas Monastery   Returning to Dipkarpaz town centre, you now need to look out for the signs saying 'Monastery' or 'Zafer Burnu Manastirsi' (Zafer Burnu being the name of the headland at the very easternmost tip of the island).

A few minutes out of Dipkarpaz, the smooth tarmac ends. Until its proposed extension occurs, you should slow your pace in anticipation of straying sheep and the inevitable donkeys. And shocking potholes.

Scenically, this stretch of isolated road along to the tip is the most magnificent on the island. There are no villages at all, and the only life you are likely to see is the occasional shepherd with his sheep and goats. The bucolic landscape has an old-world charm, and the gentle hills occasionally give way to magnificent vistas over huge sweeping bays. Scattered about all over the fields are fine buildings made from beautifully crafted stone. They look sufficiently grand to have been the residences of local mayors, but in fact they are simply storage barns and stables built by the former Greek inhabitants. Sometimes they even have crosses carved above the door.

As the road winds down through the hills from Dipkarpaz towards the sea, the landscape is covered in thick scrub. In certain seasons, the roadside is milling with vehicles disgorging men wearing camouflage gear, with rifles and a glint in their eyes. This is not, however, some relic of intercommunal strife, but the hunting season for birds. The hunters are legion, and as they quiver in the bushes, the chances of them shooting each other must be quite high. The prey is mainly partridge and francolin, and the season, only on Sundays, and sometimes on Wednesdays, from November to January, is strictly controlled by the police. The sport is so popular that hunters travel all the way from Güzelyurt at the other end of the island for what is reckoned to be the best shooting. The catch is then taken home for eating. Cyprus is used by millions of birds as a stepping stone on their migrations between Europe and the Nile Delta. The best birdwatching spot for these migrants is at the Gönyeli reservoir on the northern edge of Lefkoşa.

Just where the road leaves the hunters in the hills and swoops around to the coast, you come to the **Blue Sea Hotel and Restaurant** (pages 174–6), opened in 1989, in a lovely spot on a promontory a little above a beach and harbour. The location and willing service make a stop here very relaxing, either just for a meal, a swim on the tiny beach or overnight stay.

The spot is known as **Khelones**, from the Greek for turtle, probably because turtles have always come here to lay their eggs in the sand. The former carob store and customs house, a relic of the days when carobs were exported from here, has now been beautifully restored and put into service as self-catering units. A dozen fishing boats operate from the old harbour below, guaranteeing fresh fish for dinner.

The road from here onwards stays more or less within sight of the coast, every corner bringing new panoramas over endless deserted bays. Just beyond Golden Sands Beach, a small entrance fee is usually charged to fund donkey protection, though the beasts hardly help their cause by stubbornly occupying the middle of the road – they expect food. Soon you emerge at the **Apostolos Andreas Monastery**, arriving at a large open courtyard with one-roomed cells round the edge for pilgrims' accommodation. For 2015 and at least half of 2016, the monastery will be closed due to a 2-year renovation project being undertaken with input from both the North Cyprus government and the Greek Orthodox Church. The current buildings date from 1867, though in their pre-renovation state you could have been forgiven for thinking them older as they had been crumbling steadily for years. Dozens of cats hang around the car park and those North Cyprus donkeys can usually be seen grazing in the scrubland.

It may come as something of a surprise to find several tour buses already at the monastery, which is likely at the busiest times of year. Showing that capitalism knows no bounds, you'll also find an army of retailers peddling all sorts of generic junk. Heaven only knows how they got their stalls here, but such is the level of crime that their goods are simply left in the stalls overnight.

The monastery has traditionally been the Lourdes of Cyprus, with pilgrims coming from afar seeking cures for their afflictions. St Andrew was the great miracle worker and protector of travellers. Brother of Peter, and a fisherman like him, Andrew preached his mission in Greece and Turkey. On one such trip, the ship in which he was sailing ran out of drinking water as they were passing Cyprus, so he told the one-eyed captain to put ashore here on the rocky headland. The sailors returned with water, and Andrew restored the captain's full sight. The captain and crew were converted and baptised by Andrew, and on his return trip the captain placed an icon of Andrew beside the wells. Hence the sanctity of the spot grew up. Andrew eventually settled in Patras on the Greek mainland, where he was crucified aged 80.

Note: The description below applies to the pre-renovation position: by mid-2016, when the church is due to reopen, it may be significantly different. The modern church beneath the bell tower is bare and unexciting, housing an icon of the saint, and hosts of wax effigies of adults, children, limbs and even a cow, all seeking cures for long-term illnesses. Below the church, closer to the sea, is the **rock grotto** (the chapel was a 15th-century addition) where you can still see the tiny spring of freshwater that Andrew is said to have endowed with special healing powers. Enough stories of cures exist to encourage the shrine to keep its reputation. A recent one tells of a paralysed girl whose parents reluctantly brought her here for the saint to effect a cure. They were both highly sceptical, but the girl insisted. It was late evening and she persuaded one of the monks to carry her into the rock chapel and leave her there. Two hours passed and the monk was suddenly startled by a cry. He turned to see the girl coming up the path, on all fours at first, but then staggering weakly on her thin legs.

On Assumption Day, 15 August, and St Andrew's Day, 30 November, many pilgrims still come, Muslims and Christians alike, bringing offerings. Pre-1974 they would come on Sundays in their hundreds from Famagusta for family outings, and the priests were asked to perform so many baptisms that the font was fitted out with hot and cold taps. Numbers have dwindled somewhat since then. An old woman speaking Greek is often still to be found holding the key to the church and the grotto. She'll open the doors, pull back the curtains to show icons of the saint, and expect you to kiss them. Just beyond the monastery is the Seabird 'Motel' and its beautiful beach (page 177).

Zafer Burnu (Cape Andreas)

Having come all this way, if you still have a spare half-hour you will probably want to complete your pilgrimage by driving the remaining 5km to the very tip of the island. The track is stony and bumpy but quite driveable in a saloon car, ending at the abandoned meteorological customs hut. It takes 15–20 minutes one-way from the monastery but, though the landscape is fairly flat, you cannot see the sea on both sides until the final 200m when the track approaches the bulbous rocky outcrop. Scramble up to the summit of this rock (where immense Turkish and TRNC flags are flying) for the best views of all.

A **Neolithic fort**, the oldest yet found on Cyprus along with Petra Tou Limniti and Khirokhitia (c6000BC), was excavated on this summit in 1971–73, but only a few shapeless walls and foundations remain to the layman's eye.

Perched on the top, there is almost a climatic change, and the rock gives way to grass and lovely white flowers, alive with butterflies and gentle wafts of breeze. A temple of Aphrodite once stood here to protect sailors from the treacherous rocks or to lure them in, according to her whim. It's a wonderful spot for a picnic, here, at the end of the earth, lolling on the grass, flags flying overhead, gazing out at the string of little islands opposite, the Klides, the Keys of Cyprus, home only to the rare Audouin's Gull.

Appendix 1

LANGUAGE

Turkish is a fiendishly difficult language for foreigners to learn but, fortunately, English and German are widely understood in North Cyprus. Its grammatical structure is unrelated to Indo-European and Romance languages and the major stumbling block to forming a sentence is the word order, which almost requires you to think 'backwards'. For example, a sentence like 'The cake which I bought for you is on the table' retains the same shape in French, German, Spanish, Greek and even Arabic. In Turkish it becomes 'You-for buy-in-the-past-pertaining-to-me cake, table's surface-thereof-at is'. Not only is the order reversed, but the 11 English words become six in Turkish because of the Turkish habit of what is graphically called 'agglutinating', that is sticking on extra words to the base word.

For those who would just like to have the bare minimum of vocabulary and expressions, see the following list.

PRONUNCIATION AND ALPHABET Vowels and consonants are pronounced as in English and German except for:

- the dotless 'i' (ı) which is peculiar to Turkish and is pronounced like the initial 'a' in 'away'. (Note that the upper-case letters are respectively written İ for i and I for ı.)
- Turkish 'c', pronounced as English 'j', so cami meaning mosque = jami, and Ercan Airport = Erjan Airport
- Turkish 'ç', pronounced as English 'ch', so Akçiçek = Akchichek
- Turkish 'ş', pronounced as English 'sh', so Lefkoşa = Lefkosha
- Turkish 'ğ', unpronounced at the end of a word, or in the middle of a word, so Gazimağusa = Gazima'usa

BASIC GRAMMAR
Essentials

Good morning	*günaydın*
Good afternoon	*iyi günler*
Good evening	*iyi akşamlar*
Hello	*merhaba*
Goodbye (by person staying)	*güle güle*
Goodbye (by person leaving)	*allaha ısmarladık* or *iyi günler* (lit 'good day')
My name is ...	*benim adım ...*
What is your name?	*sizin adiniz ne?*
I am ...	*ben ...*
... from England	*... İngilteredenim*
... from Scotland	*... İskoçyalıyım*
... from Ireland	*... İrlandalıyım*

... from Wales	... Gallerdenim
... from the United States	... Amerikalıyım
... from Australia	... Avustralyalıyım
How are you?	nasılsınız?
Pleased to meet you	tanıştığımıza memnun oldum
Thank you	teşekkür ederim
Please	lütfen
Don't mention it	rica ederim
Cheers	bravo or şerefe
Yes	evet or var
No	hayır or yok
I don't understand	anlamadım
Please would you speak more slowly	lütfen daha yavaş konuşunuz
Do you understand?	anladınızmı?

Questions

how?	nasıl?	when?	ne zaman?
what?	ne?	why?	neden?
where?	nerede?	who?	kim?
what is it?	bu ne?	how much?	kaç?
which?	hangi?		

Numbers

1	bir	16	on altı
2	iki	17	on yedi
3	üç	18	onsekiz
4	dört	19	on dokuz
5	beş	20	yirmi
6	altı	21	yirmi bir
7	yedi	30	otuz
8	sekiz	40	kırk
9	dokuz	50	elli
10	on	60	altmış
11	onbir	70	yetmiş
12	on iki	80	seksen
13	on üç	90	doksan
14	on dört	100	yüz
15	onbeş	1,000	bin

Time

What time is it?	saat kaç?	tomorrow	yarın
it's ... am/pm	öğleden once or	yesterday	dün
	sabah	morning	sabah
today	bugün	afternoon	öğle
tonight	bu gece or bu akşam	evening	akşam

Days

Monday	Pazartesi	Friday	Cuma
Tuesday	Salı	Saturday	Cumartesi
Wednesday	Çarşamba	Sunday	Pazar
Thursday	Perşembe		

Months

January	*ocak*	July	*temmuz*
February	*şubat*	August	*ağustos*
March	*mart*	September	*eylül*
April	*nisan*	October	*ekim*
May	*mayıs*	November	*kasım*
June	*haziran*	December	*aralık*

Getting around
Public transport

I'd like…	*istiyprum*	bus	*otobüs*
… a one-way ticket	*tekyön bilet*	plane	*uçak*
… a return ticket	*… gidiş dönüş bilet*	boat	*kayık*
I want to go to …	*gitmek istiyorum*	ferry	*feribot*
How much is it?	*kaç para*	car	*otomobil*
What time does it leave?	*kaçta ayrılıyor*	4x4	*cip*
What time is it now?	*şimdi saat kaç?*	taxi	*taksi*
ticket office	*bilet gişe*	minibus	*minibüs*
timetable	*tarife*	motorbike/moped	*motosiklet/moped*
from	*den* or *dan*	bicycle	*bisiklet*
to	*a* or *e*	arrival/departure	*geliş/gidiş*
bus station	*otobüs garı*	here	*burada*
airport	*havaalanı*	there	*şurada*
port	*liman*	bon voyage!	*hayırlı yolculuklar*

Private transport

Is this the road to …?	*bu yol … a gidiyormu?* or *bu yol … e gidiyormu*
Where is the service station?	*benzin istayonu nerede?*
Please fill it up	*doldur lütfen*
I'd like … litres	*… litre istiyorum*
diesel	*dizel*
leaded petrol	*kurşunlu*
unleaded petrol	*kurşunsuz*
I have broken down	*arabam bozuldu*

Road signs

give way	*yol ver*	toll	*yol parası*
danger	*tehlike*	no entry	*giriş yok*
entry	*giriş*	exit	*çıkış*
detour	*dolambaçlı*	keep clear	*yolaçık tutulsun*
one-way	*tek yön*		

Directions

Where is it?	*nerede*	south	*güney*
go straight ahead	*düz devam ediniz*	east	*doğu*
turn left	*sola dön*	west	*batı*
turn right	*sağa dön*	behind	*arka*
… at the traffic lights	*… trafik ışığında*	in front of	*ilerde*
… at the roundabout	*… çemberde*	near	*yakın*
north	*kuzey*	opposite	*karşıt* or *karşı*

Street signs

entrance	*giriş*	toilets – men/women	*tuvalet-baylar/*
exit	*çikiş*		*bayanlar*
open	*açik*	information	*bilgi*
closed	*kapalı*		

Accommodation

Where is a cheap/good hotel?	*ucuz/iyi otel nerede var?*
Could you please write the address?	*adresi yazarmısınız?*
Do you have any rooms available?	*boş adanız varmı?*
I'd like …	*istiyorum…*
… a single room	*… tek kisilik oda*
… a double room	*… çift kişilik oda*
… a room with two beds	*… iki yataklı oda*
… a room with a bathroom	*… banyolu oda*
… to share a dorm	*… koğuşunuz varmı*
How much it is per night/person?	*tek geceliği/tek kişilik kaç para?*
Where is the toilet?	*tuvalet nerede?*
Where is the bathroom?	*banyo nerede?*
Is there hot water?	*sicak su varmı?*
Is there electricity?	*elektrik varmı?*
Is breakfast included?	*kahvalti dahilmi?*
I am leaving today	*bügün ayrılıorum*

Food

Do you have a table for … people?	*… kişilik masaniz varmı?*
… a children's menu?	*çucuk menünüz varmı?*
I am a vegetarian	*vejeteryanım*
Do you have any vegetarian dishes?	*vejeteryen menünüz varmı?*
Please bring me …	*bana … getirirmisiniz lütfen*
… a fork/knife/spoon	*çatal/bıçak/kaşık*
Please may I have the bill?	*hesap, lütfen*

Basics

bread	*ekmek*	pepper	*biber*
butter	*tereyağı*	salt	*tuz*
cheese	*peynir*	sugar	*şeker*
oil	*yağ*		

Fruit

apple	*elma*	mango	*mango*
banana	*muz*	melon	*kavun*
grapes	*üzüm*	orange	*portakal*
lemon	*limon*	pears	*armut*

Vegetables

broccoli	*brokoli*	onion	*soğan*
carrot	*havuç*	pepper	*biber*
garlic	*sarımsak*	potatoes	*patates*

Help!	*imdat*	police	*polis*
Call a doctor!	*doktor cağırınız*	fire	*angın*
There's been an		ambulance	*ambulans*
accident	*kaza oldu*	thief	*hırsız*
I'm lost	*kayboldum*	hospital	*hastahane*
Go away!	*git!*	I am ill	*hastayım*

Fish

| mackerel | *uskumru* | salmon | *somon* |
| mussels | *midye* | tuna | *ton baliğı* |

Meat

beef	*et*	lamb	*kuzu*
chicken	*piliç* or *tavuk*	sausage	*sosis*
pork	*domuz*		

Drinks

beer	*bira*	tea	*çay*
coffee	*kahve*	water	*su*
fruit juice	*meyve suyu*	wine	*şarap*
milk	*süt*		

Shopping

I'd like to buy …	*… almak istiyorum*	Do you accept …?	*… alıyormusunuz*
How much is it?	*kaç para*	credit cards	*kredi kartı*
I don't like it	*beğenmedim*	travellers' cheques	*seyahat çeki*
I'm just looking	*sadece bakıyorum*	more	*daha çok*
It's too expensive	*çok pahalı*	less	*daha az*
I'll take it	*alayım*	smaller	*daha küçük*
Please may I have …	*… verirmisin*	bigger	*daha büyük*

Communications

I am looking for …	*… arıyorum*	embassy	*elçilik*
bank	*banka*	exchange office	*döviz bürosu* or *kambio*
post office	*postahane*	telephone centre	*telefon*
church	*kilise*	tourist office	*turist ofis*

Health

diarrhoea	*ishal*	contraceptive	*doğum kontrol hapı*
nausea	*mide bulantısı*	sun block	*güneş yağı*
doctor	*doktor*	I am asthmatic	*astımlıy[ım*
prescription	*reçete*	I am epileptic	*saralıyım*
pharmacy	*eczane*	I am diabetic	*diabetikim*
painkiller	*ağri kesici*	I'm allergic to …	*… karşıalerjim var*
antibiotic	*antibiyotik*	penicillin	*penisilin*
antiseptic	*antiseptik*	nuts	*kuru yemiş*
tampon	*tampon*	bees	*arı*
condom	*prezervatif*		

Travel with children

Is there a …?	… varmı?
… baby changing room	bebek odası …
… a children's menu?	çocuk menüsü …?
Do you have …?	… varmı?
… infant milk formula	bebek için süt …
nappy	bebek bezi …
potty	lazımlık
babysitter	dadı …
highchair	çocuk sandalyesi
Are children allowed?	çocuk alıyormusunuz?

Other

my/mine/	benim/benim	beautiful/ugly	güzel/çirkin
ours/yours	bizimki/seninki or	old/new	eski/yeni
	sizinki	good/bad	iyi/kötu
and/some/but	ve/biraz/fakat	early/late	erken/geç
this/that	bu/o	hot/cold	sicak/soğuk
cheap	ucuz	difficult/easy	zor/kolay
expensive	pahalı	boring/interesting	sikici/ilginç

Appendix 2

PLACE NAMES

Turkish	Greek	Turkish	Greek
Akçiçek	Sisklipos	Karaağaç	Kharcha
Akdeniz	Ayia Irini	Karakum	Karakoumi
Akova	Gypsos	Karaoğlanoğlu	Ayios Yeoryios
Alevkaya	Halevga	Karaman	Karmi
Alsancak	Karavas	Karşıyaka	Vasilia
Ardahan	Ardhana	Kayalar	Orga
Avtepe	Ayios Symeon	Kaynakköy	Sykhari
Bafra	Vokolidha	Kırpasa	Karpas
Bahçeli	Kalogrea	Koruçam	Kormakitis
Bellabayıs	Bellapais	Kuruova	Korovia
Beşparmak	Pentadaktylos	Lapta	Lapithos
Boğaz	Boghaz	Lefke	Lefka
Boğaztepe	Monarga	Lefkoşa	Nicosia
Boltaşlı	Lythrangomi	Malatya	Paleosophos
Çamlıbel	Myrtou	Maraş	Varosha
Çatalköy	Ayios Epiktitos	Mutluyaka	Styllos
Çayırova	Ayios Theodhoros	Ozanköy	Kazaphani
Değirmenlik	Kythrea	Paşaköy	Asha
Derince	Vathylakkas	Sazlıköy	Lavidhia
Dikmen	Dhikomo	Şehitler	Sandlaris
Dipkarpaz	Rizokarpaso	Sınırüstü	Syngrasis
Edremit	Trimithi	Sipahi	Ayia Trias
Ercan	Tymbou	Şirinevler	Ayios Ermolaos
Erenköy	Kokkina	Taşkent	Vouno
Erdenli	Tremetousha	Tatlısu	Akanthou
Esentepe	Ayios Amvrosios	Tepebası	Dhiorios
Gaziköy	Aphania	Tirmen	Trypimeni
Gazimağusa	Famagusta	Turnalar	Yerani
Geçitkale	Lefkoniko	Turunçlu	Strongylos
Gemikonağı	Karavostasi	Tuzla	Engomi
Girne	Kyrenia	Yedidalga	Potamos tou
Güngör	Koutsovendis		Kambou
Gürpınar	Ayia Mani	Yeni Erenköy	Yialousa
Güzelyurt	Morphou	Yıldırım	Milea
İlgaz	Phterykha	Yılmazköy	Skylloura
İskele	Trikomo	Zafer Burnu	Cape Apostolos
Kaleburnu	Galinoporni		Andreas
Kalecık	Gastria	Zeydn Burnu	Cape Elea
Kaplıca	Dhavlos	Ziyamet	Leonarisso

Appendix 3

FURTHER INFORMATION

BOOKS

Background and history Any assessment of the literature available on the island's history is prone to being influenced by the reader's view of 'who is right, and who is wrong' on the 'Cyprus question'. The following list includes a selection that should at least prompt the relevant questions, if not actually providing definitive answers.

Bijl, Nick van der *The Cyprus Emergency* Pen & Sword, 2010. Mainly for military aficionados, but with a concise summary of events between 1955 and 1974.

Dodd, Clement H *The Cyprus Imbroglio* Eothen Press, 1998. With a good introduction, concise for those not wishing to delve too deep into history.

Durrell, Lawrence *Bitter Lemons* Faber and Faber, 1957. Entertaining and moving account of Durrell's years at Bellapais from 1953 to 1956. The title is taken from an evocative poem he wrote about the island's political turmoil.

Gunnis, Rupert *Historic Cyprus* Methuen, 1936, republished Lefkoşa 1973. Architectural description of all the churches and monuments on the island.

Halliday, Sonia and Lushington, Laura *High above Kibris* Angus Hudson Ltd, 1985. Coffee-table book with many splendid aerial photos.

Hitchens, Christopher *Hostage to History: Cyprus from the Ottomans to Kissinger* Verso, 1997. Absorbing study examining how the world's powers helped to turn a local dispute between the Greeks and Turks on Cyprus into a full-scale war.

Home, Gordon *Cyprus Then and Now* J M Dent & Sons, 1960. Good for historical background before partition.

Luke, Sir Harry *Cyprus under the Turks 1571–1878* Hurst, 1971. Interesting historical account based on British consular archives.

Mallinson, William *Cyprus: a Modern History* I B Tauris & Co Ltd, 2009. An interesting and, at times, opinionated discourse that sets out the context and issues that shape the island's future.

Oberling, Pierre *The Road to Bellapais* Columbia University Press, 1982. Account of intercommunal strife and events leading up to partition.

O'Malley, Brendan and Craig, Ian *The Cyprus Conspiracy: America, Espionage and the Turkish Invasion* I B Tauris & Co Ltd, 1999. An interesting contribution, particularly for those who like geopolitics.

Papadakis, Yiannis *Echoes From the Dead Zone* I B Taurus & Co Ltd, 2005. Written by a Greek Cypriot social anthropology student who spent time with Turks, Greeks, Greek Cypriots and Turkish Cypriots, documenting their views on pre- and post-division Cyprus. A good, balanced insight into the experiences and views of 'ordinary' Cypriots about living on a divided island.

Stephen, Michael *The Cyprus Question: A Concise Guide to the History, Politics and Law of the Cyprus Question* Northgate Publications, 2001. Becoming difficult to obtain.

Thubron, Colin *Journey into Cyprus* Heinemann, 1975. Fascinating description of his 600-mile walk through the island in 1972.

Volkan, Vamik D and Itzkowitz, Norman *Turks and Greeks: Neighbours in Conflict* Eothen Press, 1995. Not a light holiday read, being fairly academic in style, but well researched.

Flora, fauna and walks
The following reference material will be of particular interest:

Anderson, B and Anderson, E *North Cyprus: Walk and Eat* Sunflower, 2010.

Dowey, Alison *Walks in North Cyprus* Self-published, 6th edition, 2009. Available in bookshops in North Cyprus (page 52), or in the UK from The Map Shop (*www.themapshop.co.uk*).

Flint, P and Stewart, P *The Birds of Cyprus: An Annotated Checklist* British Ornithologists' Union (BOU), 1992.

Goetz, R and Round, G *Cyprus – South and North: Rother Walking Guide* Rother, 2010.

Haines, D and Haines, H *The Butterflies of North Cyprus* Spiderwize, 2010.

Meikle, R D *The Flora of Cyprus* Bentham-Moxon Trust, 1985. Two volumes, becoming hard and expensive to get hold of.

Oddie, B and Moore, D *A Birdwatcher's Guide to the Birds of Cyprus* Suffolk Wildlife Trust, 1993 (out of print).

Pantelas, V, Papachristophorou, T and Christodoulou, P *Cyprus Flora in Colour: The Endemics* MAM, 1993.

Took, J M E *Birds of Cyprus* Char J Philippides, 1992.

Language
Eat Smart in Turkey Ginkgo Press Inc, 2005. To help the nervous diner decipher Turkish-language menus.

Just Enough Turkish McGraw-Hill, 1990.

Turkish Compact Dictonary Berlitz, 2006.

Turkish Phrasebook Collins Gem, 2nd edition, 2010.

WEBSITES North Cyprus has now built a whole range of web pages and sites. Listed below are a few that may help as starting points in arranging a holiday or in simply reading about what the country has to offer. Some of those listed do not appear to be updated very regularly, but are included as they still contain useful background and historical information.

www.brstrnc.com Website of the British Residents Society of North Cyprus. Useful information, especially for those thinking about buying property in North Cyprus.

www.cypnet.com & www.cypnet.co.uk Comprehensive sites on North Cyprus tourism, though much information needs updating.

www.cyprus44.com General travel resource.

www.cyprusive.com General resource.

www.emu.edu.tr Website of the Eastern Mediterranean University.

www.cypruswildlifeecology.com Birdwatching, nature and conservation in North Cyprus.

www.gau.edu.tr Website of Girne American University.

www.kartnc.org Website of Kyrenia Animal Rescue, a charity set up by expats to look after strays and wild animals on the island.

www.lgcnews.com One of the better and more frequently updated English-language websites for news, weather and general information.

www.mc-med.org Website of the Management Centre in Lefkoşa, involved in the development of sustainable tourism options in North Cyprus.

www.northcyprus.net Northern Cyprus Hoteliers Association website, with listings of hotels, including eco tourism establishments.

www.north-cyprus.com General tourism site on northern Cyprus.
www.northcyprusonline.com General tourism website.
www.turkishcyprus.com A useful site for general information and contact details.
www.welcometonorthcyprus.co.uk New official website of the North Cyprus Tourism Centre in London, with much useful information for all aspects of your visit.

We're 40...
how did that happen?

How did it all happen? George (my then husband) and I wrote the first Bradt guide – about hiking in Peru and Bolivia – on an Amazon river barge, and typed it up on a borrowed typewriter. We had no money for the next two books so George went to work for a printer and was paid in books rather than money.

Forty years on, Bradt publishes over 200 titles that sell all over the world. I still suffer from Imposter Syndrome – how did it all happen? I hadn't even worked in an office before! Well, I've been extraordinarily lucky with the people around me. George provided the belief to get us started (and the mother to run our US office). Then, in 1977, I recruited a helper, Janet Mears, who is still working for us. She and the many dedicated staff who followed have been the foundations on which the company is built. But the bricks and mortar have been our authors and readers. Without them there would be no Bradt Travel Guides. Thank you all for making it happen.

Hilary Bradt

Index

INDEX OF ADVERTISERS